NEW RESEARCH IN
FINANCIAL MARKETS

Centre for Economic Policy Research

The Centre for Economic Policy Research is a network of over 530 Research Fellows and Affiliates, based primarily in European universities. The Centre coordinates the research activities of its Fellows and Affiliates and communicates the results to the public and private sectors. CEPR is an entrepreneur, developing research initiatives with the producers, consumers, and sponsors of research. Established in 1983, CEPR is a European economics research organization with uniquely wide-ranging scope and activities.

CEPR is a registered educational charity. Institutional (core) finance for the Centre is provided by major grants from the Economic and Social Research Council, under which an ESRC Resource Centre operates within CEPR; the Esmée Fairbairn Charitable Trust; and the Bank of England. The Centre is also supported by the European Central Bank; the Bank for International Settlements; 22 national central banks; and 45 companies. None of these organizations gives prior review to the Centre's publications, nor do they necessarily endorse the views expressed therein.

The Centre is pluralist and non-partisan, bringing economic research to bear on the analysis of medium- and long-run policy questions. CEPR research may include views on policy, but the Executive Committee of the Centre does not give prior review to its publications, and the Centre takes no institutional policy positions. The opinions expressed in this report are those of the authors and not those of the Centre for Economic Policy Research.

Centre for Economic Policy Research
90–98 Goswell Road
London EC1V 7RR
UK

Tel: (44 20) 7878 2900   Fax: (44 20) 7878 2999
Email: cepr@cepr.org   Website: www.cepr.org

New Research in
Financial Markets

Edited by

BRUNO BIAIS

and

MARCO PAGANO

OXFORD

UNIVERSITY PRESS

OXFORD

UNIVERSITY PRESS

Great Clarendon Street, Oxford OX2 6DP

Oxford University Press is a department of the University of Oxford.
It furthers the University's objective of excellence in research, scholarship,
and education by publishing worldwide in

Oxford New York

Athens Auckland Bangkok Bogotá Buenos Aires Cape Town
Chennai Dar es Salaam Delhi Florence Hong Kong Istanbul Karachi
Kolkata Kuala Lumpur Madrid Melbourne Mexico City Mumbai Nairobi
Paris São Paulo Shanghai Singapore Taipei Tokyo Toronto Warsaw

with associated companies in Berlin Ibadan

Oxford is a registered trade mark of Oxford University Press
in the UK and in certain other countries

Published in the United States
by Oxford University Press Inc., New York

Selection and editorial matter © Oxford University Press, 2001

The moral rights of the authors have been asserted
Database right Oxford University Press (maker)

First published 2001

British Library Cataloguing in Publication Data

Data available

Library of Congress Cataloging in Publication Data

Data available

ISBN 0-19-924321-2
ISBN 0-19-924322-0 (pbk.)

10 9 8 7 6 5 4 3 2 1

Typeset by Newgen Imaging Systems (P) Ltd., Chennai, India
Printed in Great Britain
on acid-free paper by
T.J. International Ltd., Padstow, Cornwall

Contents

Contents

PART IV. ASSET PRICING AND CORPORATE FINANCE

Introduction

This volume collects some of the best writings that European researchers have contributed to research in asset pricing and market microstructure in the last decade. Asset pricing, which relates asset prices to their fundamental determinants, lies at the very core of finance—at the same time the most traditional and the most technically sophisticated field of the subject. Market microstructure, instead, is a relatively young field, which focuses on the effect that market interactions between investors and intermediaries have on asset price formation. The two fields complement each other, the first being concerned with fundamental valuations and the second with how such valuations get impounded in prices via trading. The chapters in this volume bear witness to the impressive quality and span of the results that European research has recently achieved in both of these fields, where the frontiers of research have been traditionally dominated by US researchers.

I. ASSET PRICING

Though apparently diverse, the chapters in this volume are all connected by a common approach, which is at the basis of modern asset pricing theory. Since the seminal work of Lucas (1978), a key relationship in asset pricing theory states that the price $P_{i,t}$ of asset i at time t is its expected cash flow multiplied by a stochastic discount factor or pricing kernel, often denoted by m. For example, in a discrete time context, where the cash flow generated by asset i at time $t+1$ is denoted by $F_i(\omega_{t+1})$, and ω_{t+1} is the state of the world at time $t+1$:

$$P_{i,t} = E[F_i(\omega_{t+1})m_t(\omega_{t+1})]. \tag{1}$$

In models of intertemporal choice, the pricing kernel m_t is the intertemporal marginal rate of substitution of the investor, and the pricing equation is the first-order condition of the consumption and investment optimization programme. For example, with a representative agent, who consumes C_t at time t and $C_{t+1}(\omega_{t+1})$ at time $t+1$, this first-order condition becomes:

$$P_{i,t} = E\left[F_i(\omega_{t+1}) \cdot \frac{\rho U'(C_{t+1}(\omega_{t+1}))}{U'(C_t)}\right], \tag{2}$$

where the $U(\cdot)$ is the instantaneous utility function and ρ is the rate of time preference. Thus in this case:

$$m_t(\omega_{t+1}) = \frac{\rho U'(C_{t+1}(\omega_{t+1}))}{U'(C_t)}. \tag{3}$$

Alternatively, the pricing kernel can be obtained by imposing the absence of arbitrage opportunities. This kernel is unique if and only if the market is complete. Relying on Hansen's (1982) GMM approach, the seminal paper of Hansen and Singleton (1982) offers a direct test of the first-order condition (2) along with an estimation of the risk-aversion parameter of the representative agent.

The pricing kernel is related to the notion of Arrow–Debreu securities. The Arrow–Debreu security corresponding to state ω_{t+1} is the asset paying 1 unit of consumption at time $t+1$ if state ω_{t+1} is realized and 0 otherwise. Denote $p_t(\omega_{t+1})$ the price of the Arrow–Debreu security corresponding to state ω_{t+1}. If the state space is discrete, the pricing equation can be rewritten as:

$$P_{i,t} = \sum_\omega p_t(\omega_{t+1}) F_i(\omega_{t+1}). \tag{3}$$

Hence, the value of the stochastic discount factor for a given state of the world ω_{t+1} is equal to the Arrow–Debreu price of that state, $p_t(\omega_{t+1})$ divided by its probability $\mu_t(\omega_{t+1})$:

$$m_t(\omega_{t+1}) = \frac{p_t(\omega_{t+1})}{\mu_t(\omega_{t+1})}.$$

Further, note that a portfolio composed of all the Arrow–Debreu securities, corresponding to all the possible states, generates with certainty a payoff of one for the next period. Hence the sum of the state prices must be equal to the price of the riskless bond yielding a unit pay-off next period. Denoting that price by B_t and the free rate by r, in discrete time we have:

$$\sum_\omega p_t(\omega_{t+1}) = B_t = \frac{1}{1+r}.$$

Finally, the state prices, divided by the price of the unit riskless bond, have the properties of a probability: they are positive and add up to one over the set of all possible states. This is often referred to as the risk-neutral probability $\pi_t(\omega_{t+1})$:

$$\pi_t(\omega_{t+1}) = \frac{p_t(\omega_{t+1})}{(1+r_t)}. \tag{4}$$

Correspondingly, the pricing equation can be written, in terms of the risk neutral probabilities:

$$P_{i,t} = \frac{\sum_{\omega} \pi_t(\omega_{t+1}) F_i(\omega_{t+1})}{1 + r_t}$$

or:

$$P_{i,t} = \frac{E^*[F_i(\omega_{t+1})]}{1 + r_t}. \tag{5}$$

where $E^*[\cdot]$ is the expectation operator taken with respect to the risk-neutral probability.

Performance Evaluation: Dahlquist and Soderlind (1999)

Relying on the pricing kernel paradigm, Dahlquist and Soderlind (1999) revisit standard portfolio performance evaluation. Traditionally, performance evaluation relies on mean-variance analysis and involves such tools as Jensen's alpha. These traditional approaches are often limited to the extent that they are parametric and fail to take into account changes in expected returns and risk. Instead of starting from a mean variance program, Dahlquist and Soderlind (1999) start from the pricing kernel equation (1). They estimate the pricing kernel consistent with observed prices for a benchmark portfolio. Denoting by F_1 the cash flow generated by this benchmark portfolio, equation (1) yields:

$$P_{1,t} = E[F_1(\omega_{t+1}) m_t(\omega_{t+1})]. \tag{6}$$

The pricing kernel m_t is estimated under the constraint that this equation holds. Then, to test if a given fund (with cash flow F_2) outperforms the benchmark portfolio, they test if it is also priced by the same kernel. That is, they test if the condition:

$$P_{2,t} = E[F_2(\omega_{t+1}) m_t(\omega_{t+1})].$$

holds, where $m_t(\omega_{t+1})$ is the pricing kernel estimated based on equation (6).

Dahlquist and Soderlind (1999) perform this test using the Hansen (1982) GMM approach. This enables them to conduct the empirical analysis without making specific assumptions about distributions, to handle conditional heteroskedasticity and serial correlation, and to incorporate conditional information. Applying their methodology to Swedish mutual funds, they reject the hypothesis that these funds never had abnormal performance.

Option Prices: Dumas, Fleming and Whaley (1998)

The analysis of Dumas, Fleming, and Whaley (1998) also offers an innovative methodology, to estimate Arrow–Debreu state prices, which are an important component of the pricing kernel (as shown by the pricing equation (3) above), and uses these to construct empirical tests of asset pricing theories.

Rubinstein (1994) offered an interesting new approach to the pricing of options relying on implied binomial trees. Intuitively, the approach is the following:

1. First, as shown by Breeden and Litzenberger (1978), from the current stock and bond prices price and option prices with maturity T and different strike prices, one can infer the current state prices $\{p_t(\omega_T)\}_\omega$ or equivalently the corresponding risk-neutral probabilities $\{\pi_t(\omega_T)\}_\omega$, since:

$$\pi_t(\omega_T) = \frac{p_t(\omega_T)}{(1+r)^T}.$$

2. The second step is to characterize a corresponding implied binomial tree. A binomial tree is a sequence of possible up or down movements for the stock price along with the associated risk-neutral probabilities. The implied binomial tree is such that the sum of the probabilities of all the paths leading to one node (ω_T) is equal to the risk-neutral probability of that node, $\pi_t(\omega_T)$ (computed at the first step). To pin down the risk-neutral probabilities along the implied binomial tree, one needs to make some (arbitrary) identification assumptions. Rubinstein (1994) proposes to assume that paths leading to the same terminal stock price have equal probability.

Dumas, Fleming, and Whaley (1998) propose a stimulating empirical strategy to test the consistency of this implied binomial trees method. The intuition of their test is the following. At time t they use the Rubinstein approach to compute an implied binomial tree, using the information contained in the current stock price and in the prices of options maturing at time T. Then, at time $t+1$ (in fact one week later), they replicate the same computations, using again the implied state prices corresponding to time T. If the Rubinstein model is well specified, the implied probabilities starting from the node reached at time $t+1$ should be the same, irrespective of whether they are computed at time t or at time $t+1$. In fact, they reject this hypothesis. They trace back the cause of this rejection to the overfitting nature of the Rubinstein method. They also show that the pricing error generated by the implied binomial tree approach exceeds that stemming from a simple extension of the Black-Scholes formula.

Concluding Remarks

Although they explore different areas (namely performance evaluation and option pricing), the two papers of Dumas, Fleming, and Whaley (1998) and Dahlquist and Soderlind (1999) share common features. In both cases the theoretical background of the analysis is the pricing kernel approach. In both cases the empirical strategy is to test if the pricing kernel is robust, across assets in the analysis of Dahlquist and Soderlind (1999), or over time in the analysis of Dumas,

Fleming, and Whaley (1998). In both cases, the paper brings an elegant theoretical approach to financial markets data, and tests the model.

II. MARKET MICROSTRUCTURE

The second set of papers in this volume deals with market microstructure. While, in the asset pricing literature the focus is mainly on how to adjust probabilities for risk, the microstructure literature takes an alternative perspective, where the focus is on how to adjust probabilities for the informational content of trades. In contrast with the perfect market assumption made by the asset pricing literature briefly discussed above, market microstructure endeavours to analyse the consequences of market imperfections.

The market imperfection on which this literature has focused the most is asymmetric information. When some investors have private information, the other investors must infer the information content of their trades. The seminal papers by Kyle (1985) and Glosten and Milgrom (1985) analyse the interaction between informed traders and (relatively) uninformed market makers, and show how the latter come up with an adjusted expectation operator, to compute the price of the asset, while rationally taking into account the informational content of the order flow. Denote X the order flow they observe, and E^{**} this adjusted expectation operator. Then, when the uninformed agents are risk-neutral, the price equation can be written, in a manner similar to equation (5):

$$ P_{i,t} = \frac{E^{**}[F_i(\omega_{t+1})]}{1 + r_t} \tag{7} $$

or

$$ P_{i,t} = \frac{\sum_{\omega} \pi_t^{**}(\omega_{t+1}) F_i(\omega_{t+1})}{1 + r_t} \tag{8} $$

where $\{\pi_t^{**}(\omega_{t+1})\}$ are the probabilities of the different states, updated using Bayes law, conditionally on the observed order flow X. In fact, computing these updated probabilities, and the corresponding adjusted expectation, involves more than simply using Bayes rule. It also requires correctly anticipating the informed agent's strategy. Indeed, the price function (7) is a Nash equilibrium of the trading game. In general, Nash equilibria are not unique, and consequently, there may be several possible probability measures in equilibrium.

Equilibrium Uniqueness: Rochet and Vila (1994)

Rochet and Vila (1994) keep the major assumptions in Kyle (1985) and Glosten and Milgrom (1985): there is an informed trader along with exogenous noise traders, and risk-neutral competitive market makers post quotes after observing the order flow. The assumption that there are noise traders ensures that the order flow does not immediately fully reveal the informed agent's private signal. Rochet and Vila (1994) considerably generalize the Kyle (1985) framework because they consider general (bounded support) distributions and do not restrict their analysis to linear equilibria. In this context, and under the assumption that the informed agent observes the noise traders' orders, they prove that there exists a unique equilibrium of the trading game. Hence, the information adjusted probability measure $\{\pi_t^{**}(\omega_{t+1})\}_\omega$ in equation (8) is unique. The proof offered in the paper is very general and elegant, and it has an interesting economic interpretation. Trading games à la Kyle (1985) are zero-sum games: the gains of the informed agent are the losses of the noise traders. Rochet and Vila (1994) show that the fixed-point problem of finding the Nash equilibrium in such games is equivalent to an optimization problem: that of finding the price function that minimizes the losses of the noise traders. The paper shows that such a price function exists and is unique, which implies that the Nash equilibrium of the trading game also exists and is unique.

Option Prices: Biais and Hillion (1995)

Like Rubinstein (1994), and Dumas, Fleming, and Whaley (1998), Biais and Hillion analyse the adjusted probability or state price that is relevant to price stocks and options. In contrast to the asset pricing literature, however, Biais and Hillion (1995) assume asymmetric information. As in Kyle (1985), Glosten and Milgrom (1985) and Rochet and Vila (1994), the adjustment in the probability reflects the information content of orders, but in Biais and Hillion's model, the randomness of the order flow does not stem from exogenous noise traders. Instead, it reflects optimal order placement by rational but uninformed hedgers who face random endowment shocks. In this context, Biais and Hillion (1995) analyse stock and option prices when (i) only the stock and the bond are traded and the market is incomplete, and when (ii) in addition to the stock and the bond, there is an option that completes the market.[1]

They analyse how the introduction of this non-redundant option induces a change in the state prices (or correspondingly the adjusted probability measure), and how this alters the informational efficiency of the market. They find that, when the option is traded (and correspondingly hedging opportunities are potentially enhanced), potential market breakdown problems are alleviated. Not only does this enhance the welfare of the uninformed agents, it also enables prices

---

[1]Considering optimizing hedgers, as opposed to exogenous noise trades, is particularly important in the present context where the focus is on the comparison between the complete and the incomplete market. Indeed, changing the set of securities traded, and correspondingly the set of hedging opportunities, is bound to have an impact on the trades of the uninformed agents. Other papers where the randomness in the order flow stem from rational risk-sharing motivations include Glosten (1989), Dow and Gorton (1994), which is discussed below, and Biais, Martimort, and Rochet (2000).

to be established and reveal information in situations where otherwise no trade would occur. But the introduction of the option can reduce the informational efficiency of prices in situations in which the incomplete market would not break down. This is because, when the option can be traded, the informed agent has access to a wider set of venues to exploit her private information, and correspondingly can better camouflage her identity.

The Speed of Learning: Vives (1995)

While Rochet and Vila (1994) and Biais and Hillion (1995) focus on one-shot games, Vives considers a dynamic problem, like Kyle (1985), Glosten and Milgrom (1985), or the asset pricing papers discussed above. He proposes a novel analysis of the dynamics of information revelation and, in particular, the speed at which prices converge to full revelation. To do so he considers a tâtonnement mechanism whereby heterogeneously informed, risk-averse, and competitive investors place orders and tentative prices are set. This process is repeated over time until the market opens and trades actually take place. The market opening time is exogenously and randomly determined.

An important previous paper (Vives, 1993) studies the case where only two types of agents interact in the market: noise traders and limit order traders. In this context, Vives (1993) shows that the convergence of prices towards values is relatively slow. This is because, as prices become more and more informative, traders place less and less weight on their private signals relative to the public information conveyed by the price. Consequently, the order flow brings about less and less incremental information.

Vives (1995) extends this analysis to the case where there is a third type of player: risk-neutral market makers setting the price equal to the expected value of the asset, conditional on the order flow. In that setup there is a countervailing effect to that highlighted in Vives (1993): as private information gets progressively revealed, market makers' prices become less and less reactive to the order flow. This pushes the informed agents to trade more and more aggressively. Thus they place more weight on their private signals than in the case analysed in Vives (1993), and the market learns faster.

Concluding Remarks

As can be seen from the above remarks, recent research in market microstructure ranges from the study of deep theoretical economics issues, such as existence and uniqueness of equilibrium in signalling games, to more applied finance questions, such as the pricing of options. Also, while there is a certain (substantial as well as formal) similarity between the results obtained in market microstructure and those obtained in asset pricing (as brought out by the similarity between equations (5) and (7)), there is still a considerable gap between the two approaches. As noted in Biais, Glosten, and Spatt (2000), asset pricing focuses on the long-term dynamics of fundamental valuations observed at relatively low frequencies, while market microstructure focuses more on convergence to—or deviations from—these fundamental valuations in high frequency data. An important avenue for further research should be to better integrate the two perspectives.

III. SPECULATION

Preliminary Remarks

The study of speculation in financial markets may well be a promising area for the development of theories linking the asset pricing and market microstructure paradigms. On the one hand, papers analysing speculation often aim at characterizing economically and statistically the dynamics of stock prices so as to fit observed times series data (often at relatively low frequencies). This is in the spirit of asset pricing research. On the other hand, in line with market microstructure research, papers analysing speculation often focus on trading strategies, and on the consequences of investors' beliefs for asset prices. Harrison and Kreps (QJE 1978), in their seminal paper, define speculation as follows: 'An investor may buy the stock now, so as to sell it later for more than he thinks it is actually worth, thereby reaping capital gains.' One of the central questions in the analysis of speculation is: how can it be the case that such a resale can take place? That is, how can it be the case that the initial buyer of the asset can find somebody who is willing to buy from him, at a price which he thinks is excessively high?

In Harrison and Kreps (1978) this can happen because different classes of investors are assumed to have different beliefs about the stochastic process that generates dividends.[2] With such inconsistent beliefs, both the initial buyer and the trader to whom he sells think they are making a good deal. The former thinks that the latter is too optimistic about future dividends, and symmetrically the latter thinks the former is too pessimistic about future dividends! In this context, Harrison and Kreps (1978) show how the valuation of the stock by the investors can be decomposed into the sum of two terms: the fundamental value of the asset (the present value of expected future dividends as perceived by the investor) and a non-negative term, reflecting the value of the option of selling the asset in the future to another investor with a greater assessment of the fundamental value.

The four chapters dealing with speculation in this volume offer insights that are complementary to the analysis of Harrison and Kreps (1978). Dow and Gorton (1994) and Morris and Shin (1998) tackle the issue in the context of rational expectations equilibria where different investors have different private signals. Balduzzi, Bertola, and Foresi (1995) rely on exogenous positive or negative

---

[2] In addition, to simplify the analysis, Harrison and Kreps (1978) make the (rather extreme) assumption that investors do not alter these beliefs as they observe new data.

feedback traders. Biais and Bossaerts (1998) consider agents with different priors, in line with Harrison and Kreps (1978).

Arbitrage Chains: Dow and Gorton (1994)

Dow and Gorton (1994) consider an asymmetric information trading game in the line of Glosten and Milgrom (1985) or Kyle (1985). A key ingredient of their analysis is the assumption that the informed investors have limited trading horizons. That is, informed investors are constrained to sell back their holdings of the risky asset before a given date. Because of this constraint, they must act as speculators, i.e. they are willing to buy after receiving good news only if they anticipate being able to resell in the future at a favourable price. Interestingly, this implies that while they are buying the asset they prefer their information not to be revealed, but after they have built up their position they are better off if their private positive signal is revealed to the market. They anticipate that this will be the case if they expect that other informed speculators will buy after them, and before they must unwind their position. Such sequences of informed speculators constitute arbitrage chains. The essay offers a very elegant, general equilibrium analysis of these chains in a dynamic model where all agents are fully rational.

While in Harrison and Kreps (1978)[3] speculation arises because the initial buyer disagrees with the investor to whom he resells the asset, in Dow and Gorton (1994) the situation is exactly the opposite. Speculation arises, and the informed investor initially purchases the asset after observing a good signal if he anticipates that in the future he will encounter another investor with whom he will agree that the asset value is high, so that he will be able to unwind his inventory at a fair price.

Asset Prices with Speculators and Feedback Traders: Balduzzi, Bertola, and Foresi (1995)

Balduzzi, Bertola, and Foresi (1995) analyse the situation where two types of trader coexist in the market: (i) rational, infinitely lived, risk averse, competitive speculators are permanently present, while (ii) feedback traders intervene once. In the case of negative feedback traders, Balduzzi, Bertola, and Foresi (1995) assume that they have initially bought all the stock, but will sell their entire holdings if the stock price reaches a certain lower bound. Although this behaviour is not modelled in the chapter as reflecting optimal decisions, it is qualitatively similar to a simple form of portfolio insurance strategy. The chapter also analyses the case of negative feedback traders, who initially do not own shares but will offer to buy the entire holdings of the speculators if the stock price reaches a certain upper bound. Balduzzi, Bertola, and Foresi (1995) show that the asset price is equal to

---

[3]Or in Biais and Bossaerts (1998) discussed below.

the sum of two terms. The first term is in the spirit of the pricing equation (2) and reflects the fundamental value of the asset for the speculators:

$$P_{i,t} = E\left[\sum_s F_i(\omega_{t+1}) \cdot \frac{\rho^s U'(C_{t+1}(\omega_{t+1}))}{U'(C_t)}\right], \tag{9}$$

where C is the consumption of the speculators, U their utility function, ρ their rate of time preference, F the dividend flow, and P the asset price. The second term reflects the value for the speculators of the option to buy the asset (in the case of positive feedback) or to sell it (in the case of negative feedback).

Balduzzi, Bertola, and Foresi (1995) show that positive feedback trading amplifies the response of stock prices to dividend news as well as the volatility of the market, while negative feedback trading make prices less responsive to dividends.

Asset Prices when Speculation Reflects Heterogeneous Beliefs: Biais and Bossaerts (1998)

In the spirit of Harrison and Kreps (1978), Biais and Bossaerts (1998) analyse how differences in beliefs can induce speculation, where certain investors buy the assets hoping to resell them further to agents with more optimistic beliefs. Unlike Harrison and Kreps (1978), however, Biais and Bossaerts (1998) do not assume that the agents stick to their initial beliefs. Rather, they analyse how agents update their prior beliefs, in a Bayesian way, based on the observation of market outcomes. The chapter analyses the cases where priors are identical or include common knowledge, consistent with the Harsanyi doctrine. It also analyses the more complex case where agents are not supposed to have identical priors and furthermore their different priors are not assumed to be common knowledge. In general this can give rise to formidable difficulties. Agents must form (first-order) beliefs about the consumption flow from the asset. They must also form (second-order) beliefs about the first-order beliefs of the others. Iterating, an infinite hierarchy of beliefs obtains, and this is a complicated object to deal with. However, Biais and Bossaerts (1998) show that this infinite regress problem can be avoided by assuming a common knowledge one-to-one mapping between each agent's utility function (which determines her valuation of a given consumption flow) and her first-order prior belief. Thanks to this shortcut, Biais and Bossaerts (1998) are able to analyse speculation generated by differences in (not common knowledge) beliefs. In their analysis, as in Harrison and Kreps (1978) and Balduzzi, Bertola, and Foresi (1995), prices can be written as the sum of an expected fundamental value and a speculative option. Agents disagree in their evaluation of this option because they have different beliefs. This is what generates speculative trading. Several statistics, computed from readily observable quote, return, and volume data, are evaluated in terms of their power to discriminate the

Harsanyian case and the case where agents have different priors that are not common knowledge. Only statistics that relate volume to volatility, or volume and changes in best offers, have the necessary discriminatory power.

Speculation and Currency Attacks: Morris and Shin (1998)

Morris and Shin (1998) also underscore the role of agents' beliefs, and beliefs about beliefs, in the context of a speculative market. When a currency is 'ripe' for an attack, speculators considering whether to sell or not must form beliefs about whether the others will also decide to attack or not. This gives rise to higher-order beliefs and belief hierarchies, where each potential speculator must ask herself what the others think about the currency, what the others think about what the others think about the currency, etc. This problem is complicated by the fact that there are complementarities between the strategies of the speculators: the expected profit from my attack depends on whether the others will also attack or not. In the previous literature, this complementarity gave rise to equilibrium multiplicity, which made it difficult to rely on theory to obtain clear-cut guidance. By assuming heterogeneous information among speculators, Morris and Shin (1998) are able to offer a very elegant characterization of equilibrium uniqueness in a model of currency attacks. In their model, each speculator receives a piece of private information about the fundamental, and is uncertain as to what information the others have received. In equilibrium, she will decide to attack if and only if her own signal is below a critical threshold. As the strength of the speculators' attacks is increasing with the amount of 'hot' money they handle, the greater this amount, the greater the critical threshold under which speculators attack, and correspondingly the more likely it is that currency attacks will be observed.

Concluding Remarks

The above-discussed papers illustrate how rigorous economic thinking about difficult problems, involving dynamic strategies or market imperfections, can help shed light on important practical issues. Morris and Shin (1998) offer analytical tools helpful for discussing policy proposals to deflect currency attacks. Thus they offer insights on the effectiveness of policies directed at increasing transparency in the market. Dow and Gorton (1994) show how large cost of carry can break arbitrage chains and thus reduce the informational efficiency of the market. This suggests that policies aimed at reducing the cost of carry could enhance the workings of the market. Balduzzi, Bertola, and Foresi (1995) (and Biais and Bossaerts (1998)) shed light on the empirical consequences of positive feedback trading (and diversity of beliefs) on the joint dynamic behaviour of stock prices and volume.

IV. ASSET PRICING AND CORPORATE FINANCE

Along with the integration of asset pricing and market microstructure, the integration of asset pricing and corporate finance is one of the most important items in the research agenda of financial economists. While in the area of asset pricing researchers have developed elegant dynamic models extremely useful for practitioners, they have often failed to take into account the richness and complexity of the contractual relations and agency problems associated with the issuing of financial assets. On the other hand, while corporate finance has shed light on many important contracting issues in the presence of conflicts of interests and information asymmetries, it has not entirely succeeded in delivering precise quantitative formulae directly applicable by practitioners.

Debt Valuation in the Presence of Moral Hazard: Anderson and Sundaresan (1996)

Anderson and Sundaresan (1996) offer a pathbreaking contribution to the unification of the corporate finance and asset pricing approaches. As in standard asset pricing theory, they consider a firm, the underlying value of which follows a binomial (up and down) process. In the spirit of Black and Scholes (1973) and Merton (1974) the classical asset pricing approach would entail pricing its debt and equity using risk-neutral expectations of discounted cash flows, similar to equation (5) in Section I above. Yet Anderson and Sundaresan (1996) depart from this approach by taking into account agency problems between the manager and the outside debtholders. They assume that at each point in time the manager can choose between servicing the debt or offering a lower pay out to the debtholders. If the latter refuse, then the firm is liquidated and the corresponding proceeds are allocated to the debtholders. Otherwise, if the debtholders accept the offer made by the manager, they receive the monetary transfer and the game continues as if the debt had been fully served. An important assumption at this stage is that, if the firm is liquidated, the debtholders receive its fundamental value minus a liquidation cost. To avoid bearing this cost, it may be optimal for them to accept less than full debt service, rather than forcing liquidation. Taking advantage of that, managers opt for 'strategic default' (and offer less than contractual debt service, which they know will not be rejected by the debtholders) when the value of the firm is rather low. Having accounted for the equilibrium strategy of the manager, Anderson and Sundaresan then proceed to value straight debt contracts by computing risk-neutral expectations. This generates yield spreads over Treasuries which are more in line with stylized facts than those generated by a standard asset pricing model such as Merton (1974). Anderson and Sundaresan (1996) then push their analysis even further by delineating the implication of their model for the design of debt contracts. For example, the analysis delivers the implications that high growth firms and highly levered firms tend to use low-coupon debt contracts, while low growth firms use high-coupon debt.

Foreign Equity Investment Restrictions: Stulz and Wasserfallen (1995)

Stulz and Wasserfallen (1995) also analyse what type of security firm managers should issue and the corresponding asset prices. If the demand for shares of a given country differs between domestic and foreign investors, then standard discrimination theory implies that shares should be offered at different prices to the two categories of investor. For countries benefiting from capital flight, like Switzerland, the demand for shares by foreigners is likely to be different from domestic demand. Stulz and Wasserfallen (1995) offer evidence from Swiss share prices consistent with this analysis.

REFERENCES

Black, Fisher and Myron Scholes (1973), 'The Pricing of Options and Corporate Liabilities', *Journal of Political Economy*, 81, 637–54.

Breeden, D. T. and Robert, H. Litzenberger (1978), 'Prices of State-Contingent Claims Implicit in Option Prices', *Journal of Business*, 51(4), 621–51.

Biais, Bruno, Lawrence Glosten, and Chester Spatt (2000), 'Market Microstructure', working paper, September.

Biais, Bruno, David Martimort, and Jean-Charles Rochet (2000), 'Competing Mechanisms in a Common Value Environment', *Econometrica*, 68(4), 799–837.

Glosten, Larry, R. and Paul Milgrom (1985), 'Bid, Ask, and Transaction Prices in a Specialist Market with Heterogeneously Informed Traders', *Journal of Financial Economics*, 14(1), 71–100.

Hansen, Lars Peter (1982), 'Large Sample Properties of Generalized Method of Moments Estimators', *Econometrica*, 50(4), 1029–54.

Hansen and Kenneth Singleton (1982), 'Generalized Instrumental Variables Estimation of Nonlinear Rational Expectations Models', *Econometrica*, 50(5), 1269–86.

Harrison, J. Michael and David M. Kreps (1978), 'Speculative Investor Behavior in a Stock Market with Heterogeneous Expectations', *Quarterly Journal of Economics*, 92, 323–36.

Kyle, Albert S. (1985), 'Continuous Auctions and Insider Trading', *Econometrica*, 53(6), 1315–36.

Lucas, Robert (1978), 'Asset Prices in an Exchange Economy', *Econometrica*, 42, 1429–45.

Merton, Robert (1974), 'On the Pricing of Corporate Debt: The Risk Structure of Interest Rate', *Journal of Finance*, 29(2).

Rubinstein, Mark (1994), 'Implied Binomial Trees', *Journal of Finance*, 49(3), 771–818.

Vives, Xavier (1993), 'How Fast Do Rational Agents Learn?', *Review of Economic Studies*, 60(2), 329–47.

B.B.

M.P.

PART I

ASSET PRICING

1

Evaluating Portfolio Performance with Stochastic Discount Factors

MAGNUS DAHLQUIST AND PAUL SÖDERLIND

I. INTRODUCTION

Performance evaluation has recently received increased attention. Apart from the obvious interest for investors to evaluate portfolio strategies, this can be traced to at least two distinct developments in the asset-pricing literature.

The first development is the use of efficient benchmark portfolios. Performance evaluation is essentially a question of comparing the risk-adjusted return on one portfolio with certain benchmarks. It is, however, well known that the use of inefficient benchmarks can cause ambiguity in an evaluation. The use of two inefficient benchmark portfolios could, for instance, reverse the ranking of passive portfolios, and portfolios that have superior performance using one benchmark may have inferior performance with another benchmark.[1] The second development is the use of conditional information variables in tests of asset-pricing theories. Traditional approaches to performance measurement are unconditional, in the sense that average returns are being used to estimate the expected performance. These measures do not account for time variation in expected returns and risk, which can mask truly inferior or superior performance.[2]

Bansal and Harvey (1996), Chen and Knez (1996), and Farnsworth, Ferson, Jackson, and Todd (1996) combine these developments and implement the performance measures in a conditional setting using efficient benchmarks. The

We have benefited from the comments of Ravi Bansal, John Cochrane (the editor), Hans Fahlin, Wayne Ferson, an anonymous referee, and seminar participants at the 1997 EFA Meeting in Vienna, the 1998 CEPR Conference in Gerzensee, Erasmus University in Rotterdam, the HEC School of Management, the Institute for International Economic Studies, London Business School, the 1997 Nordic Finance Symposium in Stockholm, the Norwegian School of Management, and the 1996 Financial Econometrics Workshop at Tilburg University. Research assistance by Anne Boschini is appreciated. Correspondence to Magnus Dahlquist, Stockholm School of Economics, Department of Finance, P.O. Box 6501, S-11383 Stockholm, Sweden.

[1] For further elaborations on this, see, for instance, Roll (1978) and Dybvig and Ross (1985).

[2] Ferson and Schadt (1996) develop this reasoning and extend the traditional measures of performance and market timing by using predetermined information variables.

evaluations are done in the context of Hansen and Richard (1987), Hansen and Jagannathan (1991), and Snow (1991). Basically, a stochastic discount factor (SDF) that prices all benchmarks (and is in this sense efficient) is constructed and then used in evaluations. The methodology is related to the recent spanning tests in De Santis (1995) and Bekaert and Urias (1996).

In this article, we provide further evidence on the use of stochastic discount factors in an evaluation of portfolio performance. Our study is close in spirit to the work of Chen and Knez (1996) that deals with the theoretical strengths and weaknesses in SDF performance measures. We extend the interpretation of the performance measures and relate those measures to the traditional mean-variance analysis. We focus on the implementational aspects of the approach. Using simulations, we examine the properties of the measures in small samples. We consider SDFs with and without positivity imposed. We allow the benchmarks to be either fixed-weight strategies or dynamic strategies formed via available public information. Moreover, we consider unconditional as well as conditional evaluations.

In the case without positivity imposed on the SDF, there is an appealing duality between the performance measure and the traditional mean-variance analysis. In fact, the test of neutral performance can be interpreted as an intersection test. That is, the evaluation boils down to a test of whether additional assets (here mutual funds) expand the mean-variance frontier. The intersection test becomes equivalent to an evaluation of a fund's pricing error with respect to an ex post efficient mean-variance portfolio (an 'alpha'). Following Chen and Knez (1996), we also consider evaluation measures where positivity is imposed on the SDFs. The positivity of the SDF prevents situations where one can find arbitrage opportunities, but there is no enlargement of the mean-variance frontier. Moreover, the SDFs are efficient by construction (as in Hansen and Jagannathan 1991), and require only the returns on the benchmark assets. The analysis does not rely on a specific model and, hence, on its accuracy.

Another strength of the approach is that estimation and testing can be done with the generalized method of moment (GMM) of Hansen (1982). This means that specific distributional assumptions of the asset returns are not required, and we do not need to work in a normal independently and identically distributed (i.i.d) setting. We can handle both conditional heteroskedasticity and serial correlation in pricing errors. Moreover, it is straightforward to incorporate both conditional information, and nonlinearities (by positivity constraints on the SDFs) can be dealt with.

This framework is used in a comparison of actively managed mutual funds with some benchmark portfolios. Do fund managers possess information that provides superior returns or can simple portfolios price the returns of mutual funds? Does the incorporation of conditional (public) information via scaled returns matter? Given the interest of these questions, can our measures really distinguish superior performance from neutral performance? What do the empirical small sample distributions for the evaluation statistics look like under the null and alternative hypotheses? These are some of the questions we address.

We discuss the use and implementation of stochastic discount factors in a portfolio evaluation in Section II. We also relate the evaluation to the traditional mean-variance analysis. We especially highlight the importance of getting the mean of the SDF right. Otherwise, the evaluation could be undertaken at an arbitrary (and misleading) point in the mean-variance space. We also show how to select predetermined information variables in order to undertake a correct conditional evaluation. In Section III, we describe the data and Swedish benchmarks, instruments, and funds that we employ in the study. Monte Carlo experiments are used in Section IV to examine the small sample properties of the GMM estimators. Both size and power properties are characterized using various GMM approaches. Overall, the test statistics are well described by their asymptotic distributions, although serious size distortions are found in conditional evaluations. The simulations also show that either a significant excess return or a long sample is needed to reject neutral performance. In Section V, we apply the method to the Swedish data. We undertake an unconditional as well as a conditional evaluation. The conditional evaluation indicates that funds may have had nonneutral performance over the sample period, as revealed by the predictability of the unconditional performance measure. Finally, we draw our conclusions in Section VI.

II. STOCHASTIC DISCOUNT FACTORS AND PERFORMANCE EVALUATION

We use the same basic approach for testing fund performance as did Chen and Knez (1996). We first estimate a stochastic discount factor that 'prices' some benchmark portfolios, then use GMM to test if it also prices the funds. The SDF is estimated from asset returns, as in Hansen and Jagannathan (1991), and we compare the results from SDFs both with and without positivity imposed.

This section shows how to set up the GMM moment conditions to guarantee that simple trading rules are assigned neutral performance, both unconditionally and conditionally. The simple trading rules we consider are either fixed-weight portfolios or dynamic portfolios, where the portfolio weights are allowed to depend linearly on some publicly available information.

Without positivity of the SDF, the GMM-SDF test is equivalent to investigating if the mean-variance frontier is expanded by adding funds. In this case, the main reason for using the GMM-SDF test is that it is easy to handle nonnormal and non-i.i.d. pricing errors. Furthermore, to our knowledge, there is no alternative to the GMM-SDF test if we want to impose positivity of the SDF, which may have some advantages as discussed by Chen and Knez (1996). For instance, a fund may offer arbitrage opportunities without expanding the mean-variance frontier, and this will (sampling errors apart) be picked up by a positive SDF. Similarly, a positive SDF also guarantees that a fund that does systematically better than another fund is assigned a higher performance.

A. Performance Evaluation and Benchmark Portfolios

Investors form portfolios of certain 'benchmark' assets. The 1-period gross return on such a portfolio is

$$R_t = w'_{t-1} R_{1t}, \quad \text{with } w'_{t-1} 1 = 1, \tag{2.1}$$

where R_{1t} is a vector of the 1-period gross returns on benchmark assets, and w_{t-1} are the portfolio weights chosen in $t - 1$. We assume that the information set and preferences lead investors to use simple trading rules where w_t could be any linear function of some publicly available information, x_t,

$$w_t = \delta' x_t, \quad \text{such that } w'_t 1 = 1. \tag{2.2}$$

We will focus on two cases. First, with *fixed-weight benchmark portfolios*, x_t is just a constant. Second, with *dynamic benchmark portfolios*, x_t is a vector with a constant and some information variables that have been proven to predict stock market data. We assume that the time series process of the benchmark asset returns, R_{1t}, is exogenous and is the same for both cases.

Let z_{t-1} be a vector of instruments known at $t - 1$. The law of one price implies the existence of an SDF, m_t, such that

$$E\lambda_{1t} = 0, \tag{2.3}$$

with

$$\lambda_{1t} = z_{t-1} R_t m_t - z_{t-1}. \tag{2.4}$$

In some cases we also impose the restriction that the SDF must be positive, as suggested by Hansen and Jagannathan (1991).[3]

Suppose we now allow investors to take an infinitesimal position in a fund. The fund invests in the same benchmark assets as do investors but does so using potentially more sophisticated trading rules, for instance, because it has superior information. We study if these trading rules add anything to the opportunity set of investors. The flavor of the testing approach is first to find an SDF that 'prices' the benchmark strategies, that is, satisfies (2.3)–(2.4). Then, we see whether it also prices the fund, that is, if the following conditions are satisfied:

$$E\lambda_{2t} = 0, \tag{2.5}$$

with

$$\lambda_{2t} = z_{t-1} R_{2t} m_t - z_{t-1}. \tag{2.6}$$

---

[3] In a conditional asset-pricing model, the absence of arbitrage opportunities (nonnegative payoffs with negative prices) implies that there must be some SDF which is positive almost surely.

Different choices of the instruments give tests of different aspects of the fund performance. We focus on two cases. First, we obtain an *unconditional performance measure* by letting z_t be a constant. It is straightforward to show that $E\lambda_{2t}$ is then the average return of the fund minus what the SDF implies for the risk free rate and the risk premium.[4]

Second, we get a *conditional performance measure* by using both a constant and some information variables in z_t.[5] The element in $E\lambda_{2t}$, corresponding to the constant, is still a measure of average performance, while the other elements capture the predictability of the fund return. For simplicity, suppose the average performance is zero. It is then straightforward to show that the remaining elements in $E\lambda_{2t}$ are the covariances between the predetermined variables and the period t performance of the fund.[6]

B. Construction of the SDFs and GMM Testing

We need to estimate SDFs that price the returns from the two different classes of simple trading rules discussed above. This can be done by replacing (2.4) with

$$\lambda_{1t} = (z_{t-1} \otimes x_{t-1} \otimes R_{1t})m_t - z_{t-1} \otimes x_{t-1}1, \qquad (2.7)$$

and then finding an m_t such that $E\lambda_{1t} = 0$. As shown in Appendix A, *any* portfolio that has weights that are linear in the information variables x_{t-1} and that sum to one in *every* period will, by definition, have a neutral performance that is, $E\lambda_{2t} = 0$ in (2.5)–(2.6).

We will later show that it is important to tie the mean of the SDF to a reasonable value. This can be achieved by adding a moment condition related to an asset whose return, R_{ft}, is a suitable level for a hypothetical risk-free rate,

$$E\lambda_{ft} = 0, \qquad (2.8)$$

with

$$\lambda_{ft} = m_t - 1/R_{ft}. \qquad (2.9)$$

---

[4] If z_{t-1} is a constant, then (2.3) can be written $ER_t - 1/EM_t = -\text{Cov}(R_t, m_t)/Em_t + E\lambda_1 t/Em_t$. Since m_t prices R_t, $E\lambda_{1t} = 0$, any risk-free rate has the mean $1/Em_t$ and the risk premium is captured by the covariance term. Equation (2.5) can be written in the same form, which gives the result in the text.

[5] Ferson and Schadt (1996) conduct a 'conditional' evaluation in a linear beta framework by allowing the betas to vary with predetermined information variables. This corresponds to our unconditional evaluation of dynamic strategies.

[6] Let λ_{1t}^{uc} and λ_{1t}^{c} be the elements in λ_{1t} corresponding to the constant (unconditional evaluation) and an information variable z_{t-1}^{uc} (conditional evaluation), respectively. Clearly, $\lambda_{1t}^{uc} = R_t m_t - 1$ and $\lambda_{1t}^{c} = \lambda_{1t}^{uc} z_{t-1}^{c}$, so $E\lambda_{1t}^{c} = \text{cov}(\lambda_{1t}^{uc}, z_{t-1}^{c}) + E\lambda_{1t}^{uc} E z_{t-1}^{c}$. Since m_t prices R_t both $E\lambda_{1t}^{uc}$ and $E\lambda_{1t}^{c}$ are zero, the average performance of R_t is zero and the performance in t, λ_{1t}^{uc}, is not correlated with z_{t-1}^{c}. Equation (2.5) can be written in the same form, which gives the result in the text.

We follow Hansen and Jagannathan (1991) and Chen and Knez (1996) and construct the SDFs from the sample of $\{1, R_{1t}, x_{t-1}, z_{t-1}\}$. Without positivity, m_t is a linear function of the cross product of the four vectors. Positivity is imposed by cutting off the linear function at zero in an optionlike fashion. In principle, the testing approach could be to choose the vector γ in

$$m_t^* = [1(z_{t-1} \otimes x_{t-1} \otimes R_{1t})']\gamma, \tag{2.10}$$

or

$$m_t^+ = \max\{[1(z_{t-1} \otimes x_{t-1} \otimes R_{1t})']\gamma, 0\} \tag{2.11}$$

to make the sample average of λ_{1t} in (2.7) and λ_{ft} in (2.9) equal to a vector of zeros.[7] (This is possible since there are as many elements in γ as there are equations.) The series of estimated m_t^* or m_t^+ could then be used to test whether (2.5) holds. Noteworthy is that if there are common variables in the z_{t-1} and x_{t-1} series, *only* the unique cross products in $z_{t-1} \otimes x_{t-1}$ have to be used in (2.10) and (2.11) to price the benchmarks under the null hypothesis.

However, to take into account the sampling error in the estimated SDF, we employ the following 1-pass procedure instead. The vector γ is estimated by minimizing a quadratic loss function of the sample averages of not only λ_{1t} and λ_{ft}, but also λ_{2t}:

$$\left(\frac{1}{T}\sum_{t=1}^{T}\begin{bmatrix}\lambda_{1t}\\\lambda_{ft}\\\lambda_{2t}\end{bmatrix}\right)' W \left(\frac{1}{T}\sum_{t=1}^{T}\begin{bmatrix}\lambda_{1t}\\\lambda_{ft}\\\lambda_{2t}\end{bmatrix}\right). \tag{2.12}$$

The weighting matrix W is positive definite but need not be the inverse of the covariance matrix of the moment conditions as is most often the case. Each element in $\sum_{t=1}^{T} \lambda_{2t}/T$ is an overidentifying restriction, and we can test if they are all satisfied by using the χ^2-test in Hansen (1982) (see Appendix B for details). Without positivity, we have a linear model that can be solved analytically, but positivity introduces a nonlinearity that requires a numerical optimization algorithm.

C. The Relation to Mean-Variance Analysis

Hansen and Jagannathan (1991) show the relation between the mean-variance frontiers for asset returns and for the SDF without positivity. We use this framework to discuss how the GMM-SDF test without positivity relates to traditional mean-variance tests. We focus on the unconditional case with fixed-weight benchmark portfolios, $x_t = z_t = 1$ but the results can also be applied to the managed portfolio returns, $z_{t-1} \otimes x_{t-1} \otimes R_{1t}$ and $z_{t-1} \otimes R_{2t}$.

---

[7] Bansal and Viswanathan (1993) consider SDFs which are nonlinear in asset returns, and Glosten and Jagannathan (1994) discuss nonlinearities for performance evaluation.

Huberman and Kandel (1987) construct a test of whether the mean-variance frontier of R_{2t} intersects the mean-variance frontier of R_{1t} and R_{2t}. Suppose the fund return is

$$R_{2t} = a + BR_{1t} + \epsilon_t, \quad \text{with } E\epsilon_t = 0 \text{ and } ER_{1t}\epsilon_t' = 0. \tag{2.13}$$

Huberman and Kandel (1987) show that intersection is equivalent to the restriction

$$a = R^0(1 - B1), \tag{2.14}$$

where R^0 is the zero beta rate associated with the portfolio at the intersection point. The relation to the GMM-SDF test of $E\lambda_{2t} = 0$ is seen by using (2.13) to substitute for R_{2t} in (2.6). If the fund has neutral performance, then

$$a = \frac{1 - \text{cov}(m_t^*, BR_{1t})}{Em_t^*} - BER_{1t}. \tag{2.15}$$

It is straightforward to show that this is equivalent to (2.14). See, for instance, Ferson (1995) and Bekaert and Urias (1996). The GMM-SDF test is thus an intersection test.

It is then intuitively clear that the GMM-SDF measure of performance, $E\lambda_{2t}$, must be a kind of Jensen's alpha. To show that, we combine the following facts: (i) (2.5) implies a beta relation between ER_{2t} and the SDF; (ii) the SDF portfolio return, $R_{bt}^* = m_t^*/Em_t^{*2}$, is on the mean-variance frontier with a risk-free asset (Chamberlain and Rothschild 1983); and (iii) the tangency portfolio, R_{Tt}^*, is perfectly correlated with the SDF portfolio. Together, these facts imply

$$\frac{E\lambda_{2t}}{Em_t^*} = ER_{2t} - \frac{1}{Em_t^*} - \frac{\text{cov}(R_{2t}, R_{Tt}^*)}{\text{var}(R_{Tt}^*)} \left(ER_{Tt}^* - \frac{1}{Em_t^*} \right), \tag{2.16}$$

which is a Jensen's alpha computed against an *efficient* tangency portfolio. The pitfall of evaluating against an inefficient asset is thus avoided. Finally, recall that this duality result holds only for the SDF without positivity.

We illustrate this in Figure 1 by plotting the mean–standard deviation frontiers of our data (to be described later). In Figure 1a, the frontier for the benchmarks, R_{1t}, is the thick solid hyperbola. Adding one hypothetical fund with neutral performance gives the thick dashed hyperbola. These two frontiers intersect at the tangency portfolio, R_T^* (marked by a circle), corresponding to a risk-free return, $1/Em_t^*$, of about 10%. In Figure 1b, the fund has been given a 5% excess return, so the two frontiers no longer intersect at the tangency portfolio.

The moment condition (2.8) was included to tie the mean of the SDF to a reasonable value. Figure 1b illustrates why this is necessary. Suppose we would incorrectly estimate $1/Em_t^*$ to 28% (marked by R^0 on the vertical axis). This

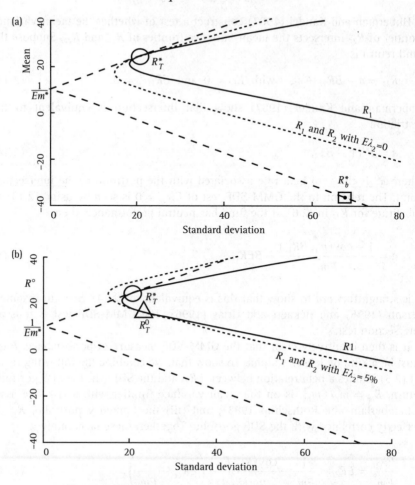

Figure 1. *The relation to mean–standard deviation frontiers*

Note: The figures show the relation between the SDF tests (without positivity imposed) and mean–standard deviation frontiers. a, Neutral performance. This shows the mean–standard deviation frontier of the benchmarks assets R_{1t} (solid hyperbola) and the frontier of the benchmarks plus a fund, R_{2t}, with neutral performance (dashed hyperbola). The frontiers intersect at the tangency portfolio R^*_{Tt}, marked by a circle. The return on the SDF, R^*_{bt}, is marked by a square. The implied risk-free rate from the SDF is $1/Em^*_t$. b, 5% excess return. This shows the frontiers when the fund has an excess return of 5%. The frontiers still intersect but now at the inefficient part, marked by a triangle. This tangency portfolio, R^0_{Tt}, corresponds to a risk-free rate of R^0.

would imply a tangency portfolio at R^0_T (marked by a triangle). Evaluated at this point, the fund with a 5% excess return appears to have a neutral performance. Chen and Knez (1996) use only stock market data to estimate the SDF. In our data set, this leads to an implied risk-free rate that differs significantly between different sets of benchmark assets, and the estimated rate is often unreasonable.

This is the reason why we include the moment condition (2.8) and use the return on a short-term bond portfolio to capture the level of the risk-free rate.[8]

III. DATA

In this section, we describe the benchmarks, information variables, and funds we use in the Monte Carlo simulations and the performance evaluation of the funds. We employ a weekly Swedish data set covering the period from January 1986 to December 1995.

Ideally, in an evaluation we would like to have access to all of the assets that comprise the investment opportunity set of the different managers. However, practical problems (like the handling of large econometric systems) prevent us from having that. For this reason we consider various portfolios of assets as benchmarks and evaluate the performance of the funds relative to these portfolios.

The first type of assets we include are truly passive buy-and-hold stock portfolios. The raw data used for the construction of the portfolios include weekly observations of Swedish stocks listed on the official A-list at the Stockholm Stock Exchange (SSE). They are obtained from *Findata*. Stocks on the A-list correspond to, on average, 97% of the total market value and 96% of the total trading volume at the SSE over the sample period.[9] We sort the firms into five industry groups: manufacturing, wood and pulp, retail services and constructing, bank and insurance, and miscellaneous. We also consider a general portfolio based on all firms. The stocks are selected based on liquidity (the value of trade) and size (market capitalization value). The portfolio weights represent initial market capitalization, and they are rebalanced only once a year (to reflect changes in the market capitalizations of the individual stocks). We also employ a data set of five portfolios formed on the basis of market capitalization (size). A detailed description of the construction of the portfolios is given in Dahlquist and Söderlind (1997).

The second type of asset we consider is a proxy for cash. We use the return on a short-term bond portfolio as a proxy for cash. It is constructed from a series of yields on a 6-month Treasury bill.

To allow for dynamic trading strategies and to study conditional performance, we use a set of predetermined economic variables that are meant to capture the state of the economy. There is considerable empirical evidence that the term structure of interest rates contains information about future economic variables (including stock returns). Two variables are used to capture the shape of the yield curve. The first is a 'level' variable based on the annualized yield of the 6-month

---

[8] Farnsworth, Ferson, Jackson, and Todd (1996) also discuss the importance of getting the mean of the SDF right.

[9] Stocks are traded under different listings, and the official A-list has the most stringent listing requirements on the records and stability of the company, as well as on the distribution and the liquidity of the company's stock.

T-bill. It is stochastically detrended by subtracting a lagged moving average (2 months) in order to decrease the persistence in the original yield. The second variable is the return on a bond portfolio with a maturity between 3 and 5 years in excess of the return on the bill portfolio. This is basically capturing changes related to the 'slope' of the yield curve; it will be referred to as the bond excess return. Moreover, the two variables are scaled so that their expected values are equal to one and their variances are of about the same magnitude as those of the original portfolio returns. The data series is obtained from *Datastream*. The lagged return on the general stock portfolio is used as a third information variable.

Table 1 reports the distributional characteristics of the industry portfolios and the bond portfolio, as well as those of the instrument variables (not scaled). The average net returns of the stock portfolios range from 14% to 21% per year. The standard deviations of the stock portfolios are between 18% and 30% per year. The low average return of the short-term bond portfolio (about 10% per year) is associated with a low volatility of 1.3%.

Furthermore, the table shows the coefficients of skewness and excess kurtosis of the portfolio returns. If they are normally distributed, then they should be equal to zero. There is no evidence of skewness—some are positive and some are negative. However, there is strong evidence of excess kurtosis, indicating that the peakness is higher and the tails are thicker than in a normal distribution. This is economically and statistically significant as revealed by the magnitudes of the

Table 1. *Distributional characteristics of benchmarks and information variables*

	Mean	Standard deviation	Skewness	Excess kurtosis	Autocorrelation
Benchmarks:					
Manufacturing	17.43	23.25	−0.03	3.31	0.12
Wood and pulp	16.65	29.83	0.95	9.25	0.11
Retail and construction	13.64	29.29	0.97	6.91	0.14
Bank and insurance	15.39	27.60	0.35	4.13	0.15
Miscellaneous	20.57	18.07	−0.46	2.94	0.11
Short-term bond	10.04	1.29	−0.08	24.82	−0.10
Information variables:					
Yield curve level	0.02	0.15	1.65	8.90	0.87
Bond excess return	1.70	5.46	−0.26	9.02	−0.11
General stock index	16.74	20.40	−0.25	3.67	0.16

Note: The table shows moments for the information variables and the weekly gross returns of the benchmark portfolios. The benchmark portfolios are passive buy-and-hold industry portfolios. The short-term bond return is a holding return on a 6-month Treasury bill. The information variables are as follows: first, the annualized yield on the 6-month Treasury detrended with a lagged 2-month moving average; second, the return on a long-term bond (maturity between 3 and 5 years) in excess of the return on the short-term bond; third, the gross return on a passive buy-and-hold portfolio of the general stock market. The mean and standard deviations of returns are expressed as net returns and in % per year. The kurtosis is in excess of the kurtosis for a normally distributed variable (3).

coefficients and the p-values (not reported).[10] A joint hypothesis of normality (not reported) can clearly be rejected at the 5% level for the portfolios.

The first-order serial correlations of the weekly returns are also reported in Table 1. All correlation coefficients are greater than 0.11. We computed standard errors as in Richardson and Smith (1994), allowing for persistence in the variances; this revealed that they all have p-values of about 5%.

Finally, the estimated moments for the two term structure variables are reported. The yield curve level has low volatility, positive skewness, and very high autocorrelation. The bond excess return, in contrast, has high volatility and no skewness or autocorrelation. These two variables seem to capture different aspects of the yield curve movements. The general (buy-and-hold) stock portfolio shows characteristics similar to those of the industry portfolios.

We have obtained data on mutual funds from *Findata*. These are available as net asset values per share adjusted for management fees and are collected on the same weekday as are the data for the benchmarks. Dividends are reinvested, by purchases of shares, in the fund. The mutual funds have some load and sale charges that are not included. We choose to study funds that invest mainly in Swedish stocks. The benchmarks above should therefore correspond to the investment styles of the funds. The data set includes only funds that existed at the end of the sample period, and potential survivorship biases are not dealt with. The funds have different inclusion dates, and we mainly present results for the period from July 1991 to December 1995 (235 observations). This gives us 24 funds in total. However, we also report the results for a subsample of six funds, covering the period from January 1987 to December 1995 (465 observations).

The funds show characteristics similar to those of the benchmarks (not reported). The average returns and standard deviations are in the same ranges as the stock portfolios. There is little evidence of skewness different from zero, but there are significant excess kurtosis and serial correlation.

IV. A MONTE CARLO EXPERIMENT

A. Motivation

Generalized method of moment is a very flexible approach that allows us to handle both non-i.i.d. and nonnormal pricing errors and positivity restrictions. In contrast, traditional tests for mean-variance intersection/spanning (see, for instance, Huberman and Kandel 1987) rely on i.d.d. normally distributed errors and linearity.

The asymptotic properties of GMM estimators and test statistics are well known, but less is known about the finite sample properties of GMM-based performance tests. Bekaert and Urias (1996) provide some simulation evidence for tests of unconditional mean-variance spanning. They find that it may be important to

---

[10] The moments in the table are estimated within a GMM system that gives us standard errors (and p-values) and by which different hypotheses can be tested.

account for serial correlation and that the properties of large systems are very unsatisfactory. However, their simulations leave several important questions unanswered. First, how does a prespecified weighting matrix (motivated below) compare with the usual 'efficient' weighting matrix? Second, do the tests have the power to detect superior performance? Third, can we rely on overlapping data? These are some of the questions we try to answer by performing a series of Monte Carlo simulations. Moreover, we extend their results to a conditional setting where data are consistently generated to allow for time variation in expected returns via information variables. We also use the opportunity to compare the small sample properties of intersection and spanning tests.

B. Setup

We estimate a time-series process from data on the information variables and the benchmarks described in Section III. The estimated process is then used in the simulations.

We want a parsimonious modeling, but one that still captures the time variation in the first and second moments. The information variables are therefore modeled as a VAR(1) system with conditionally heteroskedastic errors following a BEKK GARCH process (see Engle and Kroner 1995). The benchmark returns are generated as linear functions of the information variables and the fund returns, in accordance with Huberman and Kandel's (1987) restriction (2.13) under the assumption of mean-variance spanning, $B1 = 1$. The reason for generating data under spanning is that it certainly implies intersection (which we test for) and we want to compare intersection and spanning tests. A constant is added to the fund return when we simulate a fund with excess return. More details are found in Appendix C.

For each experiment, we construct 3,000 Monte Carlo samples, each of which has either 250 or 500 observations. A sample size of 250 (500) corresponds to approximately 5 (10) years of weekly data. From the simulations, we compute the empirical (small sample) distribution of the test statistic of neutral performance, that is, of the overidentifying restrictions that $E\lambda_{2t} = 0$.[11]

The number of simulations quickly gets very large. We therefore show results from just a representative subset of the simulations and make a few remarks about the others.

C. Choice of Weighting Matrix

In this section, we study how the small sample properties of the GMM-SDF test are affected by the choice of weighting matrix W in (2.12). We compare four versions of 'efficient' weighting matrices (giving the smallest asymptotic variance matrix) with each other and with a prespecified 'inefficient' weighting matrix.

---

[11] We have also looked at the sample averages of the performance measure itself. We find no evidence of bias, and the distribution appears symmetric and similar to a normal distribution.

The first efficient weighting matrix is a two-step estimator. Start by setting W to an identity matrix and estimate the model parameters. Use these to estimate the covariance matrix of the sample averages of the moment conditions. Then, use the inverse of the covariance matrix as the new weighting matrix and estimate the model parameters again. The second efficient weighting matrix continues from the two-step estimator by reestimating the covariance matrix and the parameters until the loss function value converges—that is, it is an iterated estimator.

The covariance matrix of a sample average is a sum of the autocovariances of the series. Estimators of this covariance matrix differ with respect to how many autocovariances are used and which coefficients they have in the sum. In the first two efficient weighting matrices, we assume a first-order autocorrelation (since returns show no partial autocorrelations beyond the first lag), and the coefficients follow Bartlett's 'tent shaped' scheme, as in Newey and West (1987). The third and fourth efficient weighting matrices are similar to the second, except that they use the automatic selection of the order of autocorrelation suggested by Newey and West (1994) and Andrews (1991), respectively.

Cochrane (1997) argues that a prespecified weighting matrix may give more robust results and that it facilitates comparison between estimations (here funds). We therefore try the inverse of the second moment matrix of (managed) returns suggested by Hansen and Jagannathan (1997). This matrix may be of particular interest, since the minimized GMM loss function value can then be interpreted as the distance between the SDF estimated with the overidentifying restrictions and the SDF that prices all assets (including the fund).

We use three tests in this article: unconditional performance with fixed-weight benchmarks, unconditional performance with dynamic benchmarks, and conditional performance with dynamic benchmarks. For the first two tests, the different weighting matrices give virtually the same result. In contrast, for the test of conditional performance with dynamic benchmarks, the choice of weighting matrix matters.

The test of conditional performance with dynamic benchmarks has a much larger system of equations than do the first two tests (the number of estimated parameters are 6, 21, and 51, respectively). Simulations reveal that this difference is important in small samples, but that it gets less and less important as the sample size increases. The number of observations per parameter, the saturation ratio, seems to be a key feature of these and of several subsequent simulations.[12] Here, it is 51, 20, and 9 for the three tests, respectively. A value below 10 is often considered an indicator of potential problems.

Figure 2 shows the empirical probability of rejecting a true null hypothesis of neutral performance (the 'size' of the test) as a function of the level of the critical

---

[12] The saturation ratio (measured as the number of observations per parameter, including the unique ones in the weighting matrix) discussed in Gallant and Tauchen (1989) can be seen as a guide to whether the dimension of the econometric system is too large. Ferson and Foerster (1994) improve the accuracy of GMM standard errors by adjusting for the total number of parameters. The saturation ratios in our setting are shown in Appendix D.

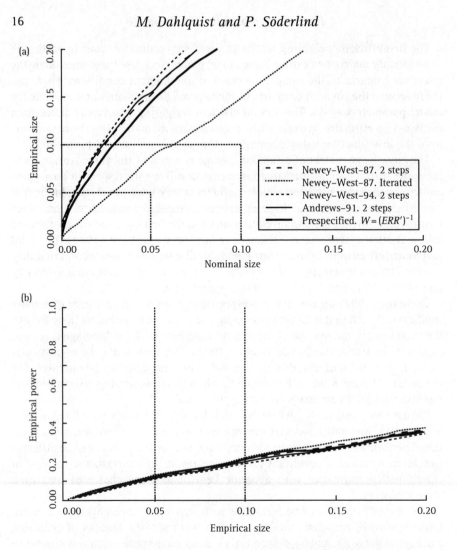

Figure 2. *Empirical size and power; choice of weighting matrix*

Note: The figures show the size and power for five different weighting matrices (see below). The results are for the test of unconditional performance with dynamic benchmarks on a sample of 250 weekly observations. a, Size. This shows the empirical size versus nominal size. b, Power at 5% excess return. This shows the corresponding power, using empirical critical values from a, when the fund has 5% excess return. The first estimator is a two-step GMM. It uses an identity matrix as a weighting matrix in the first step and the inverse of a Newey and West (1987) covariance estimator with one lag in the second step. The second weighting matrix is similar to the first but iterates until the change in loss function value is less than 1% of the expected value under the null hypothesis (here, one). The third and fourth weighting matrices are similar to the first, but use the covariance estimator with automatic lag order selection suggested by Newey and West (1994) and Andrews (1991), respectively. The fifth weighting matrix is a one-step estimator using the inverse of the second moments of the managed portfolios and the fund return.

value from the asymptotic distribution (nominal size). The closer the curves are to a 45 degree line, the closer are the small sample distributions to the asymptotic (chi-square) distribution.

The prespecified weighting matrix is slightly better than the two-step estimators, which are all very similar. However, the iterated estimator (in this case based on Bartlett's scheme, but this is not important) clearly has a smaller size distortion than do the other estimators. It can be shown that the differences between the weighting matrices are smaller when the sample is longer.

Suppose we forget about the x% critical values from the asymptotic distribution and instead take those values that give rejections in x% of the simulations in Figure 2a. We now apply these 'empirical critical values' on simulated data where the fund has 5% excess return per year to see how often the false hypothesis of neutral performance is rejected (the 'power' of the test). Figure 2b shows—once we use the empirical critical values—that all estimators do equally well.

This simulation exercise suggests that it might be important to use small sample (simulated) critical values. However, once that is done, all the estimators considered here appear equally good. The prespecified weighting matrix has some practical advantages, so this is our main choice for carrying out the subsequent simulations and for the evaluation of Swedish mutual funds. However, none of the results depends on this choice.

D. Power Issues

In this section, we investigate whether it is possible to reject the hypothesis of neutral performance when it is false.

In Figure 3 we compare the three tests used in this article on a sample of 250 weekly observations. Figure 3a shows that there are small overrejections in the two unconditional tests. For instance, a 5% critical value from the asymptotic distribution, which is $\chi^2(1)$, generates rejections in 6–7% of the simulations.[13] The overrejection is more pronounced in the conditional test: the 5% asymptotic critical value, from a $\chi^2(4)$ table, gives rejections in 13% of the simulations.

Figure 3b shows that the power of the two unconditional tests is not too impressive, even if we allow the fund to have 5% excess return per year. The power of the conditional test is even lower. The basic reason for this is that the fund returns are very volatile and the 'managed fund' returns, $z_{t-1} \otimes R_{2t}$, are even more so. To illustrate this effect, disregard the risk adjustment and suppose that a fund has a 5% excess return in a sample of τ years. If the excess return is serially uncorrelated and has a standard deviation of 10% per year, then it takes more than 10 years of data to reject neutral performance using a 10% critical value (solving $5/(10/\sqrt{\tau}) = 1.64$ gives $\tau \approx 10.8$).

---

[13] The Monte Carlo results have sampling errors since they are based on a finite number of simulations (i.e., 3,000). A 10% Kolmogorov-Smirnov confidence interval of the distributions in the figure would be approximately ±0.02 around the point estimate.

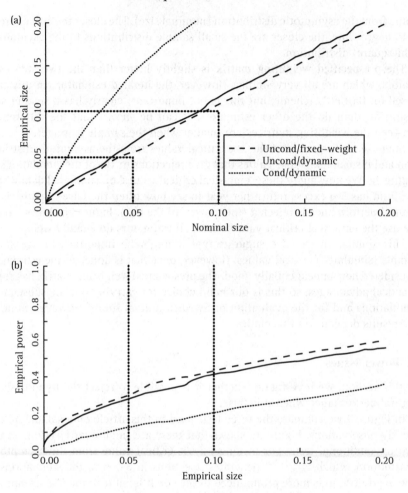

Figure 3. *Empirical size and power: different performance tests*

Note: The figures show the size and power of the three performance tests used in the article; unconditional performance with fixed-weight or dynamic benchmarks and conditional performance with dynamic benchmarks. a, Size. This shows the empirical size versus nominal size. The sample has 250 weekly observations and a prespecified weighting matrix is used. b, Power at 5% excess return. This shows the corresponding power, using empirical critical values from a, when the fund has 5% excess return.

 In Figure 4, we take a closer look at how the sample length and the excess return affect the size and the power. In this case, we show results for the unconditional test with dynamic benchmarks. Figure 4a shows that the size is not affected very much by increasing the sample length from 250 to 500 weekly observations. This is true also in the unconditional test of fixed-weight benchmarks. In the conditional test, we notice that size distortions decrease substantially for the two-step estimators and the prespecified weighting matrix, but not for the iterated estimator. The

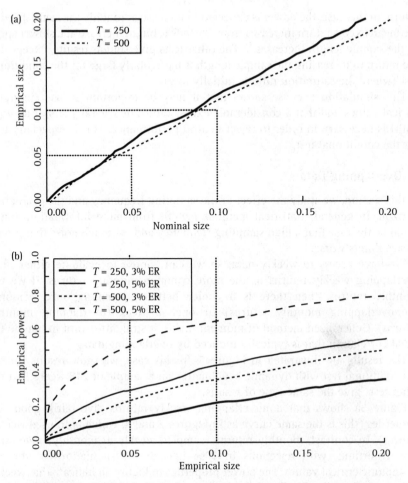

Figure 4. *Empirical size and power: sample length and excess return*

Note: The figures show the size and power for two different sample sizes and excess returns. The results are for the test of unconditional performance with dynamic benchmarks, using a prespecified weighting matrix. a, Size. This shows the empirical size versus nominal size for samples of 250 and 500 weekly observations. b, Power at 3% and 5% excess returns. This shows the corresponding power, using empirical critical values from a, when the fund has 3% or 5% excess return.

relative advantage of the iterated estimator for the conditional test on a small sample, shown in Figure 2a, is therefore almost eliminated in the longer sample.

Figure 4b shows that the power increases significantly when the excess return goes from 3% to 5% per year or when the sample length is increased from 250 to 500. For instance, at the empirical 10% critical values, the power increases from 20% to 40% when the excess return goes from 3% to 5%. Similarly, increasing the sample length from 250 to 500 increases the power at 5% excess return from 40% to 70%. As a comparison, consider once again a *t*-test of an i.i.d. normal excess return. In this case, the power is expected to increase at roughly the same speed as the mean excess return increases from 3% to 5%, but to increase at a slower speed as the sample length increases.[14] The other tests give similar results, except that the return to increasing the sample length is particularly large for the conditional test (where the saturation ratio is initially low).

This simulation exercise shows that it may be important to use simulated critical values and that a considerable excess return or several years of data (or both) is necessary in order to reject neutral performance. This is especially true for the conditional test.

E. Overlapping Data

In this section, we study the effect of the sampling frequency and the evaluation horizon. In general, statistical methods benefit from more information, but it could be the case that a high sampling frequency adds so much noise that it only makes things worse.

We have access to weekly data, so we can choose to evaluate either non-overlapping weekly returns or the more common monthly returns. If we use monthly returns, then there is a choice between sampling once a month (nonoverlapping monthly returns) or once a week (overlapping monthly returns). Generalized method of moment makes it straightforward to handle the serial correlation that is typically induced by overlapping data.

The results are illustrated in Figure 5. In this case, we show results for the unconditional test with dynamic benchmarks on a sample of 248 weeks, but the other tests give the same type of results.

Figure 5a shows that nonoverlapping weekly returns give fairly good size properties (this is the same curve as in Figures 2 and 4, which both used weekly returns). In contrast, monthly returns (sampled weekly or monthly) give large size distortions, with rejections in 10%–12% of the simulations at the 5% asymptotic critical values. The power properties in Figure 5b indicate that weekly data (either nonoverlapping weekly returns or overlapping monthly returns) deliver somewhat higher power than monthly data.

This simulation exercise suggests that we should use either of the two weekly data series. It seems somewhat more straightforward to use nonoverlapping data, so our main choice for the evaluation of the Swedish funds and the simulations (perhaps already noticed) is to use nonoverlapping weekly returns.

F. Intersection versus Spanning Tests

In this section, we round off the simulation experiments with a simple comparison of the intersection test we use and the spanning test used in De Santis (1995) and Bekaert and Urias (1996).

---

[14] If x is distributed as $N(\mu, \sigma^2)$, the probability that the t-statistics of the sample mean exceeds 1.64 is $P = 1 - \Phi(1.64 - \sqrt{T}\mu/\sigma)$. Set $\{P, T, \mu\} = \{0.2, 250, 0.03\}$ and solve for σ. With this value of σ, P is 0.38 at $\{T, \mu\} = \{250, 0.05\}$ and 0.63 at $\{T, \mu\} = \{500, 0.05\}$.

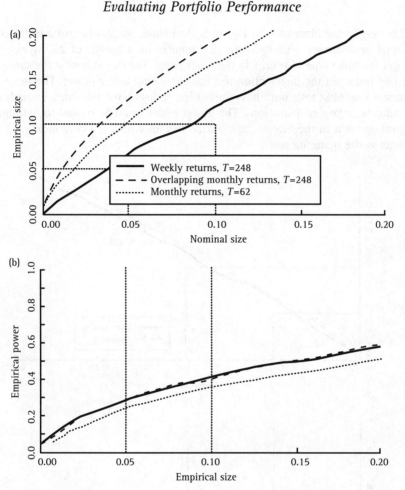

Figure 5. *Empirical size and power: evaluation horizon and sampling frequency*

Note: The figures show the size and power for three different types of data sampling from a sample of 248 weeks: weekly returns, weekly sampled monthly returns, and monthly sampled monthly returns. The results are for the test of unconditional performance with dynamic benchmarks, using a prespecified weighting matrix. a, Size. This shows the empirical size versus nominal size. b, Power at 5% excess return. This shows the corresponding power, using empirical critical values from a, when the fund has 5% excess return.

All portfolios on the mean–standard deviation frontier can be written as combinations of two portfolios on the frontier, so intersection at two distinct points is the same as spanning. This is the basis for the spanning test of Bekaert and Urias (1996), which tests for intersection at two prespecified points (0% and 10%). We compare this with a test of intersection at one prespecified point (10%), which is a slight modification of our performance test (we no longer use [2.8] to tie down the intersection point).

The results are illustrated in Figure 6. As before, we show results for unconditional performance with dynamic benchmarks on a sample of 250 weeks, but
we get the same type of results in the other cases. The size is almost the same for
the two tests, but the intersection test has somewhat better power. The intersection and spanning tests both have saturation ratios above 10—high enough not
to indicate large size distortions. The power result could be related to the higher
saturation ratio in the intersection test (it has only half as many moment conditions as the spanning test).

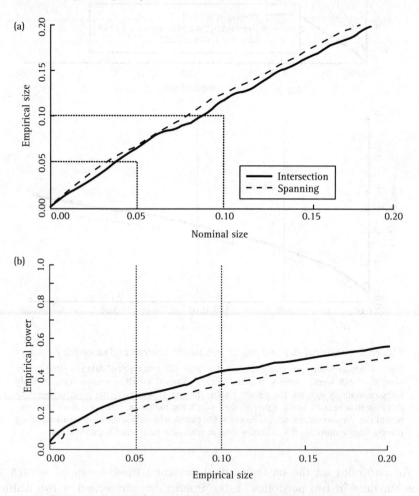

Figure 6. *Empirical size and power: intersection versus spanning*

Note: The figures show the size and power of intersection and spanning tests of unconditional performance with dynamic benchmarks. A prespecified weighting matrix is used
on a sample with 250 weekly observations. a, Size. This shows the empirical size versus
nominal size. b, Power at 5% excess return. This shows the corresponding power, using
empirical critical values from a, when the fund has 5% excess return.

G. Positive SDF

The SDF without positivity gives a linear model with an analytical solution, while positivity introduces a nonlinearity that requires a numerical optimization algorithm.

In the unconditional tests, it was quite straightforward to solve the nonlinear minimization problem, and the small sample properties were very similar to those for the SDF without positivity reported above. We interpret this as good news since there are typically reasons to worry about the small sample properties of nonlinear estimation methods.

However, in the conditional test, the solution algorithms (we tried quite a few) proved unreliable. In this case, there are 51 parameters to estimate from 55 moment conditions, which is a fairly large system of nonlinear equations. The gradient-based methods often got stuck at local minima, and other methods were too slow for performing a meaningful Monte Carlo experiment.

This simulation exercise shows that the small sample properties of the test with positivity of SDF are very similar to those of the SDF without positivity—at least in the case of an unconditional test.

H. Conclusions from the Simulation Exercises

The main results on the small sample properties of the GMM-SDF test are as follows. First, asymptotic critical values should not be used, especially when the number of observations per estimated parameter, the saturation ratio, is low. Second, it takes a considerable excess return and a long sample to reject neutral performance. Third, a prespecified weighting matrix does as well as the other weighting matrices—once empirical critical values are used. Fourth, non-overlapping weekly returns give better size and power than monthly returns. Fifth, the intersection test has better power than does the spanning test. Sixth, and last, imposing positivity on the SDF is only feasible for the unconditional tests; the positivity, however, has no effect on the statistical properties.

We have only reported a subset of the simulations. In other simulations, we have looked at the effect of using fewer/more benchmark assets, a shorter/longer sample, weaker/stronger instruments, combinations of the various experiments reported above, and different types of data-generating processes. Given the previous results, these additional simulations did not reveal anything new.

V. EVALUATING SWEDISH MUTUAL FUNDS

We now evaluate the performance of a sample of Swedish mutual funds. The returns are nonoverlapping weekly returns, and a prespecified weighting matrix (inverse of second moment matrix) is used—as suggested by the simulation results. We study mainly the sample period July 1991 to December 1995. This period is shorter than the total sample period, but it includes more funds than does the total sample. We also report results for the period January 1987 to December 1995. First we evaluate the mutual funds using fixed-weight strategies. We then extend the analysis by incorporating dynamic strategies and undertaking a conditional evaluation.

The stated goal of many funds is to provide investors with well-diversified portfolios composed of Swedish stocks. Our buy-and-hold stock portfolios are meant to describe the investment opportunity set and should capture passive investment strategies of the funds (some properties of these portfolios are summarized in Table 1). The return on the short-term bond is used to tie down the mean of the stochastic discount factor, which was shown to be of importance.

We estimated the systems for all funds separately. For the unconditional evaluations, we initially estimated the models without imposing positivity on the SDF; we then proceeded to check whether the estimated SDF was always positive. If it was not, we then reestimated with positivity imposed. In the conditional evaluation with a large GMM system, however, we did not impose positivity because we ran into numerical problems when attempting to do so.

What kind of results should we expect? Superior performance may be present if fund managers have information that is not publicly available and the skill to use it. The mutual fund returns we have (changes in net asset values) are adjusted for management fees that are not considered in the construction of the passive buy-and-hold portfolios or in the dynamic strategies we allow for. Significant management costs would then affect the measures downward. However, load charges and sales costs faced by the investors in the mutual funds are not incorporated in the net asset values. These would affect the measures upward. In total, it is hard to see a systematic bias (in either direction) of these transaction/rebalancing costs. However, the data may suffer from survivorship biases. If it is the case that only the funds that have performed well during the studied period are in the sample, we can expect an upward bias in the performance measures.

We illustrate the results in Figures. Consider first the unconditional evaluation, where the original benchmarks are assumed to reflect *fixed-weight strategies*. Figure 7a shows the frequency of the statistic of the test for neutral performance (the overidentifying restriction). This is compared with the empirical density function under the null hypothesis (which corresponds asymptotically to the $\chi^2(1)$-distribution).[15] Empirical critical values from the simulations are also reported (the vertical dotted lines mark the 5% and 10% values). About 17% of the funds are to the right of the 5% critical value. This indicates that a somewhat larger portion of the funds than expected have nonneutral performance.

In Figure 7b the distribution of the performance measure, $E\lambda_{2t}$, which utilizes a positive SDF, is reported. We see that most of the values are concentrated around zero but that some funds seem to have nonneutral performance. The distribution is somewhat skewed to the right, as indicated by the higher average (0.5%)

---

[15] The empirical densities shown in this and subsequent figures are estimated with a Gaussian kernel where the bandwidth parameter is chosen automatically (See Silverman 1996).

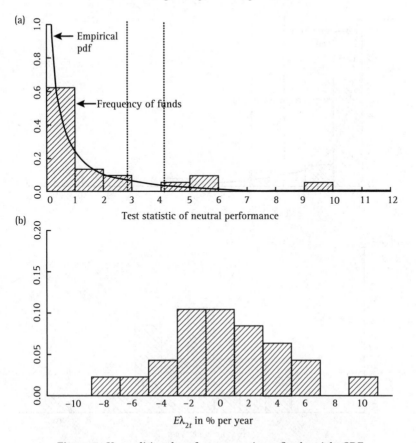

(a)

Empirical pdf

Frequency of funds

Test statistic of neutral performance

(b)

$E\lambda_{2t}$ in % per year

Figure 7. *Unconditional performance using a fixed-weight SDF*

Note: The figures show the result of an unconditional evaluation using a fixed-weight benchmark. a, Test statistic. This shows the frequency distribution of the test statistic of neutral performance (one overidentifying restriction). The empirical density function (asymptotically corresponding to a $\chi^2(1)$-distribution under the null hypothesis) is also depicted. The vertical dotted lines mark the empirical critical values at the 5% and 10% significance level. b, Performance measure. This shows the distribution of performance measures, $E\lambda_{2t}$ that are based on a positive SDF.

compared to the median (0.1%) of the distribution. Out of 24 funds, five have absolute deviations (inferior or superior performance) that are greater than 5% (per year) from zero. Still, there is no general tendency in the distribution.

The benchmark portfolios can be seen as fixed-weight portfolios. We find that the average (risk-adjusted) performance is slightly positive. Can this be explained by dynamic asset allocation based on publicly available information? Alternatively, is the actual performance masked by variations in expected returns and risk premia? Above we discussed dynamic strategies as a partial solution to this problem. We therefore consider dynamic strategies using the

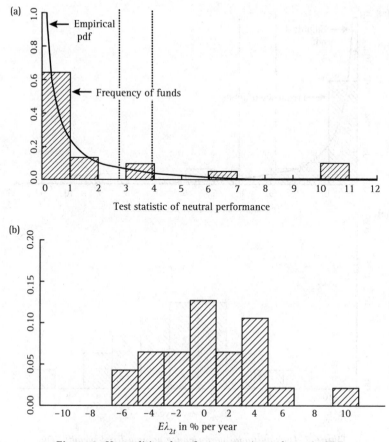

Figure 8. *Unconditional performance using a dynamic SDF*

The figures show the result of an unconditional evaluation using a dynamic benchmark. a, Test statistic. This shows the frequency distribution of the test statistic of neutral performance (one overidentifying restriction). The empirical density function (asymptotically corresponding to a $\chi^2(1)$-distribution under the null hypothesis) is also depicted. The vertical dotted lines mark the empirical critical values at the 5% and 10% significance level. b, Performance measure. This shows the distribution of performance measures $E\lambda_{2t}$ that are based on a positive SDF.

lagged level of the yield curve, the lagged excess return on the bond portfolio, and the lagged return on the general stock portfolio as instruments. Put differently, we now analyze the unconditional performance against five managed portfolios. The results are shown in Figure 8. Observing Figures 8a and 8b, we can, however, see that the results are not very different. The distribution of the moment conditions for the funds in Figure 8b is somewhat flatter with a mean and median of 0.4% and 0.1% , respectively. Again, five funds have an absolute overperformance that is greater than 5%. The test for overidentifying restriction in Figure 8a shows no distinct differences from the asymptotic distribution, and the findings are the same as with fixed-weight strategies. Notice that the use of the asymptotic critical values would cause an overrejection of neutral performance (as was shown in Figure 4), whereas the empirical critical values overcome this.

In Section IIc we argued that it is important to tie the mean of the SDF to a reasonable value. Otherwise we may evaluate at a misleading tangency point. We therefore investigate how sensitive the results are to deviations from $Em_t = E(1/R_{ft})$. Adding $\pm 1\%$ (on an annual basis) to Em_t changes the distributions of the performance measures (both fixed-weight and dynamic m_t) fairly little. Adding (subtracting) 1% moves the distributions somewhat to the left (right), yielding a somewhat more negative (positive) performance. The deviations are not enough, though, to overturn the results.

Up to now we have analyzed unconditional (average) performance. It is also of interest to test the conditional performance of the funds, again using dynamic benchmark strategies. We condition the unconditional performance measure on the state of the economy to study if the funds have superior/inferior performance in some (predictable) states of the economy. Note that the specification of the SDF has to be changed in order to price these conditional strategies under the null (see Section IIB). In Figure 9a, the test statistics and the empirical distribution of the test statistics are depicted (it now corresponds asymptotically to a $\chi^2(4)$-distributed variable).[16] The nonneutral performance appears this time to be more significant for a large portion of the funds. The null is rejected even though we use the empirical critical values which are significantly larger than the asymptotic ones. In Figure 9b, we show the performance measure that corresponds to the constant in z_{t-1}. Recall that the performance measures related to the non-constant elements in z_{t-1} (the z_{t-1}^c:s) can be written as:

$$E\lambda_{2t}^c = \operatorname{cov}(\lambda_{2t}^{uc}, z_{t-1}^c) + E\lambda_{2t}^{uc} E z_{t-1}^c. \tag{5.1}$$

Since $E z_{t-1}^c$ is set to one, the $E\lambda_{2t}^c$ measures the sum of the covariance of the unconditional performance and the information variables and the unconditional performance. In Figures 9c–e, we show the covariances in (5.1), that is, the $\operatorname{cov}(\lambda_{2t}^{uc}, z_{t-1}^c)$. The average unconditional performance across the funds (the average of the $E\lambda_{2t}^{uc}$) is slightly higher than before (about 0.9% per year). The unconditional performance measure seems to be positively related to two of the information variables—the general market and the level of the yield curve—as measured by the covariances. Hence, the tendency for nonneutral performance is strengthened (they show a performance of 1.1%–1.2% on average with medians of about 1.4%). That is, when we have experienced an increase in the stock market or a high level of interest rates in general, the funds have performed better than on average. The opposite is the case for the bond excess return instrument. Overall, the stronger case for nonneutral performance appears to stem from the fact that the unconditional performance can be predicted by the information variables.

---

[16] In the conditional evaluation, one fund is not examined because of numerical difficulties in forming the test statistic.

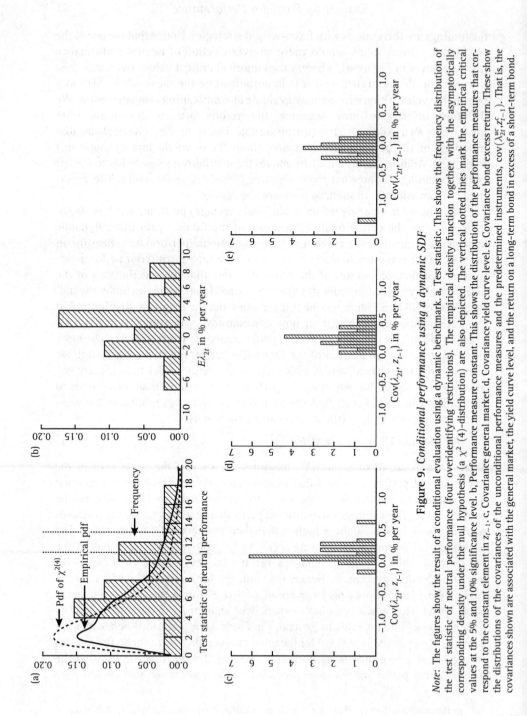

Figure 9. *Conditional performance using a dynamic SDF*

Note: The figures show the result of a conditional evaluation using a dynamic benchmark. a, Test statistic. This shows the frequency distribution of the test statistic of neutral performance (four overidentifying restrictions). The empirical density function together with the asymptotically corresponding density under the null hypothesis (a χ^2 (4)-distribution) are also depicted. The vertical dotted lines mark the empirical critical values at the 5% and 10% significance level. b, Performance measure constant. This shows the distribution of the performance measures that correspond to the constant element in z_{t-1}. c, Covariance general market. d, Covariance yield curve level. e, Covariance bond excess return. These show the distributions of the covariances of the unconditional performance measures and the predetermined instruments, $\text{cov}(\lambda_{2t}^{uc}, z_{t-1}^c)$. That is, the covariances shown are associated with the general market, the yield curve level, and the return on a long-term bond in excess of a short-term bond.

To sum up, we present the means and medians of the performance measures for the three cases in Table 2. Decompositions of the performance measures are also given. Using (2.6), the performance measures can be written as:

$$E\lambda_{2t}/Em_t = [E(z_{t-1} \otimes R_{2t}) - 1/Em_t] - [-\text{cov}(z_{t-1} \otimes R_{2t}, m_t)/Em_t], \quad (5.2)$$

where we have used the fact that the instrument is normalized such that $Ez_{t-1} = 1$. The first term within brackets can be interpreted as the managed returns of the funds in excess over the implied risk-free rate. The second term within brackets is then the 'risk premium.' From the table, we see that the average excess return over a risk-free rate in the unconditional evaluation is about 3.4% and the risk premium is about 2.9%, yielding a superior performance of about 0.5% per year. It is noteworthy that, in the conditional evaluation, the excess returns (for the different information variables) are about the same magnitude or higher, whereas the risk premia are smaller.

An assessment of the various stochastic discount factors used reveals that their means are similar (since they are tied to the bill portfolio, the only differences come from the positivity imposed). On average, the SDFs imply a risk-free rate of about 9% per year. It is evident that when strategies based on the information variables are allowed, the standard deviations of the SDFs increase significantly. The dynamic SDFs show a correlation of about 56%, whereas their correlations to the fixed-weight SDF are fairly low (about 20%). This indicates that risk premia would be very different if the 'correct' specifications of the SDF were not being used.

Table 2. *A summary of the performance evaluations*

	Unconditional fixed-weight constant	Unconditional dynamic constant	Conditional dynamic			
			Constant	General	Yield	Bond
Performance measures:						
Mean	0.48	0.42	0.90	1.12	1.18	0.73
Median	0.08	0.14	1.24	1.42	1.40	0.78
Decomposition:						
Excess return	3.43	3.16	3.43	3.97	3.72	4.15
Risk premium	2.95	2.74	2.53	2.85	2.54	3.42

Note: The table summarizes the results of the three evaluations that are undertaken on a sample of Swedish mutual funds. The first evaluation is unconditional and utilizes a fixed-weight benchmark. The second evaluation is also unconditional but allows for dynamic strategies through predetermined information variables. The variables (in addition to a constant) are the general market return, the level of the yield curve (detrended), and the return on a long-term bond in excess of the return on the short-term bond. The third evaluation is conditional on the state of the economy, captured by the above noted information variables. Again, dynamic strategies are allowed. The conditional evaluation yields a several-dimensional performance measure—one per information variable. The first two rows in the table show the means and medians (in % per year) across the funds. In the subsequent rows, the average performance is decomposed into an excess return and a risk premium, as expressed in (5.2). All measures are in % per year.

For six of the funds, we have data from 1987. Applying the above tests on the funds over this longer sample period shows that for five of the six funds, the performances have been worse during he period 1987–95 compared to the period 1991–95. This holds for both the unconditional setting and the conditional setting. Two funds change from positive to negative performance as the sample is extended backward.

Finally, we assess the robustness of the results by undertaking the evaluation using size portfolios instead of industry portfolios as benchmarks. This changes the unconditional performance measures very little; the distributions are still centered around zero. The evaluation using a dynamic SDF indicates better performance, but the null of neutral performance cannot be rejected.

VI. CONCLUSIONS

In this article, we provide evidence on the use of stochastic discount factors in the evaluation of portfolio performance. The article is divided into three major parts. In the first part, we build on papers by Bansal and Harvey (1996), Chen and Knez (1996), and Farnsworth, Ferson, Jackson, and Todd (1996) and discuss performance evaluation using efficient (by construction) benchmarks and allowing for dynamic strategies. We relate the performance measures in Chen and Knez (1996) to the traditional mean-variance analysis. In particular, we make an explicit interpretation of the performance measures in terms of a specific Jensen's alpha measure computed against efficient benchmarks. Moreover, we highlight the importance of getting the mean of the SDF right. Otherwise, the evaluation could be undertaken at an arbitrary (and misleading) point in the mean-variance space. Finally, we show how to select the instruments in order to undertake a correct conditional evaluation that allows for dynamic strategies. If we fail to use the correct instruments in constructing the SDF, then a fund with a neutral dynamic trading strategy can incorrectly show either inferior or superior performance.

In the second part of the article, we examine the small sample properties of GMM estimators in this setting using a series of Monte Carlo simulations. The results provide no evidence against using a prespecified weighting matrix. We do find evidence in favor of using weekly nonoverlapping returns instead of monthly returns. We also show that the size of the test can sometimes be seriously distorted such that empirical critical values should be used. However, when we correct for the size, the power is about the same in the different settings. Moreover, we highlight the case in which an economically significant excess return is needed in order to reject the null of neutral performance unless the sample is very long. The power properties are better in the unconditional setting compared to the conditional setting and/or when the econometric systems are large. Moreover, the intersection test appears to have higher power than the spanning test.

In the third part, we apply the methodology to Swedish-based mutual funds and offer an actual evaluation. An unconditional as well as a conditional evaluation is undertaken. In the unconditional evaluation, using either fixed-weight or dynamic strategies (via returns scaled by available public information), we cannot find strong evidence of non-neutral performance. The performance of the funds is, on average, positive, but it cannot be confirmed statistically. However, when we evaluate conditionally, again allowing for dynamic strategies, the results indicate a tendency toward nonneutral performance. This captures the degree of predictability in the performance measure.

Appendix A. Simple Benchmark Strategies and Performance Measures

Let R_{1t} be an $n_1 \times 1$ vector, x_t a $k \times 1$ vector, and z_t an $l \times 1$ vector. Take expectations of (2.7)

$$E\lambda_{1t} = E(z_{t-1} \otimes x_{t-1} \otimes R_{1t})m_t - Ez_{t-1} \otimes x_{t-1} \otimes 1_{n_1}, \tag{A1}$$

which is set to zero by the choice of m_t. (The case with a fixed-weight benchmark portfolio is obtained by setting $x_t = 1$.) This appendix shows that any portfolio with weights that are linear in the information variables x_{t-1} and that sum to one in every period will then be assigned a neutral performance.

Combine (2.1) and (2.2) to get

$$R_t = x'_{t-1}\delta R_{1t}, \quad \text{such that } x'_{t-1}\delta 1_{n_1} = 1, \tag{A2}$$

where δ is a $k \times n_1$ matrix.

For simplicity, suppose x_t has only two elements: a constant and a random variable, $x'_t = [1 \quad \tilde{x}_t]$. The portfolio weights are then

$$x'_t\delta = [1 \quad \tilde{x}_t] \begin{bmatrix} \delta_{11} \cdots \delta_{1n_1} \\ \delta_{21} \cdots \delta_{2n_1} \end{bmatrix}. \tag{A3}$$

The portfolio weights must sum to one in every period, that is,

$$1 = x'_t\delta 1_{n_1} = [1 \quad \tilde{x}_t] \begin{bmatrix} \delta_{11} + \cdots + \delta_{1n_1} \\ \delta_{21} + \cdots + \delta_{2n_1} \end{bmatrix}. \tag{A4}$$

The only way to guarantee that this holds in every period is to have the first row in δ summing to one and the second row summing to zero. This means that movements in the stochastic information variables are only allowed to change the portfolio weights in a zero investment portfolio of R_{1t}. More formally, we have the requirement that

$$\delta 1_{n_1} = \begin{bmatrix} 1 \\ 0 \end{bmatrix}. \tag{A5}$$

The $l \times 1$ vector of performance measures of the scalar benchmark portfolio R_t in (A2) is (one for each instrument in z_{t-1})

$$E\lambda_t = E(z_{t-1}x'_{t-1}\delta R_{1t})m_t - Ez_{t-1}. \tag{A6}$$

Pick out the elements in $E\lambda_{1t}$ from (A1) and $E\lambda_t$ from (A6) which correspond to the jth element in $z_{t-1}, z_{t-1,j}$, and write them as

$$E\lambda_{1t,j} = E(z_{t-1,j}x_{t-1} \otimes R_{1t})m_t - Ez_{t-1,j}x_{t-1} \otimes 1_{n_1}, \tag{A7}$$

and

$$E\lambda_{t,j} = E(z_{t-1,j}x'_{t-1}\delta R_{1t})m_t - Ez_{t-1,j}. \tag{A8}$$

Let δ_i be the ith row of δ, so

$$x'_{t-1}\delta R_{1t} = \delta_1 R_{1t} + \tilde{x}_{t-1}\delta_2 R_{1t}. \tag{A9}$$

This allows us to rewrite (A8) as

$$E\lambda_{t,j} = \delta_1 E(z_{t-1,j}R_{1t}m_t) + \delta_2 E(z_{t-1,j}\tilde{x}_{t-1}R_{1t}m_t) - Ez_{t-1,j}. \tag{A10}$$

Since the first element in x_{t-1} is a constant, (A7) shows that each of the elements in the vector $E(z_{t-1,j}R_{1t}m_t)$ equals $Ez_{t-1,j}$. From (A5) we also know that $\delta_1 1 = 1$. Combining these facts gives that $\delta_1 E(z_{t-1,j} R_{1t}m_t)$ in (A10) equals $Ez_{t-1,1}$.

Similarly, by (A7), each of the elements in $E(z_{t-1,j}\tilde{x}_{t-1}R_{1t}m_t)$ equals $E(z_{t-1,j}\tilde{x}_{t-1})$. Since $\delta_2 1 = 0$, we get that $\delta_2 E(z_{t-1,j}, \tilde{x}_{t-1}R_{1t}m_t)$ in (A10) is zero. Together, these results give $E\lambda_{t,j} = 0$ in (A10). To sum up, any portfolio with weights that are linear in the information variables x_{t-1} and that sum to one in every period has a neutral performance if $E\lambda_{1t} = 0$ in (A1).

Appendix B. GMM Estimation and Testing

In this appendix we briefly review the limiting distributions of the parameter estimate and the test for overidentifying restrictions.

Let Λ_t be the stacked moment conditions in (2.12), and let Q denote the Jacobian of the sample moment conditions, that is,

$$Q = \frac{\partial \bar{\Lambda}}{\partial \gamma'}, \tag{B1}$$

where $\bar{\Lambda} = 1/T \sum_{t=1}^{T} \Lambda_t$. The general (for an arbitrary weighting matrix) expression for the asymptotic covariance matrix of $\sqrt{T}(\hat{\gamma} - \gamma)$ is equal to

$$V = (Q'WQ)^{-1}Q'WSWQ(Q'WQ)^{-1}, \tag{B2}$$

where

$$S = \text{cov}(\sqrt{T}\bar{\Lambda}) = \lim_{T \to \infty} \sum_{s=-(T-1)}^{T-1} \text{cov}(\Lambda_t, \Lambda_{t-s}). \tag{B3}$$

It is common to set $W = S^{-1}$, and (B2) then simplifies to $V = (Q'S^{-1}Q)^{-1}$. Regarding the overidentifying restrictions, Hansen (1982) shows (lemma 4) that the asymptotic covariance matrix of the moment restrictions $\sqrt{T}(\bar{\Lambda} - \Lambda)$ is

$$\Omega = [I - Q(Q'WQ)^{-1}Q'W]S[I - WQ(Q'WQ)^{-1}Q']. \tag{B4}$$

When $W = S^{-1}$, this simplifies to $\Omega = S - Q(Q'S^{-1}Q)^{-1}Q'$ which is numerically equal to S (see Cochrane 1997). In either case, Ω has reduced rank equal to the number of overidentifying restrictions, denoted q below. We can therefore construct a χ^2-distributed test statistic,

$$T\bar{\Lambda}'\Omega^+\bar{\Lambda} \sim \chi^2(q), \tag{B5}$$

where $^+$ indicates a generalized inverse (see Cochrane 1996). It is tricky to calculate Ω^+ with reasonable accuracy. According to our experience, it is very useful to impose the known rank of Ω in these calculations. This is done in several steps. First, calculate the singular value decomposition such that $usv' = \Omega$ and reorder u, s, and v so that the singular values come in decreasing order. Second, partition

$$s = \begin{bmatrix} s_1 & 0 \\ 0 & s_2 \end{bmatrix}, \quad u = [u_1 \quad u_2], \quad \text{and} \quad v = [v_1 \quad v_2],$$

so that the first block contains the q largest singular values (the remaining singular values should, in principle, be zero). Third, calculate the generalized inverse as $\Omega^+ = v_1 s_1^{-1} u_1'$.

Appendix C. The Data-Generating Processes

This appendix describes the data-generating processes for the reference assets and the portfolios under evaluation in the Monte Carlo simulations. We want a parsimonious modeling for the reference assets but still want to capture time variation in the first and second moments. We therefore use a first-order vector autoregressive model (VAR) for the first moments. The dynamics of the second moment is a simple version of the general BEKK model in Engle and Kroner (1995). The advantage of the BEKK model for conditional covariances is that it guarantees positive definite conditional covariance matrices under weak conditions. Moreover, compared to other models, it uses few parameters but still allows for conditional correlations and is able to capture potential cross-volatility interactions as well. For tractability, the model is here restricted to be of order $(1, 1)$. The specification below allows us to model simultaneously conditional means, variances, covariances, and correlations.

Let $\tilde{z}_t$ be a $k - 1$ vector of instruments. The dynamics for the $\ln \tilde{z}_t$ is a VAR(1) with BEKK errors

$$\ln \tilde{z}_t = \mu + A \ln \tilde{z}_{t-1} + \epsilon_t, \tag{C1}$$

where μ is a $k - 1$ parameter vector, A is a $(k - 1) \times (k - 1)$ parameter matrix, and ϵ_t is a $k - 1$ vector of error terms that are assumed to be conditionally multivariate normal distributed but serially uncorrelated. That is,

$$\epsilon_t | \Omega_{t-1} \sim N(0, H_t), \tag{C2}$$

where Ω_{t-1} denotes the information set at time $t - 1$. Assuming that the dynamics of the conditional covariance matrix is covariance stationary with an unconditional covariance matrix equal to H_0, we estimate a diagonal BEKK model that can be written as

$$H_t = H_0 \odot (1_n 1'_n - bb' - cc') + bb' \odot \epsilon_{t-1} \epsilon'_{t-1} + cc' \odot H_{t-1}, \tag{C3}$$

where $\odot$ denotes the Hamadard product (element-by-element), and b and c are parameter vectors.

The parameters are estimated in a two-step procedure. In the first step, we estimate the VAR system (using least squares) and the parameters in H_0. In the second step, the BEKK parameters, b and c, are estimated by maximum likelihood.

The dynamics of the benchmark portfolios are

$$\ln R_{1t} = C \left| \begin{array}{c} 1 \\ \vdots \\ \ln \tilde{z}_{t-1} \end{array} \right| + \eta_t, \tag{C4}$$

where C is an $n_1 \times k$ parameter matrix, and η_t a vector of i.i.d. normally distributed error terms with covariance matrix Σ. The matrices C and Σ are estimated using least squares.

The data-generating process of the portfolios that are being evaluated under the null hypothesis is

$$R_{2t} = BR_{1t} + u_t, \tag{C5}$$

where $B1 = 1$ and u_t is a vector of i.i.d. normally distributed errors with covariance matrix Ψ. The matrix Ψ is taken from a least squares estimation of (C5) of a typical mutual fund, and B is also based on the estimate but is adjusted to satisfy the condition $B1 = 1$ exactly. Note that (C5) is actually the case of spanning in Huberman and Kandel (1987). The advantage of this approach is that the funds are generated only by the benchmarks and not at all by the zero-beta asset, which is important for the conditional evaluation. In the actual evaluation we still use the intersection test. Under the alternative hypothesis of superior performance, we add a constant yielding, for instance, a 5% excess return on an annual basis.

Appendix D. Saturation Ratios

In GMM estimation, the total number of observations divided by the number of parameters to be estimated (including the number of unique parameters in the weighting matrix) is sometimes referred to as the saturation ratio. The total number of observations is equal to the number of moment conditions times the length of the data. The saturation ratios for the three systems we consider in this article are given by

$$SR^1 = \frac{(n_1 + n_2 + 1)T}{\left[n_1 + 1 + \dfrac{(n_1 + n_2 + 1)(n_1 + n_2 + 2)}{2}\right]}, \tag{D1}$$

$$SR^2 = \frac{(kn_1 + n_2 + 1)T}{\left[kn_1 + 1 + \dfrac{(kn_1 + n_2 + 1)(kn_1 + n_2 + 2)}{2}\right]}, \tag{D2}$$

and

$$SR^3 = \frac{\left(\dfrac{k(k+1)}{2}n_1 + kn_2 + 1\right)T}{\left[\dfrac{k(k+1)}{2}n_1 + 1 + \dfrac{\left(\dfrac{k(k+1)}{2}n_1 + kn_2 + 1\right)\left(\dfrac{k(k+1)}{2}n_1 + kn_2 + 2\right)}{2}\right]}, \tag{D3}$$

where SR^1 refers to the fixed-weight/unconditional case, SR^2 to the dynamic/unconditional case, and SR^3 to the dynamic/conditional case.

REFERENCES

Andrews, D. W. K. 1991. Heteroskedasticity and autocorrelation consistent covariance matrix estimation. *Econometrica* 59: 817–58.

Bansal, R., and Harvey, C. R. 1996. Performance evaluation in the presence of dynamic trading strategies. Working paper. Durham, N.C.: Duke University, Fuqua School of Business.

——, and Viswanathan, S. 1993. No arbitrage and arbitrage pricing: A new approach. *Journal of Finance* 48: 1231–62.

Bekaert, G., and Urias, M. S. 1996. Diversification, integration and emerging market closed-end funds. *Journal of Finance* 51: 835–69.

Chamberlain, G., and Rothschild, M. 1983. Arbitrage factor structure, and mean-variance analysis on large asset markets. *Econometrica* 51: 1281–1304.

Chen, Z., and Knez, P. J. 1996. Portfolio measurement: Theory and applications. *Review of Financial Studies* 9: 511–55.

Cochrane, J. H. 1996. A cross-sectional test of an investment-based asset pricing model. *Journal of Political Economy* 104: 572–621.

—— 1997. Asset pricing. Unpublished manuscript. Chicago: University of Chicago.

Dahlquist, M., and Söderlind, P. 1997. Swedish buy-and-hold stock portfolios: 1985 to 1995. Working paper. Stockholm: Stockholm School of Economics.

De Santis, G. 1995. Volatility bounds for stochastic discount factors: Tests and implications from international financial markets. Working paper. Los Angeles: University of Southern California, Department of Finance and Business Economics.

Dybvig, P. H., and Ross, S. A. 1985. The analytics of performance measurement using a security market line. *Journal of Finance* 40: 401–16.

Engle, R. F., and Kroner, K. F. 1995. Multivariate simultaneous generalized ARCH. *Econometric Theory* 11: 122–50.

Farnsworth, H., Ferson, W., Jackson. D., and Todd, S. 1996. Conditional performance evaluation. Working paper. Seattle: University of Washington.

Ferson, W. E. 1995. Theory and empirical testing of asset pricing models. In R. A. Jarrow, V. Maksimovic, and W. T. Ziemba (eds.), *Handbooks in Operations Research and Management Science.* Amsterdam: North-Holland.

Ferson, W. E., and Foerster, S. R. 1994. Finite sample properties of the Generalized Method of Moments in tests of conditional asset pricing models. *Journal of Financial Economics* 36: 29–55.

——, and Schadt, R. 1996. Measuring fund strategy and performance in changing economic conditions. *Journal of Finance* 51: 425–61.

Gallant, R. A., and Tauchen, G. 1989. Seminonparametric estimation of conditionally constrained heterogeneous processes: Asset pricing implications. *Econometrica* 57: 1091–1120.

Glosten, L., and Jagannathan, R. 1994. A contingent claims approach to performance evaluation. *Journal of Empirical Finance* 1: 133–66.

Hansen, L. P. 1982. Large sample properties of generalized method of moments estimators. *Econometrica* 50: 1029–54.

——, and Jagannathan, R. 1991. Implications of security market data for models of dynamic economies. *Journal of Political Economy* 99: 225–62.

——, and Jagannathan, R. 1997. Assessing specification errors in stochastic discount factor models. *Journal of Finance* 52: 557–90.

——, and Richard, S. F. 1987. The role of conditioning information in deducing testable restrictions implied by dynamic asset pricing models. *Econometrica* 55: 587–613.

Huberman, G., and Kandel, S. 1987. Mean-variance spanning. *Journal of Finance* 42: 873–88.

Newey, W. K., and West, K. D. 1987. A simple positive semi-definite heteroskedasticity and autocorrelation consistent covariance matrix. *Econometrica* 55: 703–8.

——, and —— 1994. Automatic lag selection in covariance matrix estimation. *Review of Economic Studies* 61: 631–54.

Richardson, M., and Smith, T. 1994. A unified approach to testing for serial correlation on stock returns. *Journal of Business* 67: 371–99.

Roll, R. 1978. Ambiguity when performance is measured by the security market line. *Journal of Finance* 38: 1051–69.

Silverman, B. W. 1986. *Density Estimation for Statistics and Data Analysis.* London: Chapman & Hall.

Snow, K. N. 1991. Diagnosing asset pricing models using the distribution of asset returns. *Journal of Finance* 46: 955–83.

2

Implied Volatility Functions:
Empirical Tests

BERNARD DUMAS, JEFF FLEMING, AND ROBERT E. WHALEY

Expected future volatility plays a central role in finance theory. Consequently, accurately estimating this parameter is crucial to meaningful financial decision making. Finance researchers generally rely on the past behavior of asset prices to develop expectations about volatility, documenting movements in volatility as they relate to prior volatility and/or variables in the investors' information set. As useful as such investigations have been, they are by nature backward looking, using past behavior to project forward. An alternative approach, albeit less explored in the literature, is to use reported option prices to infer volatility expectations.[1] Because option value depends critically on expected future volatility, the volatility expectation of market participants can be recovered by inverting the option valuation formula.

The volatility expectation derived from reported option prices depends on the assumptions underlying the option valuation formula. The Black–Scholes (1973) model, for example, assumes the asset price follows geometric Brownian motion with constant volatility. Consequently, all options on the same asset should

This research was supported by the HEC School of Management and the Futures and Options Research Center at the Fuqua School of Business, Duke University. We gratefully acknowledge discussions with Jens Jackwerth and Mark Rubinstein and comments and suggestions by Blaise Allaz, Denis Alexandre, Suleyman Basak, David Bates, Greg Bauer, Peter Bossaerts, Andrea Buraschi, Peter Carr, Gilles Demonsant, Jin-Chuan Duan, Bruno Dupire, Gary Gorton, Sanford Grossman, Bruce Grundy, Philippe Henrotte, Steve Heston, John Hull, Eric Jacquier, Jean-Paul Laurent, Hayne Leland, Angelo Melino, Krishna Ramaswamy, Ehud Ronn, Hersh Sheffrin, Robert Stambaugh, Denis Talay, Ken West, Alan White, Stanley Zin, three anonymous referees, René Stulz (the editor) and the seminar participants at HEC, the Isaac Newton Institute, Cambridge University, the Chicago Board of Trade's Nineteenth Annual Spring Research Symposium, the University of Pennsylvania, the University of New Mexico, the University of Toronto, Hong Kong Polytechnic University, the University of New South Wales, the Sixth Annual Conference of Financial Economics and Accounting at the University of Maryland, the Inquire Europe group in Barcelona, the London Business School, the NBER Asset Pricing group, the European Financial Management Association meeting in Innsbruck, the University of British Columbia, the University of Toulouse, the 'World of Fischer Black' London School of Economics/ London School of Business conference in Sardinia, Erasmus University, Rice University, the University of Amsterdam, the University of Lausanne, and the Dallas meetings of the Institute for Operations Research and the Management Sciences.

[1] See Breeden and Litzenberger (1978), Bick (1988), and Bates (1996a, 1996b).

provide the same implied volatility. In practice, however, Black–Scholes implied volatilities tend to differ across exercise prices and times to expiration.[2] S&P 500 option-implied volatilities, for example, form a 'smile' pattern prior to the October 1987 market crash. Options that are deep in the money or out of the money have higher implied volatilities than at-the-money options. After the crash, a 'sneer'[3] appears—the implied volatilities decrease monotonically as the exercise price rises relative to the index level, with the rate of decrease increasing for options with shorter time to expiration.

The failure of the Black–Scholes model to describe the structure of reported option prices is thought to arise from its constant volatility assumption.[4] It has been observed that when stock prices go up volatility goes down, and vice versa. Accounting for nonconstant volatility within an option valuation framework, however, is no easy task. With stochastic volatility, option valuation generally requires a market price of risk parameter, which, among other things, is difficult to estimate. An exception occurs when volatility is a deterministic function of asset price and/or time. In this case, option valuation based on the Black–Scholes partial differential equation remains possible, although not by means of the Black–Scholes formula itself. We refer to this special case as the 'deterministic volatility function' (DVF) hypothesis.

Derman and Kani (1994a,b), Dupire (1994), and Rubinstein (1994) develop variations of the DVF approach. Their methods attempt to decipher the cross section of option prices and deduce the future behavior of volatility as anticipated by market participants. Rather than positing a structural form for the volatility function, they search for a binomial or trinomial lattice that achieves an *exact* cross-sectional fit of reported option prices. Rubinstein, for example, uses an 'implied binomial tree' whose branches at each node are designed (either by choice of up-and-down increment sizes or probabilities) to reflect the time variation of volatility.

The goal of this paper is to assess the time-series validity of assuming volatility is a deterministic function of asset price and time. We do this by answering the question: Is the asset price behavior revealed by these methods validated by the actual, subsequent behavior of asset prices? We do not perform statistical analysis on the asset prices themselves, however, as this would require years of observations. Instead, we consider the future behavior of option prices. This approach represents a powerful statistical procedure that more rapidly yields a verdict on the validity of the DVF approach.

---

[2] Rubinstein (1994) examines the S&P 500 index market. Similar investigations have also been performed for the Philadelphia Exchange foreign currency option market (e.g., Taylor and Xu (1993)), and for stock options traded at the London International Financial Futures Exchange (e.g., Duque and Paxson (1993)) and the European Options Exchange (e.g., Heynen (1993)).

[3] Webster (1994, p. 1100) defines a sneer as 'a scornful facial expression marked by a slight raising of one corner of the upper lip.'

[4] Putting it succinctly, Black (1976, p. 177) says that 'if the volatility of a stock changes over time, the option formulas that assume a constant volatility are wrong.'

To implement this approach, we simply move out-of-sample to assess whether the volatility function implied today is the same one embedded in option prices tomorrow. If the estimated volatility function is stable through time, this finding supports the DVF approach as an important new way to identify the underlying process of financial market prices and for setting hedge ratios and valuing exotic options. On the other hand, if the estimated function is not stable, we must conclude that valuation and risk management using the DVF approach is unreliable and that other explanations for the Black–Scholes implied volatility patterns must be sought.

The paper is organized as follows. In Section I, we document the historical patterns of the Black–Scholes implied volatilities. In Section II, we provide a brief overview of the implied tree approach. Section III outlines our empirical procedure. We show how it is related to the implied tree specification, we review our computational procedure for option valuation under deterministic volatility, and we describe the data. In Section IV, we estimate the implied volatility functions using the DVF model on S&P 500 index option prices, and we describe the model's goodness-of-fit and the time-series behavior of its implied parameter values. In Sections V and VI, we assess the time-series validity of the implied volatility functions. Section V examines how well the implied functions predict option prices one week later, and Section VI assesses whether the DVF approach improves hedging performance. In Section VII, we examine several variations of the model and the procedure to ascertain the robustness of our approach. Section VIII concludes with a summary of the main results and some suggestions for future research.

I. BLACK–SCHOLES IMPLIED VOLATILITY PATTERNS

The motivation for considering deterministic volatility functions in option valuation arises from apparent deficiencies of the Black–Scholes model. These deficiencies are most commonly expressed in cross section as the relation between the Black–Scholes implied volatility and option exercise price. In this section, we illustrate this relation for S&P 500 index options and describe its implications for option valuation.

S&P 500 index options are used in our illustration because, as Rubinstein (1994) argues, this option market provides a context where the Black–Scholes conditions seem most reasonably satisfied. We use only one cross section of option prices, from April 1, 1992, but the pattern on this day is typical of those since the October 1987 stock market crash. The data for the example include all bid and ask price quotes for all call options during the half-hour interval of 2:45 to 3:15 p.m. (CST). To compute the implied volatilities, we use the Black–Scholes call option formula,

$$c = (S - PVD)N(d_1) - X_e^{-rT}N(d_2), \qquad (1)$$

where $S - PVD$ is the index level net of the present value of expected dividends paid over the option's life, X is the option's exercise price, T is the time to expiration, r is the risk-free interest rate, σ is the volatility rate,

$$d_1 = \frac{ln[(S - PVD)/X] + (r + 0.5\sigma^2)T}{\sigma\sqrt{T}}, \tag{2}$$

$$d_2 = d_1 - \sigma\sqrt{T}, \tag{3}$$

and $N(d)$ is the cumulative unit density function with upper integral limit d. To proxy for the risk-free rate, the rate on a T-bill of comparable maturity is used. The actual cash dividends paid during the option's life are used to proxy for expected dividends. For each option price, the implied volatility is computed by solving for the volatility rate (σ) that equates the model price with the observed bid or ask quote.[5]

Figure 1 illustrates the typical pattern in the S&P 500 implied volatilities. Strikingly, the volatilities do not all lie on a horizontal line. This pattern is often called the volatility 'smile' and constitutes evidence against the Black–Scholes model. In the figure, the 'smile' actually appears to be more of a 'sneer'. The smile label arose prior to the 1987 crash when, in general, the volatilities were symmetric around zero moneyness, with in-the-money and out-of-the-money options having higher implied volatilities than at-the-money options. The sneer pattern displayed in Figure 1, however, is more indicative of the pattern since the crash, with call (put) option implied volatilities decreasing monotonically as the call (put) goes deeper out of the money (in the money).

Figure 1 also illustrates that the sneer is influenced by the time to expiration of the underlying options.[6] The implied volatilities of seventeen-day-options are generally lower than the forty-five-day options, which, in turn, are lower than the eighty-day options. This pattern suggests that the local volatility rate modeled within the DVF framework is a function of time.

The differences in implied volatilities across exercise prices shown in Figure 1 appear to be economically significant. The bid-implied volatility for the short-term, in-the-money call, for example, exceeds the ask-implied volatility for the short-term, at-the-money call,[7] implying the possibility of an arbitrage profit. A strategy of selling in-the-money calls and buying at-the-money calls to capture the 'arbitrage profits' is more complex than merely spreading the options,

---

[5] We use the reported index level for this exercise. Since this index is stale, the implied volatilities of call options will be biased downward or upward depending on whether the index is above or below its true level. With puts, the bias is opposite. By using only call options, the bias for each option is in the same direction. Longstaff (1995) has shown that using the wrong index level will create a smile, but a much fainter one than observed.

[6] It is important to recognize that the moneyness variable in Figure 1 is adjusted by the square root of time. Without the adjustment, the slope of the sneer steepens as the option's life grows shorter. This is consistent with Taylor and Xu (1993), who demonstrate that more complex valuation models (such as jump diffusion) can generate time-dependence in the sneer even when volatility is constant over time.

[7] The variation in the difference between bid and ask volatilities depends on two factors. First, although bid/ask spreads are competitively determined, they tend to vary systematically with option moneyness. In part, this may be caused by the CBOE's rules governing the maximum spreads for options with different premia. The rules state that the maximum bid/ask spread is (a) 1/4 for options

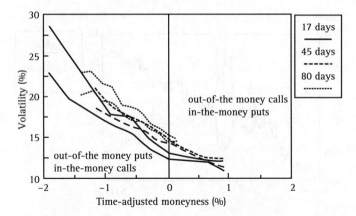

Figure 1. *Black–Scholes implied volatilities on April 1, 1992*

Note: Implied volatilities are computed from S&P 500 index call option prices for the April, May and June 1992 option expirations. The lower line of each pair is based on the option's bid price, and the upper line is based on the ask. Time-adjusted moneyness is defined as $[X/(S - PVD) - 1]/\sqrt{T}$, where S is the index level, PVD is the present value of the dividends paid during the option's life, X is the option's exercise price, and T is its number of days to expiration.

however, and requires dynamic rebalancing through time. The differences among the implied volatilities, however, are too large to be accounted for by the costs of dynamic rebalancing, as can be shown using the Constantinides (1997) bounds.

The differences raise a question concerning the source of the Black–Scholes model's apparent deficiency. One possibility is that the constant volatility assumption is violated, or that the distribution of asset prices at expiration is not lognormal. In this context, the emergence of the volatility sneer after the crash might be explained by an increase in investors' probability assessment of downward moves in the index level. The nonlognormality of prices is also consistent with what has become known as the 'Fischer Black effect.' Black (1976) writes

I have believed for a long time that stock returns are related to volatility changes. When stocks go up, volatilities seem to go down; and when stocks go down, volatilities seem to go up. (p. 177)

This inverse time-series relation between stock returns and volatility changes has been documented in a number of empirical studies. Most of the studies use stock

whose bid price is less than $2, (b) 3/8 for bid prices between $2 and $5, (c) 1/2 for bid prices between $5 and $10, (d) 3/4 for bid prices between $10 and $20, and (e) 1 for bid prices above $20. See the Chicago Board Options Exchange (1995, pp. 2123–2124). Second, the sensitivity of option price to the volatility parameter is highest for at-the-money options, with in-the-money and out-of-the-money having much lower sensitivities. As a result, for a given spread between the bid and ask price quotes, the range of Black–Scholes implied volatilities will be lowest for at-the-money options and will become larger as the options move deeper in or out of the money.

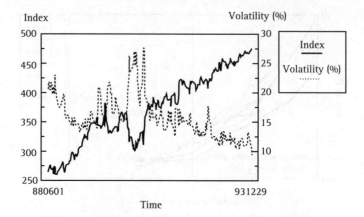

Figure 2. *S&P 500 index level and Black–Scholes implied volatility each Wednesday during the period of June 1988 through December 1993*

returns to measure volatility, but the effect is also apparent when volatility is measured using option prices. Figure 2 shows the level of Black–Scholes implied volatility during the sample period of our study, June 1, 1988 through December 31, 1993. As the S&P 500 index level trends up, the level of implied volatility trends down. The correlation in the first differences of these series is −0.570.

In addition to the DVF approach considered in this paper, a number of option valuation models are capable of explaining the behavior documented in Figures 1 and 2. The stochastic volatility models of Heston (1993) and Hull and White (1987), for example, can explain them when the asset price and volatility are negatively correlated. The negative correlation is what produces the sneer, not the stochastic feature itself. Similarly, the jump model of Bates (1996a) can generate these patterns when the mean jump is negative. Deterministic volatility models, however, are the simplest because they preserve the arbitrage argument that underlies the Black–Scholes model. Unlike stochastic volatility and jump models, they do not require additional assumptions about investor preferences for risk or additional securities that can be used to hedge volatility or jump risk. Therefore, only the parameters that govern the volatility process need be estimated.

II. THE IMPLIED TREE APPROACH

The implied tree approach developed by Derman and Kani (1994a,b), Dupire (1994), and Rubinstein (1994) assumes the local volatility rate is a flexible but deterministic function of the asset price and time. The aim of the approach is to develop an asset price lattice that is consistent with a cross section of option prices. The general procedure for doing this involves: (a) estimating the risk-neutral probability distribution of asset prices at the end of the lattice, and

(b) determining the up and down step sizes and probabilities throughout the lattice that are consistent with the implied probability distribution.

The implied probability distributions obtained from step (a) typically seem consistent with the apparent deficiencies of the Black–Scholes model. In particular, for S&P 500 options, the distributions tend to exhibit negative skewness and excess kurtosis relative to the lognormal distribution. The excess kurtosis is a well-known feature of historical stock returns and the skewness is consistent with the notion that after the crash investors increased their assessment of the probability of stock market declines. Indeed, as Rubinstein reports, the implied probability assessment of decreases is so severe that it is 'quite common' to observe a bimodal distribution. In other words, for index levels far enough below the mean, the implied probability actually increases.

Step (b) in the approach involves constructing the asset price tree. At any node in the tree, we can deduce the move volatility, which in the limit converges to the local volatility rate, $\sigma(S, t)$. The structure of these volatilities is typically consistent with the empirical evidence regarding stock volatility. Specifically, an inverse relation exists between the index level and volatility—as the index falls, volatility increases (Black (1976)). Moreover, the relation is asymmetric—the increase in volatility for decreases in the index tends to be larger than the decrease in volatility for higher index levels (Schwert (1989, 1990)).

The reasonableness of these implied dynamics provides indirect support for the implied tree approach. But, given the many potential applications stemming from this approach, more comprehensive tests seem necessary. The approach yields an estimate of how the asset price evolves over time, and this estimate could be used to value other derivatives on the same asset (e.g., American and exotic options) or as the basis for more exact hedge ratios. Moreover, to the extent that the asset is a stock market index, the estimates could be used in more general asset pricing and volatility estimation contexts. The reliability of the approach in these settings depends critically on how well we can estimate the dynamics of the underlying asset price from a cross section of option prices. This assessment is the purpose of this paper.

III. EMPIRICAL METHODOLOGY

In this section, we begin by describing the intuition for our valuation method vis-à-vis the implied tree approach. As in the implied tree approach, our method assumes the local volatility rate is a deterministic function of asset price and time. Next we provide a formal description of the deterministic volatility function valuation framework, and we specify the structure of the volatility functions that we test in our analysis. The final subsection describes the data.

A. Intuition

The implied tree approach uses a cross section of option prices to imply the tree (and, hence, to implicitly estimate the volatility function) that achieves an exact fit of observed option prices. An exact fit is possible because there are as many degrees of freedom in defining the tree as there are observed option prices. With so much freedom in parameter selection, however, the possibility exists that the approach overfits the data.

We examine this possibility by evaluating the time-series reliability of the implied parameter estimates. The logic of our test is straightforward. First, we use today's option prices to estimate the parameters of the underlying process, that is, the implied tree. Then, we step forward in time. If the original tree was correct, then the subtree stemming out of the node realized today must again be correct. Equivalently, option values from this subtree (using the new asset price) should be correct. If, however, the volatility function is not stable through time, then the out-of-sample option values are inaccurate. This finding suggests that the cross-sectional fit has not identified the true volatility function or the true stochastic process for the underlying asset.

Using a tree-based approach to implement this test suffers from a practical limitation. Suppose we estimate an implied tree today, and then step forward in time to use the remainder of the tree. The likelihood that the realized asset price falls exactly on a node of our original tree is remote. Indeed, the realized price is virtually certain to fall between nodes or entirely outside the span of the tree. Consequently, using the tree for out-of-sample option valuation would require interpolation or extrapolation techniques.

To avoid this complication, we specify from the start an interpolative functional form for the volatility process. We consider a number of alternatives based on a Taylor series approximation in S and t. Once we specify the function, we can estimate its parameters by obtaining the best fit of the option values under deterministic volatility with the observed option prices. This deterministic volatility function (DVF) approach to fitting the data is slightly different from the implied tree approach, but the spirit of the two approaches is the same. Both fundamentally concern obtaining estimates of the deterministic volatility function. What we will show is that, even with fairly parsimonious models of the volatility process, we achieve an 'almost exact' fit of observed option prices. The crucial question, then, concerns the stability of these estimates over time. Using more elaborate models such as those embedded in the lattice-based approaches presents an even greater danger of overfitting reported prices and deteriorating the quality of prediction.

The fact that we allow for pricing errors in our approach may seem inconsistent with the implied tree approach. Rubinstein requires that all option values computed using the implied tree fall within their respective bid and ask prices observed in the market—that is, that no arbitrage opportunities exist. More recent research, however, relaxes this requirement. Jackwerth and Rubinstein (1996), for example, advocate using bid/ask midpoint prices, as we do, rather than the bid/ask band due to the tendency to '(overfit) the data by following all the small wiggles' when the no-arbitrage constraint is imposed. As a result, they allow for 'small' deviations from market prices, and use the sum of squared dollar errors (as we do also) in their objective function in fitting the implied tree.

B. Option Valuation under Deterministic Volatility

Option valuation when the local volatility rate is a deterministic function of asset price and time is straightforward. In this case, the partial differential equation describing the option price dynamics is the familiar Black–Scholes (1973) equation,

$$-\frac{1}{2}\sigma^2(F,t)F^2\frac{\partial^2 c}{\partial F^2} = \frac{\partial c}{\partial t},\tag{4}$$

where F is the forward asset price for delivery on the expiration date of the option, c is the forward option price, $\sigma(F,t)$ is the *local* volatility of the price F, and t is current time.[8] We use forward prices, rather than spot prices, for both the option and the underlying asset to avoid the issue of randomly fluctuating interest rates.

Equation (4) is called the *backward* equation of the Black–Scholes model (expressed in terms of forward prices). The call option value is a function of F and t for a fixed exercise price X and date of expiration T. At time t when F is known, however, the cross section of option prices (with different exercise prices and expiration dates) can also be considered to be functionally related to X and T. For European-style options, Breeden and Litzenberger (1978) and Dupire (1994) show that the forward option value, $c(X,T)$, must be a solution of the *forward* partial differential equation,[9]

$$\frac{1}{2}\sigma^2(X,T)X^2\frac{\partial^2 c}{\partial X^2} = \frac{\partial c}{\partial T},\tag{5}$$

with the associated initial condition, $c(X,0) = \max(F-X,0)$. The volatility function in equation (5) is the same as in equation (4), but the arguments, F and t, are replaced by X and T. Equation (4) requires the local volatility that prevails at the *present time* when the date is t and the index level is F; equation (5) uses the *future* local volatility that will prevail on the expiration date, T, when the underlying index is then at level X.

The advantage of using the forward equation to value European-style options (such as those on the S&P 500 index) is that all option series with a common time to expiration can be valued simultaneously—a considerable computational cost saving when using numerical procedure.[10] To infer volatility functions from American-style option prices, however, requires solving the backward equation (4) for each option series.

---

[8] Bergman, Grundy, and Wiener (1996) examine the implications of specifying volatility as a function of the underlying spot or forward asset price. They also illustrate a number of reasons for which volatility may be a (possibly nonmonotonic) function of the asset price.

[9] Because the option price, c, and the underlying asset price, F, are expressed as forward prices (forward to the maturity date of the option), equations (4) and (5) ignore interest and dividends. We account for these factors in our definition of forward prices. See Section III.D below.

[10] We solve equation (5) using the Crank-Nicholson finite-difference method.

C. Specifying the Volatility Function

We estimate the volatility function, $\sigma(X, T)$, by fitting the DVF option valuation model to reported option prices at time t. Because $\sigma(X, T)$ is an arbitrary function, we posit a number of different structural forms including:

$$\text{Model 0:} \quad \sigma = \max(0.01, a_0); \tag{6}$$

$$\text{Model 1:} \quad \sigma = \max(0.01, a_0 + a_1 X + a_2 X^2); \tag{7}$$

$$\text{Model 2:} \quad \sigma = \max(0.01, a_0 + a_1 X + a_2 X^2 + a_3 T + a_5 XT); \text{ and} \tag{8}$$

$$\text{Model 3:} \quad \sigma = \max(0.01, a_0 + a_1 X + a_2 X^2 + a_3 T + a_4 T^2 + a_5 XT). \tag{9}$$

Model 0 is the volatility function of the Black–Scholes constant volatility model. Model 1 attempts to capture variation in volatility attributable to asset price, and Models 2 and 3 capture additional variation attributable to time. A minimum value of the local volatility rate is imposed to prevent negative values.

We choose quadratic forms for the volatility function, in part because the Black–Scholes implied volatilities for S&P 500 options tend to have a parabolic shape. The volatility function could also be estimated using more flexible non-parametric methods such as kernel regressions[11] or splines. As noted above, however, we want to avoid overparameterization. In Section VII below, we verify that the quadratic form of the DVF, despite the parabolic branches, leads to robust empirical results.

D. Data Selection

Our sample contains reported prices of S&P 500 index options traded on the Chicago Board Options Exchange (CBOE) over the period June 1988 through December 1993.[12] S&P 500 options are European-style and expire on the third Friday of the contract month. Originally, these options expired only at the market close and were denoted by the ticker symbol SPX. In June 1987, when the Chicago Mercantile Exchange (CME) changed its S&P 500 futures expiration from the close to the open, the CBOE introduced a second set of options with the ticker symbol NSX that expired at the open. Over time, the trading volume of this 'open-expiry' series grew to surpass that of the 'close-expiry' series, and on August 24, 1992, the CBOE reversed the ticker symbols of the two series. Our sample contains SPX options throughout: close-expiry until August 24, 1992, and open-expiry thereafter. During the first subperiod, the option's time to expiration is measured as the number of calendar days between the trade date and the expiration date; during the second, we use the number of calendar days remaining less one.

---

[11] See Ait-Sahalia and Lo (1998).

[12] The sample begins in June 1988 because it was the first month for which Standard and Poors began reporting daily cash dividends for the S&P 500 index portfolio. See Harvey and Whaley (1992) regarding the importance of incorporating discrete daily cash dividends in index option valuation.

As we noted earlier, we estimate each of the volatility functions once each week during the sample. We use Wednesdays for these estimations because fewer holidays fall on a Wednesday than on any other trading day. When a particular Wednesday is a holiday, we use the immediately preceding trading day.

To estimate the volatility functions, we express both the index level and option price as forward prices. Constructing the forward index level requires the term structure of default-free interest rates and the daily cash dividends on the index portfolio. We proxy for the riskless interest rate by using the T-bill rates implied by the average of the bid and ask discounts reported in the *Wall Street Journal*. The t_i-period interest rate is obtained by interpolating the rates for the two T-bills whose maturities straddle t_i. The daily cash dividends for the S&P 500 index portfolio are collected from the *S&P 500 Information Bulletin*. To compute the present value of the dividends paid during the option's life, *PVD*, the daily dividends are discounted at the rates corresponding to the ex-dividend dates and summed over the life of the option; that is,

$$PVD = \sum_{i=1}^{n} D_i e^{-r_i t_i}, \tag{10}$$

where D_i is the ith cash dividend payment, t_i is the time to ex-dividend from the current date, r_i is the t_i-period riskless interest rate, and n is the number of dividend payments during the option's life.[13] The implied forward price of the S&P 500 index is therefore

$$F = (S - PVD)e^{rT}, \tag{11}$$

where S is the reported index level and T is the time to expiration of the option. To create a forward option price, we multiply the average of the option's bid and ask price quotes[14] by the interest accumulation factor appropriate to the option's expiration, e^{rT}.

Three exclusionary criteria are applied to the data. First, we eliminate options with fewer than six or more than one hundred days to expiration. The shorter-term options have relatively small time premiums, hence the estimation of volatility is extremely sensitive to nonsynchronous option prices and other possible measurement errors. The longer-term options, on the other hand, are unnecessary because our objective is only to determine whether the volatility

---

[13] The convention introduces an inconsistency, with small consequences, between option prices of different maturities. The inconsistency takes two forms. First, our forward index level assumes that the dividends to be paid during the option's life are certain, so the index cannot fall below the promised amount of dividends during this period. This barrier is different for each maturity date. This is an inconsistency in the specification of the process for the index. Second, the volatility function that we are estimating is actually a volatility of the forward price to the maturity date of the option. To be completely rigorous, we should model the forward price process for each maturity, with the appropriate cross-maturity constraints on price imposed, and estimate a separate volatility function for each.

[14] Using bid/ask midpoints rather than trade prices reduces noise in the cross-sectional estimation of the volatility function.

function remains valid over a span of one week. Including these options would simply deteriorate the cross-sectional fit.

Second, we eliminate options whose absolute 'moneyness', $|X/F - 1|$, is greater than 10 percent. Like extremely short-term options, deep in- and out-of-the-money options have small time premiums and hence contain little information about the volatility function. Moreover, these options are not actively traded, and price quotes are generally not supported by actual trades.

Finally, we only use those options with bid/ask price quotes during the last half hour of trading (2:45 to 3:15 p.m. (CST)). Fearing imperfect synchronization with the option market,[15] we do not use the reported S&P 500 index level or the S&P 500 futures price [16] in our estimation. Instead, we infer the current index level simultaneously,[17] together with the parameters of the volatility function, from the cross section of option prices. In this way, our empirical procedure relies only on observations from a single market, with no auxiliary assumption of market integration.[18] The procedure, however, requires that the option prices are reasonably synchronous—hence the need for a tight time window. The cost of this criterion is a reduction in the number of option quotes, but the cost is not too onerous because we have quotes for an average of 44 (and a range from 14 to 87) option series during the last half-hour each Wednesday.[19] Seventeen of the 292 Wednesday cross sections had only one contract expiration available; 141 had two; 129 had three; and 5 had four.

IV. ESTIMATION RESULTS

Using the S&P 500 index option data described in the previous section, we now estimate the four volatility functions specified in equations (6) through (9). As noted earlier, Model 0 is the Black–Scholes constant volatility model. Model 1 allows the volatility rate to vary with the index level but not with time. Models 2 and 3 attempt to capture additional variation due to time. A fifth volatility function, denoted Model S, is also estimated. Model S switches among the volatility functions given by Models 1, 2, and 3, depending on whether the number of different option expiration dates in a given cross section is one, two, or three, respectively. Model S is introduced because some cross sections have fewer

---

[15] See Fleming, Ostdiek, and Whaley (1996).

[16] For a detailed description of the problems of using a reported index level in computing implied volatility, see Whaley (1993, Appendix).

[17] In doing so, we impose the 'cross-futures constraint' that the futures prices for different maturities should reflect the same underlying cash index level.

[18] This is not quite true since we use Treasury bill rates in computing forward prices.

[19] To assess the reasonableness of using the 2:45 to 3:15 p.m. window for estimation, we compute the mean absolute return and the standard deviation of return of the nearby S&P 500 futures (with at least six days to expiration) by fifteen-minute intervals throughout the trading day across the days of the sample period. The results indicate that the lowest mean absolute return and standard deviation of return occur just before noon. The end-of-day window is only slightly higher, but the beginning-of-day window is nearly double. We choose to stay with the end-of-day window for ease in interpreting the results.

expiration dates available, undermining our ability to estimate precisely the relation between the local volatility rate and time.

This section focuses on identifying the 'best' volatility function given the structure of S&P 500 index option prices. First, each local volatility function is estimated by minimizing the sum of squared dollar errors between the reported option prices and their DVF model values. Summary statistics on the goodness-of-fit and on coefficient stability are provided. Next, we illustrate the shape of the implied probability functions for options of different times to expiration.

A. Goodness-of-Fit

To assess the quality of the fitted models, five measurements are made each week. These are defined as follows:

(i) The root mean squared valuation error (RMSVE) is the square root of the average squared deviations of the reported option prices from the model's theoretical values.

(ii) The mean outside error (MOE) is the average valuation error outside the bid/ask spread. If the theoretical value is below (exceeds) the option's bid (ask) price, the error is defined as the difference between the theoretical value and the bid (ask) price, and, if the theoretical value is within the spread, the error is set equal to zero. A positive value of MOE, therefore, means that the model value is too high on average, and a negative value means the model value is too low. This measure is used primarily to detect biases in specific option categories.

(iii) The average absolute error (MAE) is the average absolute valuation error outside the bid/ask spread. This measure illustrates the exactness with which each model fits within the quoted bid and ask prices over all option categories.

(iv) The frequency (FREQ) indicates the proportion of observations where the specified model has a lower RMSVE than Model S.

(v) Finally, the Akaike (1973) Information Criterion (AIC) is calculated to appraise the potential degree of overfitting. The AIC penalizes the goodness-of-fit as more degrees of freedom are added to the model in a manner similar to an adjusted R^2. The lowest value of the AIC identifies the 'best' model based on in-sample performance. Of course, overfitting is best detected by going out of sample (see Section V).

Table I contains the average RMSVEs, MOEs, and MAEs across the 292 days (one day each week) during the sample period of June 1988 through December 1993. The average RMSVE results show a strong relationship between the local volatility rate and the asset price. Where the volatility rate is a quadratic function of asset price (Model 1), the average RMSVE of the DVF model is less than one-half that of the Black–Scholes constant volatility model (Model 0), 30.1 cents versus 65.0 cents, for all options in the sample. Time variation also appears important. In moving from Model 1 to Model 2, the average RMSVE in the full sample is reduced

Table I. *Average S&P 500 index option dollar valuation errors using the Deterministic Volatility Function (DVF) model*

Panel A: Aggregate Results

DVF model	All Options				Call Options			Put Options		
	RMSVE	MOE	MAE	AIC	RMSVE	MOE	MAE	RMSVE	MOE	MAE
0	0.650	-0.034	0.348	0.003	0.651	0.166	0.360	0.643	-0.239	0.338
1	0.301	0.002	0.095	0.257	0.300	0.036	0.095	0.296	0.009	0.096
2	0.230	-0.009	0.052	0.671	0.222	0.000	0.047	0.233	-0.020	0.058
3	0.226	-0.011	0.050	0.062	0.218	-0.002	0.044	0.230	-0.020	0.057
S	0.227	-0.010	0.050	0.007	0.218	-0.002	0.050	0.230	-0.020	0.057

Panel B: Call Options Only

Moneyness (%)		DVF model	Days to Expiration								
Lower	Upper		Less than 40			40 to 70			More than 70		
			RMSVE	MOE	FREQ	RMSVE	MOE	FREQ	RMSVE	MOE	FREQ
-10	-5	0	0.313	0.000	0.429	0.644	-0.290	0.042	1.051	-0.623	0.016
		1	0.236	-0.012	0.593	0.246	-0.021	0.491	0.342	-0.035	0.210
		2	0.257	-0.026	0.271	0.224	-0.014	0.241	0.234	-0.002	0.306
		3	0.259	-0.027	0.214	0.221	-0.013	0.264	0.220	0.003	0.073
		S	0.259	-0.027		0.223	-0.014		0.220	0.003	
-5	0	0	0.401	0.143	0.133	0.403	-0.075	0.124	0.583	-0.227	0.091
		1	0.352	0.136	0.179	0.228	0.023	0.434	0.255	-0.029	0.462
		2	0.205	0.020	0.218	0.192	0.014	0.239	0.210	0.022	0.394
		3	0.197	0.014	0.267	0.187	0.012	0.248	0.205	0.026	0.053
		S	0.198	0.014		0.187	0.012		0.205	0.026	
0	5	0	0.721	0.607	0.014	0.836	0.661	0.000	0.850	0.627	0.016
		1	0.384	0.251	0.087	0.234	0.037	0.347	0.260	-0.099	0.315
		2	0.177	0.058	0.225	0.180	0.014	0.216	0.198	-0.027	0.386
		3	0.166	0.047	0.293	0.171	0.007	0.266	0.189	-0.021	0.087
		S	0.167	0.048		0.173	0.008		0.189	-0.021	
5	10	0	0.441	0.367	0.228	0.905	0.804	0.028	1.096	0.975	0.014

		1	0.154	-0.020	0.574	0.203	-0.094	0.491	0.317	-0.205	0.108
		2	0.150	-0.081	0.277	0.204	-0.102	0.245	0.241	-0.130	0.297
		3	0.151	-0.082	0.287	0.205	-0.108	0.236	0.245	-0.135	0.068
		S	0.151	-0.082		0.207	-0.107		0.246	-0.135	

Panel C: Put Options Only

-10	-5	0	0.608	-0.524	0.000	1.193	-1.073	0.000	1.660	-1.521	0.000
		1	0.188	-0.114	0.792	0.216	-0.108	0.473	0.308	-0.176	0.177
		2	0.237	-0.163	0.242	0.201	-0.096	0.234	0.161	-0.049	0.365
		3	0.237	-0.164	0.273	0.194	-0.088	0.228	0.152	-0.035	0.073
		S	0.238	-0.165		0.196	-0.091		0.152	-0.035	
-5	0	0	0.446	-0.287	0.054	0.753	-0.546	0.010	1.018	-0.769	0.024
		1	0.291	0.123	0.200	0.197	0.006	0.406	0.218	-0.047	0.435
		2	0.166	-0.020	0.275	0.154	-0.003	0.238	0.182	0.026	0.347
		3	0.162	-0.026	0.279	0.152	-0.001	0.218	0.181	0.037	0.081
		S	0.162	-0.026		0.151	-0.002		0.181	0.037	
0	5	0	0.299	0.046	0.268	0.335	0.080	0.231	0.435	0.103	0.190
		1	0.353	0.129	0.137	0.235	0.016	0.330	0.284	-0.057	0.254
		2	0.206	0.012	0.243	0.192	0.002	0.245	0.224	-0.003	0.397
		3	0.203	0.010	0.289	0.190	0.000	0.208	0.225	-0.001	0.071
		S	0.203	0.010		0.190	0.001		0.225	-0.001	
5	10	0	0.409	-0.063	0.224	0.369	0.076	0.405	0.610	0.233	0.230
		1	0.247	0.021	0.513	0.294	-0.035	0.386	0.367	-0.058	0.190
		2	0.244	0.016	0.194	0.291	-0.036	0.203	0.314	-0.038	0.330
		3	0.243	0.016	0.259	0.291	-0.037	0.229	0.309	-0.037	0.060
		S	0.243	0.016		0.291	-0.036		0.310	-0.037	

Note: RMSVE is the root mean squared dollar valuation error averaged across all days in the sample period from June 1988 through December 1993. MOE is the average of the mean valuation error outside the observed bid/ask quotes across all days in the sample (a positive value indicates the theoretical value exceeds the ask price on average; a negative value indicates the theoretical value is below the bid price). MAE is the average of the mean absolute valuation error outside the observed bid/ask quotes across all days in the sample. AIC is the proportion of days during the sample period that the model is judged best by the Akaike Information Criterion. FREQ is the frequency of days, expressed as a ratio of the total number of days, on which a particular model has a lower daily RMSVE than Model S. Model 0 is the Black/Scholes constant volatility model. Models 1, 2, and 3 specify that the local volatility rate is linear in (a) X and X^2, (b) X, X^2, T, and XT, and (c) X, X^2, T, T^2, and XT, respectively, where X is the option's exercise price and T is its time to expiration. Model S switches between Models 1, 2, and 3 depending upon whether the number of option expirations in the cross-section is one, two or three, respectively. Moneyness is defined as $X/F - 1$, where F is the forward index level.

even more (from 30.1 cents to 23.0 cents), albeit not so dramatically. The addition of the time variable to the volatility function appears to be important, although most of the incremental explanatory power appears to come from the cross-product term, XT.[20] Adding a quadratic time to expiration term (Model 3) reduces the average RMSVE to its lowest level of the assumed specifications, 22.6 cents. Model S's RMSVE is virtually the same. The average MOE and MAE measurement criteria lead to the same conclusions for the overall sample. The MAE shows that with Model 3 an essentially exact fit, within the bid-ask spread, has been achieved because the average absolute error outside the spread is a mere 5 cents.

Once goodness-of-fit is adjusted to account for the number of parameters in the volatility function, more parsimonious volatility functions appear to work best. The AIC results are reported in Table I as the proportion of days during the sample period that a particular model is judged the best specification. The results indicate that Model 2 provides the best fit of the cross section of S&P 500 index option prices, having the lowest AIC in 67.1 percent of the 292 days in the sample. The next best performer is Model 1, which is even more parsimonious than Model 2 and does not have time variation in the local volatility rate function, out-performing the other models in 25.7 percent of the days in the sample. The more elaborate Model 3, which had the lowest RMSVE, does not perform well once the penalty for the additional variables is imposed—performing best in less than 7 percent of the days in the sample. All in all, the results indicate that the deter-ministic volatility function need not be very elaborate to describe the observed structure of index option prices accurately.

The MOE values reported for the Black–Scholes model (Model 0) show that the theoretical value exceeds the ask price on average for call options, 16.6 cents, and is below the bid price for put options, −23.9 cents. This behavior arises from the character of our sample (i.e., the number of calls versus the number of puts, and the number of in-the-money options versus the number of out-of-the-money options). When the options are stratified by option type and moneyness, the Black–Scholes model value appears to be too low (relative to the bid price) for in-the-money calls and for out-of-money puts. This is consistent with the implied volatility sneer shown in Figure 1. With all options forced to have the same volatility in the estimation of Model 0, the variation in implied volatility trans-lates into valuation errors. Options with Black–Scholes implied volatilities higher (lower) than average are valued too low (high).

Figure 3 shows the dollar valuation errors (i.e., the model values less the bid/ask midpoints) of Model 0 for the subsample of call options with 40 to 70 days to expiration. Also shown are normalized bid/ask spreads (i.e., the bid/ask prices less the bid/ask midpoint). Note first that the bid/ask spreads are as high as one dollar for deep in-the-money calls on the left of the figure. As we move right along the horizontal axis, the maximum bid/ask spread stays at a dollar until the moneyness variable is about −2.5 percent, and then the maximum spread begins to decrease as

---

[20] Model 2 is also estimated without the time variable with little difference in explanatory power.

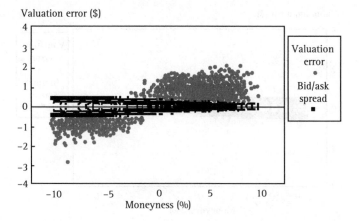

Figure 3. *Dollar valuation estimation errors of Deterministic Volatility Function Model 0 (i.e., the Black–Scholes model) for S&P 500 call options with 40 to 70 days to expiration*

Note: The solid squares correspond to normalized bid ask price quotes (i.e., the bid and ask price less the average of the bid and ask prices). The circles correspond to valuation errors (i.e., the theoretical option value less the bid/ask midpoint). Moneyness is defined as $X/F - 1$, where F is the forward index level and X is the option's exercise price.

the calls move further out-of-the-money. This spread behavior is consistent with the CBOE's maximum spread rules described earlier. The average bid/ask spread across all option series used in our estimation is approximately 47 cents.

Figure 4 shows the valuation errors of Model 3 for calls with 40 to 70 days to expiration. The DVF model improves the cross-sectional fit. Where the valuation errors are outside the bid/ask spread, they appear randomly, with a slight tendency for the DVF model to undervalue deep in-the-money and deep out-of-the-money calls and to overvalue at-the-money calls. Overall however, Model 3's fit appears quite good. The MOE across all calls in this category is just −2.6 cents, in contrast to an MOE of more than 25 cents for the Black–Scholes model.

Model 3 also appears to eliminate the relation between valuation error and the option's days to expiration. For the Black–Scholes model, the valuation errors generally increase with days to expiration. For deep in-the-money calls with fewer than 40 days to expiration, for example, the RMSVE is 31.3 cents; it is 64.4 cents for calls between 40 and 70 days to expiration; and 105.1 cents for calls with more than 70 days to expiration. For the same call options, the RMSVEs for Model 3 are 25.9, 22.1, and 22.0 cents, respectively.

The results in Table I support the notion that a relatively parsimonious model can accurately describe the observed structure of S&P 500 index option prices.[21]

---

[21] To test if the estimation results are driven by the presence of outliers, we examine the valuation errors of the various models. We identify unusually large errors for three days during the sample period. When we eliminate these days from the summary results, the magnitudes of the average errors reported in Table I are reduced by only small amounts. Consequently, we report the result for the full sample.

Valuation error ($)

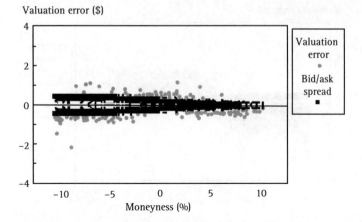

Figure 4. *Dollar valuation estimation errors of Deterministic Volatility Function Model 3 for S&P 500 call options with 40 to 70 days to expiration*

Note: The solid squares correspond to normalized bid/ask price quotes (i.e., the bid and ask prices less the average of the bid and ask prices). The circles correspond to valuation errors (i.e., the theoretical option value less the bid/ask midpoint). Moneyness is defined as $X/F - 1$, where F is the forward index level and X is the option's exercise price.

The implied tree approach can achieve an exact fit of option prices by permitting as many degrees of freedom as there are option prices. Our results suggest that such a complete parameterization may be undesirable. Based on the AIC, Model 2 does 'best,' with the local volatility rate being a function of X, X^2, T, and XT. Moreover, where Model 2 does not perform best, the more parsimonious Model 1, with local volatility being only a function of X and X^2, usually does best. Together, these two simple models outperform the others in 92.8 percent of the 292 cross sections of index option prices examined. Based on these in-sample results, parsimony in the specification of the volatility function appears to be warranted.

B. Average Parameter Estimates and Parameter Stability over Time

The average parameters estimated for each of the volatility functions are also informative. Model 0 is, of course, the constant volatility model of Black–Scholes. When this model is fitted each week during our 292-week sample period, the mean estimated coefficient, $\bar{a}_0$, is 15.72 percent. Recall Figure 2 shows the level of the Black–Scholes implied volatility on a week-by-week basis. Over the sample period, implied market volatility fell from more than 20 percent to less than 10 percent. Volatility reached a maximum of 27.16 percent on January 16, 1991, the height of the Gulf War. The minimum implied volatility, 9.43 percent, occurred on December 29, 1993, the last date of the sample period.

Table II. *Summary statistics of parameter estimates obtained for Deterministic Volatility Function (DVF) Model 3*

Coefficient Estimate	Mean			Standard Deviation
Panel A: Means and Standard Deviations				
a_0	131.8			69.5
a_1	−0.3529			0.447
a_2	0.00008611			0.00768
a_3	−0.2260			1.94
a_4	−0.0001666			0.00237
a_5	0.05275			0.0593
	a_2	a_3	a_4	a_5
Panel B: Correlations				
a_1	−0.969	0.596	−0.811	−0.291
a_2		−0.589	0.853	0.182
a_3			−0.114	−0.232
a_4				0.093

Note: Summary statistics from fitting Model 3 to the cross section of S&P 500 index option prices each week during the sample period from June 1988 through December 1993. Model 3 specifies that the local volatility rate is linear in X, X^2, T, T^2, and XT, where X is the option's exercise price and T is its time to expiration. The parameter estimates, a_1, a_2, a_3, a_4, and a_5, are the estimated coefficients of each of these terms, respectively. The parameter estimate, a_0, is the estimated intercept term.

Model 3 has six parameters, and the averages (standard deviations) of the model's six parameter estimates across the 292 cross sections are reported in Panel A of Table II. The standard deviation of the parameter estimates indicates that there is considerable variation in the coefficient estimates from week to week, implying perhaps that the volatility function is not stable through time. If the parameter estimates are highly correlated, however, the errors affecting them may cancel out when option prices are looked at. To check this possibility, we compute the correlation among the parameter estimates across the 292 weeks in the sample period and report them in Panel B of Table II. As the values show, the correlations are generally quite large. The correlation between the linear and quadratic terms in Model 3, for example, is − 0.969, indicating that in weeks where a_1 is high, a_2 is low and vice versa.

In order to examine explicitly the issue of coefficient stability, Figure 5 has four panels containing plots of the time-series estimates of the Black–Scholes implied volatility (i.e., $\hat{a}_0$ in Model 0) as well as of the time-series estimates of the three main coefficients of Model 3 (i.e., $\hat{a}_0$, $\hat{a}_1$, and $\hat{a}_2$). The figures in Panels A and B indicate that the intercept coefficient of the DVF function fluctuates largely in unison with Black–Scholes implied volatility. Week after week, the coefficient appears to simply record the movements in the level of the volatility. It is to be suspected that, were the coefficients kept constant from one week to the next,

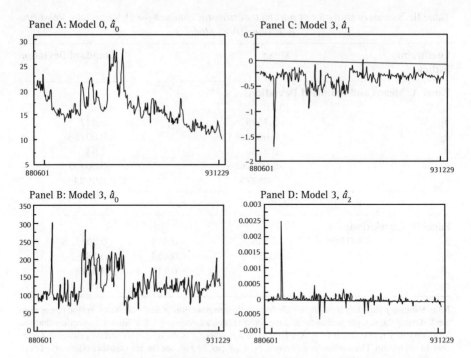

Figure 5. *Parameter estimates for a_0 of Model 0 (Panel A) and $\hat{a}_0$, $\hat{a}_1$, and $\hat{a}_2$ of Model 3 (Panels B, C, and D, respectively) each Wednesday during the sample period of June 1988 through December 1993*

Note: The parameter estimates are obtained by fitting Model 0 and Model 3 to the cross section of S&P 500 index option prices each week.

very little of the volatility movement would be captured by the movement in the level of the index itself. The plots in Figure 5 themselves are not entirely meaningful, however, since the movements in the individual coefficients are highly correlated, and they may, to some extent, offset each other when combined to generate fitted volatility levels. We are ultimately interested in the movements of the fitted volatility in the neighborhood of the money.

To examine this further, Figure 6 shows the time series of the explained at-the-money volatility of each week (with contemporaneous coefficients) minus the explained at-the-money volatility of the same week calculated on the basis of the *previous week's* coefficients. The figure, therefore, portrays the week-to-week changes in the coefficients, and which remain 'unexplained' by the DVF function and index level changes. It is apparent that these unexplained weekly changes in (annualized) volatility are very large and routinely reach several percentage points.

This evidence indicates that the in-sample estimates for the DVF model seem to be unstable. This inference implies that changes in the coefficient estimates may

Changes in volatility (%)

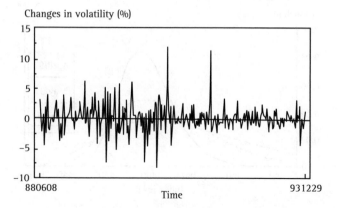

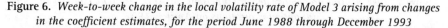

Time

Figure 6. *Week-to-week change in the local volatility rate of Model 3 arising from changes in the coefficient estimates, for the period June 1988 through December 1993*

Note: The change is defined as the difference between the estimated local volatility rate at the current index level using contemporaneous coefficient estimates of Model 3 less the estimated local volatility rate using the previous week's coefficient estimates.

not be entirely due to economic factors, but may be the result of overfitting. Therefore, it seems critical that we should measure the economic significance of the DVF model in terms of valuation prediction errors. This is exactly the procedure applied in Section V.

C. Implied Probability Distribution

The estimated coefficient of the volatility functions can also be used to deduce the shape of the risk-neutral probability distribution at the option expiration dates.[22] To illustrate, we first use the estimated coefficients of Model 3 on April 1, 1992. On April 1, 1992, the S&P 500 options had three different expiration months, April, May, and June 1992, with 17, 45, and 80 days to expiration, respectively. Based on these expirations, the estimated volatility function implies the three probability distributions shown in Figure 7. All distributions are skewed to the left, exactly the opposite of the right-skewness implied by the Black–Scholes assumption of lognormally distributed asset prices. The wider variances for the May and then June expirations merely reflect the greater probability of large price moves over a longer period of time. Our implied distributions do not exhibit the bimodality that was present in Rubinstein (1994). This likely results from the fact that our volatility functions are more parsimonious than those implicitly used within his binomial lattice framework.

---

[22] The identification of state price densities from option prices has been the goal of much of David Bates' work. See Bates (1996a, 1996b). See also Ait-Sahalia and Lo (1998).

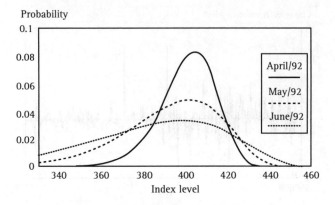

Figure 7. *Risk-neutral probability density functions for April, May, and June 1992 S&P 500 option expirations on April 1, 1992*

Note: The probability distributions are based on the parameter estimates of Deterministic Volatility Function Model 3.

V. PREDICTION RESULTS

The estimation results reported in the last section indicate that the volatility function embedded in index option prices is not particularly elaborate. The AIC indicates that only linear and quadratic terms in asset price are necessary and only linear terms in time. A critical assumption of the model, however, is that the volatility function is stable through time, an assumption we already have reason to doubt. In this section, we evaluate how well each week's estimated volatility function values the same options one week later.

A. Goodness-of-Fit

Table III provides the summary statistics for the prediction errors. The RMSVE, MOE, and MAE values in the table are computed in the same manner as in the previous section. The prediction errors are generally quite large, at least relative to the estimation errors reported in Table I. The average RMSVE reported in Panel A is about 56 cents out-of-sample across all days for all DVF models except Model 0, and the in-sample error for these models is about 23 cents. The MAE statistics tell essentially the same story but more dramatically: The almost exact fit achieved for Model 3 (i.e., 5-cent MAE in sample) has deteriorated to nearly 30 cents within a week. New market information induces a shift in the level of overall market volatility from week to week.

The prediction errors for calls and puts reported in Panel A are about the same size. As in the case of the estimation errors, the average MOE for Model 0 is positive for calls and negative for puts, depending on the character of the sample. When the options are stratified by option type and moneyness, we see that the Black–Scholes model value is too low (relative to the bid price) for in-the-money calls and out-of-the-money puts and is too high (relative to the ask price) for out-of-the-money calls and in-the-money puts. This pattern is particularly clear in Figure 8, which is the analogue of Figure 3, but for the prediction stage.

Interestingly, the average MOE is smaller for Model 1 than for Models 2, 3, and S. This suggests that the time variable in the more elaborate volatility functions is unnecessary. Apparently, the time variable serves only to overfit the data at the estimation stage. The fact that the valuation prediction errors for the models that include the time variable are more negative than those of Model 1 indicates that the implied volatility functions predict a larger decrease in volatility over the week than actually transpires.

At-the-money options have the largest valuation prediction errors for all times to expiration. This arises because at-the-money options are the most sensitive to volatility (where time premium is the highest). For a given error in the estimated volatility rate, the dollar valuation error is larger for at-the-money options than for either in-the-money or out-of-the-money options. Figure 9, which is the analogue of Figure 4, illustrates that the prediction errors of Model 4 do not display the characteristic patterns across the spectrum of moneyness that we identify above for Model 0.

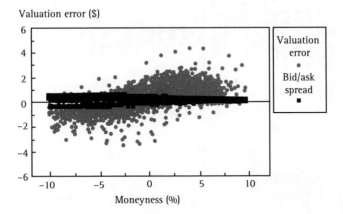

Figure 8. *Dollar valuation prediction errors of Deterministic Volatility Function Model 0 (i.e., the Black–Scholes model) for S&P 500 call options with 40 to 70 days to expiration*

Note: The theoretical values are based on the implied volatility function from the previous week. The solid squares correspond to normalized bid/ask price quotes (i.e., the bid and ask prices less the average of the bid and ask prices). The circles correspond to valuation errors (i.e., the theoretical option value less the bid/ask midpoint). Moneyness is defined as $X/F - 1$, where F is the forward index level and X is the option's exercise price.

Table III. *Average S&P 500 index option dollar prediction errors using the Deterministic Volatility Function (DVF) Model*

Panel A: Aggregate Results

DVF Model	All Options					Call Options					Put options				
	RMSVE	ΔRMSVE	t-ratio	MOE	MAE	RMSVE	ΔRMSVE	t-ratio	MOE	MAE	RMSVE	ΔRMSVE	t-ratio	MOE	MAE
0	0.784			−0.017	0.449	0.790			0.180	0.458	0.762			−0.219	0.440
1	0.557	−0.227	−7.26	−0.043	0.285	0.556	−0.234	−7.85	−0.022	0.284	0.551	−0.211	−6.62	−0.064	0.289
2	0.559	0.002	0.15	−0.067	0.294	0.551	−0.005	−0.28	−0.045	0.287	0.562	0.011	0.78	−0.091	0.305
3	0.556	−0.003	−1.19	−0.065	0.291	0.549	−0.002	−0.60	−0.044	0.285	0.557	−0.005	−1.82	−0.088	0.300
S	0.555	−0.001	−0.61	−0.066	0.292	0.548	−0.001	−1.05	−0.045	0.286	0.557	0.000	−0.09	−0.090	0.301
AH	0.498	−0.057	−2.46	−0.054	0.238	0.491	−0.057	−2.19	−0.002	0.235	0.493	−0.064	−2.85	−0.107	0.243

Panel B: Call Options Only

Moneyness (%)		DVF Model	Days to Expiration								
Lower	Upper		Less than 40			40 to 70			More than 70		
			RMSVE	MOE	FREQ	RMSVE	MOE	FREQ	RMSVE	MOE	FREQ
−10	−5	0	0.348	−0.004	0.484	0.640	−0.290	0.332	0.106	−0.688	0.073
		1	0.310	−0.024	0.609	0.436	−0.082	0.469	0.602	−0.180	0.419
		2	0.324	−0.045	0.534	0.458	−0.096	0.417	0.607	−0.057	0.476
		3	0.330	−0.045	0.523	0.461	−0.098	0.417	0.604	−0.049	0.444
		S	0.328	−0.047	0.516	0.459	−0.098	0.427	0.603	−0.051	0.452
		AH	0.344	−0.016		0.443	−0.079		0.553	−0.107	
−5	0	0	0.524	0.179	0.377	0.625	−0.063	0.347	0.794	−0.325	0.212
		1	0.472	0.136	0.444	0.547	−0.014	0.400	0.691	−0.252	0.364
		2	0.425	0.015	0.489	0.577	−0.067	0.396	0.713	−0.057	0.386
		3	0.428	0.010	0.500	0.583	−0.069	0.382	0.706	−0.036	0.379
		S	0.426	0.009	0.500	0.581	−0.069	0.382	0.707	−0.040	0.379
		AH	0.428	0.084		0.469	−0.023		0.545	−0.119	
0	5	0	0.799	0.656	0.142	0.989	0.743	0.149	0.930	0.599	0.213
		1	0.504	0.234	0.396	0.571	−0.025	0.385	0.664	−0.313	0.409
		2	0.428	0.062	0.458	0.589	−0.108	0.353	0.710	−0.100	0.370
		3	0.424	0.054	0.476	0.592	−0.114	0.353	0.686	−0.080	0.378
		S	0.425	0.054	0.476	0.593	−0.114	0.353	0.692	−0.082	0.370
		AH	0.408	0.163		0.443	0.008		0.507	−0.172	
5	10	0	0.475	0.397	0.257	0.981	0.860	0.113	1.042	0.921	0.149
		1	0.220	−0.010	0.525	0.364	−0.105	0.472	0.461	−0.252	0.459
		2	0.222	−0.066	0.436	0.389	−0.156	0.425	0.461	−0.088	0.554

Moneyness	Model									
	3	0.221	−0.068	0.436	0.394	−0.162	0.406	0.469	−0.096	0.527
	S	0.222	−0.067	0.436	0.394	−0.162	0.406	0.466	−0.095	0.527
	AH	0.209	−0.024		0.344	−0.101		0.437	−0.237	

Panel C: Put Options Only

Moneyness	Model									
−10, −5	0	0.591	−0.502	0.039	1.176	−1.051	0.024	1.742	−1.602	0.010
	1	0.276	−0.127	0.615	0.440	−0.200	0.506	0.623	−0.362	0.313
	2	0.309	−0.176	0.459	0.479	−0.232	0.434	0.532	−0.215	0.396
	3	0.313	−0.173	0.468	0.475	−0.225	0.434	0.520	−0.189	0.438
	S	0.310	−0.177	0.468	0.477	−0.227	0.434	0.522	−0.189	0.438
	AH	0.308	−0.196		0.415	−0.244		0.497	−0.283	
−5, 0	0	0.540	−0.281	0.265	0.849	−0.551	0.144	1.135	−0.867	0.113
	1	0.466	0.109	0.416	0.540	−0.061	0.383	0.654	−0.232	0.371
	2	0.430	−0.040	0.419	0.581	−0.122	0.363	0.711	−0.018	0.355
	3	0.431	−0.042	0.409	0.580	−0.121	0.368	0.698	0.016	0.371
	S	0.429	−0.044	0.416	0.581	−0.122	0.368	0.699	0.010	0.363
	AH	0.369	−0.050		0.434	−0.115		0.511	−0.130	
0, 5	0	0.443	0.081	0.435	0.611	0.156	0.393	0.691	0.077	0.357
	1	0.484	0.117	0.406	0.579	−0.066	0.422	0.714	−0.293	0.413
	2	0.446	−0.002	0.435	0.615	−0.132	0.398	0.775	−0.135	0.405
	3	0.443	−0.003	0.435	0.615	−0.133	0.403	0.751	−0.112	0.421
	S	0.444	0.004	0.442	0.616	−0.133	0.403	0.754	−0.116	0.421
	AH	0.409	−0.001		0.486	−0.090		0.572	−0.185	
5, 10	0	0.444	−0.059	0.372	0.493	0.116	0.490	0.634	0.249	0.400
	1	0.277	0.025	0.567	0.400	−0.071	0.569	0.520	−0.143	0.500
	2	0.273	0.015	0.563	0.427	−0.094	0.497	0.562	−0.055	0.480
	3	0.273	0.015	0.532	0.424	−0.092	0.497	0.551	−0.057	0.470
	S	0.273	0.015	0.550	0.425	−0.094	0.503	0.551	−0.056	0.480
	AH	0.347	−0.037		0.459	−0.103		0.508	−0.125	

Note: RMSVE is the root mean squared dollar valuation error averaged across all days in the sample period from June 1988 through December 1993. ΔRMSVE is the incremental RMSVE when comparing successive models. The t-ratio indicates the significance of that increment. MOE is the average of the mean valuation error outside the observed bid/ask quotes across all days in the sample (a positive value indicates the theoretical value exceeds the ask price on average; a negative value indicates the theoretical value is below the bid price). MAE is the average of the mean absolute valuation error outside the observed bid/ask quotes across all days in the sample. FREQ is the frequency of days, expressed as a ratio of the total number of days, on which a particular model has a lower daily RMSVE than the Ad Hoc Model. Model 0 is the Black/Scholes constant volatility model. Models 1, 2, and 3 specify that the local volatility rate is linear in (a) X and X^2, (b) XX^2, T, T^2, and XT, and (c) X, X^2, T, T^2, and XT, respectively, where X is the option's exercise price and T its time to expiration. Model S switches between Models 1, 2, and 3 depending upon whether the number of option expiration in the cross section is one, two or three, respectively. The Ad Hoc (AH) Model specifies that Black/Scholes implied volatility is linear in (a) X and X^2, (b) X, X^2, T, and XT, and (c) X, X^2, T, T^2, and XT, respectively, depending upon whether the number of option expiration in the cross section is one, two or three. Moneyness is defined as $X/F - 1$, where F is the forward index level.

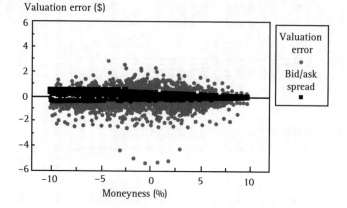

Figure 9. *Dollar valuation prediction errors of Deterministic Volatility Function Model 3 for S&P 500 call options with 40 and 70 days to expiration*

Note: The theoretical values are based on the implied volatility function from the previous week. The solid squares correspond to normalized bid/ask price quotes (i.e., the bid and ask prices less the average of the bid and ask prices). The circles correspond to valuation errors (i.e., the theoretical option value less the bid/ask midpoint). Moneyness is defined as $X/F - 1$, where F is the forward index level and X is the option's exercise price.

B. An 'Ad Hoc' Strawman

A troubling aspect of the analysis thus far is that, although the RMSVEs seem large for all practical purposes, we have not yet indicated what size of prediction error should be considered 'large.' One way to gauge the prediction errors is to measure them against a benchmark. To account for the sneer patterns in Black–Scholes implied volatilities, many marketmakers simply smooth the implied volatility relation across exercise prices (and days to expiration) and then value options using the smoothed relation. To operationalize this practice, we fit the Black–Scholes model to the reported structure of option prices each week using Model S to describe the Black–Scholes implied volatility. Obviously, applying the Black–Scholes formula in this context is internally inconsistent because the Black–Scholes formula is based on an assumption of constant volatility. Nonetheless, the procedure is a variation of what is applied in practice as a means of predicting option prices.[23] The DVF option valuation model, which is based on an internally consistent specification, should dominate this 'ad hoc' approach.

To create our strawman, we use a two-step procedure similar to the one we used for the DVF models. On day t, we fit Model S to the Black–Scholes implied volatilities, and then, on day $t + 7$, we apply the Black–Scholes formula using the volatility levels from estimated regression. The valuation prediction errors computed in this fashion are also included in Table III. As the table shows, the errors using the ad hoc model (AH) are almost uniformly smaller than those of the

---

[23] The Black–Scholes procedure cannot serve to predict American or exotic option prices from European option prices, which is the major benefit claimed for the implied volatility tree approach.

DVF approach. The average RMSVE across the entire sample period is 49.8 cents for the ad hoc Black–Scholes procedure, whereas it is more than 55 cents for the best DVF option valuation model. The average MAE is 23 cents for the ad hoc Black–Scholes procedure and 28.5 cents for Model 1. In viewing the various option categories, the greatest pricing improvement appears to be for at-the-money options, whose average RMSVEs are reduced by 10 cents or more. Put simply, the deterministic volatility approach does not appear to be an improvement over the, albeit theoretically inconsistent, ad hoc procedure used in practice. One possible interpretation of this evidence is that there is little economic meaning to the deterministic volatility function implied by option prices.

The reason the ad hoc strawman performs marginally better than the DVF model can be seen by examination of Figure 10, which is identical in its format to Figure 6; that is, we show the time series of the explained at-the-money-implied volatility of each week (with contemporaneous coefficients) minus the explained at-the-money implied volatility of the same week calculated on the basis of the *previous week's* coefficients. A comparison of Figure 10 with Figure 6 shows that the coefficients of the ad hoc model are somewhat more stable than those of the DVF Model 3.

C. A *t*-Test of Equivalence between the Various Models[24]

Panel A of Table III also reports the results of statistical tests of the equivalence between models. The tests are based on West (1996), and, for ease of reference, we

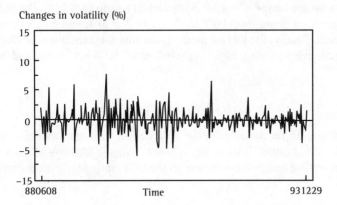

Figure 10. *Week-to-week change in the volatility rate of the ad hoc Black–Scholes model arising from changes in the coefficient estimates, for the period June 1988 through December 1993*

Note: The change is defined as the difference between the estimated volatility rate at the current index level using contemporaneous coefficient estimates of the ad hoc Black–Scholes model less the estimated volatility rate using the previous week's coefficient estimates.

[24] We are extremely grateful to Ken West for his correspondence outlining the steps of the procedure below.

use his notation. Let f_t be the (6×1) vector of root mean squared prediction errors at time t corresponding to the six models 0, 1, 2, 3, S, and AH. Let Ef be the population value, and let f be the sample average. Then, if we know the population values for all the parameters, $f - Ef$ is asymptotically normal with the variance–covariance matrix:

$$S_{ff} = \sum_{j=-\infty}^{\infty} E(f_t - Ef)(f_{t-j} - Ef)'. \tag{12}$$

On the basis of this observation and a generalized method of moments reasoning, we determine $\bar{f}$, a 6×1 constant vector, such that

$$\min_{\bar{f}} \sum_t (f_t - \bar{f})' \Omega (f_t - \bar{t}), \tag{13}$$

where Ω is the Newey-West heteroskedasticity-consistent, 6×6 variance–covariance matrix with fifteen weekly lags which accounts for the possibility of correlation across the models and serially correlated errors. In this way, we obtain asymptotic t-ratios for the root mean square prediction errors of our six models. Panel A of Table III reports both the incremental root mean squared prediction errors of each model compared to the previous one in the list as well as their corresponding t-ratios.

The test results reported in Table III indicate that DVF Model 1 is a significant improvement over the straight Black–Scholes Model 0. The incremental average root mean squared error is -22.7 cents and its t-ratio is -7.26. The incremental improvements in going from DVF Models 1 to 2, 2 to 3, and 3 to S, however, are insignificant. Finally, the ad hoc model is an improvement over the Model S. The incremental average root mean squared error is -5.7 cents and its t-ratio is -2.46.[25]

VI. HEDGING RESULTS

A key motivation for developing the DVF option valuation model is to provide better risk management. If volatility is a deterministic function of asset price and time, then setting hedge ratios based on the DVF option valuation model should

---

[25] Admittedly, the assumption that we know the population values for all the parameters is incorrect. Each time we move down one week, we calculate the errors of the new week on the basis of the parameters of the old week. The t-statistics do not take into account the standard errors of the parameter estimation performed in the old week. As shown by West (1996), the needed correction would depend on the expected value of the derivative of the prediction errors taken with respect to the parameter values. This would require repeated numerical calculation of the time series of errors, varying one parameter each time. There is no theoretical reason why this derivation would be equal to zero in our application, whereas it would have been if our estimators had been designed to optimize the prediction.

present an improvement over the constant volatility model. In this section, we evaluate the performance of a hedge portfolio formed on day t and unwound one week later. Galai (1983) shows that the return on such a discretely adjusted option hedge portfolio has three components: (a) the riskless return on investment, (b) the return from the discrete adjustment of the hedge, and (c) the return from the change in the deviation of the actual option price from the change in the theoretical value. Since all option prices used in our analysis are forward prices, the riskless return component of the hedge portfolio is zero. Furthermore, because our focus is on model performance and not on the issues raised by discrete-time readjustment, we assume that the hedge portfolio is continuously rebalanced through time. Consequently, the hedge portfolio error is defined as:

$$\epsilon_t = \Delta c_{\text{actual},t} - \Delta c_{\text{model},t}, \tag{14}$$

where $\Delta c_{\text{actual},t}$ is the change in the reported option price from day t until day $t+7$ and $\Delta c_{\text{model},t}$ is the change in the model's theoretical value.

The proof of equation (14) is straightforward. The hedging error that results from the continuous rebalancing using the hedge ratio, h, is

$$\Delta c_{\text{actual},t} - \int_t^{t+7} h(S_u, u) dS_u. \tag{15}$$

If we had the correct model to determine h, the two quantities in equation (15) would be equal to one another, not as a real number equality but with probability one or at the very least in the sense that their difference would have an expected value of zero and zero variance. Therefore, it must be the case that the integral term equals $\Delta c_{\text{model},t}$. In other words, when the hedge is continuously rebalanced, the hedging error is simply equal to the time increment in the valuation error.

Table IV contains a summary of the hedging error results. Across the over-all sample period, Model 0—the Black–Scholes constant-volatility model—performs best of all the deterministic volatility function specifications. Its average root mean squared hedging error (RMSHE) is 45.5 cents, compared with 48.9, 50.5, 50.6, and 50.5 cents for Models 1 through 3 and Model S, respectively. The intuition for this result is that, although the model's option values are systematically incorrect, its errors are stable (or, at least, strongly serially dependent as suits a specification error), unlike the less parsimonious models. Within the class of DVF models considered, the results again indicate that, the more parsimonious volatility functions provide better hedging performance.

The ad hoc Black–Scholes procedure described in the preceding section also performs well from a hedging standpoint. The average RMSHE is only 46.7 cents. Consistent with the prediction results reported in Table III, the DVF option valuation model does not appear to be an improvement.

To further distinguish between the hedging errors of the different models, we run t-tests similar to the ones we performed for the prediction errors. The results

Table IV. Average S&P 500 index option dollar hedging errors using the Deterministic Volatility Function (DVF) Model

Panel A: Aggregate Results

DVF Model	All Options			Call Options			Put Options		
	RMSHE	ΔRMSHE	t-ratio	RMSHE	ΔRMSHE	t-ratio	RMSHE	ΔRMSHE	t-ratio
0	0.455			0.445			0.443		
1	0.489	0.034	1.99	0.491	0.046	2.56	0.472	0.029	1.55
2	0.505	0.016	3.04	0.500	0.009	1.44	0.496	0.024	4.50
3	0.506	0.001	0.85	0.505	0.005	4.14	0.492	-0.004	-1.89
S	0.505	-0.001	-1.90	0.503	-0.002	-2.51	0.492	0.000	0.41
AH	0.467	-0.038	-2.13	0.454	-0.049	-2.39	0.450	-0.042	-2.42

Panel B: Call Options Only

Moneyness (%)		DVF Model	Days to Expiration					
Lower	Upper		Less than 40		40 to 70		More than 70	
			RMSHE	FREQ	RMSHE	FREQ	RMSHE	FREQ
-10	-5	0	0.367	0.519	0.349	0.541	0.454	0.455
		1	0.334	0.515	0.404	0.453	0.518	0.409
		2	0.315	0.535	0.433	0.394	0.552	0.409
		3	0.319	0.550	0.441	0.382	0.568	0.398
		S	0.316	0.554	0.439	0.382	0.568	0.398
		AH	0.370		0.388		0.482	
-5	0	0	0.406	0.534	0.394	0.591	0.489	0.473
		1	0.466	0.455	0.524	0.403	0.642	0.333
		2	0.452	0.487	0.560	0.333	0.673	0.344
		3	0.457	0.484	0.569	0.328	0.686	0.333
		S	0.454	0.487	0.567	0.328	0.686	0.333
		AH	0.432		0.444		0.510	
0	5	0	0.388	0.367	0.367	0.534	0.422	0.488
		1	0.359	0.480	0.459	0.391	0.536	0.417
		2	0.364	0.476	0.483	0.385	0.552	0.429
		3	0.364	0.476	0.486	0.379	0.555	0.417
		S	0.363	0.480	0.485	0.385	0.555	0.417
		AH	0.335		0.384		0.443	
5	10	0	0.431	0.245	0.381	0.250	0.363	0.303
		1	0.203	0.510	0.256	0.462	0.304	0.485

Moneyness	Model						
	2	0.394	0.301	0.500	0.238	0.551	0.169
	3	0.394	0.306	0.500	0.238	0.571	0.168
	S	0.394	0.307	0.500	0.237	0.571	0.169
	AH		0.285		0.238		0.228

Panel C: Put Options Only

Moneyness	Model						
−10 / −5	0	0.510	0.421	0.370	0.292	0.353	0.277
	1	0.429	0.473	0.380	0.352	0.419	0.252
	2	0.388	0.539	0.360	0.395	0.443	0.241
	3	0.367	0.540	0.360	0.395	0.455	0.240
	S	0.367	0.541	0.370	0.396	0.461	0.239
	AH		0.412		0.251		0.211
−5 / 0	0	0.553	0.443	0.466	0.407	0.510	0.352
	1	0.395	0.565	0.338	0.521	0.361	0.437
	2	0.303	0.644	0.345	0.580	0.384	0.434
	3	0.316	0.642	0.351	0.579	0.384	0.433
	S	0.316	0.643	0.351	0.579	0.384	0.432
	AH		0.464		0.402		0.348
0 / 5	0	0.607	0.479	0.509	0.443	0.506	0.420
	1	0.506	0.544	0.509	0.515	0.557	0.388
	2	0.461	0.596	0.441	0.551	0.502	0.408
	3	0.449	0.588	0.460	0.547	0.524	0.404
	S	0.449	0.588	0.460	0.547	0.531	0.405
	AH		0.522		0.467		0.425
5 / 10	0	0.410	0.453	0.491	0.442	0.473	0.358
	1	0.492	0.384	0.545	0.370	0.597	0.272
	2	0.492	0.401	0.500	0.377	0.587	0.283
	3	0.492	0.389	0.527	0.368	0.587	0.279
	S	0.492	0.397	0.527	0.369	0.602	0.280
	AH				0.429		0.359

Note: RMSHE is the root mean squared dollar hedging error averaged across all days in the sample period from June 1988 through December 1993. ΔRMSHE is the incremental RMSHE when comparing successive models. The t-ratio indicates the significance of that increment. FREQ is the frequency of days, expressed as a ratio of the total number of days, on which a particular model has a lower daily RMSHE than the Ad Hoc Model. Models 1, 2, and 3 specify that the local volatility rate is linear in (a) X and X^2, (b) X, X^2, T, T^2, and XT, and (c) X, X^2, T, T^2, and XT, respectively, where X is the option's exercise price and T is its time to expiration. Model S switches between Models 1, 2, and 3 depending upon whether the number of option expirations in the cross-section is one, two or three, respectively. The Ad Hoc (AH) Model specifies that Black–Scholes implied volatility is linear in (a) X and X^2 (b), X, X^2, T, and XT, and (c) X, $X^2 T$, T^2, and XT, respectively, depending upon whether the number of option expirations in the cross section is one, two or three. Moneyness is defined as $X/F - 1$, where F is the forward index level.

are shown in Panel A of Table IV. With a t-ratio of 1.99 Model 1 represents a significant worsening relative to the plain Black–Scholes model.

VII. ROBUSTNESS

The results reported in the last three sections offer evidence that the volatility functions implied by index option prices are not stable through time. In developing our test procedures, however, we make a number of methodological decisions, some of which could be questioned in the sense that the final results may have been different had other methodologies been adopted. In this section, we investigate the robustness of our results by checking three issues of this kind. The first issue pertains to the choice of the quadratic functional forms given in equations (6) through (9). In particular, allowing volatility to grow quadratically with the state variable violates the slow-growth assumptions necessary for the existence of a solution to the stochastic differential equation. The second issue pertains to the trade-off between the cross-sectional and the time-series goodness-of-fit. Derman and Kani (1994a,b), Dupire (1994), and Rubinstein (1994) recommend using a single cross section of option prices to parameterize the DVF model. In this way, the arbitrage-free spirit of the model is maintained. But are the model's predictions improved by using multiple cross sections simultaneously? The third issue concerns the uniformity of the results over various subsamples. Does the DVF model work better during specific subperiods? We study these three issues below.

A. Functional Form

The quadratic functional forms given in equations (6) through (9) may seem questionable for two related reasons. First, the use of the parabolic branches, for which there is no basis in fact and which are purely extrapolative in nature, may influence our results. Of course, the probability weights received by values of the underlying asset far from the current value become extremely small very quickly (at an exponential rate), so they probably play a negligible role in the analysis. Nonetheless, this conjecture is worth checking. Second, it is questionable, mathematically speaking, to let the volatility grow quadratically with the state variable because such a volatility function violates the assumptions for existence of the solution of a stochastic differential equation (so-called 'slow-growth' and 'Lipschitz' conditions).

In order to allay these two fears simultaneously, we perform a simple experiment. In place of estimating Model 3 in an unconstrained manner, we truncate the local volatility rate at a maximum level of 50 percent annually, that is,

$$\text{Model 3t}: \sigma = \max(0.01, \min(a_0 + a_1 X + a_2 X^2 + a_3 T + a_4 T^2$$
$$+ a_5 XT, 0.50)), \tag{16}$$

and then redo all of the steps of the analysis. The results appear in Table V. For convenience, the earlier results of Tables I, III, and IV for Model 3 are also presented. Examining the various entries of the table, we find that the truncation makes no difference. The in-sample valuation errors, the out-of-sample prediction errors, and the hedging errors are virtually identical to those of the unconstrained version of the model for both the overall sample and the various option categorizations. In other words, the parabolic branches of the quadratic DVF models have not, in any way, obfuscated the analysis.

B. Two-Week Estimation

The second robustness test addresses the issue of the deterministic volatility function's stationarity. If we had truly believed in the permanency of the DVF model, we would have attempted to fit it to the entire five-year data sample with the same values of the coefficients throughout. It should be apparent by now, however, that no meaningful fit would have been obtained. To give the model the benefit of the doubt, we adopt the procedure advocated by the model's developers and fit it to the cross section of options available on one day only, and then determine whether the model could survive at least one week. By using comparatively little information, however, we may have introduced sampling variation. This sampling variation, as opposed to true parameter instability, may be responsible for the poor fit one week later. In order to address this possibility, we now redo the entire analysis, using the cross sections of two successive weeks for the in-sample estimation. We then investigate the quality of the fit out of sample by moving ahead by one more week, so that a total of three weeks are involved in the test.

The results for Model 3 are shown in Table VI. Not surprisingly, the in-sample fit (estimation mode) deteriorates slightly when going from one-week to two-week estimation. Forcing the same coefficient structure on two cross sections of option prices necessarily reduces in-sample performance. For the 'All Options' category, for example, the RMSVE increases from 22.6 cents to 30.8 cents. For calls, the increase is from 21.8 cents to 29.7 cents, and, for puts, 23.0 cents to 31.4 cents.[26]

The prediction results are also reported in Table VI. Overall the improvement in out-of-sample performance is small. For the whole sample, the RMSVE is reduced from 55.5 cents to 54.4 cents. The subcategory results are mixed. For short-term options, the prediction performance is reduced, but, for intermediate and long-term options, the performance is improved. All in all, the results indicate that the additional variation in the time to expiration brought about by using two cross sections of option prices captures slightly better the relation between the local volatility rate and time.

The hedging performance results are noticeably improved as a result of the two-week estimation. For the full sample, Table VI shows that the RMSHE is reduced from 50.5 cents to 48.2 cents. Reductions in the RMSHE are also observed

---

[26] The slight differences between the one-week results reported in Table VI and those reported in Table V arise because one cross section of option prices is lost in the two-week estimation procedure.

Table V. *Average S&P 500 index option dollar valuation, prediction, and hedging errors using the Deterministic Volatility Function (DVF) Model 3 without and with maximum truncation*

Panel A: Aggregate Results

Test	DVF Model	All Options			Call Options			Put Options		
		RMSVE	MOE	MAE	RMSVE	MOE	MAE	RMSVE	MOE	MAE
Estimation	3	0.226	−0.011	0.050	0.218	−0.002	0.044	0.230	−0.020	0.057
Estimation	3t	0.228	−0.010	0.051	0.220	−0.002	0.045	0.232	−0.019	0.057
Prediction	3	0.556	−0.065	0.291	0.549	−0.044	0.285	0.557	−0.088	0.300
Prediction	3t	0.556	−0.067	0.292	0.549	−0.046	0.286	0.557	−0.089	0.301
Hedge	3	0.506			0.505			0.492		
Hedge	3t	0.506			0.504			0.492		

Panel B: Call Options Only

Moneyness (%) Lower	Upper	Test	DVF Model	Days to Expiration					
				Less than 40		40 to 70		More than 70	
				RMSVE	MOE	RMSVE	MOE	RMSVE	MOE
−10	−5	estimation	3	0.259	−0.027	0.221	−0.013	0.220	0.003
		estimation	3t	0.258	−0.027	0.222	−0.014	0.227	−0.001
		prediction	3	0.330	−0.045	0.461	−0.098	0.604	−0.049
		prediction	3t	0.327	−0.046	0.459	−0.096	0.605	−0.070
		hedge	3	0.319		0.441		0.568	
		hedge	3t	0.318		0.438		0.563	
−5	0	estimation	3	0.197	0.014	0.187	0.012	0.205	0.026
		estimation	3t	0.201	0.018	0.190	0.014	0.209	0.023
		prediction	3	0.428	0.010	0.583	−0.069	0.706	−0.036
		prediction	3t	0.425	0.014	0.579	−0.065	0.715	−0.056
		hedge	3	0.457		0.569		0.686	
		hedge	3t	0.456		0.568		0.681	
0	5	estimation	3	0.166	0.047	0.171	0.007	0.189	−0.021
		estimation	3t	0.173	0.053	0.176	0.009	0.194	−0.023
		prediction	3	0.424	0.054	0.592	−0.114	0.686	−0.080
		prediction	3t	0.424	0.058	0.588	−0.109	0.697	−0.098
		hedge	3	0.364		0.486		0.555	
		hedge	3t	0.364		0.487		0.552	
5	10	estimation	3	0.151	−0.082	0.205	−0.108	0.245	−0.135
		estimation	3t	0.151	−0.081	0.204	−0.107	0.248	−0.137

Moneyness		Type	Model						
−10	−5	prediction	3	0.221	−0.068	0.394	−0.162	0.469	−0.096
		prediction	3t	0.222	−0.068	0.390	−0.160	0.464	−0.099
		hedge	3	0.168		0.238		0.306	
		hedge	3t	0.168		0.241		0.301	

Panel C: Put Options Only

Moneyness		Type	Model						
−5	0	estimation	3	0.237	−0.164	0.194	−0.088	0.152	−0.035
		estimation	3t	0.236	−0.162	0.194	−0.089	0.156	−0.041
		prediction	3	0.313	−0.173	0.475	−0.225	0.520	−0.189
		prediction	3t	0.310	−0.174	0.473	−0.226	0.542	−0.202
		hedge	3	0.240		0.395		0.540	
		hedge	3t	0.238		0.395		0.539	
0	5	estimation	3	0.162	−0.026	0.152	−0.001	0.181	0.037
		estimation	3t	0.164	−0.021	0.150	−0.001	0.181	0.032
		prediction	3	0.431	−0.042	0.580	−0.121	0.698	0.016
		prediction	3t	0.428	−0.038	0.578	−0.118	0.712	−0.009
		hedge	3	0.433		0.579		0.642	
		hedge	3t	0.433		0.579		0.642	
5	10	estimation	3	0.203	0.010	0.190	0.000	0.225	−0.001
		estimation	3t	0.206	0.012	0.192	0.002	0.226	−0.003
		prediction	3	0.443	−0.003	0.615	−0.133	0.751	−0.112
		prediction	3t	0.442	0.000	0.612	−0.129	0.759	−0.126
		hedge	3	0.404		0.547		0.588	
		hedge	3t	0.404		0.548		0.588	
		estimation	3	0.243	0.016	0.291	−0.037	0.309	−0.037
		estimation	3t	0.244	0.016	0.292	−0.038	0.312	−0.038
		prediction	3	0.273	0.015	0.424	−0.092	0.551	−0.057
		prediction	3t	0.272	0.015	0.424	−0.094	0.550	−0.061
		hedge	3	0.279		0.368		0.389	
		hedge	3t	0.280		0.371		0.389	

Note: RMSVE is the root mean squared dollar valuation error averaged across all days in the sample period from June 1988 through December 1993. MOE is the average of the mean valuation error outside the observed bid/ask quotes across all days in the sample (a positive value indicates the theoretical value exceeds the ask price on average; a negative value indicates the theoretical value is below the bid price). MAE is the average of the mean absolute valuation error outside the observed bid/ask quotes across all days in the sample. 'Estimation' refers to in-sample valuation errors, 'prediction' refers to out-of-sample valuation errors, and 'hedge' refers to hedging errors. Model 3 specifies that the local volatility rate is linear in X, X^2, T, T^2, and XT, where X is the option's exercise price and T is its time to expiration. Model 3t has the same structural form as Model 3 except that the local volatility rate is truncated at a maximum of 50 percent. Moneyness is defined as $X/F - 1$, where F is the forward index level.

Table VI. *Average S&P 500 index option dollar valuation, prediction, and hedging errors using the Deterministic Volatility Function (DVF) Model 3*

Panel A: Aggregate Results

Test	DVF Model	All Options			Call Options			Put Options		
		RMSVE	MOE	MAE	RMSVE	MOE	MAE	RMSVE	MOE	MAE
Estimation	3-1 week	0.226	−0.011	0.050	0.218	−0.002	0.044	0.230	−0.020	0.057
Estimation	3-2 weeks	0.308	−0.018	0.098	0.297	0.009	0.087	0.314	−0.047	0.112
Prediction	3-1 week	0.555	−0.063	0.292	0.548	−0.043	0.286	0.556	−0.086	0.301
Prediction	3-2 weeks	0.544	−0.047	0.283	0.548	−0.008	0.274	0.548	−0.089	0.298
Hedge	3-1 week	0.505		0.503		0.491				
Hedge	3-2 weeks	0.482		0.476		0.473				

Panel B: Call Options Only

Moneyness (%)		Test	DVF Model	Days to Expiration					
Lower	Upper			Less than 40		40 to 70		More than 70	
				RMSVE	MOE	RMSVE	MOE	RMSVE	MOE
−10	−5	estimation	3-1 week	0.260	−0.027	0.221	−0.013	0.220	0.003
		estimation	3-2 weeks	0.265	−0.032	0.311	−0.050	0.325	−0.057
		prediction	3-1 week	0.330	−0.045	0.461	−0.098	0.604	−0.049
		prediction	3-2 weeks	0.331	−0.039	0.474	−0.104	0.585	−0.105
		hedge	3-1 week	0.316		0.438		0.563	
		hedge	3-2 weeks	0.309		0.395		0.523	
−5	0	estimation	3-1 week	0.197	0.014	0.186	0.012	0.205	0.026
		estimation	3-2 weeks	0.253	0.027	0.271	0.003	0.297	−0.007
		prediction	3-1 week	0.427	0.012	0.583	−0.069	0.706	−0.036
		prediction	3-2 weeks	0.420	0.039	0.579	−0.038	0.665	−0.066
		hedge	3-1 week	0.454		0.568		0.681	
		hedge	3-2 weeks	0.429		0.529		0.652	
0	5	estimation	3-1 week	0.166	0.047	0.172	0.007	0.189	−0.021
		estimation	3-2 weeks	0.239	0.103	0.260	0.044	0.249	0.021
		prediction	3-1 week	0.423	0.056	0.592	−0.114	0.686	−0.080
		prediction	3-2 weeks	0.427	0.124	0.560	0.014	0.621	−0.009
		hedge	3-1 week	0.364		0.487		0.552	
		hedge	3-2 weeks	0.346		0.453		0.534	

Moneyness	Type	Period						
5 / 10	estimation	3-1 week	0.151	0.205	-0.082	0.245	-0.108	-0.135
	estimation	3-2 weeks	0.151	0.217	-0.035	0.258	-0.058	-0.085
	prediction	3-1 week	0.212	0.394	-0.058	0.469	-0.162	-0.096
	prediction	3-2 weeks	0.214	0.372	-0.003	0.406	-0.031	-0.017
	hedge	3-1 week	0.168	0.241		0.301		
	hedge	3-2 weeks	0.188	0.227		0.289		

Panel C: Put Options Only

Moneyness	Type	Period						
-10	estimation	3-1 week	0.237	0.194	-0.164	0.152	-0.088	-0.035
	estimation	3-2 weeks	0.280	0.323	-0.204	0.308	-0.208	-0.166
	prediction	3-1 week	0.309	0.475	-0.170	0.520	-0.225	-0.189
	prediction	3-2 weeks	0.339	0.513	-0.209	0.544	-0.281	-0.287
	hedge	3-1 week	0.235	0.395		0.539		
	hedge	3-2 weeks	0.230	0.352		0.490		
-5	estimation	3-1 week	0.162	0.151	-0.026	0.181	-0.001	0.037
	estimation	3-2 weeks	0.243	0.268	-0.053	0.271	-0.070	-0.002
	prediction	3-1 week	0.429	0.580	-0.039	0.698	-0.121	0.016
	prediction	3-2 weeks	0.444	0.586	-0.064	0.665	-0.138	-0.046
	hedge	3-1 week	0.431	0.579		0.642		
	hedge	3-2 weeks	0.413	0.546		0.610		
0	estimation	3-1 week	0.203	0.191	0.010	0.225	0.000	-0.001
	estimation	3-2 weeks	0.264	0.276	0.017	0.299	-0.003	0.004
	prediction	3-1 week	0.441	0.615	-0.001	0.751	-0.133	-0.112
	prediction	3-2 weeks	0.450	0.593	0.008	0.670	-0.066	-0.062
	hedge	3-1 week	0.405	0.548		0.588		
	hedge	3-2 weeks	0.407	0.523		0.557		
5	estimation	3-1 week	0.243	0.291	0.016	0.309	-0.037	-0.037
	estimation	3-2 weeks	0.261	0.303	0.013	0.326	-0.038	-0.026
	prediction	3-1 week	0.271	0.424	0.017	0.551	-0.092	-0.057
	prediction	3-2 weeks	0.293	0.393	0.012	0.479	-0.062	-0.029
	hedge	3-1 week	0.280	0.371		0.389		
	hedge	3-2 weeks	0.286	0.355		0.365		

Note: RMSVE is the root mean squared valuation error averaged across all days in the sample period from June 1988 through December 1993. MOE is the average of the mean valuation error averaged across all days in the sample period from June 1988 through December 1993. MOE is the average of the mean valuation error outside the observed bid/ask quotes across all days in the sample (a positive value indicates the theoretical value exceeds the ask price on average; a negative value indicates the theoretical value is below the bid price). MAE is the average of the mean absolute valuation error outside the observed bid/ask quotes across all days in the sample. 'Estimation' refers to in-sample valuation errors, 'prediction' refers to out-of-sample valuation errors, and 'hedge' refers to hedging errors. Model '3-1 week' specifies that the local volatility rate is linear in X, X^2, T, T^2, and XT, and is fitted to a single week's cross section, where X is the option exercise price, and T is the time to expiration. Model '3-2 weeks' specifies that the local volatility rate is linear in X, X^2, T, T^2, and XT and is fitted to two weeks' cross sections. Moneyness is defined as $X/F - 1$, where F is the forward index level.

for the call and put option categories as well as for most of the option subcategories. Apparently, the two-week estimation has removed some of the sampling variation and has identified a coefficient structure that is more stable through time.

The overall performance of Model 3 estimated using two weeks of index option prices, however, still does not match the overall performance of the ad hoc Black–Scholes model fitted to a *single* cross section of prices (recall Table IV where the RMSHE is reported as 46.7 cents). Indeed, if one estimates the ad hoc Black–Scholes model using two cross sections of option prices, its sampling variation is reduced by even more than it is for Model 3. Though not shown in the table, its RMSHE falls to 40.8 cents. For calls and puts separately, the RMSHEs of the ad hoc Black–Scholes model estimated using the two-week estimation are 39.3 and 41.0 cents compared with 47.6 and 47.3 cents for Model 3. In other words, while increasing the amount of information used in estimation has identified coefficients that are more stable through time, the hedging performance of the ad hoc Black–Scholes model estimated using two cross sections of option prices shows even greater dominance over the DVF model than it does when only one cross section is used.

C. Analysis of Subsamples

The final issue has to do with performance through time. Does the DVF model perform better in some periods but not in others? To answer this question, we summarize the estimation, prediction, and hedging errors by calendar year. The results are reported in Table VII.

First, with respect to in-sample performance, the results are qualitatively robust across the sample. Using the AIC, Model 2 most frequently does best at describing the cross section of option prices in all subperiods. This is followed by the performance of Model 1. Again, parsimony in the volatility structure appears warranted. With respect to prediction, the ad hoc Black–Scholes model does best in every year except 1988, when its RMSVE is only slightly higher than Model 2's. Indeed, the outperformance is quite extraordinary in 1990, when its RMSVE is 54.2 cents versus 73.3 cents for Model 2. Finally, with respect to hedging performance, the ad hoc Black–Scholes (and the constant volatility Black–Scholes) model again dominates. All in all, the results of Table VII indicate that the poor performance of the DVF model is not driven by a particular subperiod of the sample. The DVF model performs poorly relative to an ad hoc procedure.

VIII. SUMMARY AND CONCLUSIONS

Claims that the Black and Scholes (1973) valuation formula no longer holds in financial markets are appearing with increasing frequency. When the Black–Scholes formula is used to imply volatilities from reported option prices, the volatility estimates vary systematically across exercise prices and times to expiration. Derman and Kani (1994a,b), Dupire (1994), and Rubinstein (1994) argue that this systematic behavior is driven by changes in the volatility rate of asset returns. They hypothesize that volatility is a deterministic function of asset price and time, and they provide appropriate binomial or trinomial option valuation procedures to account for this.

In this paper, we apply the deterministic volatility option valuation approach to S&P 500 index option prices during the period June 1988 through December 1993. We reach the following conclusions. First, although there is unlimited flexibility in specifying the volatility function and it is always possible to describe exactly the reported structure of option prices, our results indicate that a parsimonious model works best in sample according to the Akaike Information Criterion. Second, when the fitted volatility function is used to value options one week later, the DVF model's prediction errors grow larger as the volatility function specification becomes less parsimonious. In particular, specifications

Table VII. *Average S&P 500 index option dollar valuation, prediction, and hedging errors by year using the Deterministic Volatility Function (DVF) model*

Year	DVF Model	Overall			Calls		Puts	
		RMSVE	MAE	AIC	RMSVE	MAE	RMSVE	MAE
Panel A: Estimation								
1988	0	0.435	0.208	0.000	0.433	0.215	0.435	0.200
	1	0.229	0.063	0.258	0.205	0.050	0.248	0.075
	2	0.178	0.032	0.677	0.178	0.032	0.177	0.033
	3	0.176	0.031	0.065	0.176	0.030	0.174	0.031
	S	0.178	0.032	0.000	0.178	0.032	0.177	0.032
1989	0	0.485	0.244	0.000	0.483	0.251	0.484	0.237
	1	0.256	0.085	0.192	0.266	0.090	0.240	0.079
	2	0.164	0.028	0.808	0.159	0.025	0.167	0.032
	3	0.164	0.028	0.000	0.159	0.025	0.167	0.032
	S	0.164	0.028	0.000	0.159	0.025	0.166	0.032
1990	0	0.838	0.475	0.000	0.861	0.522	0.814	0.433
	1	0.339	0.117	0.250	0.348	0.126	0.323	0.108
	2	0.223	0.048	0.712	0.230	0.053	0.212	0.043
	3	0.216	0.043	0.000	0.220	0.046	0.206	0.040
	S	0.216	0.043	0.038	0.220	0.046	0.207	0.040
1991	0	0.621	0.332	0.000	0.613	0.326	0.622	0.335
	1	0.281	0.085	0.302	0.294	0.087	0.265	0.082
	2	0.209	0.042	0.679	0.206	0.036	0.209	0.048
	3	0.209	0.042	0.019	0.205	0.036	0.209	0.048
	S	0.209	0.042	0.000	0.206	0.036	0.209	0.048
1992	0	0.708	0.390	0.000	0.712	0.401	0.698	0.381
	1	0.284	0.082	0.135	0.288	0.081	0.278	0.086
	2	0.226	0.048	0.731	0.227	0.041	0.225	0.057
	3	0.222	0.045	0.135	0.222	0.038	0.222	0.055
	S	0.223	0.046	0.000	0.223	0.038	0.222	0.055
1993	0	0.725	0.385	0.019	0.718	0.385	0.719	0.386
	1	0.388	0.124	0.404	0.358	0.115	0.405	0.139
	2	0.359	0.104	0.423	0.316	0.088	0.386	0.125
	3	0.352	0.100	0.154	0.306	0.083	0.382	0.123
	S	0.353	0.100	0.000	0.308	0.084	0.381	0.123

Table VII *(Continued)*

Year	DVF Model	Overall RMSVE	Overall MAE	Calls RMSVE	Calls MAE	Puts RMSVE	Puts MAE	Overall RMSVE	Calls RMSVE	Puts RMSVE
Panel B: Prediction								Panel C: Hedging		
1988	0	0.546	0.290	0.554	0.308	0.524	0.273	0.308	0.299	0.305
	1	0.412	0.201	0.400	0.200	0.420	0.201	0.349	0.358	0.331
	2	0.394	0.187	0.388	0.190	0.397	0.185	0.365	0.366	0.356
	3	0.398	0.193	0.392	0.196	0.402	0.190	0.365	0.368	0.356
	S	0.394	0.188	0.388	0.191	0.397	0.185	0.365	0.367	0.355
	AH	0.397	0.185	0.373	0.174	0.414	0.194	0.329	0.300	0.344
1989	0	0.612	0.346	0.614	0.350	0.605	0.345	0.386	0.376	0.394
	1	0.494	0.258	0.497	0.258	0.483	0.261	0.411	0.389	0.429
	2	0.475	0.256	0.468	0.245	0.477	0.270	0.441	0.417	0.460
	3	0.475	0.256	0.469	0.246	0.476	0.269	0.441	0.417	0.459
	S	0.474	0.255	0.468	0.245	0.476	0.269	0.440	0.417	0.459
	AH	0.462	0.240	0.465	0.247	0.446	0.236	0.404	0.381	0.413
1990	0	0.996	0.589	1.016	0.624	0.968	0.560	0.529	0.544	0.490
	1	0.671	0.364	0.677	0.375	0.661	0.353	0.608	0.634	0.570
	2	0.733	0.424	0.746	0.443	0.718	0.407	0.649	0.675	0.613
	3	0.731	0.424	0.744	0.445	0.714	0.405	0.651	0.678	0.613
	S	0.731	0.423	0.744	0.445	0.713	0.405	0.649	0.678	0.611
	AH	0.542	0.260	0.538	0.261	0.539	0.257	0.511	0.505	0.494
1991	0	0.819	0.484	0.811	0.474	0.807	0.487	0.501	0.508	0.473
	1	0.649	0.370	0.658	0.367	0.636	0.371	0.559	0.551	0.541
	2	0.640	0.372	0.638	0.362	0.639	0.384	0.571	0.555	0.564
	3	0.642	0.374	0.641	0.364	0.640	0.385	0.572	0.557	0.564
	S	0.640	0.372	0.638	0.362	0.638	0.383	0.571	0.555	0.564
	AH	0.594	0.323	0.601	0.328	0.576	0.322	0.550	0.545	0.516
1992	0	0.820	0.474	0.829	0.479	0.784	0.459	0.435	0.410	0.432
	1	0.473	0.216	0.482	0.212	0.455	0.220	0.424	0.439	0.402
	2	0.465	0.216	0.464	0.204	0.461	0.230	0.423	0.425	0.408
	3	0.451	0.207	0.449	0.195	0.449	0.220	0.422	0.427	0.404
	S	0.451	0.206	0.449	0.195	0.448	0.220	0.423	0.429	0.403
	AH	0.403	0.164	0.412	0.162	0.386	0.167	0.372	0.371	0.352
1993	0	0.809	0.446	0.815	0.447	0.781	0.445	0.506	0.468	0.502
	1	0.581	0.266	0.553	0.253	0.596	0.288	0.523	0.518	0.495
	2	0.577	0.263	0.532	0.234	0.608	0.302	0.523	0.503	0.513
	3	0.569	0.259	0.530	0.234	0.595	0.292	0.521	0.516	0.496
	S	0.573	0.261	0.532	0.236	0.600	0.295	0.522	0.512	0.501
	AH	0.507	0.208	0.473	0.187	0.524	0.235	0.477	0.469	0.437

Note: RMSVE (RMSHE) is the root mean squared valuation (hedging) error averaged across all days in the sample period from June 1988 through December 1993. MAE is the average of the mean absolute valuation error outside the observed bid/ask quotes across all days in the sample. AIC is the proportion of days during the sample period that the model is judged best by the Akaike Information Criterion. Model 0 is the Black–Scholes constant volatility model. Models, 1, 2, and 3 specify that the local volatility rate is linear in (a) X and X^2, (b) X, X^2, T, and XT, and (c) X, X^2, T, T^2, and XT, respectively, where X is the option's exercise price and T is its time to expiration. Model S switches between Models 1, 2, and 3 depending upon whether the number of option expirations in the cross section is one, two or three. The Ad Hoc (AH) Model specifies that Black–Scholes implied volatility is linear in (a) X and X^2, (b) X, X^2, T, and XT and (c) X, X^2, T, T^2, and XT, respectively, depending upon whether the number of option expirations in the cross section is one, two or three. Moneyness is defined as $X/F - 1$, where F is the forward index level.

that include a time parameter do worst of all, indicating that the time variable is an important cause of overfitting at the estimation stage. Third, hedge ratios determined by the Black–Scholes model appear more reliable than those obtained from the DVF option valuation model. In sum, 'simpler is better.'

Overall, our results suggest at least two possible avenues for future investigation. First, the deterministic volatility framework could be generalized. The volatility surface, for example, may be related to past changes in the index level. Such a generalized volatility surface is probably the last candidate model that can be considered before resorting to fully stochastic volatility processes—processes that are difficult to estimate and that do not permit option valuation by the absence of arbitrage.[27]

Second, thought should be given to appropriate statistical test designs for competing volatility structures. The 'null hypothesis' being investigated is that volatility is an exact function of asset price and time, so that options can be valued exactly by the no-arbitrage condition. Any deviation from such a strict theory, no matter how small, should cause a test statistic to reject it.[28] If a source of error had been introduced, some restriction on the sampling distribution of the error could be deduced and could provide a basis for a testing procedure.[29]

REFERENCES

Ait-Sahalia, Yacine, and Andrew W. Lo, 1998, Nonparametric estimation of state-price densities implicit in financial asset prices, *Journal of Finance* 53, 499–547.

Akaike, Hirotugu, 1973, Information theory and the extension of the maximum likelihood principle; in Boris N. Petrov and Frigyes Csaki, eds.: *2nd International Symposium on Information Theory* (Akailseoniai-Kiudo, Budapest, Hungary).

Bakshi, Gurdip, Charles Cao, and Zhiwu Chen, 1997, Empirical performance of alternative option pricing models, *Journal of Finance* 52, 2003–2049.

Bates, David, 1996a, Dollar jump fears, 1984–1992: Distributional abnormalities implicit in currency futures options, *Journal of International Money and Finance* 15, 65–93.

——,——, 1996b, Jumps and stochastic volatility: Exchange rate processes implicit in Deusche mark options, *Review of Financial Studies* 9, 69–107.

Bergman, Yaacov Z., Bruce D. Grundy, and Zvi Wiener, 1996, General properties of option prices, *Journal of Finance* 51, 1573–1610.

Bick, Avi, 1988, Producing derivative assets with forward contracts, *Journal of Financial and Quantitative Analysis* 23, 153–160.

---

[27] For an empirical test of stochastic volatility models that uses out-of-sample performance, as we recommend, see Bakshi, Cao, and Chen (1997).

[28] The same difficulty arises in any empirical verification of an exact theory. See MacBeth and Merville (1980), Whaley (1982), and Rubinstein (1985).

[29] Jacquier and Jarrow (1995) introduce two kinds of errors in the Black–Scholes model: model error and market error, which they distinguish by assuming that market errors occur rarely. Other approaches to the problem include Lo (1986) who introduces parameter uncertainty, Clément, Gouriéroux, and Monfort (1993) who randomize the martingale pricing measure to account for an incomplete market, and Bossaerts and Hillion (1997) whose error is due to discreteness in hedging.

Black, Fischer, 1976, Studies of stock price volatility changes, *Proceedings of the 1976 Meetings of the American Statistical Association, Business and Economic Statistic Section*, 177–181.

——,——, and Myron S. Scholes, 1973, The pricing of options and corporate liabilities, *Journal of Political Economy* 81, 243–272.

Bossaerts, Peter, and Pierre Hillion, 1997, Local parameter analysis of hedging in discrete time, *Journal of Econometrics* 81, 243–272.

Breeden, Douglas, and Robert Litzenberger, 1978, Prices of state-contingent claims implicit in option prices, *Journal of Business* 51, 621–651.

Chicago Board Options Exchange, 1995, *Constitution and Rules*.

Clément, Emmanuelle, Christian Gouriéroux, and Alain Monfort, 1993, Prediction of contingent price measures, Working paper, Institut National de la Statistique et des Etudes Economiques (Paris).

Constantinides, George, 1997, Transaction costs and the implied volatility smile, Working paper, Graduate School of Business, University of Chicago.

Derman, Emanuel, and Iraj Kani, 1994a, The volatility smile and its implied tree, *Quantitative Strategies Research Notes* (Goldman Sachs, New York).

——,——, and ——, 1994b, Riding on the smile, *Risk* 7, 32–39.

Dupire, Bruno, 1993, Pricing and hedging with smiles, Working paper, Paribas Capital Markets, London.

——, 1994, Pricing with a smile, *Risk* 7, 18–20.

Duque, Joao, and Dean Paxson, 1993, Implied volatility and dynamic hedging. *Review of Futures Markets* 13, 381–421.

Fleming, Jeff, Barabara Ostdiek, and Robert E. Whaley, 1996, Trading costs and the relative rates of price discovery in the stock, futures, and option markets, *Journal of Futures Markets* 16, 353–387.

Galai, Dan, 1983, The components of the return from hedging options, *Journal of Business* 56, 45–54.

Harvey, Campbell R., and Robert E. Whaley, 1992, Dividends and S&P 100 index option valuation, *Journal of Futures Markets* 12, 123–137.

Heston, Steven L., 1993, A closed-form solution for options with stochastic volatility with applications to bond and currency options, *Review of Financial Studies* 6, 327–343.

Heynen, Ronald, 1993, An empirical investigation of observed smile patterns, *Review of Futures Markets* 13, 317–353.

Hull, John, and Alan White, 1987, The pricing of options on assets with stochastic volatility, *Journal of Finance* 42, 281–300.

Jackwerth, Jens C., and Mark Rubinstein, 1996, Recovering probability distributions from option prices, *Journal of Finance* 51, 1611–1631.

Jacquier, Eric, and Robert Jarrow, 1995, Dynamic evaluation of contingent claim models (An analysis of model error), Working paper, Cornell University.

Lo, Andrew, 1986, Statistical tests of contingent-claims asset-pricing models: A new methodology, *Journal of Financial Economics* 17, 143–173.

Longstaff, Francis A., 1995, Option pricing and the martingale restriction, *Review of Financial Studies* 8, 1091–1124.

MacBeth, James D., and Larry J. Merville, 1980, Tests of the Black/Scholes and Cox call option valuation models, *Journal of Finance* 35, 285–301.

Rubinstein, Mark, 1985, Non-parametric tests of alternative option pricing models using all reported trades and quotes on the 30 most active CBOE option classes from August 23, 1976 through August 31, 1978 *Journal of Finance* 40, 455–480.

——,——,1994, Implied binomial trees, *Journal of Finance* 49, 771–818.

Schwert, G. William, 1989, Why does stock market volatility change over time? *Journal of Finance* 44, 1115–1154.

——,——,1990, Stock volatility and the crash of '87, *Review of Financial Studies* 3, 77–102.

Taylor, Stephen J., and Xinzhong Xu, 1993, The magnitude of implied volatility smiles: Theory and empirical evidence for exchange rates, *Review of Futures Markets* 13, 355–380.

Webster's II, 1994, *New Riverside University Dictionary* (Houghton Mifflin Company, Boston, MA).

West, Kenneth D., 1996, Asymptotic inference about predictive ability, *Econometrica* 64, 1067–1084.

Whaley, Robert E., 1982, Valuation of American call options on dividend-paying stocks: Empirical tests, *Journal of Financial Economics* 10, 29–58.

——,——, 1993, Derivatives on market volatility: Hedging tools long overdue, *Journal of Derivatives* 1, 71–84.

PART II

MARKET MICROSTRUCTURE

3

Insider Trading without Normality

JEAN-CHARLES ROCHET AND JEAN-LUC VILA

I. INTRODUCTION

In his seminal paper, Kyle (1985) shows how a risk-neutral and perfectly-informed insider can profit from his private information by trading strategically and by hiding his trade behind the activity of 'noise traders'. In his model, Kyle makes specific assumptions about the distribution of uncertainty (normality) and restricts himself to a specific class of equilibria, the linear ones.[1] The argument that the linear equilibria are more tractable than the non-linear ones is not convincing. The signalling literature (see Laffont and Maskin (1989, 1990) among others) abounds in examples where multiple equilibria are the rule.[2] In the context of market trading with asymmetric information, it is important to understand whether the uniqueness of an equilibrium comes from the ad hoc linearity assumption, from the distributional assumption or from the nature of the strategic interaction.

The existence of a unique equilibrium enables the economist to answer the following questions: What are the welfare properties of non-competitive rational expectations models? What is the equilibrium amount of information revealed by prices in the presence of non-competitive behaviour?

This paper has evolved from a manuscript which was circulated under the title 'Insider Trading and Market Manipulations: Existence and Uniqueness of Equilibrium'. We are grateful to participants at the 1990 World Congress of the Econometric Society in Barcelona and at the 1990 ESF summer school on Financial markets; to seminar participants at Cambridge University, the University of Toulouse, the University of Lisboa, Cornell University and MIT; to Kerry Back, Patrick Bolton, David Easley, Frank Hahn, Oliver Hart, Jean-Jacques Laffont, Patrick Legros, Kazuhiko Ohashi, Jonathan Paul, David Scharfstein, Paul Seabright, Matt Spiegel, Jean Tirole and Xavier Vives for helpful comments and discussions. We also thank the editor Ian Jewitt and three anonymous referees for their remarks. All errors are our own. Finally, Jean-Luc Vila wishes to acknowledge financial support from the International Financial Services Research Center at the Sloan School of Management.

[1] These assumptions are commonplace in the abundant literature that has built upon Kyle's model: see among many others Admati and Pfleiderer (1988 and 1990), Chowdhry and Nanda (1990), Gorton and Pennachi (1989), Pagano (1989), Pagano and Roell (1990), Roell (1989), Subrahmanyam (1990a, b) and Vives (1990). An interesting exception can be found in Bhattacharya and Spiegel (1989) who consider the possibility of non-linear equilibria with normal distributions. Another important exception, which is more directly related to the present paper, can be found in Back (1991). We shall return to the relationship between Back's work and ours in the conclusion of this paper.

[2] See also Bhattacharya and Spiegel (1989).

J.-C. Rochet and J.-L. Vila

In this paper, we prove the existence of a unique equilibrium in the Kyle (1985) model of insider trading *with the insider observing the amount of noise trading* and in the Kyle (1989) model of informed speculation when there is one risk-neutral insider and many risk-neutral market makers. We show that these two models are equivalent and that: (i) There exists a unique equilibrium independently of the distribution of uncertainty; (ii) This equilibrium minimizes the expected gains of the informed agent under incentive compatibility constraints. The first result justifies the use of the linearity assumption in the case of normal uncertainty. The second result is interpreted as a weak invisible hand property: the decentralized market minimizes the expected cost borne by the noise traders under incentive compatibility constraints. It is the key ingredient for the uniqueness result.

Of course this property does not hold in general, as can be anticipated by the multiplicity of equilibria in similar models (see for instance Laffont and Maskin (1990)). More surprising, as we show by a counter-example, neither (i) nor (ii) above holds in the original Kyle (1985) model.[3] However, we show that these properties are valid for a whole class of signalling games, those games in which the surplus is independent of the uninformed player's action.

The paper is organized as follows: in Section II, we present our central result in a relatively informal manner. Section III is dedicated to the rigorous derivation of the uniqueness result and the invisible hand property. In Section IV, the uniqueness property is shown to hold for a whole class of signalling games. Section V is dedicated to the existence question, while Section VI presents extensions and concluding remarks.

II. AN HEURISTIC PRESENTATION

The rigorous derivation of our results involves a somewhat delicate apparatus. In this section, we shall set aside some difficult technical issues in order to focus on the central intuition. These important technical issues will be dealt with in subsequent sections.

The model is a one-shot trading game inspired by Kyle (1985). A single asset is traded by three types of traders: noise traders, market makers and the informed trader (the insider). The ex-post liquidation value of the asset is denoted by v, the quantity traded by noise traders by u, the quantity traded by the informed trader by x, and the price of the asset by p. In this model, noise traders are passive players. They buy a quantity u which is the realization of an exogenously given random variable $\tilde{u}$. Their motives for trade are not explicitly modelled: one may think of the noise trading as either tax-related trading[4] or liquidity trading.

The game unfolds as follows: In stage one, the values of u and v are realized. The informed trader observes *both* u and v,[5] and submits a market order $x(u, v)$.

---

[3] See Appendix E.   [4] See Constantinides (1983).

[5] The assumption that the insider observes u is the main difference with Kyle (1985). In Appendix A we show how, in the normal case, this assumption affects the equilibrium prices and

In stage two, market makers observe aggregate demand $y(u, v) = x(u, v) + u$ but do not directly observe u, v or x. Having observed aggregate demand, y, they engage in a competitive auction à la Bertrand to supply y. The price resulting from this auction is denoted by $p(y)$. The profits of the informed trader are given by $\pi(x, u, v) = (v - p(x + u))x$. For simplicity, we shall assume that u and v have compact supports. Without loss of generality, we can then normalize u and v so that their supports are included in $[0, 1]$. In what follows we will refer to this game as the *market order game*.

A *market equilibrium* is characterized by a trading strategy and a pricing rule p such that: (i) Given the pricing rule for every (u, v), the trading strategy $x(u, v)$ maximizes the informed trader's profits $\pi(x, u, v)$. (ii) Given the trading strategy, the pricing rule $p(\cdot)$ is semi-strong efficient in the sense that the price p is set equal to the expected value of v conditional upon public information y: $p(y) = E[v \mid y(u, v)]$. This condition is implied by our assumption of Bertrand competition between market makers.

At this stage, it is not clear that such an equilibrium exists and more importantly that it is uniquely defined. Furthermore, we do not know whether an equilibrium pricing rule, if any, is differentiable or even continuous.[6] We shall deal with the questions of existence, uniqueness and regularity later in the paper. For now, we consider a differentiable pricing rule and write the first-order condition for the insider's problem:

$$-p'(y)x + v - p(y) = 0. \tag{2.1}$$

Taking conditional expectations of (2.1) with respect to y yields

$$-p'(y)E(x \mid y) + E(v \mid y) - p(y) = 0.$$

Using the efficient pricing condition $p = E(v \mid y)$, and assuming that $p'(y) \neq 0$ we obtain that, in an equilibrium, the expected insider trading x, conditional upon the public information y, is zero, i.e.

$$E(x \mid y) = 0. \tag{2.2}$$

Condition (2.2) is easy to understand: If the market estimate of insider trading was say positive, then a risk-neutral market maker would want to imitate the insider. He would then buy, which in turn would raise p. Hence condition (2.2) is necessary in equilibrium. We will prove in Proposition 5.2 that condition (2.2) is also sufficient.

Assuming that (u, v) is normally distributed, one can show the existence of a unique equilibrium in the class of linear equilibria. This equilibrium has

---

trading strategies. On the other hand, the assumption that he observes v (complete information) is not crucial: since all agents are assumed risk-neutral it is only needed that the information structures be nested i.e. that the insider knows more than the market makers.

[6] The regularity issue is *not* merely a technical one. In fact, non-continuous pricing rules play an important role in the signalling literature (see Laffont and Maskin (1990)).

interesting comparative static properties as in Kyle (1985). For example, the sensitivity of price of quantity is well-explained by the variances of u, and v, and information is transmitted only partially by prices (see Appendix A).

The relevance of this analysis depends on two questions: What happens when uncertainty is not normally distributed, and do there exist other equilibria? In similar models with asymmetric information, a large multiplicity of (Perfect Bayesian) equilibria is usually the rule. For instance, Laffont and Maskin consider two models (1989, 1990) (the first one in the context of a monopoly producing a good of uncertain quality, the second one in the same context as Kyle's) in which any amount of information transmission is compatible with one of the equilibria.

The central result of the paper, which we present below, establishes that nothing of the sort can happen in our market order game. For any distribution of uncertainty, equilibrium is unique. The key ingredient to this result is a *weak invisible hand property*. To understand its features, imagine for the moment that the price function, instead of being determined by the market, is chosen by a Social Planner. The objective of this Social Planner, who can pre-commit himself to any price function $p(\cdot)$, is to minimize the expected cost borne by uninformed traders (market makers and noise traders) because of the presence of the insider. Since we have a zero-sum game,[7] this is equivalent to minimizing the expected profit of the insider.

We define an *optimal pricing rule* as a pricing rule which minimizes the expected profit of the insider i.e. which solves the problem

$$\min_{p(\cdot)} E[\max_x (v - p(x + u))x]. \qquad (2.3)$$

Given an optimal pricing rule, the reaction of the insider is given by a function $x(u, v)$. We claim that condition (2.2) for the efficient pricing rule also coincides with a necessary and sufficient condition for an optimal pricing rule. The intuition is as follows: consider an optimal pricing rule $p^*(\cdot)$ and a given realization of y. If the Social Planner changes $p^*(y)$ to $p^*(y) + \Delta p$ the change in the insider's expected profits is

$$\Delta p \cdot E[x \mid y].$$

This quantity must be non-negative for any value of Δp, which yields: $E[x \mid y] = 0.$[8] It therefore follows that an equilibrium pricing rule determined by

---

[7] Including the noise traders.

[8] More formally, consider an alternative pricing rule $p^*(\cdot) + \varepsilon h(\cdot)$ and let $F(\varepsilon)$ be the insider profits under this alternative pricing rule:

$$F(\varepsilon) = E\{\max_x [v - p^*(x + u) - \varepsilon h(x + u)]x\}.$$

From the optimality of $p^*(\cdot)$, $F'(0) = 0$. We now use the envelope theorem to compute $F'(\varepsilon)_{\varepsilon=0}$ and we obtain:

$$E[x(u, v)h(y(u, v))] = 0, \quad \forall h(\cdot). \qquad (2.4)$$

From a standard result in probability theory, (2.4) is equivalent to (2.2).

the market coincides with an optimal pricing rule chosen by the central planner and vice versa: This is precisely the *weak invisible hand property* (Propositions 3.2 and 5.2).

From the invisible hand property, we draw three implications. First, since an equilibrium pricing rule must be optimal, all equilibrium pricing rules give the same expected profit to the insider (Proposition 3.2). In addition we will show in Proposition 3.3, that all equilibrium pricing rules generate the same insider strategy $x(u, v)$ and the same equilibrium prices $p(x(u, v) + v)$. In this sense the equilibrium is unique. Second, proving the existence of an optimal pricing rule (an optimization problem) is easier than proving the existence of an equilibrium pricing rule (a fixed point problem).[9] In Section V, we establish the existence of an optimal pricing rule and then use the weak invisible hand property to show that an equilibrium exists. Third and finally, we interpret the weak invisible hand property as a weak welfare property: even in the presence of asymmetric information and a monopsonistic insider, the decentralized market minimizes the expected losses borne by noise traders. However, without a utility-based model of noise trading, the issue of Pareto optimality cannot be addressed so that our welfare property is a weak one.

We next show how our game is related to Kyle's (1989) model of informed speculation. For this purpose, we specify a trading game which we call the *limit order game* and show that any equilibrium of this game corresponds to a market equilibrium in our sense.

The limit order game has the same structure as Kyle (1989): The informed trader (insider) observes v *but not* u and submits a demand schedule $X(p, v)$, which depends on his private information v; similarly uninformed traders (market makers) submit supply schedules $Y_i(p)i \in I$. All demands are centralized (together with noise trading u) and price is set by a Walrasian auctioneer to equalize total supply and total demand.

The differences with Kyle (1989) are that we assume (i) a continuum of risk-neutral market makers and (ii) a unique risk-neutral informed trader. The equilibrium price is thus given by the market clearing rule

$$\int Y_i(p)\, di = X(p, v) + u.^{10}$$

Since no market maker has market power, in the limit order game equilibrium prices are semi-strong efficient ($p(y) = E[v \mid y]$). Furthermore, in an equilibrium of the limit order game the equilibrium price will be a function $p(u, v)$ of (u, v). Hence if the insider observes u and submits *market orders* $x'(u, v) = X(p(u, v), v)$ he will get the same profits as with limit orders. Reciprocally, any noise trading

---

[9] A similar property (namely that a competitive market works like a team which maximizes his total expected surplus) has been obtained in different contexts by Radner (1962) and more recently by Vives (1998).   [10] See Section III for a more precise definition of the market clearing rule.

dependent market order $x'(u, v)$ can be replicated by a limit order $X(p, v) = x'(p^{-1}(p, v), v)$ where $p^{-1}(p, v)$ is the amount of noise trading u[11] which give rise to price p, i.e. $p(u, v) = p$. Therefore limit orders $X(p, v)$ are equivalent to market orders $x(u, v)$.

In other words, we have shown that *when we specify Kyle's (1989) model of informed speculation with a unique insider and a large number of uninformed traders, we obtain Kyle's (1985) model of insider trading where the insider observes the amount of noise trading.* In our terminology, it means that the market order game and the limit order game are equivalent. However, the latter is technically more difficult to define and analyse. Indeed, in the limit order game, the market clearing price must be defined for *every* possible strategy $Y_i(p)$ and $X(p, v)$ which is somewhat cumbersome. Hence for pedagogical reasons, we have decided to present our results in the context of the market order game as opposed to the limit order game.

In the next two sections, we present the rigorous derivation of the invisible hand property and show that this property can be extended to a whole class of signalling games.

III. UNIQUENESS OF EQUILIBRIUM AND THE INVISIBLE HAND PROPERTY

In this section, we reconsider the market order game of Section II: u is the noise trading, v the asset's liquidation value, x, the insider's trade, $y = x + u$ the aggregate demand and p the price. Formally, we define our equilibrium as follows:

Definition 3.1. A market equilibrium is defined as a pair $(P(\cdot), Z(\cdot, \cdot))$ such that:

(i) $P(\cdot)$ is a upper hemicontinuous convex-valued correspondence from R to R
(ii) $Z(\cdot, \cdot) = (y(\cdot, \cdot), p(\cdot, \cdot))$ is a measurable function from $[0, 1] \times [0, 1]$ to R^2.
(iii) For almost every $(u, v), Z(u, v) \in \text{ArgMax}_{(y,p); p \in P(y)} (v - p)(y - u)$ (3.1)
(iv) For almost every $(u, v), p(u, v) = E[v \mid Z(u, v)]$.   (3.2)

Technical comments on the definitions: (a) For technical reasons (see Section V), we have allowed the pricing rule to be multivalued for some values of y, with the convention that the insider can choose whatever price maximizes his profits in the set $P(y)$ of market prices at y. If the correspondence $P(\cdot)$ is a function then our equilibrium concept is standard. As it turns out, any equilibrium price correspondence $P(\cdot)$ is single valued at $y(u, v)$ with probability 1 (see Proposition 3.1 below) and thus condition (iv) is equivalent to Kyle's condition:

$$P(y) = E[v \mid y(u, v) = y].$$

(b) The reader will notice the notational difference between the pricing rule $P(y)$ and the resulting price $p(u, v)$.

---

[11] We will show in Section III that such a u is uniquely defined.

(c) The reader will also note that for convenience, we have expressed the strategy of the insider in the terms of the aggregate demand y as opposed to the insider trade x.

(d) In (iii) and (iv), as well as in the remainder of the paper, 'almost every' refers to Lebesgue's measure.

As opposed to Kyle, we do not assume any specific distribution of (u, v). For instance, we do not rule out the possibility that (u, v) be correlated. The compact support assumption is essentially technical and can be relaxed.

As we shall see later in Section IV, *existence* of such a (pure-strategy) equilibrium is not guaranteed in general, except with a continuous distribution of uncertainty. Thus we assume:

Assumption 1. *The distribution of (u, v) has a continuous density w.r.t. Lebesgue measure.*

One of the simplifications introduced by Assumption 1 stems from the following lemma:

Lemma 3.1. *For any price correspondence $P(\cdot)$ the set of (u, v) such that the insider's problem (3.1) has several maxima, is Lebesgue negligible.*

Proof. See Appendix B. □

Another important consequence of Assumption 1 is the fact that we can restrict our attention to price correspondences which are (1) non-decreasing and (2) almost surely single-valued, continuous and differentiable at $y(u, v)$. The latter property enables us to write the first-order condition for (3.1).

Definition 3.2. A market equilibrium (P, Z) is supported by a price correspondence P_1 if and only if for almost every (u, v),

$$Z(u, v) \in \text{ArgMax}_{p_1 \in P_1(y)} (v - P_1)(y - u).$$

The next proposition shows that any equilibrium can be supported by a 'well-behaved' price correspondence:

Proposition 3.1. *Under Assumption 1, every market equilibrium (P, Z) can be supported by a non-decreasing correspondence P_1[12] such that:*

(i) *For a.e. (u, v), P_1 is single-valued, continuous and differentiable[13] at $y(u, v)$ and $P_1(y(u, v)) > 0$.*

(ii) *$P_1(y) = 0$ for $y \leq 0$, $P_1(y) = 1$ for $y \geq 1$.*

---

[12] P_1 non-decreasing means that $y_1 < y_2, p_1 \in P(y_1)$ and $p_2 \in P(y_2) \Rightarrow p_1 \leq p_1$.

[13] i.e. all selections are continuous and differentiable.

Proof. See Appendix B.   □

Proposition 3.1 yields the following simplifications:

(a) Since P_1 is a non-decreasing correspondence which is single-valued at $y(u, v)$, we shall, when convenient,[14] think of $P(\cdot)$ as a *function* as opposed to a *correspondence*. However, in Section V, we shall prove the existence of an equilibrium pricing correspondence. Our proof uses the local compactness of the space of closed graph correspondences endowed with the Hausdorf topology (See Section V).
(b) Since $P(\cdot)$ is differentiable at $y(u, v)$, we can write the first-order condition for the insider's maximization problem (3.1).
(c) From (ii) above and for further reference, we will take $P(y) = 0$ for $y \le 0$ and $P(y) = 1$ for $y \ge 1$.

Let C be the set of compact graph correspondences from $[0, 1]$ to R endowed with the Hausdorf topology. We define the functional $W(\cdot)$ by:

$$\forall P \in C, \quad W(P) = E\left[\mathrm{Max}_{p \in P(y)}(v - p)(y - u)\right].$$

Definition 3.3. An optimal pricing rule is any element of C that minimizes W:

$$\forall P \in C, \quad W(\bar{P}) \le W(P).$$

The next lemma shows that an optimal pricing rule can be taken to be non-decreasing.

Lemma 3.2. *For any optimal pricing rule $P(\cdot)$, there exists a non-decreasing correspondence $P_1(\cdot)$ such that:*

(i) $W(P) = W(P_1)$
(ii) $\mathrm{ArgMax}_{p \in P(y)}\, (v - p)(y - u) \cap \mathrm{ArgMax}_{p \in P_1(y)}\, (v - p)(y - u) \ne \varnothing,$ *almost surely.*

Proof. See Appendix B.   □

The next proposition shows that an equilibrium pricing rule is an optimal pricing rule.

Proposition 3.2. *Under Assumption 1, let (P, Z) be a market equilibrium. Then P is an optimal pricing rule. As a consequence, all market equilibria give the same expected profit to the insider.*

Proof. See Appendix B.   □

---

[14] That is for any economic application.

We now prove a stronger uniqueness result, namely that equilibrium prices and quantities are uniquely determined.

Proposition 3.3. *Under Assumption* 1, *let* (P_1, Z_1) *and* (P_2, Z_2) *be two market equilibria. Then for almost every* (u, v), $Z_1(u, v) = Z_2(u, v)$.

Proof. See Appendix B. □

The market order game trading model thus possesses something specific that prevents the inconvenient multiplicity of Bayesian equilibria that is usual in similar contexts, as for instance in Laffont-Maskin (1989, 1990). In order to understand this specificity, we will study the uniqueness question in a more general set up, namely that of signalling games à la Cho-Kreps (1987). This is the objective of the next section.

For the moment, we devote that last part of this section to the equivalence between the market order game and the limit order game. This will clarify the exact relations between our model and those of Kyle (1985, 1989). For that purpose we specify a trading game and show that all the equilibria of this game give rise to a market equilibrium in our sense (Definition 3.1).

The rules of the limit order game are as follows: The informed trader (insider) submits a demand schedule $X(p, v)$ which depends on his private information v; similarly uninformed traders (market makers) submit supply schedules $Y_i(p) i \in I$. All demands are centralized (together with noise trading u) and price is set to equalize total supply and total demand.

The differences with Kyle (1989) are that we assume (i) a continuum of market makers[15] and (ii) a unique informed trader. Total supply is thus given by

$$Y(p) = \int Y_1(p) \, di. \tag{3.3}$$

As in Kyle (1989), supply and demand schedules can be multivalued: we allow for upper hemicontinuous convex-valued correspondences. Market clearing rules are defined as follows: as in Kyle (1989), $p(u, v, X, Y)$ is the smallest price compatible with the equilibrium condition

$$Y(p) \cap \{u + X(p, y)\} = \oslash. \tag{3.4}$$

The total supply $y(u, v, X, Y)$ is the smallest quantity that belongs to that intersection.

We can now express the traders expected profits as functions of their strategies $X, (Y_i)_{i \in I}$:

$$\pi(X, Y) = E[(v - p(u, v, X, Y))(y(u, v, X, Y) - u)] \tag{3.5}$$

---

[15] For example, $I = [0, 1]$ endowed with Lebesgue's measure.

for the insider, and for market maker i:

$$\pi(X, Y) = E[(p(u, v, X, Y) - v)Y_i(p(u, v, X, Y))]. \tag{3.6}$$

Next we show that any Nash Equilibrium of this trading game corresponds indeed to a Market Equilibrium in our sense (Definition 3.1).

Proposition 3.4. *Every Nash Equilibrium of the limit order game is a Market Equilibrium.*

Proof. Let thus $(X^*, (Y_i^*)_{i \in I})$ be a Nash Equilibrium of the game defined by (3.5), (3.6). Since each uninformed trader has a negligible market power we easily obtain market efficiency: For any measurable function $y_i(\cdot)$:

$$\pi_i(X, Y) \leq E[(p(u, v, X^*, Y^*) - v)y_i(p(u, v, X^*, Y^*))].$$

This is also true for $\lambda y_i(\cdot)$ for arbitrary λ. Thus we obtain that both sides of this inequality are zero, which clearly implies (3.2).

Condition (3.1) is more difficult to obtain: the first argument is that $Y^*(\cdot)$ is necessarily strictly increasing[16] (and thus its inverse is a function). We prove this by contradiction: suppose that there exist $p_1 < p_2$ and $y_1 \geq y_2$ such that $y_1 \in Y^*(p_1)$ and $y_2 \in Y^*(p_2)$. Since (y_1, p_1) corresponds to a (weakly) larger quantity at a lower price, it can only be obtained when the insider is buying. Similarly, (y_2, p_2) can only be obtained when he is selling. But this implies:

$$E[v \mid (y_1, p_1)] < p_1 \text{ and } E[v \mid (y_2, p_2)] > p_2$$

which contradicts (3.2).

Let us define now $Z_0(u, v) = (y_0(u, v), p_0(u, v))$ as the solution of:

$$\text{Max}_{(y,p); y \in Y^*(p)} (v - p)(y - u). \tag{3.7}$$

We have to prove that Z_0 equals $Z(\cdot, \cdot, X^*, Y^*)$ almost everywhere, and (3.1) will be established. We first prove that p_0 is non-decreasing in u. Indeed (3.7) implies the classical incentive compatibility constraints.

$$(v - p_1)(y_1 - u_1) \geq (v - p_2)(y_2 - u_1)$$
$$(v - p_2)(y_2 - u_2) \geq (v - p_1)(y_1 - u_2)$$

where $p_i = p_0(u_i, v)$ and $y_i = Y^*(p_i) i = 1, 2$. Adding up the above conditions, we obtain after simplifications:

$$(p_1 - p_2)(u_1 - u_2) \geq 0.$$

---

[16] A correspondence $Y(p)$ is strictly increasing if, for every $p_1 < p_2$ and $y_1 \in Y(p_1), y_2 \in Y(p_2)$, one has $y_1 < y_2$.

Let P_0 be the smallest closed-graph correspondence having p_0 as a selection and

$$X(p, u) = \{Y^*(p) - u, \text{ for } u \text{ such that } p \in P_0(u, v)\}$$

with the conventions that

$$X(p, v) = 1 \quad \text{if } p < p_0(0, v)$$
$$X(p, v) = 0 \quad \text{if } p > p_0(1, v)$$

It is immediate that X is an upper hemicontinuous correspondence with convex values. Moreover by submitting X, the insider obtains $Z_0(u, v)$, which is the best he can get given the supply function $Y^*(\cdot)$. Thus $Z = Z_0$ almost everywhere and we are done. In other words, we have proved that the insider can do as well with limit orders as with market orders conditional on noise trading. $\qquad\square$

IV. THE UNIQUENESS PROPERTY FOR A PARTICULAR CLASS OF SIGNALLING GAMES

In this section, we consider signalling games à la Cho-Kreps (1987), i.e. two-player games with the following structure: pay-offs depend on a random variable ω (the state of nature) that is observed only by the first player (the informer player). This informed player sends a signal s to the second player, who then reacts by choosing some action r. The only difference with the formulation of Cho-Kreps is that the sets Σ (possible signals) and Γ (possible reactions) are not finite, but are instead compact convex subsets of a linear space E. This will allow us to focus on pure-strategy equilibria. The parameter ω takes its value in a set Ω, in accord with a probability measure η that is common knowledge. Finally, the pay-off functions are denoted $U(\omega, s, r)$ for the informed player and $V(\omega, s, r)$ for the other player. We shall assume that these pay-off functions are continuous w.r.t. (s, r) and η-measurable w.r.t. ω.

A strategy for the informed player is a η-measurable mapping $S(\cdot)$ from Ω to Σ. The set of such strategies will be denoted $\mathcal{S}$, it is a convex subset of $L^*(\Omega, E)$ the linear space of bounded η-measurable mapping from Ω to E.

Similarly a strategy for the uninformed player is a Borel-measurable mapping R from Σ to Γ. The set $\mathcal{R}$ of such strategies is a convex subset of $B(\Sigma, E)$, the linear space of Borel-measurable mappings from Σ to E.

The expected pay-offs that are associated to a couple of strategies (S, R) are given by:

$$\bar{U}(S, R) = \int U(\omega, S(\omega), R(S(\omega))) \, d\eta(\omega);$$

$$\bar{V}(S, R) = \int V(\omega, S(\omega), R(S(\omega))) \, d\eta(\omega).$$

Definition 4.1. A Bayesian Nash Equilibrium is composed of a pair of strategies (S^*, R^*) and a family $\eta(\cdot \mid s)$ of probability measures on Ω, indexed by $s \in \Sigma$ such that:

(i)   For almost every ω in Σ, $S^*(\omega) \in \text{ArgMax}_s \, U(\omega, s, R^*(s))$;
(ii) For all s in Σ, $R^*(s) \in \text{ArgMax}_r \int V(\omega, s, r) d\eta(\omega \mid S^*(\omega) = s)$;
(iii) For all s in the support of $S^*(\omega)$, $\eta(\cdot \mid s)$ deduced from η by application of Bayes's rule.

In particular, for all such equilibria, we have:

$$\text{For all } S \in \mathcal{S}, \quad \bar{U}(S, R^*) \le \bar{U}(S^*, R^*); \tag{4.1}$$

$$\text{For all } R \in \mathcal{R}, \quad \bar{V}(S^*, R) \le \bar{V}(S^*, R^*). \tag{4.2}$$

Thus for any Bayesian Nash Equilibrium $(S^*, R^*, \eta(\cdot \mid \cdot))$, (S^*, R^*) is a Nash Equilibrium of the game $(\bar{U}, \bar{V})$ but the converse is not true in general.

It is well known that signalling games typically admit a large multiplicity of Bayesian equilibria.[17] However, we shall restrict our attention to a particular class of such games, in which the total payoff is independent of the uninformed player's action:

Assumption 2. $U(\omega, s, r) + V(\omega, s, r) = \phi(\omega, s)$.[18]

The main result of this section is that all Bayesian equilibria of such games give the same expected payoff to the informed agent. Before we state and prove this result, we need two definitions:

Definition 4.2. Let $(\bar{S}, \bar{R})$ be a pair of strategies. We say that $\bar{S}$ is a best response to $\bar{R}$ if and only if: $\forall S \in \mathcal{S}, \bar{U}(S, \bar{R}) \le \bar{U}(\bar{S}, \bar{R})$.

Definition 4.3. Let $\bar{R}$ be a strategy of the uninformed agent. We say that $\bar{R}$ is an optimal reaction function if and only if: $\forall R \in \mathcal{R}, \, W(\bar{R}) \le W(R)$ where $W(R) = \text{Max}_S \bar{U}(S, R)$.

Next, we prove that a Bayesian equilibrium involves an optimal reaction function.

Proposition 4.1. *Under Assumption 2, for any Bayesian equilibrium* (S^*, R^*):

(i) R^* *is an optimal reaction function and*
(ii) S^* *is a best response to* R^*.

As a consequence, all Bayesian equilibria give the same expected payoff to the informed player.

---

[17] See, for instance, Laffont and Maskin (1989).
[18] Assumption 2 generalizes the concept of zero-sum game; the invisible hand property generalizes the min–max property.

Proof. See Appendix C. □

Under an additional assumption, one can prove that all Bayesian equilibria also give the same payoff to the uninformed player.

Assumption 3. V is concave with respect to r.

Proposition 4.2. *Under Assumptions 2 and 3, let* (S_1, R_1) *and* (S_2, R_2) *be two Bayesian equilibria. Then* $S_1 = S_2$ *almost everywhere and* $\bar{V}(S_1, R_1) = \bar{V}(S_2, R_2)$.

Proof See Appendix C. □

So far, we have not considered the problem of existence of a Nash Equilibrium of the game $(\bar{U}, \bar{V})$ (a slightly more general concept than that of Bayesian equilibrium). Under additional regularity assumptions, this problem is solved by establishing the converse to Proposition 4.1.

Assumption 4. V is differentiable w.r.t. r, $\partial V / \partial r(\omega, s, r)$ is continuous with respect to (s, r) and measurable with respect to ω.

Proposition 4.3. *Under Assumptions 2, 3, 4, let* $\bar{R}$ *be an optimal reaction function and* $\bar{S}$ *be a best response to* $\bar{R}$. *Consider the following subset of* Ω:

$$\Omega_0 = \{\omega : s \rightarrow (\omega, s, \bar{R}(s)) \text{ has at least two maxima}\}$$

Then, if $\eta(\Omega_0) = 0$, $(\bar{S}, \bar{R})$ *is a Nash equilibrium of the game* $(\bar{U}, \bar{V})$.

Proof. See Appendix C. □

Remark. When $\eta(\Omega_0) = 0$, then in general pure-strategy equilibria fail to exist. However there exists a (unique) mixed-strategy equilibrium as in the example that we study in Rochet and Vila (1992).

We are now in a position to clarify the key difference between the market order game and other models (like the Laffont–Maskin models) that do not possess the uniqueness property. For that purpose, we will construct artificial signalling games that possess the same Bayesian Equilibria as the models under study.

Example 1. *The market order game.* Surprisingly, it turns out that the strategy of the insider (the informed player) has to be a price (and not a quantity). This is related to the fact that the second player is supposed to represent the aggregate behaviour of competitive market makers. Using the notation introduced above, we must set:

$$\omega = (u, v) \qquad \text{information of the first player}$$
$$s = P(u, v) \qquad \text{strategy of the first player (price)}$$
$$r = Y(p) \qquad \text{strategy of the second player (quantity)}$$
$$U(\omega, s, r) = (v - s)(r - u) \qquad \text{utility of the first player}$$
$$V(\omega, s, r) = (s - v)r \qquad \text{utility of the second player.}$$

If (P, Y) is a perfect Bayesian Equilibrium of this game, then one must have:

$$\forall p, \quad Y(p) \in \text{ArgMax}_y (E[v \,|\, p] - p)y,$$

and

$$\forall \omega, \quad P(\omega) \in \text{ArgMax}_p (v - p)(Y(p) - u).$$

The first condition implies semi-strong efficiency: $E[v \,|\, p] = p$. Likewise, if we define $P_1 = Y^{-1}$, and $Z(p) = (Y(p), p)$, the second condition can also be stated as:

$$\forall (u, v), \quad Z(u, v) \in \text{ArgMax}_{(y, p),\, p \in P_1(y)} (v - p)(y - u)$$

so that (P_1, Z) is a market equilibrium. The uniqueness property comes from Assumption 2:

$$U(\omega, x, r) + V(\omega, s, r) = u(s - v) = \phi(\omega, s).$$

Example 2. *The Laffont–Maskin monopoly model* (1990). In this model the informed player is a monopolist and ω is a quality parameter unknown to the buyer (the second player). The signal sent by the monopolist is a price and the response of the second player is a quantity. Thus we have to set:

$$s = P(\omega) \quad \text{and} \quad r = Q(p),$$
$$U(\omega, s, r) = (s - v(\omega))r,$$
$$V(\omega, s, r) = (\omega - s)r$$

where $v(\omega)$ and ω denote respectively marginal cost and marginal utility of the good. The multiplicity of Perfect Bayesian Equilibria comes from the fact that Assumption 2 is not satisfied:

$$U(\omega, s, r) + V(\omega, s, r) = (\omega - v(\omega))r$$

which is independent of s, but not of r!

Example 3. *The Laffont–Maskin insider trading model* (1989). The model presents close similarities to the market order game: the informed player is an insider who possesses some (imperfect) information on the liquidation value of some risky asset. The two main differences with the market order game are: (a) There is no uncertainty on aggregate demand (there are no noise traders) and (b) market makers are risk averse. Because of (a), the case where market makers are risk neutral is not interesting: the unique equilibrium is completely revealing, and there is no trade. But then, when market makers are risk averse, Assumption 2 ceases to be true for the corresponding signalling games and there may exist many equilibria (Laffont–Maskin (1989)). Again, because of (a) this result does not apply to the market order game model with risk aversion, and we do not know if the uniqueness property is preserved when market makers are risk averse. However, one can show that equilibrium is unique in the Laffont–Maskin model when risk aversion is small.

V. EXISTENCE OF EQUILIBRIUM IN THE MARKET ORDER GAME

As far as we know, no general existence result is available for a market equilibrium in the market order game. It turns out that our invisible hand model gives the key ingredient in that direction. We begin by proving the existence of an optimal pricing rule.

Proposition 5.1. *Under Assumption 1, there exists an optimal price correspondence.*

Proof. The proof is immediate by continuity of $W(\cdot)$ and compactness of C when C is endowed with the Hausdorff topology.   □

We now establish the converse to Proposition 3.2.

Proposition 5.2. *Under Assumption 1, let $\bar{P}$ be an optimal pricing rule (in the sense of Definition 3.3) and $\bar{Y}$ be a best response to $\bar{P}$. For almost every (u, v), $\bar{P}$ is differentiable at $\bar{Y}(u, v)$ and $(\bar{P}, \bar{Z})$ is a market equilibrium where $\bar{Z}$ is defined by: $\bar{Z}(u, v) = (\bar{Y}, \bar{P}(\bar{Y}(u, v)))$.*

Proof. See Appendix D.   □

Therefore, *existence* of the equilibrium is also a consequence of the weak invisible-hand property. The proof is easy, since we only have to use continuity and compactness arguments instead of a fixed point theorem. A similar technique, in a different context, is known as Negishi's method for proving existence (and uniqueness) of Arrow–Debreu equilibrium in the presence of gross substitutability. It has been extended to infinite-dimensional spaces, with applications to continuous-time finance (see for instance Mas-Colell (1986)).

VI. CONCLUSIONS

The main result of this paper is that the equilibrium is always unique in the version of the Kyle (1985) model of insider trading where the insider observes the amount of noise trading. This uniqueness result holds for any distribution of noise and asset returns. In addition since, as we show in this paper, there is an equivalence between the aforementioned model and Kyle's (1989) game with a unique insider and a large number of uninformed traders, equilibrium is unique in this game as well. This contrasts markedly with similar models of asymmetric information (like Laffont–Maskin (1989, 1990)), which admit a large multiplicity of perfect Bayesian Equilibria. The key ingredient to our uniqueness result is a weak invisible hand property: The equilibrium price function is the one that minimizes expected profits of the insider under incentive-compatibility constraints.

We also establish this uniqueness result for a particular class of signalling games, in which, once the informed player has played, the interests of the two players are completely opposed.

The invisible hand property also allows us to prove existence of a pure-strategy equilibrium in the case of continuous uncertainty. In the case of a discrete distribution, there is a one-to-one relation between optimal pricing rules and mixed-strategy equilibria. As a consequence, there exists a unique mixed-strategy equilibrium.[19]

Finally, our uniqueness result can also be shown to hold in the context of market manipulations, where the value of the asset is endogenous as in Kyle (1984), Kyle and Vila (1991), Vila (1987, 1988 and 1989).[20]

By contrast, the uniqueness result cannot be extended to the original Kyle model where the insider does not observe the amount of noise trading (see Appendix E).

Several extensions of these results can be thought of: for instance, it is reasonable to conjecture that the uniqueness result passes to the dynamic version of the Kyle model. Indeed if trading occurs continuously and if the price process has continuous sample paths then the insider knows at which price he is trading and therefore the information sets of market makers and the insider become nested. Recent work by Back (1991) shows that if noise trading u_t follows a Brownian process, then there exists a unique equilibrium within a general class of pricing rules for any distribution of v. Back's result differs from ours in the sense that: (i) it applies to the continuous-time version of Kyle (1985); (ii) the distribution of noise trading is not arbitrary (it must be a Brownian motion); (iii) the techniques that are used are quite different. However, the key condition in Back's paper is that the aggregate cumulative trade $y_t = x_t + u_t$ be a martingale from the point of view of market makers, i.e.

$$E(y_t \mid y_s; s < t) = y_s. \tag{6.1}$$

---

[19] However a pure-strategy equilibrium may fail to exist (see Rochet and Vila (1992) for an example).   [20] See Rochet and Vila (1992).

Given that future values of noise trading flows are unpredictable, condition (6.1) means that future trades of the insider are unpredictable which is analogous to our condition (2.2). It is therefore reasonable to conjecture that Back's uniqueness result (and ours) will hold in *continuous time* for *any* noise trading process.

By contrast, it is not clear to us whether it would also pass in the case of risk aversion, since our invisible hand property does not hold anymore. Similarly, we do not know what happens when there are several insiders, as in Kyle (1989).

Appendix A

Comparison between Kyle (1985) and the Market Order Game:

In this appendix, we assume that u and v are independent normal random variables with mean 0 and standard deviation σ_v and σ_u, respectively. We compare the linear equilibrium of (i) Kyle's (1985) model (where the insider does not observe the amount of noise trading) and (ii) our market order game (where the insider does observe the amount of noise trading).

The derivation of the results below is standard and left to the reader (see Kyle (1985) for more details). When the insider observes the amount of noise trading, he trades less aggressively in response to a good signal and his trading offsets 50% of the noise trading. As a result the aggregate demand and the market liquidity $(dp/dy)^{-1}$ fall by 50%. Finally, prices and profits are unchanged.

	Kyle (1985)	The market order game
Insider's strategy	$x(v) = \dfrac{\sigma_u}{\sigma_u} v$	$x(u, v) = -u/2 + \dfrac{\sigma_u}{2\sigma_u} v$
Aggregate demand	$y = u + \dfrac{\sigma_u}{\sigma_v} v$	$y = u/2 + \dfrac{\sigma_u}{2\sigma_v} v$
Pricing function	$p(y) = \dfrac{\sigma}{2\sigma_u} y$	$p(y) = \dfrac{\sigma}{\sigma_u} y$
Prices	$p(u, v) = \dfrac{\sigma}{2\sigma_u} u + v/2$	$p(u, v) = \dfrac{\sigma}{2\sigma_u} u + v/2$
Informativeness of prices	Var $(v\|p) = \sigma_u^2/2$	Var $(v\|p) = \sigma_u^2/2$
Insider's expected profits	$E[(v - p)x] = \sigma_u\sigma_v/2$	$E[(v - p)x] = \sigma_u\sigma_v/2$

Appendix B

Proof of Lemma 3.1. Let $P(\cdot)$ be any price correspondence and $\pi(P, u, v)$ denote the maximum in (3.1), i.e.

$$\pi(P, u, v) = \max_{(y,p);p\in P(y)} (v - p)(y - u).$$

If we add uv to both sides of this equality, the expression to be maximized becomes linear with respect to (u, v), which implies that $G(P, u, v) = \pi(P, u, v) + uv$ is a convex function of (u, v). Moreover, if the maximum is attained at $(y(u, v), p(u, v))$ then by the envelope theorem, we have

$$\text{For almost every } (u, v), \quad \begin{pmatrix} p(u, v) \\ y(u, v) \end{pmatrix} \in \partial G$$

where ∂G denotes the sub-differential[21] of the convex function G. A convex function on a finite-dimensional space being differentiable except on a Lebesgue-negligible set, we obtain our uniqueness result. More precisely:

$$\text{For almost every } (u, v), \quad p(u, v) = \frac{\partial G}{\partial u}(P, u, v); \quad y(u, v) = \frac{\partial G}{\partial v}(P, u, v).$$

$\square$

Proof of Proposition 3.1. The proof builds upon the following steps:

Step 1. For every pricing correspondence $P(\cdot)$, the insider's profits $\pi(P, u, v)$ are positive for almost every (u, v). Indeed, for $\pi(P, u, v)$ to be zero it must be that:

$$p > v \quad \text{for all } y > u \text{ and } p \in P(y)$$

and

$$p < v \quad \text{for all } y < u \text{ and } p \in P(y).$$

which occurs only for (u, v) in a set of measure zero.

Step 2. The price is almost surely non-fully revealing. Indeed, if there is a unique (u, v) such that $p(u, v) = p$, then condition (3.2) implies $p = v$ and thus $\pi(P, u, v) = 0$ which happens only with probability zero (step 1). Consequently, $p(u, v) \neq v$ for almost every (u, v).

Step 3. Almost every buyer pools with at least one seller and vice versa. For almost every (u, v), there exists (u', v') such that:

$$Z(u, v) = Z(u', v') \quad \text{and} \quad (y(u, v) - u)(y(u', v') - u') < 0.$$

Indeed since $p(u, v) \neq v$ and $p(u, v) = E(v \mid Z(u, v))$ it follows that the signal $Z(u, v)$ is sent by both buyers and sellers.

Step 4. For almost every (u, v), $P(\cdot)$ is differentiable at $y(u, v)$.

Using the previous step, we take $u < y(u, v) = y(u', v') < u'; p(u, v) = p(u', v')$. Both (u, v) and (u', v') send the same signal (y, p). It follows that the graph of $P(\cdot)$ must separate the sets:

$$A = \{(y, p) : y > u \text{ and } (y - u)(v - p) > (y(u, v) - u)(v - p(u, v))\}$$

---

[21] See for instance Aubin (1979) p. 105.

and

$$B = \{(y, p) : y < u' \text{ and } (u' - y)(p - v') > (u' - y(u', v'))(p(u', v') - v')\}.$$

Hence, $P(\cdot)$ must be single-valued, continuous and differentiable[22] at $y(u, v)$. Furthermore $P(\cdot)$ satisfies the following monotonicity property:

For all $y > y(u, v)$ and $p \in P(y)$, $p > p(u, v)$ and for all $y < y(u, v)$ and $p \in P(y)$, $p < p(u, v)$.

*Step 5. $P(\cdot)$ can be taken to be non-decreasing. For this purpose, let

$$f_p(y) = \max_{p \in P(z); z \leq y} p.$$

The function $f_p(\cdot)$ is non-decreasing and left continuous. Let $P_1(\cdot)$ be the convex closure of $f_p(\cdot)$ i.e.

$$P_1(y) = [f_p(y); \inf_{z \leq y} f_p(z)].$$

It follows from the monotonicity property above that $P_1(\cdot)$ supports the equilibrium (P, Z) (details are left to the reader).

*Step 6. From the differentiability of $P(\cdot)$ and the first order condition in (3.1), it follows that:

$$v - P(y(u, v)) - (y - u)P'(y(u, v)) = 0.$$

We know that $v \neq P(y(u, v))$ almost surely (step 2). Hence: $P'(y(u, v)) \neq 0$ almost surely and since $P(\cdot)$ is non-decreasing $P'(y(u, v)) > 0$.

*Step 7. The proof of 3.1(ii) is immediate and left to the reader. □

Proof of Lemma 3.2. An optimal pricing rule can be taken to be non-decreasing. Indeed, let $P(\cdot)$ be an optimal pricing rule and $P_1(\cdot)$ defined as in the proof of Proposition 3.1, Step 5.

Let:

$$(p_1(u, v), y_1(u, v)) \text{ belongs to } \text{ArgMax}_{p_1 \in P_1(y')}(v - p_1)(y_1 - u)$$

and

$$(p(u, v), y(u, v)) \text{ belongs to } \text{ArgMax}_{p \in P_y}(v - p)(y - u).$$

$P_1(y)$ is by construction greater than $P(y)$ for every y. Therefore, buyers make smaller profits with $P_1(\cdot)$ than with $P(\cdot)$. Formally, if $y_1(u, v) \geq u$ then $(v - p_1(u, v))(y_1(u, v) - u) \leq (v - p)(y_1(u, v) - u)$ for some p in $P(y_1(u, v))$. Thus, $\pi(P, u, v) \geq \pi(P_1, u, v)$ (see the proof of Lemma 3.1 for a definition of π).

Now, suppose that $y_1(u, v) < u$. By construction, there exists $z \leq y_1(u, v)$ and $p \in P(z)$ such that $p \geq p_1(u, v)$. Therefore,

$$\pi(P_1, u, v) = (p_1(u, v) - v)(u - y_1(u, v)) \leq (p - v)(u - z) \leq \pi(P, u, v).$$

Hence, $W(P) \geq W(P_1)$ so that $P_1(\cdot)$ is also an optimal pricing rule.

[22] In the sense that every selection is differentiable.

Furthermore, since $P(\cdot)$ is optimal, it must be that $\pi(P, u, v) = \pi(P_1, u, v)$ almost surely, which implies that the inequalities above must be equalities. Lemma 3.2 follows. □

Proof of Proposition 3.2. Let (P, Z) be a market equilibrium. By Proposition 3.1 this equilibrium can be supported by a non-decreasing P_1 such that, for almost every (u, v), P_1 is differentiable at $y(u, v)$ and $P_1(y(u, v)) > 0$. Thus we can write the first-order condition corresponding to condition (3.1):

For almost every (u, v), $\quad v - p_1(y(u, v)) - P'_1(y(u, v))(y(u, v) - u) = 0.$

By taking expectations conditional upon $y(u, v)$, and using the fact that $P'_1(y(u, v))$ is positive, it follows that the market efficiency condition (3.2) is equivalent to:

$$E[u \mid y(u, v)] = y(u, v) \tag{A.1}$$

We have to prove that P (or P_1) is a minimum of W: Let H be any bounded measurable function from $[0, 1]$ to R. Condition (3.1) above implies:

$$E[H(y(u, v))(y(u, v) - u)] = 0.$$

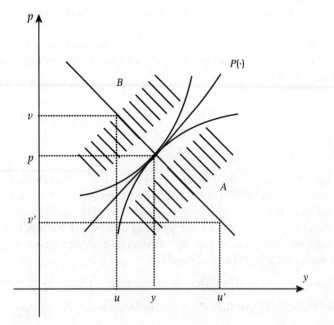

Figure 1

Thus:

$$W(P) = E[\{v - (P + H)(y(u, v))\}\{y(u, v) - u\}]$$
$$\leq \text{Max}_{0 \leq r \leq 1} E[\{v - (P + H)(y)\}\{y - u\}] = W(P + H).$$

Finally, for all bounded $H : W(P) \leq W(P + H)$. Hence P minimizes W in the space of bounded functions. By Lemma 3.1 it follows that P minimizes W in the space of compact graph correspondences. □

Proof of Proposition 3.3. By Proposition 3.1, we can assume without loss of generality that P_1 and P_2 are non-decreasing *functions*. Proposition 3.2 then implies:

$$W(P_1) = W(P_2) = \text{Min}_{P \in C} W(P).$$

W being convex, this implies in turn:

$$W(P_1) = W(P_2) = W(\tfrac{1}{2} P_1 + \tfrac{1}{2} P_2). \tag{A.2}$$

For any measurable $Y : [0, 1] \times [0, 1] \to R$ let us define

$$B(P, Y) = E[(v - P(Y(u, v))(Y(u, v)) - u)].$$

We have by definition:

$$W(P) = \text{Max}_Y B(P, Y)$$

and by linearity of B with respect to P

$$B\left(\frac{P_1 + P_2}{2}\right) = \tfrac{1}{2} B(P_1, Y) + \tfrac{1}{2} B(P_2, Y).$$

But then condition (A.2) implies:

$$\text{Max}_Y [\tfrac{1}{2} B(P_1, Y) + \tfrac{1}{2} B(P_2, Y)] = \tfrac{1}{2} \text{Max}_Y B(P_1, Y) + \tfrac{1}{2} \text{Max}_Y B(P_2, Y).$$

This is only possible if the two maxima on the right-hand side are attained for the same Y_1 i.e. if : $Y_1(u, v) = Y_2(u, v)$, for almost every (u, v). Using again condition (3.2) $(p(u, v) = E[v \mid Y(u, v)])$, this implies: $P_1(Y_1(u, v)) = P_2(Y_2(u, v))$ for almost every (u, v). □

Appendix C

Proof of Proposition 4.1. Let (S^*, R^*) be a Bayesian equilibrium (ii) is simply a reformulation of condition (4.1). We have to prove that R^* is a minimum of W.

By Assumption 2 we have:

$$W(R^*) = \bar{U}(S^*, R^*) = \int \phi(\omega, S^*(\omega))\, d\eta(\omega) - \bar{V}(S^*, R^*).$$

Now we use condition (4.2):

$$\forall R, \quad W(R^*) \leq \int \phi(\omega, S^*(\omega))d\eta(\omega) - \bar{V}(S^*, R)$$
$$\leq \bar{U}(S^*, R) \leq \text{Max}_{S \in \S}\, \bar{U}(S, R) = W(R).$$

As a consequence, if (S_1, R_1) and (S_2, R_2) are two Bayesian equilibria, we have:

$$\bar{U}(S_1, R_1) = \bar{U}(S_2, R_2) = \text{Min}_{R \in R}\, W(R).$$

$\square$

Proof of Proposition 4.2. Assumptions 2 and 3 imply that U is convex with respect to R and thus that W is also convex, as a supremum of convex mappings. Let (S_1, R_1) and (S_2, R_2) be two Bayesian equilibria. By Proposition 1, we know that: $W(R_1) = W(R_2) = \text{Min}_{R \in R}W(R)$. By convexity of W this is also equal to $W(\frac{1}{2}R_1 + \frac{1}{2}R_2)$. Thus, for almost every ω, we have:

$$\text{Max}_s\{U(\omega, s, (\tfrac{1}{2}R_1 + \tfrac{1}{2}R_2)(s))\} = \text{Max}_s\, U(\omega, s, R_1(S))$$
$$= \text{Max}_s\, U(\omega, s, R_2(s)) \text{ almost surely.}$$

Using again the convexity of U with respect to r, we have:

$$\text{Max}_s\{U(\omega, s, R_1(s)) + U(\omega, s, R_2(s))\} = \text{Max}_s\, U(\omega, s, R_1(S))$$
$$+ \text{Max}_s\,(\omega, s, R_2(s)) \text{ almost surely.}$$

This is only possible if the maximum is attained for the same s:

$$S_1(\omega) = S_2(\omega) \quad \text{for almost every } \omega.$$

Thus:

$$\int \phi(\omega_1, S_1(\omega))\, d\eta(\omega) = \int \phi(\omega, S_2(\omega))\, d\eta(\omega).$$

Using again Assumption 2 and Proposition 4.1, we conclude: $\bar{V}(S_1, R_1) = \bar{V}(S_2, R_2)$.

$\square$

Proof of Proposition 4.3. Let R be any element of $\R$ and define, for all $t > 0$ and ω in Ω:

$$a(t, \omega) = \text{Max}_{s \in \Sigma} U(\omega, s, (1 - t)\bar{R}(S) + tR(s)).$$

By a standard result of convex analysis,[23] Assumptions 3 and 4 imply that

$$\lim_{t \to 0^+} \frac{a(t,\omega) - a(0,\omega)}{t} = \sup_{s \in S_0(\omega)} \left\{ \frac{\partial U}{\partial r} (\omega, s, \bar{R}(s))(R(s) - \bar{R}(s)) \right\}$$

where

$$S_0(\omega) = \text{ArgMax}_{s \in \Sigma} U(\omega, s, \bar{R}(s)).$$

Since $\eta(\Omega_0) = 0$ and $\bar{S}$ is supported by $\bar{R}$ we have for almost every ω:

$$\lim_{t \to 0^+} \frac{a(t,\omega) - a(0,\omega)}{t} = \frac{\partial U}{\partial r} (\omega, \bar{S}(\omega), \bar{R}(\bar{S}(\omega)))(R(\bar{S}(\omega)) - \bar{R}(\bar{S}(\omega))).$$

Since U is convex with respect to r, $t \to (1/t)(a(t,\omega) - a(0,\omega))$ is non-decreasing, and we can apply Lebesgue's monotone convergence result:

$$\lim_{t \to 0^+} \int \frac{a(t,\omega) - a(0,\omega)}{t} \, d\eta(\omega)$$

$$= \int \frac{\partial U}{\partial r} (\omega, \bar{S}(\omega), \bar{R}(\bar{S}(\omega)))(R(\bar{S}(\omega)) - \bar{R}(\bar{S}(\omega))) d\eta(\omega).$$

Moreover,

$$\int a(t,\omega) \, d\eta(\omega) = W((1-t)\bar{R}(s) + tR(s))$$

so that

$$\int \frac{a(t,\omega) - a(0,\omega)}{t} \, d\eta(\omega) = \frac{1}{t} [W((1-t)\bar{R}(s) + tR(s)) - W(\bar{R}(s))],$$

$\bar{R}$ being a minimum of W, this quantity is non-negative, thus we have proved:

$$\forall R \in \bar{R}, \quad 0 \le \int \frac{\partial U}{\partial r} (\omega, \bar{S}(\omega), \bar{R}(\bar{S}(\omega)))[R(\bar{S}(\omega)) - \bar{R}(\bar{S}(\omega))] \, d\eta(\omega).$$

By Assumption A2, this implies:

$$\forall R \in \bar{R}, \quad 0 \le \int \frac{\partial V}{\partial r} (\omega, \bar{S}(\omega), \bar{R}(\bar{S}(\omega)))[R(\bar{S}(\omega)) - \bar{R}(\bar{S}(\omega))] \, d\eta(\omega).$$

V being concave with respect to r we also have:

$$\frac{\partial V}{\partial t} (\omega, \bar{S}(\omega), \bar{R}(\bar{S}(\omega)))[R(\bar{S}(\omega)) - \bar{R}(\bar{S}(\omega))]$$

$$\ge V(\omega, \bar{S}(\omega), R(\bar{S}(\omega))) - V(\omega, \bar{S}(\omega), \bar{R}(\bar{S}(\omega))).$$

[23] Aubin (1979, Proposition 6, 118–119).

By integrating over ω we deduce: $0 \geq V(\bar{S}, R) - V(\bar{S}, \bar{R})$ which implies that $(\bar{S}, \bar{R})$ is indeed a Nash Equilibrium of the game (U, V).   □

Appendix D

Proof of Proposition 5.2. The proof of Proposition 5.2 combines arguments from the proofs of Propositions 3.1 and 4.3. Recall the definition of the function W:

$$W(P) = E[\text{Max}_{p \in P_{(y)}}(v - p)(y - u)].$$

Because of Assumption 1, Lemma 3.1 implies that the maximum above is attained almost everywhere at a single $y(u, v)$. Thus W, which is convex as a supremum of linear functionals, is also Gateaux-differentiable.[24] For any H, element of C, one has:

$$\lim_{t \to 0} \frac{W(\bar{P} + tH) - W(\bar{P})}{t} = \int H(\bar{Y})(\bar{Y}(u, v) - u) \, dv(u, v).$$

Since $\bar{P}$ is a minimum of W, this quantity has to be zero for all H. This is equivalent to:

$$E[u \mid \bar{Y}] = \bar{Y}. \tag{C.1}$$

If $\bar{P}$ is differentiable at $\bar{Y}(u, v)$ for almost every (u, v) we can write the first-order condition to the insider maximization problem:

$$\text{for almost every } (u, v), \quad v - \bar{P}(\bar{Y}(u, v)) - \bar{P}'(\bar{Y})(\bar{Y}(u, v) - u) = 0.$$

By taking expectations conditional on $\bar{Y}$, we get:

$$E[v \mid \bar{Y}] - \bar{P}(\bar{Y}) = \bar{P}'(\bar{Y})(\bar{Y} - E(u \mid \bar{Y}))$$

which is zero by condition (C.1).

It now remains to be seen that $\bar{P}$ is differentiable. The proof follows the reasoning in Appendix B (proof of Proposition 3.1). First, we recall that

(i) $\pi(P, u, v) > 0$ almost surely
(ii) $E(u \mid Z(u, v)) = y(u, v)$ almost surely   (C.1)

It follows from (i) that $u \neq y$ almost surely. Using (ii), we get that every buyer must pool with a seller and differentiability follows (see the proof of Proposition 3.1, step 4).   □

Appendix E

The Uniqueness Issue in the Kyle (1985) Model

The version of the Kyle (1985) model that we have considered (i.e. the market order game) assumes that the insider observes the noise trading, u, or

---

[24] Aubin (1979, p. 111).

equivalently is able to submit limit orders. If, as in the original Kyle model, the insider does not observe u then neither the market makers who observe p but not u, nor the insider who observes v but not p, have superior information. In this case, the uniqueness issue becomes more delicate as we shall see.

First, if the support of u is bounded, say $[0, 1]$, then, for every $x \neq 0$, the probability that insider trading will be detected is positive. Indeed if x is positive and $x + u$ is greater than 1, the market makers know that the insider is buying. Hence, there exists a Nash equilibrium where no trade occurs:

$$x(v) = 0;$$
$$p(y) = -\infty \quad \text{if } y < 0;$$
$$p(y) = +\infty \quad \text{if } y > 1;$$
$$p(y) = E(v) \quad \text{otherwise}$$

This no-trade equilibrium[25] is not a Bayesian equilibrium since $+\infty$ and $-\infty$ do not belong to the support of v. However, we see that we already need a refinement (support restriction) of Definition 3.1 to rule out this trivial equilibrium, which was *not* the case in Section III.

Second, even with the support restriction, uniqueness is not guaranteed in general as can be seen from the example below.

We consider the following case:

(i) The distribution of u is discrete and takes the values $+1$ and -1 with equal probability $\frac{1}{2}$.
(ii) v takes the values $+2, +1, -1$ and -2 with probability $\frac{1}{4}$.
(iii) u and v are independent.

With these assumptions, we can construct equilibria $(x(v), p(y))$ with the following features:

(i) $x(+2) = 1 + a, x(1) = 1 - a, x(-v) = -x(v)$ for every $v, 0 < a < 1$.
(ii) $p(-y) = -p(y)$ for every y.

In this equilibrium, the types $(u = -1; v = +2)$ and $(u = +1; v = -1)$ (respectively $(u = +1; v = -2)$ and $(u = -1; v = +1)$) are pooled in the sense that $x(+2) - 1 = x(-1) + 1$ (respectively $(x(1) - 1 = x(-2) + 1)$. It follows that in this equilibrium, the following equalities must hold:

$$p(2 + a) = 2; \quad p(2 - a) = 1; \quad p(a) = \tfrac{1}{2}; \quad p(-a) = -\tfrac{1}{2};$$
$$p(a - 2) = -1 \quad \text{and} \quad p(-a - 2) = -2.$$

We next define the function: $\phi(x) = \tfrac{1}{2}p(x + 1) + \tfrac{1}{2}p(x - 1)$. $\phi(x)$ is the average price paid for x. It is easy to check that:

$$\phi(1 + a) = \tfrac{5}{4}; \quad \phi(1 - a) = \tfrac{1}{4}; \quad \phi(a - 1) = \tfrac{1}{4}; \quad \phi(-1 - a) = -\tfrac{5}{4}.$$

---

[25] Of course, the no-trade equilibrium minimizes the insider's expected profits.

Next, we verify the incentive compatibility constraints. The only one that may cause a problem is the constraint that $v = +2(v = -2)$ must not imitate $v = +1$ $(v = -1)$, i.e.

$$(2 - \phi(1 + a))(1 + a) \geq (2 - \phi(1 - a))(1 - a)$$

i.e.

$$a \geq \tfrac{2}{5}.$$

The final step is to define $p(y)$ for every value of y. This can be done for $1 > a \geq \tfrac{2}{5}$ by following the construction in Kyle and Vila (1991) (the details are left to the reader).

An interesting question remains, namely the multiplicity of equilibria for the case where u and v are normal as in Kyle (1985). At this point this question is, as far as we know, still open. □

REFERENCES

Admati, A. (1985), 'A Noisy Rational Expectations Equilibrium for Multi Asset Securities Markets', *Econometrica*, 53, 629–657.

— and Pfleiderer, P. (1988), 'A Theory of Intraday Patterns: Volume and Price Variability', *Review of Financial Studies*, 1, 3–40.

— and Pfleiderer, P. (1990), 'Sunshine Trading: The Effects of Pre-announcement of Traders' Welfare and on Price variability' (Stanford, mimeo).

Aubin, J. P. (1979), *Mathematical Methods of Games and Economic Theory* (Amsterdam: North Holland).

Back, K. (1991), 'Continuous Insider Trading and the Distribution of Asset Prices' (Washington University, mimeo).

Bhattacharya, U. and Spiegel, M. (1991), 'Insiders, Outsiders and Market Breakdowns', *Review of Financial Studies*, 4, 255–282.

Cho, I. K. and Kreps, D. M. (1987), 'Signalling games and Stable Equilibria', *Quarterly Journal of Economics*, 102, 179–221.

Chowdhry, B. and Nanda, V. (1990), 'Multi-Market Trading and Market Liquidity' (UCLA, mimeo).

Chung, K. L. (1974), *A Course in Probability Theory* (London: Academic Press).

Constantinides, G. M. (1983), 'Capital Market Equilibrium with Personal Tax', *Econometrica*, 51, 611–637.

Diamond, D. and Verrechia, R. (1981), 'Information Aggregation in a Noisy Rational Expectations Economy', *Journal of Financial Economics*, 9, 221–235.

Hellwig, M. (1980), 'On the Aggregation of Information in Competitive Markets', *Journal of Economic Theory*, 22, 477–498.

Gorton, G. and Pennachi, G. (1989), 'Security Baskets and Index-Linked Securities' (Wharton School, mimeo).

Grossman, S. (1979), 'An Introduction to the Theory of Rational Expectations Under Asymmetric Information', *Review of Economic Studies*, 48, 541–559.

— and Stiglitz, J. E. (1980), 'On the Impossibility of Informationally Efficient markets', *American Economic Review*, 70, 393–408.

Hirshleifer, J. (1971), 'The Private and Social Value of Information and the Reward to Speculative Activity', *American Economic Review*, 61, 561–574.

Kyle, A. S. (1984), 'A Theory of Futures Markets Manipulations', in R. W. Anderson (ed.), *The Industrial Organization of Futures Markets* (Lexington, Mass: Lexington Books), 141–173.

— (1985), 'Continuous Auctions and Insider Trading', *Econometrica*, 53, 1335–1355.

Kyle, A. (1989), 'Informed Speculation with Imperfect Competition', *Review of Economic Studies*, 56, 317–356.

Kyle, A. S. and Vila, J.-L. (1991), 'Noise Trading and Takeovers', *Rand Journal of Economics*, 22, 54–71.

Laffont, J.-J. and Maskin, E. S. (1989), 'Rational Expectations with Imperfect Competition: A Bertrand-Edgeworth Example', *Economic Letters*, 30, 269–274.

— and Maskin, E. S.(1990), 'The Efficient Market Hypothesis and Insider Trading on the Stock Market', *Journal of Political Economy*, 98, 70–93.

Mas-Colell, A. (1986), 'The Price Equilibrium Existence Problem in Topological Vector Lattices', *Econometrica*, 54, 1039–1053.

Pagano, M. (1989), 'Trading Volume and Asset Liquidity', *Quarterly Journal of Economics*, 104, 255–274.

— and Roell, A. (1990), 'Front Running and Stock Market Liquidity' (mimeo).

Radner, R. (1962), 'Team Decision Problems', *Annals of Mathematical Statistics*, 33, 857–881.

— (1972), 'Existence of Equilibrium of Plans, Prices and Price Expectations in a Sequence of Markets', *Econometrica*, 40, 289–303.

Rochet, J.-C. and Vila, J.-L. (1992), 'Insider Trading and Market Manipulations: Existence and Uniqueness of Equilibrium' (Sloan School of Management Working Paper No. 3438-92EFA).

Roell, A. (1989), 'Dual Capacity Trading and the Quality of the Market' (London School of Economics, mimeo).

Subrahmanyam, A. (1990*a*), 'Risk Aversion, Market Liquidity, and Price Efficiency' (Columbia University, mimeo).

— (1990*b*), 'A Theory of Trading in Stock Index Futures' (Columbia University, mimeo).

Vila, J.-L. (1987), 'Speculation et Interet Collectif', *L'Actualite Economique*, 63, 138–152.

— (1988), 'The Role of Information in Futures Market Manipulations' (unpublished).

— (1989), 'Simple Games of Market Manipulations', *Economic Letters*, 29, 21–26.

Vives, X. (1988), 'Aggregation of Information in Large Cournot Markets', *Econometrica*, 56, 851–876.

— (1990), 'Financial Markets Dynamics with Risk Averse Agents' (Universitat Autònoma de Barcelona, mimeo).

4

Insider and Liquidity Trading in Stock and Options Markets

BRUNO BIAIS AND PIERRE HILLION

What are options useful for? In incomplete markets, they can be used to improve hedging opportunities for risk-averse agents [see Ross (1976)]. Financial markets are not only useful to reallocate risk across agents, however. Financial prices can reveal private information. Easley, O'Hara, and Srinivas (1993) provide empirical evidence that insiders trade in options markets. The present article analyzes how the introduction of a nonredundant option that completes the market affects information revelation and risk sharing. In this way we are able to evaluate the interaction between information asymmetry and market incompleteness.

We consider a simple one-period model where risk-neutral market makers serve market orders placed either by an insider or by a liquidity trader. The liquidity traders are rational expected utility maximizers. They trade to hedge their risk exposure to state-dependent random shocks on their final wealth. There are three final states, determining the value of the liquidity shocks and the stock. Without the option, the market is incomplete, but the introduction of the option completes the markets. The insider knows the final state of the world in advance. To exploit her private information, while avoiding full revelation, she mimics the stock and option liquidity trades that maximize her profits.

In the incomplete market, the liquidity traders can only partially hedge their risk exposure. When the option is traded, state-contingent claims (SCC) can be traded separately. Other things being equal, this additional flexibility enables the liquidity traders to better hedge their risk exposure. Without the option the insider with good news buys the stock (and sells it after bad news), but she cannot earn profits when a neutral state is realized. With the option, the full set of contingencies can be spanned. So the insider can conduct profitable trades in all

We gratefully acknowledge the helpful comments of the editor, Rick Green, and the referee. We also thank seminar participants at Basel Universität, Carnegie Mellon University, Cornell University, Dauphine University, Delta, Banque de France, the London Business School, the London School of Economics, the Séminaire d'Economie Théorique René Roy, the Stockholm School of Economics, UCLA, Université Libre de Bruxelles, Vanderbilt University, and at the Fédération Francaise des Sociétés d'Assurance seminar in Université de Toulouse. Address correspondence to B. Biais, Institut d'Economie Industrielle, Université des Sciences Sociales, Place Anatole France, FR-31042 Toulouse Cedex, France. E-mail: Biais@cix.cict.Fr states. Hence, other things being equal, the introduction of the option is beneficial to the insider because it enables her to design trades that better match her private information.

This line of reasoning can be misleading, however. The 'other things being equal' argument does not hold because in equilibrium the insider trades and liquidity trades are interdependent. On the one hand, the insider mimics the liquidity trades, to obtain camouflage.[1] On the other hand, the presence of the insider creates an adverse selection cost of trading for the liquidity traders who respond to this cost by reducing their trades.[2] Consider the example of the insider with good news about the asset value. When the option is traded and the states can be spanned, a naive strategy would be to buy contingent claims associated with the good news state and to sell the other 'out of the money' claims. This can be implemented by buying the call with strike K larger than the unconditional value of the stock. This makes the good news SCC expensive, however, which deters the liquidity traders from buying it. Now, if the liquidity traders do not trade this security, the strategic insider also may choose to avoid it, so there will not be excessive information revelation. This exemplifies the importance of endogenizing liquidity trading when assessing the influence of the option, one contribution of the present article.[3]

We find that the introduction of the option can reduce the profits of the insider. This is because (i) in equilibrium the insider mimics the liquidity trades to avoid being spotted and (ii) the introduction of the option can generate liquidity trading patterns that are less attractive for the insider than those prevailing in the incomplete market.

We find that the introduction of the option mitigates the market breakdown problems created by asymmetric information. Asymmetric information imposes trading costs on the liquidity traders. To determine their optimal trades, they compare these trading costs to the risk-sharing gains from trade. If the costs exceed the benefits, there is a market breakdown.[4] Market incompleteness makes the market breakdown problem more severe. In the incomplete market the liquidity traders must trade predetermined bundles of state-contingent claims, namely the stock and the risk-free asset. These may include certain claims that are

[1] See, for example, Kyle (1985) or, in the case of options, Back (1993) and Easley, O'Hara, and Srinivas (1993).

[2] Glosten (1989), Madhavan (1992), Bhattacharya and Spiegel (1991), and Bossaerts and Hughson (1993) analyze the effects of asymmetric information on risk sharing in the stock market.

[3] This differs from Back (1993), Easley, O'Hara, and Srinivas (1993), or John, Koticha, and Subrahmanyam (1992), who consider exogenous liquidity trades.

[4] Glosten (1989), Madhavan (1992), Bhattacharya and Spiegel (1991), and Bossaerts and Hughson (1993) analyze market breakdown problems in the stock market. Our analysis differs from theirs because we consider a situation where, even without information asymmetry, markets would be incomplete. When only the stock and the bond are traded, the liquidity traders cannot hedge their endowment shocks contingent on the medium state. In contrast, in Glosten (1989), Madhavan (1992), Bhattacharya and Spiegel (1991), and Bossaerts and Hughson (1993) in absence of asymmetric information, agents can perfectly hedge their risk exposure, since the latter stems from stock holdings.

not useful for hedging the liquidity traders' shocks. Hence, market incompleteness is costly for the liquidity traders because it compels them to buy unnecessary contingent claims. Asymmetric information increases the cost of purchasing these claims. As a result, the introduction of the option reduces the likelihood of market breakdowns. This is beneficial to the liquidity traders because it makes it more likely that they will be able to hedge at least part of their risk exposure.

We also find that the introduction of the option has ambiguous consequences on the informational efficiency of the market. It enables trades to take place in cases where there would have been a market breakdown in the incomplete market. In these cases there is some information revelation in the complete market and none in the incomplete market. The introduction of the option can also reduce the informational efficiency of the market, however. The introduction of the option increases the set of possible trades for the insider. This complexifies the trading strategies of the insider and can make it more difficult for the market makers to interpret the information content of trades. This results in a decrease in the informational efficiency of the market.

In the next section of this article, we present the model. In Section 2, we present the benchmark case where there is no asymmetric information. In Section 3 and 4, we analyze successively the equilibrium in the incomplete market and the equilibrium with the option. Sections 5 and 6 are devoted to analysis of the complete market equilibria and their comparison to the incomplete market case. Section 7 analyzes the trades in the stock and the option and the corresponding prices in the different equilibria and discusses the relation between our findings and previous empirical results. Section 8 provides concluding remarks. All proofs are in the Appendix.

1. THE MODEL

Price formation is analyzed in a market where the risk-free asset, one stock, and one (nonredundant) option are simultaneously traded. For simplicity, the return on the risk-free asset is normalized to zero. Risk-neutral market makers face *either* one strategic, perfectly informed insider *or* one rational, competitive, risk-averse liquidity trader.[5] The market makers cannot determine whether the agent is informed. The only signal they observe is the order placed by the agent.

There is one period. The state of the world and the final value of the securities at the end of the period follow a three-point distribution. The stock, the bond, *and the option* are needed to complete the markets and span the three states. The strategic insider knows the true final state of the world in advance. The risk-averse liquidity traders are exposed to state-dependent liquidity shocks. They trade to hedge their risk exposure.

---

[5] The assumption that the market makers face only one agent is similar to Glosten and Milgrom (1985). It differs from Kyle (1985), where the market makers serve the aggregate net order flow from the insider *and* liquidity traders.

B. Biais and P. Hillion

1.1. The Final Value of the Securities and the Market Structure

The final value of the stock is u, d, or m, with equal probability. For simplicity, the distribution of the final value of the stock is symmetric around m. That is, $u \equiv m + \sigma$, and $d \equiv m - \sigma$, where $\sigma > 0$. The option can be any call or put with strike price strictly between u and d, expiring at the end of the period.

For simplicity, only market orders are considered. Market makers stand ready to serve buy or sell orders in the stock and the option.[6]

1.2. The Insider

With probability α, the market order stems from the insider. Before trading, the insider perfectly observes the realization of the state of the world, u, m, or d. The insider is risk neutral and strategic. She maximizes her expected trading profits. She does not have any leverage or short selling constraints.

1.3. The Liquidity Traders

With probability $1 - \alpha$ the market order stems from one liquidity trader. The liquidity traders are assumed to behave competitively. They do not recognize that their trades affect the prices. They do have rational expectations, however. They select their trading strategy to maximize their expected utility on the basis of the correct expectation of the price at which their trade will be executed in equilibrium.[7] For simplicity the liquidity traders are assumed to have identical constant absolute-risk aversion parameter $(\gamma) : U(x) = -e^{-\gamma x}$. Like the insiders, they have no short selling or leverage constraints.

The liquidity traders have initial cash endowment C. They also have state-dependent endowments and place orders in the stock and the option to hedge

---

[6] An alternative, equivalent assumption in the present model is that market makers in the stock and in the option markets have the same information set; that is, they can monitor perfectly and simultaneously orders and trades in both markets. In most actual exchanges, the stock and the options are traded separately. For example, options on stocks listed on the NYSE are traded on the AMEX or in Chicago. Information flows rapidly across markets, however. In particular, the options market makers monitor actively the trades and orders in the stock market. For example, in the Paris Bourse and the French options markets, the traders working for the same brokerage houses actively communicate, using screens or telephones. Berkman's (1992) analysis of the European Options Exchange, in Amsterdam, suggests that the option market makers closely monitor the stock market. Note also that, in trading rooms, traders in different but related securities sit close to one another and monitor the orders, trades, and prices in the different securities.

[7] Because they are price takers, the liquidity traders consider only the equilibrium price. They do not recognize that out-of-equilibrium trades would execute at different prices, reflecting out-of-equilibrium beliefs. Assuming strategic liquidity traders would have made the analysis less tractable. In particular, it would have given rise to multiple equilibria. In the case of stock markets, Laffont and Maskin (1990) and Bhattacharya and Spiegel (1991) also consider competitive liquidity traders. For an analysis of strategic liquidity traders, see Spiegel and Subrahmanyam (1992).

their risk exposure. The assumption reflects the idea that the securities market is used to reallocate the risk from the real economy.[8]

There are three different types of liquidity traders, likely to enter the market with equal probability $\frac{1}{3}$. The state-dependent endowment of the type 1 agent is $-L$ in state u, $-l$ in state m, and 0 in state d, with $L > l$. The type 2 agent has no risk exposure. His endowment is constant (normalized to 0) in the three states. The endowment of the type 3 agent is 0 in state u, $-l$ in state m, and $-L$ in state d.

The type 1 (type 3) risk exposure can be interpreted as a 'short' ('long') position. His liquidity shock is negatively (positively) correlated with the final value of the stock. Intuitively, since the type 1 liquidity trader is 'short,' he will engage in trades that will be attractive for the insider in state u. Symmetrically, mimicking the type 3 trades will be attractive for the insider in state d.

How would our results be affected by alterations of our simple model?

- For simplicity the endowment shocks of the type 1 and type 3 traders are assumed to be symmetric. This enables one to focus on symmetric equilibria, in which the attractiveness of the type 1 trades for the insider in state u is equal to the attractiveness of the type 3 trades for the insider in state d. Asymmetric shocks would lead to different equilibrium trades. Consider the example where the type 1 u-state shock would be $-L_1$ and the type 3 d-state shock would be $-L_3$, where $L_1 > L_3$. In this case, mimicking the type 1 trades in state u would be more attractive for the insider than mimicking the type 3 trades in state d. Consequently, the insider would trade more aggressively in state u than in state d. As a result more information would be revealed in the former than in the latter. However, the basic intuition developed in the current article (that the insider mimics the liquidity trades that best fit her information) would still hold.[9]

- The type 2 liquidity trader is not subject to any shock and consequently does not trade. We could consider type 1 and type 3 only, without altering the qualitative nature of the results. However, because it enhances the symmetry of the model (three possible final values for the stock and three types of liquidity traders), the introduction of the type 2 liquidity trader actually simplifies the computations and enables us to obtain simpler expressions.

- Alternatively, one could have considered an intermediate liquidity shock, neither short nor long, equal to 0 in the u and d state and negative in the medium state. Agents with such an endowment shock would benefit from the introduction of the option, since when only the stock and the bond are traded they cannot obtain any risk sharing from the financial markets. Hence, this

---

[8] For a similar analysis of liquidity trading, in the case of stocks, see Dow and Gorton (1993).

[9] If we considered more than one trading period, asymmetry in the liquidity shocks (and hence in the liquidity trades) would raise the possibility of manipulation. That is, strategic agents without private information could trade in one direction to move the prices up or down and then unwind their inventory at a profit [see Allen and Gorron (1992)]. Our simple one trading period set-up precludes such behavior.

extension of the model would not alter our result that liquidity traders benefit from the introduction of the option.

1.4. The Equilibrium

In equilibrium the following conditions are satisfied. First, the agents take optimal actions: (i) the market order chosen by each liquidity trader maximizes his expected utility, (ii) the trade of the insider maximizes her expected profits, and (iii) the prices quoted by the market makers are such that they earn zero expected profits.

Second, the agents have rational expectations: (i) when they compute their final wealth, the liquidity traders correctly anticipate the price at which their trades are executed; (ii) the insider correctly anticipates the reaction of the market makers to her trades; and (iii) in interpreting the information content of the trade, the market makers apply Bayes' rule and correctly conjecture the trading strategies of the other agents.

This is similar to the equilibrium concept in Kyle (1985), Laffont and Maskin (1990), Rochet and Vila (1994), or Vila (1989). The zero expected profit condition for the market makers stems from Bertrand competition between identical, risk-neutral agents.

2. EQUILIBRIUM PRICES AND TRADES WITHOUT ASYMMETRIC INFORMATION

2.1. The Incomplete Market

The type 1 liquidity trader is exposed to the negative liquidity shocks $-L$ in state u and $-l$ in state m. To hedge the u-state risk exposure, he buys Q_1 shares of the stock, at the ask price A. The risk-free rate is normalized to zero. The type 1 agent must solve the following problem:

$$\text{Max}_{Q_1}[U(C - Q_1A + Q_1u - L) + U(C - Q_1A + Q_1m - l)$$
$$+ U(C - Q_1A + Q_1d)]/3.$$

Without asymmetric information, the ask price A is equal to the unconditional expected final value of the stock m. Noting that $u - m = \sigma$ and $m - d = -\sigma$, the objective of the type 1 liquidity trader can be rewritten:

$$\text{Max}_{Q_1} \frac{U(C + Q_1\sigma - L) + U(C - l) + U(C - Q_1\sigma)}{3}.$$

Buying the stock provides a hedge against the u-state exposure but creates new exposure to the d-state risk. One can easily check that the optimal compromise between these two effects is to hedge half of the u-state risk by trading $L/2\sigma$.[10] Note that the m-state wealth of the agent is not affected by the amount traded. The

---

[10] We do not prove the results presented in this section. They are particular cases of those presented in the next sections, in the case $\alpha = 0$.

negative side of this is that the m-state shock cannot be hedged. The positive side is that exposure to the m-state shock does not prevent the liquidity trader from hedging the u-state shock. As a result, the optimal trade does not depend on l. In the next section we show that this is no longer the case with asymmetric information.

2.2. The Complete Market

The stock, the bond, and the option span the three states. In this case the agents can trade the u-, m-, and d-state-contingent claims. Because it simplifies the exposition and the proofs, we analyze trades in the complete market in terms of the SCC rather than in terms of the stock and the option. For example, the type 1 liquidity trader seeks to hedge his w-state and m-state risk exposures. To do so he purchases the u SCC and the m SCC in exchange for money (the risk-free asset).[11]

Since the market makers are risk-neutral, they are willing to trade the SCC at a price equal to the probability of the corresponding states, updated conditionally on the informational content of the trade. Let these conditional probabilities be denoted: π_u, π_m, and π_d. Note that they can also be interpreted as state prices. When there is no asymmetric information, they are simply the unconditional probabilities, equal to $\frac{1}{3}$. In this case the final wealth of the type 1 liquidity trader who purchases $Q_{u,1}$ units of the u SCC and $Q_{m,1}$ units of the m SCC is

$$
\begin{cases}
C - L + Q_{u,1} - \left(\dfrac{Q_{u,1} + Q_{m,1}}{3} \right) & \text{in state } u, \\[2mm]
C - l + Q_{m,1} - \left(\dfrac{Q_{u,1} + Q_{m,1}}{3} \right) & \text{in state } m, \\[2mm]
C - \left(\dfrac{Q_{u,1} + Q_{m,1}}{3} \right) & \text{in state } d.
\end{cases}
\tag{1}
$$

Because the prices are set by risk-neutral competitive market makers, who have the same information as the liquidity trader, the optimal trade is to hedge the risk exposure fully by purchasing L units of the u SCC and l units of the m SCC. This generates the same final wealth in all three states: $-[(L + l)/3]$. This contrasts with the previous, incomplete market, case.

3. EQUILIBRIUM IN THE INCOMPLETE MARKET, WITH ASYMMETRIC INFORMATION

3.1. The Insider Trades

The market makers quote ask and bid prices (A and B) equal to the conditional expectation of the final value of the stock. Because of interdealer competition

---

[11] Instead of considering the u and m SCC and the risk-free asset, we could have equivalently focused on the u, m, and d SCC.

$A \leq u$ and $B \geq d$. In state u the insider buys the stock at a profit (selling would generate losses). In state d she sells. Hence, the market makers know that purchases stem either from the type l liquidity trader (in which case they should quote $A = m$) or from the insider in state u (in which case they should quote $A = u$). As a result, the ask price must be between u and m. Similarly, the bid is between m and d. Now consider the insider in state m. If she bought the stock, she would make losses because $A > m$. If she sold the stock, she would also make losses because $B < m$. Hence, the insider in state m does not trade. In that respect, the insider suffers from the incompleteness of the market.

3.2. The Liquidity Trades

As in the symmetric information case, the type 1 liquidity trader can buy the stock to hedge his μ-state risk exposure. With asymmetric information, this trade is costly because the ask price is $A > m$. In this case, the final wealth of the type 1 liquidity trader if he buys the stock is

$$
\begin{cases}
C - L + Q_1(u - A) & \text{in state } u, \\
C - l + Q_1(m - A) & \text{in state } m, \\
C + Q_1(d - A) & \text{in state } d.
\end{cases}
\tag{2}
$$

From now on the cash endowment of the liquidity trader (C) is normalized to zero. This does not affect the results, since the agents have CARA utilities, which do not exhibit wealth effects. In all states, the wealth of the liquidity trader is lower in the asymmetric information case than in the symmetric information case. This reflects the higher stock price. As a result the liquidity trade is smaller with asymmetric information than with symmetric information. Also, in contrast with the symmetric information case, the final wealth of the agent in state m is now affected by the trade. Buying the stock creates losses for the agent in the m state. Such losses are particularly damaging for the agent if his marginal utility in that state is high because his m state liquidity shock l is high. As a result the liquidity trade is decreasing in the m-state shock, l. The optimal demand is given in the following lemma.

Lemma 1. *The type 1 liquidity trader buys Q_1 shares, the type 2 agent does not trade, and the type 3 liquidity trader sells Q_3 shares, where*

$$
Q_1 = \text{Max} \left[0, \frac{1}{\gamma\sigma} \ln \left(\frac{2(u - A)e^{\gamma L}}{(A - m)e^{\gamma l} + \sqrt{(A - m)^2 e^{2\gamma l} + 4(u - A)(A - d)e^{\gamma L}}} \right) \right]
$$

and

$$Q_3 = \text{Max}\left[0, \frac{1}{\gamma\sigma}\ln\left(\frac{2(B-d)e^{\gamma L}}{(m-B)e^{\gamma l} + \sqrt{(m-B)^2 e^{2\gamma l} + 4(u-B)(B-d)e^{\gamma L}}}\right)\right].$$

If the degree of information asymmetry is sufficiently high, the cost it imposes on the liquidity traders is such that they choose not to hedge. This can be interpreted as a market breakdown, to the extent that efficient risk-sharing trades cannot take place. The condition under which this market breakdown occurs is stated in the following corollary:

Corollary to Lemma 1. *If $e^{\gamma L} < (A-d)/(u-A) + (A-m)/(u-A)e^{\gamma l}$, then the type 1 agent does not trade $(Q_1 = 0)$.*

The right-hand side of this inequality is increasing in A, which increases with the degree of asymmetric information. Also, there is a market breakdown if l is sufficiently large with respect to L. This reflects the trade-off faced by the agent between (i) hedging his u-state shock efficiently by buying a large amount of shares (which is particularly attractive if L is large) and (ii) creating losses in the m state, which is particularly damaging if his marginal utility is high in that state because l is large.

3.3. The Equilibrium

Proposition 1. *When only the stock and the bond are traded, equilibrium prices and trades are as follows: The type 2 agent does not trade. The type 1 (3) liquidity trader buys (sells) Q stocks where*

$$Q = \text{Max}\left[\frac{1}{\gamma\sigma}\ln\left(\frac{2(1-\alpha)e^{\gamma L}}{\alpha e^{\gamma l} + \sqrt{\alpha^2 e^{2\gamma l} + 4(1-\alpha^2)e^{\gamma L}}}\right), 0\right].$$

In state u the insider buys Q stocks; in state d she sells Q stocks; in state m she does not trade. The ask price of the stock is $A = m + \alpha\sigma$ and the bid price is $B = m - \alpha\sigma$.

The proposition states that the insider mimics the liquidity trades. This is because, if the insider traded other quantities, she would be spotted by the market makers and unable to earn profits. Note also that the bid-ask spread is $2\alpha\sigma$, consistent with the intuition that the spread increases as the volatility or the degree of asymmetric information increases. Finally, using Proposition 1 and the corollary to Lemma 1, the condition under which the quantity traded by the agent is positive is

$$e^{\gamma L} > \frac{1+\alpha}{1-\alpha} + \frac{\alpha}{1-\alpha}e^{\gamma l}. \tag{3}$$

The right-hand side is increasing in α. If the degree of asymmetric information is high, the market breaks down.

4. EQUILIBRIUM IN THE COMPLETE MARKET WITH ASYMMETRIC INFORMATION

4.1. The Liquidity Trades

The liquidity trades are given in the following lemma:

Lemma 2. *The type 1 liquidity trader buys* $Q_{u,1}$ *units of the u SCC and* $Q_{m,1}$ *of the m SCC where*

$$Q_{u,1} = \text{Max}\left[0, L - \frac{1}{\gamma}\ln\left(\frac{\pi_{u,1}}{\pi_{d,1}}\right)\right] \quad and$$

$$Q_{m,1} = \text{Max}\left[0, l - \frac{1}{\gamma}\ln\left(\frac{\pi_{m,1}}{\pi_{d,1}}\right)\right].$$

The type 2 agent does not trade. The type 3 agent buys $Q_{d,3}$ *units of the d SCC and* $Q_{m,3}$ *of the m SCC where*

$$Q_{d,3} = \text{Max}\left[0, L - \frac{1}{\gamma}\ln\left(\frac{\pi_{d,3}}{\pi_{u,3}}\right)\right] \quad and$$

$$Q_{m,3} = \text{Max}\left[0, l - \frac{1}{\gamma}\ln\left(\frac{\pi_{m,3}}{\pi_{u,3}}\right)\right].$$

The quantities $Q_{u,1}$ and $Q_{m,1}$ are equal to the difference between the liquidity shocks in the corresponding states (L and l, respectively) and a price elasticity component that reflects the sensitivity of the liquidity trader to the prices of the contingent claims. As in the perfect information case, to hedge his risk exposure perfectly the agent can buy L units of the u SCC and l units of the m SCC.[12] When hedging is costly because $\pi_{u,1}$ or $\pi_{m,1}$ is higher than the unconditional probabilities, the liquidity trader chooses to underhedge ($Q_{u,1} < L$ and $Q_{m,1} < l$).

4.2. The Equilibrium Prices and Trades

On the one hand, the insider would like to buy as many claims contingent on the realized state as possible and to sell the claims contingent on the other states. Such aggressive trades are not optimal, however, because they involve too much information revelation. Rather, the insider mimics the liquidity trades to avoid being spotted by the market makers. Thus, the strategy of the insider is to mimic the liquidity trades that enable her to buy as many claims on the realized state as

---

[12] The perfect hedge is the actual trade when the agent is infinitely risk-averse ($\gamma \to \infty$) so that the price elasticity component of the liquidity demand is irrelevant.

Table 1. *Equilibrium prices and trades in the complete market*

Equ.	Q_u	Q_m	λ	μ	π_u	π_m
Pure	$L - \frac{1}{\gamma}\ln\left(\frac{1+2\alpha}{1-\alpha}\right)$	l	1	0	$\frac{1+2\alpha}{3}$	$\frac{1-\alpha}{3}$
Mixed 1	$L - \frac{1}{\gamma}\ln\left(\frac{1+2\alpha}{1-\alpha}\right)$	$l - \frac{1}{\gamma}\ln\left[\frac{1+\alpha(3\mu-1)}{1-\alpha}\right]$	1	$\mu \in \,]0, \tfrac{1}{2}]$	$\dfrac{\alpha + \frac{1-\alpha}{3}}{1+\alpha\mu}$	$\dfrac{\alpha\mu + \frac{1-\alpha}{3}}{1+\alpha\mu}$
Mixed 2	$L - \frac{1}{\gamma}\ln\left[\frac{\alpha\lambda+(1-\alpha)/3}{(1-\alpha)/3}\right]$	$l - \frac{1}{\gamma}\ln\left[\frac{\alpha/2+(1-\alpha)/3}{(1-\alpha)/3}\right]$	$\lambda \in [0,1]$	$\tfrac{1}{2}$	$\dfrac{\alpha\lambda + \frac{1-\alpha}{3}}{1-\alpha/2+\alpha\lambda}$	$\dfrac{\alpha/2 + \frac{1-\alpha}{3}}{1-\alpha/2+\alpha\lambda}$

possible, while minimizing the number of worthless SSC purchased.[13] To the extent that the liquidity trades depend on the liquidity shocks (L and l), the insider's strategy also depends on these shocks.

Consider the trade of the type 1 liquidity trade, which involves buying the u SCC (to hedge his state-u shock, L) and the m SCC (to hedge his state-m shock, l). If L is large and l is small, the number of u SCCs bought is large and the number of m SCC is small. As a result this trade is attractive for the insider in state u. As L gets closer to l, the liquidity trade involves buying a larger number of m SCC and it becomes less attractive for the insider in state u and more attractive for the insider in state m. The next three propositions describe how the insider's strategy changes as the relative magnitudes of L and l vary.

When L is sufficiently larger than l, the insider in state u finds it optimal always to mimic the type 1 liquidity trade. In contrast, mimicking this trade would imply losses for the insider in state m. As a result, as in the incomplete market, the insider in state m does not trade, like the type 2 trader. This is described in the next proposition.

Proposition 2. Pure strategy equilibrium: *If*

$$L > \frac{1}{\gamma}\ln\left(\frac{1+2\alpha}{1-\alpha}\right) + \frac{2+\alpha}{1+2\alpha}l, \tag{4}$$

then the insider in state u buys $L - 1/\gamma[(1+2\alpha)/(1-\alpha)]$ units of the u SCC and l units of the m SCC, like the type 1 liquidity trader; the insider in state m does not trade, like the type 2 liquidity trader; and the insider in state d buys l units of the m SCC and $L - 1/[\gamma(1+2\alpha)/(1-\alpha)]$ units of the d SCC, like the type 3 liquidity trader.[14]

---

[13] When the insider is indifferent between two liquidity trades, her strategy involves mixing over these trades. Easley and O'Hara (1987) and Easley, O'Hara, and Srinivas (1993) also show that the insider uses mixed strategies to limit information revelation.

[14] In this proposition as well as in Propositions 3 and 4, the numbers of SCC bought by the agents and the corresponding state prices are in Table 1.

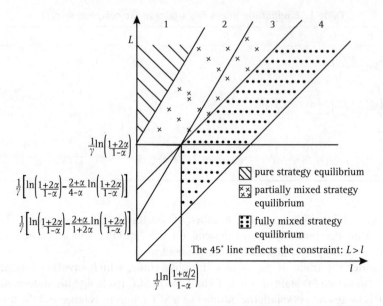

Figure 1. *The equilibria in the complete market*

Note: The parameter values for which the different equilibria arise are graphically represented in Figure 1. The larger the value of the u-state liquidity shock (L) relative to the value of the m-state shock, the more likely it is that the pure strategy equilibrium prevails.

The set of parameter values for which the pure strategy equilibrium prevails is region 1 in Figure 1. As l increases relative to L, the number of m SCC purchased by the type 1 or type 3 liquidity trader increases. Above a certain cut-off level for l, mimicking the type 1 or 3 trades no longer results in losses for the insider in state m. Consequently, she mixes between the type 1 and 3 trades (and the type 2 trade as long as the type 1 and 3 trades do not yield strictly positive profits). This is described more precisely in the next proposition.

Proposition 3. Partially mixed strategy equilibrium: *If*

$$\frac{1}{\gamma}\ln\left(\frac{1+2\alpha}{1+\alpha}\right) + \frac{2+\alpha}{1+2\alpha}l > L > \text{Max}\left[\frac{1}{\gamma}\ln\left(\frac{1+2\alpha}{1-\alpha}\right),\right.$$

$$\left.\frac{1}{\gamma}\left[\ln\left(\frac{1+2\alpha}{1-\alpha}\right) - \frac{2+\alpha}{4-\alpha}\ln\left(\frac{1+\alpha/2}{1-\alpha}\right)\right] + \frac{2+\alpha}{4-\alpha}l\right],$$

then the insider in state u (d) buys the u (d) and m SCC, like the type 1 (3) liquidity trader. Further, there is a $\mu \in\,]0, \frac{1}{2}]$ such that the insider in state m mixes between (i) buying the u and m SCC, like the type 1 liquidity trader, with probability

$\mu \in]0, \frac{1}{2}]$, (*ii*) *not trading with probability* $1 - 2\mu$, *and* (*iii*) *buying the m and d SCC, like the type 3 liquidity trader, with probability* μ.

The set of parameter values for which the partially mixed strategy equilibrium prevails is represented in regions 2 and 3 in Figure 1. Region 2 corresponds to the case where the insider in state m mixes over the type 1, 2, *and* 3 trades (i.e., $\mu < \frac{1}{2}$), whereas region 3 corresponds to the case where she mixes between the type 1 and 3 trades only (i.e., $\mu = \frac{1}{2}$).

As l keeps increasing relative to L, the type 1 trade becomes less attractive for the insider in state μ. Above a certain cut-off level for l, mimicking the type 1 trade generates zero profits for the insider in u. Hence, she is indifferent (and mixes) between the type 1 and 2 trades. Symmetrically, the insider in d mixes between type 2 and 3 trades. In contrast, because l is large, the type 1 and 3 trades are very attractive for the insider in state m, so she mixes between these two trades. This is stated in the next proposition.

Proposition 4. Fully mixed strategy equilibrium: *If*

$$\frac{1}{\gamma}\left[\ln\left(\frac{1+2\alpha}{1-\alpha}\right) - \frac{2+\alpha}{4-\alpha}\ln\left(\frac{1+\alpha/2}{1-\alpha}\right)\right] + \frac{2+\alpha}{4-\alpha}l > L \ and$$

$$l > \frac{1}{\gamma}\ln\left(\frac{1+\alpha/2}{1-\alpha}\right),$$

then there is a $\lambda \in [0, 1]$ *such that the insider in state u mixes between* (*i*) *buying the u and m SCC, like the type 1 liquidity trader, with probability* λ, *and* (*ii*) *not trading, like the type 2 agent, with probability* $1 - \lambda$. *Symmetrically, the insider in state d mixes between the type 2 and type 3 liquidity trades. Further, the insider in state m mixes between the type 1 and 3 liquidity trades with equal probability.*

The set of parameter values for which the fully mixed strategy equilibrium prevails is region 4 in Figure 1. To conclude this section we offer some economic intuition for mixed strategies. Mixed strategies arise in our discrete model because they enable the insider to convexify the strategy space. For example, always mimicking the type 1 liquidity trade after observing that u is realized can be too aggressive a trading strategy because it would lead to too much information revelation. If the insider wants to pursue a less aggressive strategy (to reduce information revelation), she can mix between the type 1 and the type 2 trade. Mixing is more attractive (and arises more often) in the complete market because the introduction of options increases the set of pay-offs which can be attained. For example, insiders with good news can buy either the stock or different calls. To the extent that these trades are substitutable, the insider may find it optimal to mix.

5. ANALYSIS OF THE PURE STRATEGY EQUILIBRIUM

In this section we compare the complete and the incomplete markets in terms of pricing and welfare, for the parameter values such that the pure strategy equilibrium prevails in the incomplete market.

5.1. State Prices

Proposition 5. *When the pure strategy equilibrium prevails in the complete market, the prices of the u, m, and d SCCs are the same in the complete and the incomplete markets.*

The proposition obtains because in both market structures the insider in state u, m, or d, respectively, mimics the trades of the type 1, type 2, and type 3 liquidity traders, respectively. As a result the information structure of the market makers (defined in the proof of the proposition) is the same in the complete market and the incomplete market. Consequently, the updated probabilities (and hence the state prices) of u, m, and d are the same in the two market structures.

5.2. The Profits Earned by the Insider

The numbers of the three SCC which the liquidity traders would buy in a perfect and complete market depend on their liquidity shocks. For example, if L is very large with respect to l, the type 1 liquidity trader would like to buy many u SCC and relatively few m SCC, other things being equal. Now, in the incomplete market, the liquidity trades are constrained by the pay-off patterns of the available securities. In particular, the pay-off pattern of the stock determines the relative number of the u, m, and d SCC that the agents can buy. If L is very large relative to l, the type 1 liquidity trader is constrained by this pay-off pattern. He cannot buy as many u SCC as he would like to because this would involve also buying too many m SCC. This constraint is relaxed in the complete market. Other things being equal (and, in particular, holding prices constant), when L is very large relative to l the type 1 liquidity trader will buy more u SCC and less many m SCC in the complete than in the incomplete market.

Now, the profits of the insider are constrained by the liquidity trades because she must mimic them.[15] In state u the insider would like to buy as many u SCC (and as few m and d SCC) as possible. Consequently, the insider in state u will earn larger profits in the complete market if the type 1 liquidity trader buys more u SCC and less many m SCC in the complete than in the incomplete market.[16] As discussed above this is the case if L is sufficiently large with respect to l. The following proposition states this more precisely:

---

[15] In that sense, the market is not complete for the insider even when the option is traded. Even in that case she cannot freely choose which bundles of SCC to buy, lest she might have too strong an influence on prices.
[16] The case of the insider in state d is symmetric. The insider in state m does not trade in the incomplete market as well as in the complete market when the pure strategies equilibrium prevails.

Proposition 6. *The profits of the insider in the complete market when the pure strategies equilibrium prevails are larger than in the incomplete market if and only if*

$$L > \frac{1}{\gamma} \ln\left(\frac{1 + 2\alpha}{1 - \alpha}\right) + 2l. \tag{5}$$

5.3. The Utility of the Liquidity Traders

In general, there are two differences between the complete and incomplete market cases. First, in the complete market, the liquidity trader can span the three states. Other things being equal this improves his welfare. Second, the prices at which his order is executed are, *in general*, different in the complete and the incomplete markets. Still, as stated in Proposition 5, when the pure strategy equilibrium prevails in the complete market, there is no difference in pricing between the two cases. As a result, for the liquidity trader the only difference between the complete and the incomplete market is that in the latter there is a constraint on the relative numbers of u, m, and d SCC that he can buy. The solution of the maximization problem of the liquidity trader is more efficient without the constraint than with the constraint. Consequently, the introduction of the option increases the welfare of the liquidity traders.[17] Combining this and Proposition 6, the following proposition obtains:

Proposition 7. *If*

$$L > \frac{1}{\gamma} \ln\left(\frac{1 + 2\alpha}{1 - \alpha}\right) + 2l, \tag{6}$$

then the introduction of the option leads to a Pareto improvement.

Under the condition stated in the proposition, both the liquidity trader's expected utility *and* the insider's profits are larger when the option is traded. This is because the introduction of the option creates additional surplus from trade, part of which accrues to the liquidity traders and part of which accrues to the insider.[18]

6. COMPARING THE EQUILIBRIA WITH AND WITHOUT THE OPTION

6.1. Market Breakdown With and Without the Option

As shown in Section 3.2, in the incomplete market case, the condition for no market breakdown relates to the u and m-state shocks. In contrast, in the

---

[17] Note that the expected utility of the liquidity traders is larger in this case when the option is traded, whatever their type (1, 2, or 3).

[18] Note that when the pure strategy equilibrium prevails, but condition 5 is not satisfied, the introduction of the option does not lead to a Pareto improvement, since it reduces the welfare of the insider.

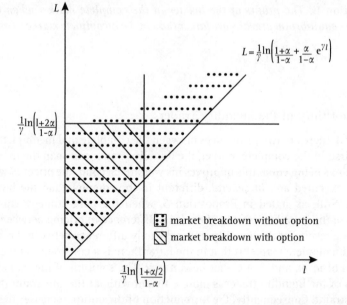

Figure 2. *Market breakdown in the complete and the incomplete markets*

Note: The sets of parameter values for which there is a market breakdown in the complete or in the incomplete market are represented in Figure 2. The former is strictly included in the latter. That is, market breakdown is less likely to occur in the complete market than in the incomplete market.

complete market, as shown in Lemma 2, the condition under which there is no trading in the complete market does not rely on the relative magnitude of the different liquidity shocks. Instead, it is a condition relating to each of the shocks separately. This condition is stated more precisely in the next proposition and is illustrated in Figure 2.

Proposition 8. *When the option is traded, there is no market breakdown if*

$$L > \frac{1}{\gamma} \ln\left(\frac{1 + 2\alpha}{1 - \alpha}\right) \quad or \quad l > \frac{1}{\gamma} \ln\left(\frac{1 + \alpha/2}{1 - \alpha}\right).$$

The right-hand side of the two inequalities is increasing in α. The higher the degree of information asymmetry, the more likely the market breakdown. Also, because the two SCC can be unbundled, there is no market breakdown (i.e., some risk sharing occurs), as long as *one* of the liquidity shocks is large enough to generate trading in the corresponding SCC. Hence, the condition for no market breakdown is less demanding than in the incomplete market case. This is stated in the next corollary and illustrated in Figure 2.

Corollary to Proposition 8. *The set of parameters for which there is a market breakdown when the option is traded is strictly included in the set of parameters for which there is a market breakdown when the option is not traded.*

This is one beneficial consequence of the option for the liquidity traders. By reducing the set of parameters for which there is a market breakdown, the introduction of the option facilitates risk sharing. In particular, if the structure of the liquidity shocks is unlike the payoff structure of the stocks (e.g., if the *u* shock *L* is close to the *m* shock *l*), risk sharing can take place only if the option is traded. This result could be examined empirically by studying the occurrence of trading halts (proxying for market breakdowns) for optioned versus nonoptioned stocks.

6.2. Information Revelation

The stock price (S) is the expectation of the final value of the state (θ), conditional on the order flow. The difference between this conditional expectation and the realized final value of the state, $(S - \theta)$, can be interpreted as an estimation error. The lower the variance of this estimation error, the higher the informational efficiency of the market. So we define the informational efficiency of the market as $[V(S - \theta)]^{-1}$.[19] When there is a market breakdown, there is no trade on which the market makers can condition their expectations. Hence, the estimation error is simply the unconditional variance of the final state variable $(2/3\sigma^2)$.

Proposition 9

- *When there is no market breakdown in the incomplete market and the pure strategy equilibrium prevails in the complete market, then the informational efficiency of the market is not altered by the introduction of the option.*
- *When there is no market breakdown in the incomplete market and the (partially or fully) mixed equilibrium prevails in the complete market, then the informational efficiency of the market is lower when the option is traded.*
- *When there is a market breakdown in the incomplete but not in the complete market, then the informational efficiency of the market is higher when the option is traded.*

The introduction of the option increases the set of payoff profiles that can be traded. This has two countervailing effects on the informational efficiency of the market. On the one hand, as shown above, the introduction of the option makes it less likely that the market will break down. Consequently, it enables trades to take place and information to be revealed through trades. This tends to increase the informational efficiency of the market. On the other hand, the introduction of the

---

[19] Kyle (1985) or Grossman and Stiglitz (1980) use conditional variances to measure the informational efficiency of the market. This is because, in their normal distribution setting, conditional variances are constant. Our approach is similar to theirs, however.

option increases the set of profitable trades for the insider. For example, without the option the insider can only buy the stock in u and sell it in d but cannot trade profitably in m. In contrast, when the option is traded, in the two mixed equilibria, the insider in state m can mix over the type 1 and type 2 liquidity trades. This mixing blurs the informational content of the type 1 (or type 3) trades and hence reduces the informational efficiency of the market.

7. THE INFORMATIVENESS OF THE TRADES IN THE STOCK AND THE OPTION AND THE BID-ASK SPREAD

7.1. The Informativeness of the Trades in the Stock and the Option

We now describe the equilibrium prices and trades in terms of the actual securities, rather than in terms of the state contingent claims. For simplicity, normalize m to σ.[20]

When several options with different strikes are written on the stock, all but one of these options are redundant. As a result there is an indeterminacy in the trades in the actual securities. Any given payoff profile can be generated by several different trades. We focus on one reasonable trading pattern by assuming that the liquidity traders first use the stock to hedge the bulk of their risk exposure and then select the simplest option trade that matches their actual trades to their optimal hedge.

For example, in the case where there is no asymmetric information, the type 1 liquidity trader wants to buy L units of the u SCC and l units of the m SCC. To do this he can buy l/σ shares of stock. This yields $2l$ in u, l in m, and 0 in d. Thus, the trader is perfectly hedged in states m and d. Given this stock purchase, the type 1 agent need only trade $(L - 2l)/(u - K)$ calls with strike $K(m < K < u)$ to achieve perfect hedging of the u-state shock. This call can be interpreted as an out-of-the-money call, to the extent that the strike is above the initial value of the stock, its unconditional expectation, m. Note that the trade in the out-of-the-money call is a purchase or a sale according to whether L is larger or smaller than $2l$.

Now consider the liquidity trades in the complete market with asymmetric information described in Lemma 2. To hedge his m-state shock, the type 1 liquidity trader can buy $[l - (1/\gamma)\ln(\pi_{m,1}/\pi_{d,1})]/\sigma$ stocks. This yields $2[l - (1/\gamma)\ln(\pi_{m,1}/\pi_{d,1})]$ SCC in state u and $[l - (1/\gamma)\ln(\pi_{m,1}/\pi_{d,1})]$ SCC in state m. To fine tune his state-u hedge, the type 1 liquidity trader can trade

$$\frac{L - (1/\gamma)\ln(\pi_{u,1}/\pi_{d,1}) - 2[l - (1/\gamma)\ln(\pi_{m,1}/\pi_{d,1})]}{u - K}$$

---

[20] This simplifies the analysis without altering the nature of the problem. This normalization amounts to subtracting $m - \sigma$ to the payoff of the stock in each state. This corresponds to the payoff generated by a levered position in the stock.

out-of-the-money calls, with strike $K \in]m, u[$. Note that, as in the symmetric information case, this can be a purchase or a sale. Consider, for example, the pure strategy equilibrium (described in Proposition 2). Substituting the values of the state prices (given in Table 1), it is easy to check that the type 1 trade in the out-of-the-money call is a purchase if and only if

$$L > \frac{1}{\gamma} \ln \left(\frac{1 + 2\alpha}{1 - \alpha} \right) + 2l.$$

Now the insider in state u mimics this trade; hence, if the above inequality does not hold she sells the call. Consequently, the sale of the call is not necessarily a negative signal. This is consistent with empirical results that options trades have little predictive power about the future evolution of the stock [see, for example, Vijh (1990) or Berkman (1993)].[21] Our description of the insider trades contrasts with the theoretical results of Back (1993), where the insider with good news buys the out-of-the-money call. This difference reflects the fact that Back (1993) considers exogenous liquidity trading, unaffected by the in- or out-of-the-moneyness of the call. In contrast, in our analysis, liquidity trading is endogenous. As a result, lack of liquidity trading in far out-of-the-money options can arise endogenously (consistent with casual empirical observation) and deter the insider from trading too aggressively in these options.

7.2. The Bid–Ask Spread in the Stock Market

Our analysis can also be related to empirical studies of the effect of the introduction of options on the bid-ask spread in the stock market. For example, Fedenia and Grammatikos (1992) find that the reaction of the spread is ambiguous—it can either increase or decrease after the introduction of the option. To shed some light on this issue in our simple model, consider the case described in the previous subsection, where the type 1 liquidity trader buys the stock while the type 3 liquidity trader sells it (whether the option is traded or not, as long as there is no market breakdown). In this case the ask and bid prices are

$$A = \pi_{u,1} u + \pi_{m,1} m + \pi_{d,1} d = m + (\pi_{u,1} - \pi_{d,1})\sigma \quad \text{and}$$
$$B = \pi_{u,3} u + \pi_{m,3} m + \pi_{d,3} d = m + (\pi_{u,3} - \pi_{d,3})\sigma.$$

The ask price is the sum of (i) the unconditional expectation of the final value of the stock (m) and (ii) the update reflecting the informational content of the purchase $[(\pi_{u,1} - \pi_{d,1})\sigma]$. The latter is strong if the insider buys aggressively when she observes good news about the final value of the stock. Symmetrically, the

---

[21] Our theoretical analysis points at a potential statistical problem in Vijh (1990). He regresses changes in option prices on simultaneous changes in the stock price. In contrast, our analysis shows that both the option and the stock price changes are likely to result from the insider trades and be jointly endogenous. Easley, O'Hara, and Srinivas (1993) analyze this joint endogeneity.

informational content of a sale is $(\pi_{u,3} - \pi_{d,3})\sigma$. The spread $(A - B)$ is the sum of the informational content of the purchase of the stock and the informational content of the sale. The spread is large when the insider responds strongly to her private information. Consequently, the spread is larger (tighter) when the option is traded when it is not if the insider responds more (less) aggressively to her private information.

The aggressiveness of the insider's strategy depends on the attractiveness of the liquidity trade she can mimic. A polar case is the fully mixed strategy equilibrium analyzed in Proposition 4. In this case the insider in state u is indifferent between mimicking the type 1 trade (which involves buying the stock) and not trading. This is because she earns zero profits when mimicking the type 1 trade. In this case the insider in state u does not react aggressively to her private information; when she observes that the final state of the world is u, she only buys the stock with probability λ. The bid and ask quotes in this equilibrium reflect this weak response of the insider to her private signal. The ask is $A = m + \alpha\lambda/[(1 - \alpha)/(2 + \alpha\lambda)]\sigma$, and the bid is $B = m - \alpha\lambda/[(1 - \alpha)/(2 + \alpha\lambda)]\sigma$. The spread is $2\alpha\lambda/[(1 - \alpha)/(2 + \alpha\lambda)]\sigma$. In contrast, in the incomplete market, the insider reacts more strongly to strong private signals: she always buys the stock on observing that the final value of the stock is u and sells it on observing d. As shown in Section 3.3, in this case the ask and bid prices are $A = m + \alpha\sigma$ and $B = m - \alpha\sigma$ and the spread is $2\alpha\sigma$. Consequently, the spread in the stock market is larger in the incomplete market than in the complete market when the fully mixed strategies equilibrium prevails.

The general point underlying this example is that the introduction of the option leads to a change in the spread because it alters the portfolios of SCC which the insider can trade and, as a result, her responsiveness to the private signal. If the introduction of the option leads to less (more) attractive trades for insiders with strong signals (u or d), it reduces (increases) the responsiveness of the insider to these signals and consequently reduces (increases) the spread.

8. CONCLUSION

This article studies the effect of the introduction of an option that completes the market on risk sharing and information revelation. Thus, we study the interaction between information asymmetry and market incompleteness.

Market incompleteness reduces the *effectiveness* of hedging. In incomplete markets, the payoff structure of the securities does not perfectly match the structure of the risks faced by the liquidity traders. For example, in our model, this problem arises when the only risky security is the stock and when there is not much difference between the state-dependent endowment shocks of the liquidity trader in the good state and in the bad state. In this case the liquidity trader cannot efficiently hedge by trading the stock.

On the other hand, asymmetric information increases the *cost* of trading in financial markets. Thus, when the market is incomplete and the proportion of insiders is large, it is both ineffective and costly to trade. Consequently, the market can break down (i.e., there is no liquidity trading). Completing the market by introducing the option alleviates this problem and can permit some risk sharing.

To the extent that the option is necessary for trading to occur, it is also necessary for private information to be revealed. In contrast, when there is no market breakdown in the complete market, the introduction of the option can reduce the degree of information revelation. In the incomplete market the insider with very good (or very bad) information buys (or sells) the stock, while the insider with more neutral signals does not trade. In the complete market, when the endowment shocks of the liquidity traders are not too different across states, they design less extreme trades than the purchase (or the sale) of the stock. For example they can buy the stock and sell the out-of-the-money call. Such trades can be attractive both for the insider with strong signals and for the insider with more neutral signals. That insiders with different signals mimic these trades blurs their information content. More generally, the introduction of the option complexifies the strategies of the insiders. As a result the information content of trades is more difficult to interpret for the market makers. This tends to reduce the degree of information revelation in the marketplace.

Similarly, the introduction of the option has ambiguous consequences on the profitability of insider trades. When the option is needed to avoid market breakdown, its introduction increases the insider's profit. When the liquidity trades in the complete market are less attractive for the insider, the introduction of the option reduces her profits.

Our analysis has implications for the study of endogenous market creation or security design. To the extent that the option increases the profits of the informed agent, the latter has an incentive to set up nonredundant markets. Note that, even if it is well known that the insider trades in this newly set-up market, liquidity traders may find it optimal to use it. In the pure strategy equilibrium (described in Proposition 2), the adverse selection cost is outweighed by the improved hedging opportunities. This could explain why markets created by agents who are likely to be informed attract trades. Examples of this phenomenon are the over-the-counter markets in derivatives on oil or commodities set up by nonfinancial firms that are likely to have private information, such as Elf Aquitaine (Elf Trading) or Cargill.

Another example of the interaction between securities design, asymmetric information, and market completeness is the case of corporations issuing securities. Managers designing securities are likely to subsequently obtain private information on the basis of which they can trade at the expense of the shareholders [see Diamond and Verrecchia (1991)]. To reduce the cost of capital, the managers may want to precommit not to trade on the basis of such private information. Our analysis sheds some light on this issue. If the introduction of the option reduces the profits of the insider (as is the case, for example, in the pure strategy equilibrium, when condition 5 does not hold), the managers might have an incentive, ex ante, to issue securities that improve the spanning of the markets.

Appendix

Proof of Lemma 1. The objective of the type 1 liquidity trader is

$$\max_{Q_1} = \tfrac{1}{3} U(-L + Q_1(u - A)) + \tfrac{1}{3} U(-l + Q_1(m - A))$$
$$+ \tfrac{1}{3} U(Q_1(d - A)),$$

where the utility function is exponential with CARA coefficient equal to γ. The first-order condition is

$$(u - A)e^{-\gamma(-L + Q_1(u - A))} + (m - A)e^{-\gamma(-l + Q_1(m - A))}$$
$$+ (d - A)e^{-\gamma(Q_1(d - A))} = 0.$$

Simplifying by $e^{-\gamma Q_1(d - A)}$:

$$(u - A)e^{-\gamma(-L + 2Q_1\sigma)} + (m - A)e^{-\gamma(-l + Q_1\sigma)} + (d - A) = 0.$$

Changing variables, we set $X = e^{-\gamma Q_1\sigma}$, or equivalently, $Q_1 = (1/\gamma\sigma)\ln(1/X)$, and we get a quadratic equation:

$$(u - A)e^{-\gamma(-L)}X^2 + (m - A)e^{-\gamma(-l)}X + (d - A) = 0.$$

Since $(u - A)e^{-\gamma(-L)} > 0$ and $d - A < 0$, there is a unique positive root. The discriminant is

$$\Delta = (m - A)^2 e^{2\gamma l} + 4(u - A)(A - d)e^{\gamma L} > 0.$$

The positive solution is

$$\frac{(A - m)e^{\gamma l} + \sqrt{(A - m)^2 e^{\gamma l} + 4(u - A)(A - d)e^{\gamma L}}}{2(u - A)e^{\gamma L}}.$$

Imposing that Q_1 must be positive (otherwise, the price is the bid B):

$$Q_1 = \text{Max}\left[0, \frac{1}{\gamma\sigma}\ln\left(\frac{2(u - A)e^{\gamma L}}{(A - m)e^{\gamma l} + \sqrt{(A - m)^2 e^{2\gamma l} + 4(u - A)(A - d)e^{\gamma L}}}\right)\right].$$

$\square$

Proof of Corollary to Lemma 1. The corollary to Lemma 1 obtains after straightforward manipulations of the expression in the lemma. $\square$

Proof of Proposition 1. If the insider buys Q, in state u, sells Q in state d, and does not trade in state m, then

$$\pi_{u,1} \equiv P(u \mid \text{buy} Q) = \frac{P(\text{buy} Q \mid u)P(u)}{P(\text{buy} Q, u) + P(\text{buy} Q, m) + P(\text{buy} Q, d)}$$

$$= \frac{P(\text{buy} Q \mid u)P(u)}{P(\text{buy} Q \mid u)P(u) + P(\text{buy} Q \mid m)P(m) + P(\text{buy} Q \mid d)P(d)}.$$

Now $P(u) = P(m) = P(d) = \frac{1}{3}$, so we can simplify the state probabilities. Also,

$$P(\text{buy} Q \mid u) = P(\text{buy} Q \mid u, \text{insider})P(\text{insider})$$
$$+ P(\text{buy} Q \mid u, \text{liquidity})P(\text{liquidity})$$
$$= P(\text{buy} Q \mid u, \text{insider})\alpha$$
$$+ P(\text{buy} Q \mid u, \text{liquidity})(1 - \alpha).$$

Using the insider's strategy and given that the only liquidity trader who buys the stock is the type 1 trader, $P(\text{buy} Q \mid u) = \alpha + (1 - \alpha)/3$. Similarly, $P(\text{buy } Q \mid m) = P(\text{buy} Q \mid d) = (1 - \alpha)/3$. Hence, $\pi_{u,1} = \alpha + (1 - \alpha)/3 = (1 + 2\alpha)/3$. Similarly, $\pi_{m,1} \equiv P(m \mid \text{buy } Q) = \pi_{d,1} \equiv P(d \mid \text{buy } Q) = (1 - \alpha)/3$. As a result, $A = \pi_{u,1}u + \pi_{m,1}m + \pi_{d,1}d = m + (\pi_{u,1} - \pi_{d,1})\sigma = m + \alpha\sigma$. Similarly, $B = m - \alpha\sigma$.

The value of Q, the quantity traded by the type 1 liquidity trader, is obtained by substituting the value of the asking price in Lemma 1.

Finally, we discuss the insider trades. Consider the insider in state u. First consider the equilibrium trades. The insider may either buy Q stocks, sell Q stocks, or do nothing. The insider is obviously better off buying the stock than selling it or doing nothing. Now consider deviations from the equilibrium trades. Could the insider be better off buying any other amount of shares than Q? The answer depends on the out-of-equilibrium beliefs of the market makers. One set of beliefs that support the equilibrium is that the market makers give probability 1 to the $u(d)$ state if they observe any other purchase (sale) than the equilibrium amount Q. These beliefs are reasonable because of the following.

- Obviously, no purchase could stem from the insider in d.
- Neither could it stem from the insider in m. This is because, since the insider in d never buys the stock, the conditional expectation of the final value of the stock given a buy order must be at least as large as the unconditional expectation, m.
- The purchase of any other amount than Q could not stem from the liquidity traders either. This is because the liquidity traders are price takers, so they do not anticipate the price to change as they alter their trades. As a result they have no reason to deviate from Q, which is their optimal demand at the equilibrium price.

The last argument actually implies that, *with price-taking liquidity traders*, the equilibrium is unique. Consider a candidate equilibrium where the quantity traded would be different from Q, say Q'. In that case, the insider in u would buy Q', the insider in state d would sell it, and the insider in m would not trade. As a result the equilibrium asking price for quantity Q' would be $m + \alpha\sigma$ as in the equilibrium described in Proposition 1. Could that be an equilibrium? No, because at that price the optimal amount for the liquidity traders would be $Q \neq Q'$. So, because they are price takers, the liquidity traders would deviate from the equilibrium and trade Q. Given that deviation, the market makers would have no reason to quote an asking price higher than $m + \alpha\sigma$ (even if the insider also deviated to Q). So the liquidity traders would be actually better off deviating. This result simply reflects that multiplicity problems arising with strategic agents are mitigated with competitive agents. If liquidity traders were strategic (i.e., if they anticipated that the difference quantities would be executed at different prices, reflecting out-of-equilibrium as well as equilibrium beliefs), then we would get multiple equilibria.   □

Proof of Lemma 2. The objective of the type 1 liquidity trader to choose $Q_{u,1}$ and $Q_{m,1}$ to maximize

$$\tfrac{1}{3} U(-L + Q_{u,1}(1 - \pi_{u,1}) - Q_{m,1}\pi_{m,1})$$
$$+ \tfrac{1}{3} U(-l - Q_{u,1}\pi_{u,1} + Q_{m,1}(1 - \pi_{m,1}))$$
$$+ \tfrac{1}{3} U(-Q_{u,1}\pi_{u,1} - Q_{m,1}\pi_{m,1}),$$

where the utility function is exponential with CARA coefficient equal to γ. The first-order condition with respect to $Q_{u,1}$ is

$$(1 - \pi_{u,1}) e^{-\gamma(-L + Q_{u,1}(1-\pi_{u,1}) - Q_{m,1}\pi_{m,1})} - \pi_{u,1} e^{-\gamma(-l - Q_{u,1}\pi_{u,1} + Q_{m,1}(1-\pi_{m,1}))}$$
$$- \pi_{u,1} e^{-\gamma(-Q_{u,1}\pi_{u,1} - Q_{m,1}\pi_{m,1})} = 0.$$

Simplifying by $e^{-\gamma(-Q_{u,1}\pi_{u,1} - Q_{m,1}\pi_{m,1})}$,

$$(1 - \pi_{u,1}) e^{\gamma(L - Q_{u,1})} - \pi_{u,1} e^{\gamma(l - Q_{m,1})} - \pi_{u,1} = 0.$$

Similarly the first-order condition with respect to $Q_{m,1}$ is

$$-\pi_{m,1} e^{\gamma(L - Q_{u,1})} + (1 - \pi_{m,1}) e^{\gamma(l - Q_{m,1})} - \pi_{m,1} = 0.$$

Setting $X_{u,1} \equiv e^{-\gamma Q_{u,1}}$ and $X_{m,1} \equiv e^{-\gamma Q_{m,1}}$, we have a linear system. The determinant is $D = \pi_{d,1} > 0$. The solutions are $X_{u,1} = (\pi_{u,1}/\pi_{d,1})e^{\gamma L}$ and $X_{m,1} = (\pi_{m,1}/\pi_{d,1})e^{\gamma L}$, which yields the values of $Q_{u,1}$ and $Q_{m,1}$ in the lemma.   □

Proof of Proposition 2. First consider the liquidity trades. Suppose that, in equilibrium, the insider in state $u(d)$ always mimics the trade of the type 1 (3) liquidity trader $T_1(T_3)$ and that the insider in state m never trades. As a result the updated probabilities of the market makers are the same as in the incomplete market. Substituting these probabilities in the quantities in Lemma 2, we obtain the equilibrium quantities given in Table 1. In particular, one can check that, for the parameter set where the pure strategy equilibrium prevails (condition 4),

$$L > \frac{1}{\gamma} \ln\left(\frac{1 + 2\alpha}{1 - \alpha}\right) + \frac{2 + \alpha}{1 + 2\alpha} l,$$

and, for the equilibrium prices and quantities, there is no market breakdown, $Q_{u,1}$ and $Q_{m,1}$ are strictly positive.

We now turn to the insider's trades. We show that under condition 4 the insider finds it optimal to use the pure strategy described in the proposition. We consider only the choice by the insider between the different equilibrium trades (used by the type 1, 2, and 3 liquidity traders). Out-of-equilibrium trades can be eliminated by invoking similar arguments, as in Proposition 1.

For the insider in state u, the incentive compatibility constraint is that she must be better off using the same trade as the type 1 liquidity trader than using the same trade as the type 2 liquidity trader. The condition is $Q_{u,1}(1 - \pi_{u,1}) - Q_{m,1}\pi_{m,1} > 0$ or $Q_{u,1} > Q_{m,1}\pi_{m,1}/(1 - \pi_{u,1})$. The incentive compatibility condition for the insider in state m is

$$-\pi_{u,1}Q_{u,1} + (1 - \pi_{m,1})Q_{m,1} < 0$$

or

$$Q_{u,1} > Q_{m,1}\frac{1 - \pi_{m,1}}{\pi_{u,1}}.$$

Only the type m constraint is relevant because $(1 - \pi_{m,1})/(\pi_{u,1}) > (\pi_{m,1})/(1 - \pi_{u,1})$. Substituting the values of $Q_{u,1}, Q_{m,1}, \pi_{u,1}, \pi_{m,1}$, the type m incentive compatibility constraint can be rewritten

$$L > \frac{1}{\gamma} \ln\left(\frac{1 + 2\alpha}{1 - \alpha}\right) + l\frac{2 + \alpha}{1 + 2\alpha},$$

which is condition 4 in the proposition. ☐

Proof of Proposition 3. In the partially mixed strategy equilibrium described in Proposition 3, the insider in state u mimics the type 1 liquidity trade (T_1), the insider in state d mimics the type 3 liquidity trade (T_3), and the insider in state m mixes over the type 1 liquidity trade (with probability $\mu \in [0, \frac{1}{2}]$), the type 3 liquidity trade (with probability $\mu \in [0, \frac{1}{2}]$), and the type 2 liquidity trade (T_2) (with probability $1 - 2\mu$). For these trades, the probability of the state u, conditional on the type 1 trade, is

$$\pi_{u,1} \equiv P(u \mid T_1) = \frac{P(T_1 \mid u)P(u)}{P(T_1, u) + P(T_1, m) + P(T_1, d)}$$

$$= \frac{P(T_1 \mid u)P(u)}{P(T_1, u)P(u) + P(T_1, m)P(m) + P(\text{buy}T_1 \mid d)P(d)}.$$

Now $P(u) = P(m) = P(d) = \frac{1}{3}$, so we can simplify the state probabilities. Also,

$$P(T_1 \mid u) = P(T_1 \mid u, \text{insider})P(\text{insider})$$
$$+ P(T_1 \mid u, \text{liquidity})P(\text{liquidity})$$
$$= P(T_1 \mid u, \text{insider})\alpha + P(T_1 \mid u, \text{liquidity})(1 - \alpha).$$

Given that the liquidity trader can be of type 1 with probability $\frac{1}{3}$, that the insider in state u always mimics T_1, and that the insider in state m mimics T_1 with probability μ,

$$\pi_{u,1} = \frac{\alpha + \dfrac{1-\alpha}{3}}{\left(\alpha + \dfrac{1-\alpha}{3}\right) + \left(\alpha\mu + \dfrac{1-\alpha}{3}\right) + \left(\dfrac{1-\alpha}{3}\right)} = \frac{\alpha + \dfrac{1-\alpha}{3}}{1 + \alpha\mu}.$$

Similarly, $\pi_{m,1} = [\alpha\mu + (1 - \alpha)/3]/(1 + \alpha\mu)$ and $\pi_{d,1} = [(1 - \alpha)/3]/(1 + \alpha\mu)$.

Substituting these conditional probabilities in Lemma 2, one obtains the liquidity trades described in Table 1. One can check that, when

$$\frac{1}{\gamma}\ln\left(\frac{1+2\alpha}{1-\alpha}\right) + \frac{2+\alpha}{1+2\alpha}l > L > \max\left\{\frac{1}{\gamma}\ln\left(\frac{1+2\alpha}{1-\alpha}\right),\right.$$

$$\left.\frac{1}{\gamma}\left[\ln\left(\frac{1+2\alpha}{1-\alpha}\right) - \frac{2+\alpha}{4-\alpha}\ln\left(\frac{1+\alpha/2}{1-\alpha}\right)\right] + \frac{2+\alpha}{4-\alpha}l\right\},$$

there is no market breakdown; $Q_{u,1}$ and $Q_{m,1}$ are strictly positive.

Finally, we check that for these parameter values the insider finds it optimal to mimic T_1 in u and T_3 and d and is indifferent between T_1, T_2, and T_3 in m. Consider the insider in state u. (The case of the insider in state d is symmetric and is not described.) Obviously, she will not mimic the type 3 trade (which involves buying the m and d SCC). The incentive compatibility condition for her is that mimicking the type 1 trade be more profitable than mimicking the type 2 trade; that is,[22] $Q_{u,1}(1 - \pi_{u,1}) - Q_{m,1}\pi_{m,1} > 0$. Or

$$Q_{u,1} > Q_{m,1}\frac{\pi_{m,1}}{1 - \pi_{u,1}}.$$

---

[22] As in the previous proposition, we focus on equilibrium trades only.

Consider the insider in state m. Two cases must be distinguished. Either $\mu < \frac{1}{2}$ and the incentive compatibility condition is

$$-\pi_{u,1} Q_{u,1} + (1 - \pi_{m,1}) Q_{m,1} = 0.$$

Or $\mu = \frac{1}{2}$ and the incentive compatibility condition is

$$-\pi_{u,1} Q_{u,1} + (1 - \pi_{m,1}) Q_{m,1} > 0.$$

1. We first analyze the case where $\mu = \frac{1}{2}$. In this case the i.c. condition for the insider in state m is

$$Q_{u,1} < Q_{m,1} \frac{1 - \pi_{m,1}}{\pi_{u,1}}.$$

In contrast with the pure strategy equilibrium, both the type u and type m constraints are relevant. They combine to

$$\frac{1 - \pi_{m,1}}{\pi_{u,1}} Q_{m,1} > Q_{u,1} > \frac{\pi_{m,1}}{1 - \pi_{u,1}} Q_{m,1}. \tag{A1}$$

Substituting the quantities from Lemma 2 and the conditional probabilities evaluated at $\mu = \frac{1}{2}$, the i.c. condition (7) is

$$\frac{2 + \alpha}{1 + 2\alpha} \left[1 - \frac{1}{\gamma} \ln\left(\frac{1 + \alpha/2}{1 - \alpha} \right) \right] > L$$

$$- \frac{1}{\gamma} \ln\left(\frac{1 + 2\alpha}{1 - \alpha} \right) > \frac{\alpha + 2}{4 - \alpha} \left[1 - \frac{1}{\gamma} \ln\left(\frac{1 + \alpha/2}{1 - \alpha} \right) \right].$$

Or

$$\frac{1}{\gamma} \ln\left[\left(\frac{1 + 2\alpha}{1 - \alpha} \right) - \frac{2 + \alpha}{1 + 2\alpha} \ln\left(\frac{1 + \alpha/2}{1 - \alpha} \right) \right] + \left(\frac{2 + \alpha}{1 + 2\alpha} \right) l > L$$

$$> \frac{1}{\gamma} \left[\ln\left(\frac{1 + 2\alpha}{1 - \alpha} \right) - \left(\frac{2 + \alpha}{4 - \alpha} \right) \ln\left(\frac{1 + \alpha/2}{1 - \alpha} \right) \right] + \left(\frac{2 + \alpha}{4 - \alpha} \right) l.$$

This corresponds to region 3 in Figure 1. One can check that, in this region, when the insider follows the partially mixed strategy with $\mu = \frac{1}{2}$, $Q_{u,1}$ and $Q_{m,1}$ are strictly positive.

2. Second, we analyze the case where $\mu < \frac{1}{2}$. In this case the i.c. condition for the insider in state m is

$$Q_{u,1} = Q_{m,1} \frac{1 - \pi_{m,1}}{\pi_{u,1}}.$$

As in the pure strategy equilibrium, the type u constraint is not relevant; only the type m constraint is relevant. Substituting the quantities from Lemma 2 and the updated probabilities, for $\mu \in [0, \frac{1}{2}]$ the condition is

$$\left[L - \frac{1}{\gamma}\ln\left(\frac{1+2\alpha}{1-\alpha}\right)\right] = \left[t - \frac{1}{\gamma}\ln\left(\frac{1+\alpha(3\mu-1)}{1-\alpha}\right)\right]\left(\frac{2+\alpha}{1+2\alpha}\right).$$

The right-hand side of this equation is continuous, decreasing in μ, and equal to $l(2+\alpha)/(1+2\alpha)$ for $\mu = 0$ and $[(2+\alpha)/(1+2\alpha)]\{l - (1/\gamma)\ln[(1+\alpha/2)/(1-\alpha)]\}$ for $\mu = \frac{1}{2}$. When

$$\frac{1}{\gamma}\ln\left(\frac{1+2\alpha}{1-\alpha}\right) + l\frac{2+\alpha}{1+2\alpha} > L$$

$$> \frac{1}{\gamma}\left[\ln\left(\frac{1+2\alpha}{1-\alpha}\right) - \frac{2+\alpha}{1+2\alpha}\ln\left(\frac{1+\alpha/2}{1-\alpha}\right)\right] + l\frac{2+\alpha}{1+2\alpha},$$

which corresponds to region 2 in Figure 1, one can see from Figure 3A that there exists a probability $\mu \in]0, \frac{1}{2}[$ such that the incentive compatibility condition holds. To conclude the proof, one can check that, for the parameter values in region 2, when the insider plays the partially mixed strategy with $u \in]0, \frac{1}{2}[$ there is no market breakdown. □

Proof of Proposition 4. In the fully mixed strategies equilibrium, the insider mixes between the type 1 trade (T_1), with probability λ, and the type 2 trade (T_2), with probability $1 - \lambda$. The insider mixes with equal probabilities between (T_1) and (T_2).

First, we analyze the conditional probabilities in this equilibrium. Following the same reasoning as in the two previous propositions,

$$\pi_{u,1} \equiv P(u \,|\, T_1) = \frac{\alpha\lambda + (1-\alpha)/3}{1 + \alpha\lambda - \alpha/2},$$

$$\pi_{m,1} \equiv P(m \,|\, T_1) = \frac{\alpha/2 + (1-\alpha)/3}{1 + \alpha\lambda - \alpha/2},$$

and

$$\pi_{d,1} \equiv P(d \,|\, T_1) = \frac{(1-\alpha)/3}{1 + \alpha\lambda - \alpha/2}.$$

Next, we turn to the incentive compatibility condition of the insider.[23] The incentive compatibility of the insider in state u is

$$Q_{u,1} = Q_{m,1}\frac{\pi_{m,1}}{1 - \pi_{u,1}}.$$

---

[23] Again we focus on the equilibrium actions.

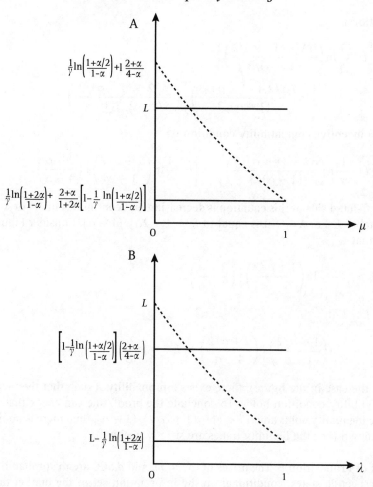

Figure 3. *Graphical analysis of the existence of equilibrium mixing probabilities in the partially and fully mixed strategy equilibria*

Note: Figure 3A illustrates that, in the partially mixed strategy equilibrium, there exists a value of μ (the mixing probability) for which the equilibrium indifference condition is satisfied. This value is at the intersection of the horizontal line (L) and the downward sloping curve.

Figure 3B illustrates that, in the fully mixed strategy equilibrium, there exists a value of λ (the mixing probability) for which the equilibrium indifference condition is satisfied. This value is at the intersection of the horizontal line (L) and the downward sloping curve.

In state m it is

$$Q_{u,1} < Q_{m,1}\frac{1-\pi_{m,1}}{\pi_{u,1}}.$$

Only the u-state condition is relevant. Substituting in the condition the quantities obtained in Lemma 2 and the above-computed conditional probabilities, the condition is

$$\left[L - \frac{1}{\gamma}\ln\left(\frac{\alpha\lambda + (1-\alpha)/3}{(1-\alpha)/3}\right)\right]$$

$$= \left[l - \frac{1}{\gamma}\ln\left(\frac{\alpha/2 + (1-\alpha)/3}{(1-\alpha)/3}\right)\right]\left(\frac{\alpha/2 + (1-\alpha)/3}{\alpha/2 + 2/3(1-\alpha)}\right).$$

So the incentive compatibility condition is

$$\left[L - \frac{1}{\gamma}\ln\left(\frac{\alpha\lambda + (1-\alpha)/3}{(1-\alpha)/3}\right)\right] = \left[l - \frac{1}{\gamma}\ln\left(\frac{1+\alpha/2}{1-\alpha}\right)\right]\left(\frac{2+\alpha}{4-\alpha}\right).$$

The left-hand side of this equation is decreasing and continuous in λ. For $\lambda = 0$ it is equal to L. For $\lambda = 1$ it is equal to $L - (1 + 2\alpha)/(1 - \alpha)$. Consider Figure 3B. Note that

$$L > \left[l - \frac{1}{\gamma}\ln\left(\frac{1+\alpha/2}{1-\alpha}\right)\right]\left(\frac{2+\alpha}{4-\alpha}\right),$$

since $L > l$. If

$$\left[l - \frac{1}{\gamma}\ln\left(\frac{1+\alpha/2}{1-\alpha}\right)\right]\left(\frac{2+\alpha/2}{4-\alpha}\right) > L - \frac{1+2\alpha}{1-\alpha}$$

(as is the case in the figure), there exists a probability λ such that the incentive compatibility condition holds. To conclude the proof, one can check that, if the above inequality holds and if $l < (1/\gamma(1 + \alpha/2)/(1 - \alpha)$, then there is no market breakdown (i.e., the liquidity trades are strictly positive). □

Proof of Proposition 5. The prices of the u, m, and d SCC are the probabilities of the respective states, conditional on the information set of the market makers. These conditional probabilities are the same in the complete market and the incomplete market because the information sets of the market makers are the same. To see this, first consider the set of all possible states of the world in the two market structures. The states of the world are differentiated by the final value of the stock (u, m, or d) and the identity of the trader: insider (denoted i), type 1 (denoted T_1), type 2 (denoted T_2), or type 3 (denoted T_3) liquidity trader. So there are 12 states, and the state space Ω is

$$\Omega = \{(u, i), (u, T_1), (u, T_2), (u, T_3), (m, i), (m, T_1), (m, T_2), (m, T_3),$$
$$(d, i), (d, T_1), (d, T_2), (d, T_3)\}.$$

In the incomplete market the insider in state u always buys the stock, like the type 1 liquidity trader; the insider in state m never trades, like the type 2 liquidity trader; and the insider in state d always sells the stock, like the type 3 liquidity trader. So the information structure of the market makers is the following partition of the state space:

$$\{[(u, i), (u, T_1), (m, T_1), (d, T_1)], [(m, i), (u, T_2), (m, T_2), (d, T_2)],$$
$$[(d, i), (u, T_3), (m, T_3), (d, T_3)]\}.$$

This reflects that, for example, the market makers cannot differentiate the purchase of the stock from the insider in state u from the purchase of the stock by the type 1 liquidity trader in state m but that they can differentiate it from the sale of the stock by the type 3 liquidity trader.

Similarly, in the complete market, in the pure strategy equilibrium, the insider always mimics the type 1 trade in state u, the type 2 trade in state m, and the type 3 trade in state d. Hence, the informational structure of the market makers is the same partition as above. ☐

Proof of Proposition 6. Both in the incomplete market and in the complete market pure strategy equilibrium, the insider mimics the type 1 trade in u, the type 2 trade in m, and the type 3 trade in d. She earns no profit in state m, and, because of the symmetry of the game, her profits in u are equal to her profits in d. So we need only compare the insider profits in u when the option is traded and when it is not.

In state u the insider's profit when the option is not traded is

$$(u - A)Q = \frac{1 - \alpha}{\gamma} \ln\left(\frac{2(1 - \alpha)e^{\gamma L}}{\alpha e^{\gamma l} + \sqrt{\alpha^2 e^{2\gamma l} + 4(1 - \alpha^2)e^{\gamma L}}}\right).$$

In state u the insider's profit when the option is traded is

$$(1 - \pi_{u,1})Q_{u,1} - \pi_{m,1}Q_{m,1} = \frac{1 - \alpha}{3}\left\{2\left[L - \frac{1}{\gamma}\ln\left(\frac{1 + 2\alpha}{1 - \alpha}\right)\right] - l\right\}.$$

The insider's profit is larger when the option is traded if

$$\frac{2}{3\gamma}L - \frac{2}{3}\ln\left(\frac{1 + 2\alpha}{1 - \alpha}\right) - \frac{\gamma l}{3}$$
$$> \ln\left(\frac{2(1 - \alpha)e^{\gamma L}}{\alpha e^{\gamma l} + \sqrt{\alpha^2 e^{2\gamma l} + 4(1 - \alpha^2)e^{\gamma L}}}\right).$$

Taking exponentials on both sides and simplifying,

$$\sqrt{\alpha^2 e^{2\gamma l} + 4(1 - \alpha^2)e^{\gamma L}}$$
$$> 2(1 + 2\alpha)^{2/3}(1 - \alpha)^{1/3}e^{\gamma(L+l)/3} - \alpha e^{\gamma l}.$$

Squaring both sides of the inequality and simplifying,

$$(1 - \alpha^2)e^{2/3\gamma L} - (1 + 2\alpha)^{4/3}(1 - \alpha)^{2/3}e^{\gamma L/3}e^{2\gamma l/3}$$
$$+ \alpha(1+2\alpha)^{2/3}(1 - \alpha)^{1/3}e^{4\gamma^{1/3}} > 0.$$

Setting $X \equiv e^{\gamma L/3}$ and $Y = e^{2/3\gamma l}$, this is a quadratic in X and Y. The discriminant with respect to X is

$$\Delta_X = [(1 - \alpha)^{2/3}(1 + 2\alpha)^{1/3}Y]^2 > 0.$$

The roots are $[(1 + 2\alpha)/(1 - \alpha)]^{1/3}Y$ and $[(1 + 2\alpha)/(1 - \alpha)]^{1/3} \cdot Y[\alpha/(1 + \alpha)]$. The quadratic is negative between the roots and positive outside them. The quadratic is positive (i.e., the profit of the insider is larger with the option) iff X is larger than the highest root.[24]

$$X > \left(\frac{1 + 2\alpha}{1 - 2\alpha}\right)^{1/3}Y.$$

Substituting the values of X and Y, the above inequality hold iff $L > (1/\gamma)\ln[(1 + 2\alpha)/(1 - \alpha)] + 2l$.
    This establishes the result.   □

Proof of Proposition 8. The proposition obtains by substituting the probabilities corresponding to the pure, partially mixed, and fully mixed strategies equilibria (described in Propositions 2, 3, 4) in the quantities given in Lemma 2.   □

Proof of Corollary to Proposition 8. The corollary obtains straightforwardly, by combining Proposition 8 and condition (3).   □

Proof of Proposition 9. The information efficiency of the market increases as $V(S - \theta)$ decreases. $V(S - \theta) = V(S) + V(\theta) - 2\text{cov}(S, \theta)$ Note that $V(\theta) = \frac{2}{3}\sigma^2$. To analyze the informational efficiency of the market, we analyze how $V(S)$ and $\text{cov}(S, \theta)$ vary across equilibria.
    The first part of the proposition stems from the identity of the trading strategies and stock prices in the incomplete market and in the pure equilibrium in the complete market. The last part of the proposition stems from the fact that, when there is trading in the complete market and not in the incomplete market, there is some information revelation in the former but none in the latter. We now establish the second part of the proposition:

1. First, consider the incomplete market when there is no market breakdown.

$$V(S) = (\alpha\sigma)^2[\tfrac{2}{3}\alpha + \tfrac{2}{3}(1 - \alpha)] = \tfrac{2}{3}(\alpha\sigma)^2$$

---

[24] X cannot be below the lowest root when the pure strategy equilibrium prevails and there is no market breakdown in the complete market.

and

$$\text{cov}(S, \theta)$$
$$= P(\text{insider})[P(u)(\alpha\sigma)(\sigma) + P(m)(0)(0) + P(d)(-\alpha\sigma)(-\sigma)]$$
$$+ P(\text{liquidity})\{P(u)[P(\text{type} - 1)(\alpha\sigma)\sigma + P(\text{type} - 2)0\sigma$$
$$+ P(\text{type} - 3)(-\alpha\sigma)\sigma]$$
$$+ P(m)[P(\text{type} - 1)(\alpha\sigma)0 + P(\text{type} - 2)(0)(0)$$
$$+ P(\text{type } 3)(-\alpha\sigma)0]$$
$$+ P(d)[P(\text{type} - 1)(\alpha\sigma)(-\sigma) + P(\text{type} - 2)0(-\sigma)$$
$$+ P(\text{type} - 3)(-\alpha\sigma)(-\sigma)]\}.$$

The second term on the right-hand side [multiplied by $P(\text{liquidity})$] simplifies to 0. Substituting for the values of the probabilities, the first term simplifies to $\text{cov}(S, \theta) = \frac{2}{3}\alpha^2\sigma^2$. So, $V(S - \theta) = \frac{2}{3}(1 - a^2)\sigma^2$.

2. Second, consider the complete market, in the partially mixed equilibrium. Taking similar steps as in the previous case,

$$V(S) = \text{cov}(\theta, S) = \frac{2}{3}\frac{(\alpha\sigma)^2}{1 + \alpha\mu}.$$

So,

$$V(S - \theta) = \frac{2}{3}\sigma^2\left(1 - \frac{\alpha^2}{1 + \alpha\mu}\right).$$

Since $(\alpha, \mu) \in [0, 1]^2$, this is higher than $V(S - \theta)$ in the incomplete market case $[\frac{2}{3}(1 - \alpha^2)\sigma^2]$.

3. Third, consider the complete market, in the fully mixed equilibrium.

$$V(S) = \text{cov}(S, \theta) = \frac{2}{3}\frac{(\alpha\lambda\sigma)^2}{1 + \alpha\lambda - \alpha/2}.$$

So,

$$V(S - \theta) = \frac{2}{3}\sigma^2\left(1 - \frac{(\alpha\lambda\sigma)^2}{1 + \alpha\lambda - \alpha/2}\right).$$

So the informational efficiency of the market is lower in this case than in the incomplete market if

$$\frac{2}{3}\left[1 - \frac{(\alpha\lambda\sigma)^2}{1 + \alpha\lambda - \alpha/2}\right]\sigma^2 > \frac{2}{3}(1 - \alpha^2)\sigma^2$$

or

$$-\lambda^2 + \alpha\lambda + (1 - \alpha/2) > 0.$$

This is a quadratic inequality in λ. The unique positive root is

$$\lambda = \frac{\alpha + \sqrt{\alpha^2 + 4 - 2\alpha}}{2},$$

which is larger than 1. Note also that for $\lambda = 0$ the inequality holds. So for all $\lambda \in [0, 1]$ the inequality holds. Consequently, the informational efficiency of the market is lower in the complete market fully mixed equilibrium than in the incomplete market (when there is no market breakdown). ☐

REFERENCES

Allen, F., and G. Gorton, 1992, 'Stock Price Manipulation, Market Microstructure and Asymmetric Information,' *European Economic Review*, 36, 624–630.

Back, K., 1993, 'Asymmetric Information and Options,' *Review of Financial Studies*, 6, 435–472.

Berkman, H., 1993, 'Large Options Trades, Market Makers and Limit Orders,' Working paper, Erasmus University.

Bhattacharya, U., and M. Spiegel, 1991, 'Insiders, Outsiders and Market Breakdowns,' *Review of Financial Studies*, 4, 255–282.

Bossaerts, P., and E. Hughson, 1993, 'Noisy Signalling in Financial Markets,' Working paper, Caltech.

Diamond, D., and D. Verecchia, 1991, 'Disclosure, Liquidity and the Cost of Capital,' *Journal of Finance*, 1325–1359.

Dow, J., and G. Gorton, 1993, 'Arbitrage Chains,' working paper, London Business School; forthcoming in *Journal of Finance*.

Easley, D., and M. O'Hara, 1987, 'Price, Quantity and Information in Securities Markets,' *Journal of Financial Economics*, 19, 69–90.

——, M. O'Hara, and P. S. Srinivas, 1987, 'Option Volume and Stock Prices: Evidence on Where Informed Traders Trade,' working paper, Cornell University.

Fedenia, M., and T. Grammatikos, 1992, 'Options Trading and the Bid-Ask Spread of the Underlying Stocks,' *Journal of Business*, 335–351.

Glosten, L. R., 1989, 'Insider Trading, Liquidity and the Role of the Monopolist Specialist,' *Journal of Business*, 62, 211–325.

——, and P. R. Milgrom, 1985, 'Bid, Ask, and Transaction Prices in a Market with Heterogeneously Informed Traders,' *Journal of Financial Economics*, 14, 71–100.

Grossman, S., and J. Stiglitz, 1980, 'On the Impossibility of Informationally Efficient Markets,' *American Economic Review*, 66, 246–252.

John, K., A. Koticha, and M. Subrahmanyam, 1992, 'The Microstructure of Options Markets: Informed Trading, Liquidity, Volatility and Efficiency,' Working paper, New York University.

Kyle, A. S., 1985, 'Continuous Auctions and Insider Trading,' *Econometrica*, 53, 1315–1335.

Laffont, J. J., and E. Maskin, 1990, 'The Efficient Market Hypothesis and Insider Trading on the Stock Market,' *Journal of Political Economy*, 98, 70–94.

Madhavan, A., 1992, 'Trading Mechanisms in Securities Markets,' *Journal of Finance*, 47, 607–642.

Rochet, J. C., and J. L. Vila, 1994, 'Insider Trading without Normality,' *Review of Economic Studies*, 61, 131–152.

Ross, S., 1976, 'Options and Efficiency,' *Quarterly Journal of Economics*, 90, 75–89.

Spiegel, M., and A. Subrahmanyam, 1992, 'Informed Speculation and Hedging in a Noncompetitive Securities Market,' *Review of Financial Studies*, 5, 307–331.

Vijh, A., 1990, 'Liquidity of the CBOE Equity Options,' *Journal of Finance*, 45, 1157–1178.

Vila, J. L., 1989, 'Simple Games of Market Manipulation,' *Economics Letters*, 29, 21–26.

5

The Speed of Information Revelation in a Financial Market Mechanism

XAVIER VIVES

1. INTRODUCTION

The role of prices in transmitting information in financial markets has been extensively studied since the early work of Kihlstrom and Mirman [19] and Grossman [12]. Nevertheless, the study of the speed at which prices incorporate information is much less developed.[1] This paper studies a simple *information tâtonnement mechanism* to elicit the dispersed private information of risk averse agents on the value of a risky asset. The speed of convergence of the prices generated by the mechanism to the underlying value of the asset, that is, the speed of price discovery, is established and the role of market makers analyzed. More specifically, we address the following issues:

How fast will prices incorporate information in the presence of *risk aversion*? What factors affect the speed at which prices tend to converge to the underlying value of the asset? What is the role of *market makers* and *limit orders* in this process? What are the comparative dynamic properties in terms of basic market parameters: Degree of risk aversion, precision of private information, amount of noise, and underlying volatility of the asset?

In a world where agents have heterogeneous beliefs and where prices reveal information over time, the study of the *dynamics* of the market is, indeed, not a simple matter. The problem is compounded by the presence of risk aversion.[2] A first attempt is made here to isolate the information dynamics induced by risk averse informed agents and competitive market makers abstracting from some of the complications introduced by full-fledged dynamic trade. In order to do so we consider an information, tâtonnement (or adjustment) process inspired by the

A preliminary version of this paper was circulated in 1990 under the title 'Financial Market Dynamics with Risk Averse Agents.' I am grateful to Gerard Gennotte, Kai-Uwe Kühn, and Marco Pagano for helpful comments. Support from the Spanish Ministry of Education through Grants DGICYT PB87-0340, PB89-0074, and PB90-0132 is gratefully acknowledged. Comments from an anonymous referee proved very useful in improving the paper. Joan Ramon Palau provided excellent research assistance.

[1] A first attack on the problem is provided in Vives [34].

[2] Wang [36] and Gennotte and Kyle [10] break ground with continuous time models, and Dennert [9] and Pagano [26] consider overlapping generations models. Vives [35] studies a finite horizon model.

dynamic adjustment process to implement rational expectations equilibria studied by Jordan [17,18] and Kobayashi [20]. Indeed, the results obtained in the paper can be interpreted as providing a rate of convergence for an iterative mechanism which implements fully revealing rational expectations equilibria.

The basis for the information tâtonnement is a standard financial market model (a competitive version of the one-shot auction model in Kyle [21]): A single risky asset, with random (ex post) liquidation value v, and a riskless asset are traded among many risk averse informed agents with the intermediation of competitive market makers in the presence of noise or liquidity traders (or, perhaps, noise in the transmission of orders). Each informed agent has some (private) information about the unknown v and the collective information of informed agents reveals the v. Informed agents submit market orders to risk neutral market makers who set prices efficiently conditional on the aggregate order flow. More precisely, markets makers set prices upon observing the order book which contains the aggregate orders of informed agents plus the price sensitive orders submitted by liquidity traders. The described auction gives an information advantage to informed agents in the sense that they have private information about v, but also to market makers in the sense that they observe a noisy a signal of the aggregate information of informed agents. In this way market makers can be thought of as having better information about 'market conditions,' and informed agents private information about the fundamental value of the asset.

Consider now an infinite horizon version of the market described above in which at any stage there is a positive probability (not necessarily the same across periods) that the value v is realized and trade consummated given that there has not been trade up to then. At the beginning of stage n, informed agents, before knowing whether there will be trade in the period, submit market orders to competitive market makers conditional on their private signal and on public information (price quotations up to $n - 1$). Market makers quote prices efficiently on the basis of public information and the noisy aggregate order flow. If trade is realized this is the end of the story. Otherwise, the process starts again with informed agents having refined their information with the observation of the last period price quotation. The theoretical price quotation of the market serves the purpose of eliciting the information of agents about the fundamental value of the asset. Agents can revise their orders at any point in the process.

The information tâtonnement process does not pretend to reflect any particular market mechanism and is offered as a *benchmark* to think about the issues of interest. Nevertheless, the mechanism shares some features with the tâtonnement which takes place in the opening batch auction of some continuous stock trading systems (like in Tokyo, Toronto, Paris, and Madrid). Typically, for one hour agents submit orders to the system and *theoretical* prices are quoted periodically and frequently as orders accumulate. No trade is made till the end of the tâtonnement and at any point agents may revise their orders.[3] This opening auction is

---

[3] Although any order submitted has a chance to 'stick' if there is noise in the communication channel.

designed to decrease the uncertainty about prices after a period without trade (overnight). The cost of submitting complete demand schedules precludes the widespread use of generalized limit orders to eliminate price uncertainty.[4]

Assuming that all random variables are normally distributed and that agents display constant absolute risk aversion (CARA) utility functions, it is possible to characterize the equilibrium of the tâtonnement process and its asymptotic properties.

The results are as follows: As the number of rounds n of the tâtonnement increases, price quotations become more and more informative. Market makers induce an increasingly deep market, in the sense that the price quotation is decreasingly sensitive to the current (notional) order flow, as the information advantage of informed agents diminishes. Risk averse informed agents respond to the increased depth of the market by reacting more intensely to their private information. The outcome is that private information is incorporated into prices fast: Price quotations converge to the underlying value of the asset r at a rate of $1/\sqrt{n}$. Furthermore, the asymptotic variance of the price as an estimator of v, a refined indicator of the speed of convergence, depends positively on the degree of risk aversion and the amount of noise trading, and negatively on the precision of the private information of agents. Agents with a lower degree of risk aversion, and/or better information, and/or facing less noise, make the market more resilient, as intuition dictates.

The analysis uncovers that the presence of competitive market makers (or enough agents providing liquidity to the market using limit orders) has a crucial influence on the speed of convergence by inducing an endogenous depth of the market. Removing the market makers results in a market of constant depth, held by the price sensitive liquidity traders, and the speed of convergence of prices to v is much slower: $1/\sqrt{n^{1/q}}$. In this case, as in the model analyzed in Vives [34], informed agents respond less and less to their private information as price quotations become more informative, and in the limit they ignore their private signals. In contrast, in the presence of market makers, informed agents react more intensely to their private information when n is large, yielding faster convergence. This is so since price quoting by competitive market makers, faced by increasingly informative prices, leads to an expanding market depth.[5]

In summary, the information tâtonnement proves effective in resolving quickly the uncertainty about the fundamental value of the asset (and may provide a rationale for the theoretical price quotations in the above-mentioned opening batch auctions).

The model allows the study of the comparative dynamic properties of equilibria, in terms of informativeness and volatility of price quotations, and (notional) depth with respect to the basic parameters of the model: Degree of risk aversion,

---

[4] See, for example, Withcomb [37].
[5] Leach and Madhavan [23,24] consider the incentives and the ability of market makers to speed up price discovery through price experimentation.

precision of information, amount of noise, and underlying volatility of the asset. It is possible to show, for example, that comparing two environments, one with either a larger degree of risk aversion or a lower precision of information, or with more diffuse priors, agents respond less to the information they have (private plus prices) and prices reveal less information in any period. Further, except in the case of a higher prior variance of the value of the asset, the volatility of price quotations is also uniformly lower over time. Similarly, when n is large, the informativeness and volatility of prices is smaller if the economy has a larger amount of noise trading, and the depth of the market is also smaller if either the economy displays a larger aversion to risk or the agents have less precise private information.

The paper proceeds as follows. In Section 2 the basic static version of the model is introduced. The information tâtonnement process and its equilibrium is presented in Section 3 and the proofs are gathered in Section 4. Section 5 studies the convergence properties of the equilibrium. Section 6 analyzes the role of market makers by removing them from the basic model. Section 7 performs some comparative dynamics exercises. Concluding remarks follow.[6]

2. A STATIC FINANCIAL MARKET MODEL

The basic static financial market model is the following: A single risky asset, with random (ex post) liquidation value v, and a riskless asset, with unitary return, are traded among informed agents and noise traders with the intermediation of competitive market makers. There is a continuum of informed agents indexed in the interval $[0, 1]$ (endowed with the Lebesgue measure). Each informed agent has a little piece of (private) information about the unknown v and the collective information of informed agents reveals v. The profits of agent i buying x_i units of the asset at price p are given by $\pi_i = (v - p)x_i$. Informed agents are risk averse and have CARA utilities: $U(\pi_i) = \exp\{p\pi_i\}$, where p is the (positive) coefficient of constant absolute risk aversion. The initial wealth of informed agents is normalized to zero. Informed agent i submits a market order $X_{1i}, (s_i)$, contingent on the private signal s_i he receives. Noise traders are price sensitive and in the aggregate submit an order $u_1 - \alpha_1 p_1$, where u_1 is random and α_1 a constant.[7] Market makers are risk neutral and set prices efficiently conditional on the observation of the 'order book':

$$L_1(p_1) = \bar{x}_1 + u_1 - \alpha_1 p_1, \quad \text{with} \quad \bar{x}_1 = \int_0^1 X_{1i}(s_i)\, di.$$

Note that all the information on the order book $L_1(\cdot)$ about v is contained in the intercept $\omega_1 = \bar{x}_1 + u_1$, which, with some abuse of language, will be termed the

[6] In this paper we do not deal with the welfare analysis of informed trading (see Ausubel [7] and Leland [25] in this regard).
[7] Noise could arise also as a result of garbling added in the communication channel or transmission of orders. Gould and Verrechia [11], in a different market making model, assume the price quoted by the specialist is garbled.

order flow. In consequence, $p_1 = E(v | L_1(\cdot)) = E(v | \omega_1)$. Efficient pricing will be the outcome of Bertrand competition among risk neutral market makers who observe the order book.

Alternatively, and equivalently, prices could be set through a market clearing process. The competitive market making sector would submit demand schedules (generalized limit orders) based on public information (prices); noise traders, random demand schedules (with a fixed slope); and informed agents, market orders to a centralized auctioneer. The auctioneer would set then the price to clear the market. This process is equivalent to the previous one provided there are many (a continuum of) risk neutral market makers. Indeed, market clearing should satisfy $E(v | p_1) = P_1$ since otherwise market makers would take unbounded positions.[8] It follows then that $p_1 = E(v | \omega_1)$ since, as we will see in Proposition 2.1 below, in the linear equilibria considered p_1 is linear in ω_1.

In summary, and in any case, informed agents have an information advantage over market makers because of their private signals but market makers observe a noisy signal of the aggregate position of the informed agents.

It is assumed that all random variables are normally distributed: v with mean $\bar{v}$ and variance σ_v^2, and u_1 with zero mean and variance σ_u^2. The parameter v and u_1 are uncorrelated. Conditional on v, each signal s_i is normally distributed with mean v and variance σ_ε^2, and signals are uncorrelated across agents. The signal s_i can be thought as $s_i = v + \varepsilon_i$, where v and ε_i are uncorrelated, and errors are also uncorrelated across agents (and with the noise u_1). The usual *convention* that gives v, the average signal $\bar{s} = \int_0^1 s_i \, di$ equals almost surely (a.s.) v (i.e., errors cancel out in the aggregate, $\int_0^1 \varepsilon_i \, di = 0$) will be used. In other words, the pooled information of informed agents reveals v.[9] The precision of a random variable x, $(\sigma_x^2)^{-1}$, will be denoted τ_x.

The model is a version of the one-shot auction in Kyle [21] replacing the single risk neutral insider with a continuum of risk averse informed agents and introducing price sensitive noise traders.[10]

Let $\tau_1 \equiv [\text{Var}(v | p_i)]^1$ denote the informativeness of the price about the liquidation value v. Restricting attention to equlibria in linear strategies it is possible to show:

Proposition 2.1. *There is a unique linear equilibrium. It is symmetric and given by*

$$X_1(s_i) = a_1(s_i - \bar{v}) \quad and \quad p_1 = \lambda_1 \omega_1 + v,$$

---

[8] This is consistent with the analysis of Kyle [22, Theorem 6.1] where a finite number of insiders and market makers (uniformed agents) submit limit orders to an auctioneer. When the number of market makers increases without bound, the market prices becomes 'unbiased' in the sense that $p = E(v | p)$.

[9] There are well-known potential technical difficulties with the adopted convention (see, for example, Feldman and Giles [15]). Admati [1] justifies the convention in the context of a financial market rational expectations model, and Vives [33] in the context of a Cournot model.

[10] The issue of uniqueness of equilibria in the Kyle model, as well as in some market manipulation models (Vila [32]) has been recently studied by Rochet and Vila [30].

where $a_1 = \{\rho(\sigma_0^2 + \operatorname{Var} p_1)\}$.[1] The parameter a_1 is the unique positive root of the cubic equation $F_1(a) \equiv (\rho\tau_0 a - 1)\tau_v + \rho\lambda_1 a^2 = 0$, with $\lambda_1 = \tau_u a/\tau_1, \tau_1 = \tau_v + \tau_u a^2$.

Proof. See Section 4 below and let $n = 1$. ∎

Remark. The sensitivity of noise trading to price, x_1, does not affect the equilibrium trading of informed agents. It does affect the trading intensity of market makers (who trade according to $-(\lambda_1^{-1} - x_1)(p_1 - \bar{v})$.

For completeness let us state some basic comparative static properties of the equilibrium.

Proposition 2.2. *Comparative statics*

(i) *The responsiveness of informed agents to private signals (a_1) decreases with $\rho_1, \sigma_\varepsilon^2$, and σ_r^2, and increases with σ_u^2.*
(ii) *The informativeness of the price (τ_1) decreases with $\rho, \sigma_\varepsilon^2, \sigma_v^2$ and σ_u^2.*
(iii) *The ex ante volatility of prices ($\operatorname{Var} p_1$) decreases with $\rho, \sigma_\varepsilon^2$, and σ_u^2, and increases with σ_u^2.*
(iv) *The (expected) volume traded by informed agents ($E|\bar{x}_1| = (2/\pi)^{1/2} a_1 \sigma_v$) decreases with ρ and σ_v^2 and increases with σ_u^2.*

Proof. Omitted. For items (i) to (iii), it is similar to the proof of the Claim contained in the proof of Proposition 7.1 below. Item (iv) follows from (i). ∎

The interpretation of the comparative static properties is quite straightforward. The responsiveness of informed agents to private information decreases with the coefficient of risk aversion (ρ), with the noise in the signal (σ_v^2) and with the prior variance of the value of the asset (σ_v^2). The informativeness of prices (τ_1) also decreases with the same factors. The effects with respect to ρ and σ_v^2 accord to intuition. Increases in σ_v^2 decrease the price precision for a fixed a_1 and induce market makers to raise λ_1. Informed agents respond by trading less intensely accentuating the decrease in τ_1. Increases in noise (σ_u^2) increase a_1 since in equilibrium they induce a lower volatility of prices. Noise has a negative direct effect on the informativeness of prices (that is, for a_1 fixed) and a positive indirect effect through a_1. The direct effect dominates. This contrasts with Kyle [21] in which noise trading does not affect the informativeness of prices and is due to the presence of risk aversion.

The ex ante volatility of prices is positively related to their informativeness given a fixed prior variance (σ_v^2) of the underlying value of the asset $\operatorname{Var} p_1 = \tau_v^1 - \tau_1^1$. Therefore, all factors (except σ_v^2) which increase τ_1 will also increase $\operatorname{Var} p_1$. A higher σ_v^2 has a double impact on $\operatorname{Var} p_1$: A negative indirect effect, since it decreases τ_1, and a positive direct effect which dominates. Finally, with respect to the (expected) trading volume, informed agents trade less when they are more risk averse or have less precise information and when there is more noise. The effect of the prior variance of v is ambiguous.

3. AN INFORMATION TÂTONNEMENT PROCESS

Consider now an infinite horizon version of the market described in the last section where at stage n there is a positive probability γ_n that the value v is realized and trade consummated given that there has not been trade before stage n, and with probability $(1 - \gamma_n)$ there is no trade. Let us assume that the sequence $\{\gamma_n\}$ is nondecreasing. At the beginning of stage n, informed agents, before knowing whether there will be trade in the period, submit market orders to competitive market makers conditional on their private signal and on public information (price quotations up to $n - 1$). Market makers quote prices efficiently on the basis of public information and the aggregate order flow, which is just a noisy version of the aggregate orders of informed agents. If trade is realized this is the end of the story. Otherwise the process starts again with informed agents having refined their information with the observation of the last period price quotation. The information tâtonnement consists of rounds of notional trade where price quotations of market makers serve the purpose of eliciting (partially) the aggregate information possessed by traders about v. Prices are not fully revealing of v because of the new noise every period. The idea is that at every stage the information on which market makers quote prices is a garbled version of the fundamental value v.

We can think about the tâtonnement process as follows. The market will open at a certain point in the future and at period n (given that it has not opened up to then) there is a probability γ_n that if it opens, trade is consummated, and v realized. Informed agents submit their orders and if the market does not open they are allowed to revise them once informed of the price quotation of market makers or the auctioneer. In general, informed agents will have incentives to reconsider their market orders when receiving more public information.

In fact, in several continuous auction stock trading systems (like Tokyo, Toronto, Paris, and Madrid) there is an opening batch auction with real-time dissemination of the theoretical price at which transactions would take place if the market would open at this moment. The opening auction is designed to reduce the uncertainty about the trading price after a period without trade (overnight). At the beginning of the trading day, agents may be reluctant to submit their orders since in the absence of previous price quotations there is more uncertainty about the equilibrium price. The opening batch auction works typically as follows. For one hour (say from 9 to 10 AM) traders may enter orders into the system. As orders arrive periodically (and frequently) a new theoretical opening price is computed and publicly displayed (this is the market clearing price given the orders that have arrived). Agents can revise their orders before 10 AM when the market opens (although if there is noise in the communication channel an order may 'stick' in the sense that the market opens before the trader has been able to revise it) and the accumulated orders are executed at the theoretical 10 AM price. This system is akin therefore to an information tâtonnement with a price discovery function.[11]

A formal description of the information tâtonnement follows. The first round is like in the static model with the result that $p_1 = E(v \mid \omega_1)$. If v is realized the world ends. Otherwise, there is no trade and in the second period the information vector of informed agent i is $\{s_i, p_i\}$. He submits a market order $X_{2i}(s_i, p_i)$, and the process continues. Suppose that round n is reached. Then agent i's information vector is $\{s_i, p^{n-1}\}$, with $p^{n-1} = (p_1, \ldots, p_{n-1})$, and his strategy is given by $X_{ni}(s_i, p^{n-1})$. Noise traders are assumed to submit at round n the order $u_n - \alpha_n p_n$, with α_n being an exogenous constant.[12] The order book is then

$$L_n(p_n) = \omega_n - \alpha_n p_n, \quad \text{with } \omega_n = \tilde{x}_n + u_n, \text{ and } \tilde{x}_n = \int_0^1 X_{ni}(s_i, p^{n-1})\, di.$$

As before, the informational content of the order book $L_n(\cdot)$ is just the intercept (or 'order flow') ω_n. Competitive market makers set p_n equal to the expectation of v conditional on past public information $\omega_{n-1}^n = (\omega_1, \ldots, \omega_{n-1})$ and the current order flow $\omega_n : P_n = E(v \mid \omega^n)$.

In summary, informed agents compete repeatedly in the market having observed at date n the sequence of past prices and their own private information. Competitive market makers set prices at each period on the face of the history of order books or, what amounts to the same, (noisy) order flows. All trades are notional; that is, they can be revised, till the end of the information tâtonnement when v is realized. This happens in finite time: The probability that the information tâtonnement lasts till stage n is $\Pi_{t=1}^n (1 - \gamma_t)$, which tends to zero as n tends to infinity since the sequence $\{\gamma_t\}$ is nondecreasing. Note nevertheless that with small γ's the probability $\Pi_{t=1}^n (1 - \gamma_t)$ may be substantial even for n large. For example, for γ constant and equal to 0.0069, $(1 - \gamma)^{100}$ equals approximately $\frac{1}{2}$. The sequence $\{\gamma_n\}$ can approximate the opening batch auction case (where $\gamma_n = 0$ for n before 10 AM and $\gamma - 1$ at 10 AM) in a smooth way (approximating the step function associated to the opening auction with a smooth function giving small values to γ before 10 AM and increasing sharply at 10 AM).

Alternatively, a finite horizon model could be considered in which after N periods of tâtonnement with a zero probability of trade the market opens. The results obtained below would still hold since the model is not horizon dependent. In this case, informed traders would be indifferent about whether to submit their orders during the tâtonnement. Although they would not have incentives to misrepresent, given that a trader is negligible, they would not have a *strict*

---

[11] Note, however, that the process described is not the usual Walrasian tâtonnement, typical of oral batch auctions (à la criée), where tentative prices are called, agents respond by placing quantity bids and offers, and prices are adjusted according to excess demand. See Pagano and Roell [27]. See also Ortega [29] for the Madrid Bolsa, and CAC [8] for the Paris Bourse. Price information reported in advance of transactions via *indicated prices* is also available in Amsterdam and Vienna (see Withcomb [37]).

[12] A justification of price sensitive noise or liquidity traders in a model with myopic informed investors can be found in Singleton [31].

incentive to submit *serious* orders. (In any case, it is important to realize that since agents are negligible, no agent is able to manipulate the information contained in prices.) In summary, if this helps, the reader can forget about the γ's and think in terms of a finite horizon model.

As in the last section all random variables are normally distributed with the sequence $\{u_1, u_2, \ldots\}$ independently and identically distributed with zero mean and variance σ_u^2. The parameter v, the errors terms of signals, and the sequence $\{u_t\}$ are uncorrelated.

The information tâtonnement process can be interpreted as a mechanism to elicit the aggregate information of informed agents via price quotations. The information tâtonnement is analogous to the 'dynamic information adjustment process' considered by Jordan [17,18] and Kobayashi [20] to implement rational expectations equilibria. The essence in Jordan's adjustment process is, as in the present case, that prices serve only as public information signals and trades are *not* consummated until the iterative process has stopped. Similarly, Kobayashi [20] assumes that agents trade at any period as if it were the last. The dynamic processes in Jordan [17] and Kobayashi [20] are very much like the information tâtonnement considered in the present paper except that they consider markets with a finite number of agents with no noise added in the price system (that is, without noise traders or supply shocks). With a finite state space, convergence occurs then in a finite number of steps (Kobayashi also obtains it assuming normal distributions). In the present paper with no noise trading (and with a continuum of agents) the liquidation value v would be revealed in the first round since then p_1 would be a linear function of the average signal received by agents which, according to our convention, equals v. Jordan [18] considers the issue of learning how to form rational expectations (correct conditional distributions) in the context of the model in Jordan [17].

At stage t of the dynamic process, a strategy for agent i is a function that maps his private information s_1 and the observed past prices p^{n-1} into desired purchases. The agent behaves as if the asset were to be liquidated and trade realized in the period. This will happen with probability γ_t, and with probability $(1 - \gamma_t)$ the agent obtains the continuation (expected) utility which, given that the agent is negligible, is independent of his market order in period t. From the point of view of an agent, the only difference between periods is in the information structures. Restricting attention to equilibria in linear strategies it is possible to obtain a full characterization and show a uniqueness result in our model with risk averse agents.

Let $\tau_n \equiv [\text{Var}(v \,|\, p_n)]^{-1}$ denote the precision of the price quotation p_n in the estimation of v_1 and $p_0 \equiv v$.

Proposition 3.1. *There is a unique linear equilibrium. It is symmetric and can be characterized by (for $n = 1, 2, \ldots$)*

$$X_n(s_i, p^{n-1}) = a_n(s_i - p_{n-1}) \quad and \quad p_n = \lambda_n \omega_n + p_{n-1},$$

$$\omega_n = a_n(v - p_{n-1}) + u_n,$$

where $a_n = \varepsilon(\sigma_\varepsilon^2 + \mathrm{Var}(p_n \mid p_{n-1}))^{-1}$, and a_n is the unique positive root of the recursive cubic equation: $F_n(a_n) \equiv (\rho(\tau_\varepsilon)^{-1}a_n - 1)\tau_{n-1} + \rho\lambda_n a_n^2 = 0$, with

$$\lambda_n = \tau_n a_n / T_n, \quad T_n = \tau_n + \tau_n \sum_{t=1}^{n} a_t^2,$$

and

$$\mathrm{Var}\{p_n \mid p_{n-1}\} = (\tau_{n-1})^{-1} - (\tau_n)^{-1}.$$

Remark. As before, the (exogenous) sensitivity of noise traders to price, α_n, does not affect trading by informed agents. Market makers in period n trade according to $-(\lambda_n^{-1} - \alpha_n)(p_n - p_{n-1})$.

The equilibrium has a very intuitive feature: Agent i desires to buy or sell according to whether his private estimate of v, s_i, is larger or smaller than the market estimate, p_{n-1}. The price p_{n-1} is a sufficient statistic of all past prices $\{p^{n-1}\}$ (which are public information, observationally equivalent to the history of noisy order flows or intercepts of the order books ω^{n-1}) due to competitive market making: $E(v \mid p^{n-1}) = p_{n-1}$. Note that, because of normality, $E(v \mid p^{n-1})$ is a sufficient statistic in the estimation of v with respect to the information $\{p^{n-1}\}$. This implies that $E(v \mid p^{n-1}) = p_{n-1}$. It follows that quoted prices follow a martingale: $E(p_n \mid p^{n-1}) = p_{n-1}$.

Informed agents' response to private information, a_n, depends negatively, ceteris paribus, on the degree of risk aversion ρ, the noise in the private signal σ_ε^2, and the conditional variance of the price $\mathrm{Var}(p_n \mid p_{n-1})$. All this accords to intuition. Recall that all demands and price quotations are notional unless the value of the asset happens to be realized in the period.

Before giving the formal proof of the proposition it may be helpful to check heuristically the consistency of the proposed equilibrium.

At stage n agent i has information $\{s_i, p^{n-1}\}$. The information contained in past prices, $p^{n-1} = (p_1, \ldots, p_{n-1})$, is summarized in the last period price p_{n-1}. This is so since competitive market making implies that $p_{n-1} = E(v \mid \omega^{n-1})$, where ω^{n-1} is the history of order flows, and, from the joint normality of random variables, it follows that $E(v \mid \omega^{n-1})$ is a sufficient statistic in the estimation of v with the information ω^{n-1}. The agent faces then the problem of estimating $v - p_n$ with the information $\{s_i, p_{n-1}\}$, knowing that in the current period market makers will set $p_n = E(v \mid \omega^{n-1}, \omega_n)$, which will equal (by the same argument as before) $E(v \mid p_{n-1}, \omega_n)$. From normal distribution theory p_n can be expressed then as $\lambda_n \omega_n + p_{n-1}$, where λ_n is an appropriate constant which indicates the sensitivity of the market price to the order flow. As Kyle [21] remarks, λ_n^{-1} is a natural measure of the depth of the market.

At stage n agent i will face the following expected utility conditional on his information, $\gamma_n E\{U(\pi_{in}) \mid s_i\}, p_{n-1} + (1 - \gamma_n)E\{U_n \mid s_i, p_{n-1}\}$, where $\pi_{in} = (v - p_n)x_{in}$. $U(\pi_{in}) = -\exp\{-\rho\pi_{in}\}$, and U_n is the (random) continuation utility (which is independent of the current market order x_{in}). In consequence, to behave myopically is optimal and the informed agent will optimize choosing a market order (with the usual form in a CARA-normal model):

$$X_n(s_i, p_{n-1}) = \frac{E\{(v - p_n) \mid s_i, p_{n-1}\}}{\rho \text{Var}\{(v - p_n) \mid s_i, p_{n-1}\}}.$$

Agent i, positing that other agents use the prescribed strategy (in Proposition 3.1) will infer that $\omega_n = a_n(v - p_{n-1}) + u_n$ and will evaluate $E\{v - p_n \mid s_i, p_{n-1}\} = (1 - \lambda_n a_n) E\{(v - p_{n-1}) \mid s_i, p_{n-1}\}$, and $\text{Var}\{(v - p_n) \mid s_i, p_{n-1}\} = (1 - \lambda_n a_n)^2 \times \text{Var}\{(v - p_{n-1}) \mid s_i, p_{n-1}\} + \lambda_n^2 \sigma_u^2$. Given that $p_{n-1} = E(v \mid p_{n-1})$, it follows from normal distribution theory that $s_i - p_{n-1}$ is a sufficient statistic for $v - p_{n-1}$ with respect to the information $\{s_i, p_{n-1}\}$ and $X_n(s_i, p_{n-1})$ will have the prescribed form since the denominator is a constant and the numerator a linear function of $s_i - p_{n-1}$. The fact that the price sensitivity of noise traders (α_n) does not affect the trading strategy of informed agents should not be surprising. The information vector of the latter in period n depends on past prices, whose information is summarized in the last period price p_{n-1}. However, prices are independent of the coefficients α_n because only the intercept ω_n of the order book $L_n(\cdot) = \omega_n - \alpha_n p_n$ is informative about v and, consequently, $p_n = E(v \mid \omega^n)$.

Two elements are crucial to construct the equilibrium: (1) Agents optimize against a linear function ($p_n = \lambda_n \omega_n + p_{n-1}$), and (2) market makers determine the price function ($p_n = E(v \mid \omega_n) = E(v \mid p_n)$) making λ_n endogenous.

It is easy to check that, ceteris paribus, an increase in the depth of the market induces risk averse informed agents to respond more to their information (since $\text{Var}\{p_n \mid p_{n-1}\}$ will be lower).[13] On the contrary, an increase in a_n, again ceteris paribus, induces market makers to put more weight on the order flow in setting p_n, decreasing market depth, as the order flow is more informative. An increase in the precision of prices τ_n, holding a_n constant, would have the opposite effect.

4. PROOF OF PROPOSITION 3.1

We will proceed to establish a series of claims which prove Proposition 3.1. At a linear equilibrium and given our assumptions, all random variables are normally distributed. Maximization of CARA utility function by agent i yields then at stage n

$$X_n(s_i, p^{n-1}) = \frac{E\{(v - p_n) \mid s_i, p^{n-1}\}}{\rho \text{Var}\{(v - p_n) \mid s_i, p^{n-1}\}},$$

where $p_n = E(v \mid \omega^n)$ from the competition among market makers, and where ω_n is the n period order flow. Recall that the informational content of the order book,

---

[13] It is immediate that fixing $\lambda_n = \lambda$ the unique root of $F_n(a) = 0$ is decreasing with λ.

$L_n(p_n) = \omega_n - x_n p_n$, with $\omega_n = \bar{x}_n + u_n$, and $\bar{x}_n = \int_0^1 X_{nt}(s_i, p^{n-1})\, di$, is summarized in the intercept (order flow) ω_n. The expression is independent of i and therefore equilibria will be symmetric.

Consider the candidate equilibrium $X_n(s_i, p^{n-1}) = a_n s_i + \oslash_n(p^{n-1})$, where $a_n > 0$, and $\oslash_n(\cdot)$ is a linear function with a corresponding order flow

$$\omega_n = a_n v + \oslash_n(p^{n-1}) + u_n.$$

Claim 1. *In equilibrium, the following vectors of random variables are observationally equivalent*: $\{p^n\}$, $\{\omega^n\}$, *and* $\{z^n\}$ *where* $z_t = a_1 v + u_1$, $t = 1, \ldots, n$.

Proof. By induction. For $n = 1$, $\omega_1 = a_1 v + \oslash_1 + u_1$, which is observationally equivalent to $z_1 = a_1 v + u_1$, since at equilibrium $\oslash_1$ is known. Now, $p_1 = E(v \mid \omega_1)$ is a nondegenerate linear function of ω_1 and therefore is also observationally equivalent (o.e.), to ω_1. Now, if $\{\omega^{n-1}\}$, $\{z^{n-1}\}$, $\{p^{n-1}\}$ are o.e., then $\{\omega^n\}$, $\{z^n\}$, $\{p^n\}$ are o.e. also. This follows immediately from the expressions of ω_n, z_n and the fact that $p_n = E(v \mid \omega^n)$ is a nondegenerate linear function of ω^n. $\square$

Claim 2. $p_n = E(v \mid z^n) = (\tau v \bar{v} + \tau_u \sum_{t=1}^n a_t z_t)/\tau_n$, *where* $\tau_n = \tau_v + \tau_v A_n$, $A_n = \sum_{t=1}^n (a_t)^2$. *Note that* $p_n = E(v \mid p_n)$, $E(p_n \mid p_{n-1}) = p_{n-1}$ *and* $\mathrm{Var}\{p_n \mid p_{n-1}\} = (\tau_{n-1})^{-1} - (\tau_n)^{-1}$.

Proof. The first statement is immediate from Claim 1 and competitive market making. The computation of $E(v \mid z^n)$ is standard. Because of normality $p_n = E(v \mid z^n)$ is a sufficient statistic for the information $\{z^n\}$ in the estimation of v. In consequence, $p_n = E(v \mid p_n)$ and prices follow a martingale (from which the properties of conditional expectations and variances are derived immediately). $\square$

Claim 3. $p_n - p_{n-1} = \lambda_n \omega_n$, *where* $\lambda_n = \tau_a a_n / \tau_n$.

Proof. From Claim 2, $p_n - p_{n-1} = (\tau_u a_n z_n + (1 - \tau_n/\tau_{n-1})(\tau_n \sum_{t=1}^{n-1} a_t z_t + \tau_v \bar{v}))/\tau_n = \lambda_n(z_n - a_n p_{n-1}) = \lambda_n \omega_n$, since $(1 - \tau_n/\tau_{n-1}) = -\tau_n(a_n)^2/\tau_{n-1}$ and $p_{n-1} = E(v \mid p_{n-1})$. $\square$

Claim 4. *Under our assumptions*, $E(v \mid s_i, p_n) = E(v \mid s_i, z^n) = (\tau_\varepsilon s_i + \tau_n p_n)/\tau_{in}$, *and* $\tau_{in} = (\mathrm{Var}(v \mid s_i, z^n))^{-1} = \tau_n + \tau_n$.

Proof. Standard. $\square$

Claim 4 states that $E(v \mid s_i, p_n)$ equals a weighted average of the private signal and the price according to their contribution to the total precision $\tau_i + \tau_n$.

Claim 5. *In the estimation of $v - p_n$, $s_i - p_{n-1}$ is sufficient with respect to the information $\{s_t, p^{n-1}\}$ (or $\{s_t, z^{n-1}\}$). Furthermore, $E((v - p_n) \mid s_i, p^{n-1}) = (1 - \lambda_n a_n)\tau_\varepsilon(\tau_{in-1})^{-1}(s_i - p_{n-1})$.*

Proof. It is a consequence of the projection theorem for normal random variables that $E\{(v - p_n) \mid s_i, z^{n-1}\}$ is sufficient for $v - p_n$ with respect to $\{s_i, z^{n-1}\}$. From Claim 3 $p_n = \lambda_n a_n v + (1 - \lambda_n a_n)p_{n-1}$, and therefore $v - p_n = (1 - \lambda_n a_n) \times (v - p_{n-1})$. From Claim 4 we have that $E\{(v - p_{n-1}) \mid s_i, p_{n-1}\} = E(v \mid s_i, p_{n-1}) - p_{n-1} = (\tau_\varepsilon s_i + \tau_{n-1}p_{n-1})/\tau_{in-1} - p_{n-1}$. The result follows since $\tau_{n-1}(\tau_{in-1})^{-1} - 1 = -\tau_\varepsilon(\tau_{in-1})^{-1}$. □

Claim 6. *The solutions to the equation $F_n(a) = 0$ yield a_n. Further, $F_n(a) = 0$ has a unique positive root (which lies in the interval $(0, (\rho\sigma_\varepsilon^2)^{-1})$).*

Proof. It follows immediately from expected CARA utility maximization that

$$X(s_i, p_{n-1}) = \frac{E\{(v - p_n) \mid s_i, p_{n-1}\}}{\rho \text{Var}\{(v - p_n) \mid s_i, p_{n-1}\}},$$

which equals

$$\frac{(1 - \lambda_n a_n)E\{(v - p_{n-1}) \mid s_i, p_{n-1}\}}{\rho[(1 - \lambda_n a_n)^2 \text{Var}\{v \mid s_i, p_{n-1}\} + \lambda_n^2 \sigma_u^2]}.$$

Using the expressions for $E\{(v - p_n) \mid s_i, p_{n-1}\}$ and $\text{Var}\{v \mid s_i, p_{n-1}\}$ in Claims 5 and 4, we obtain $a_n = \rho(\sigma_\varepsilon^2 + a_n\lambda_n\text{Var}(v \mid p_{n-1}))^{-1} = \rho(\sigma_\varepsilon^2 + \text{Var}(p_n \mid p_{n-1}))^{-1}$. This yields the desired cubic equation $F_n(a_n) = (\rho(\tau_\varepsilon)^{-1}a_n - 1)\tau_{n-1} + \rho\lambda_n a_n^2 = 0$. It is clear that positive roots must lie in $(0, (\rho\sigma_\varepsilon^2)^{-1})$. It can be easily checked that $F_n(0) < 0$, $F_n((\rho\sigma_n^2)^{-1}) > 0$, and that $F_n(a) = 0$ implies that $F_n'(a) > 0$. It follows then that there is a unique positive root. □

5. THE SPEED OF INFORMATION REVELATION

How many rounds of price quotations are necessary to obtain an accurate estimate of the liquidation value v? How do market parameters like the degree of risk aversion, precision of signals, or the amount of noise in the system impinge upon the speed at which prices reveal information? In summary, what are, and what factor determine, the properties of the price quotation p_n as an estimator of v? The asymptotic analysis of the dynamic equilibrium will yield insights into these issues.

Proposition 5.1. gives the asymptotics of key endogenous market parameters while Proposition 5.2. studies the properties of the market price p_n as an estimator of the liquidation value v, establishing the speed of convergence of p_n to v. It is worth recalling again that the market parameters are notional or theoretical unless trade happens to be realized in the period.

Proposition 5.1. *As n goes to infinity:*

(i) *the responsiveness to information a_n increase monotonically to $a = (\rho\sigma_\varepsilon^2)^1$,*

(ii) *the informativeness of prices τ_n tends monotonically to infinity at a rate of n; the asymptotic value of τ_n, $A\tau_\infty \equiv \lim_{n\to\infty} n^{-1}\tau_n$, equals $\tau_u a^2$.*

(iii) *the depth of the market λ_n^{-1} tends to infinity at a rate of n.*

(iv) *the unconditional volatility of prices $\operatorname{Var} p_n$ increases monotonically to σ_u^2 the conditional volatility $\operatorname{Var}\{p_n \mid P_{n-1}\}$ tends to zero.*

(v) *the expected volume traded by informed agents $(E|\bar{x}_n| = (2/\tau)^{1/2} a_n \times \sqrt{\operatorname{Var}(v \mid p_{n-1})})$ tends to zero.*

Proof. (i) The equilibrium a_n is the unique solution to $F_n(a) = 0$. Now, $\partial F_n/\partial a > 0$ when evaluated at a_n, and F_n is strictly decreasing in $A_{n-1} = \sum_{t=1}^{n-1} a_t^2$. Therefore a_n is increasing with A_{n-1} and with n. It follows that $A_{n-1} \underset{n}{\to} \infty$ and therefore from $F_n(a) = 0$, $(\rho a_n \sigma_\varepsilon^2 - 1) \underset{n}{\to} 0$ or $a_n \underset{n}{\to} (\rho\sigma_t^2)^{-1}$.

(ii) and (iii) It follows from the expression for τ_n that it increases monotonically. The rate statements are equivalent to $A_n \underset{n}{\to} \infty$ at the rate of n. This is clear since $n(\rho\sigma_\varepsilon^2)^{-2} \geq A_n \geq na_1^2$.

(iv) For the unconditional variance, the result follows from (ii) and the fact that $\operatorname{Var} p_n = \sigma_v^2 - \operatorname{Var}(v \mid p_n)$. To check the latter note that $\sigma_v^2 = E\{\operatorname{Var}(v \mid p_n)\} + \operatorname{Var}\{E(v \mid p_n)\}$ and $E(v \mid p_n) = p_n$. Further, $E\{\operatorname{Var}(v \mid p_n)\} = \operatorname{Var}(v \mid p_n)$ since (v, p_n) are jointly normally distributed. For the conditional variance the result follows from (i), (ii), and (iii), and the expression for $\operatorname{Var}\{p_n \mid p_{n-1}\}$.

(v) It is well known that $E|\bar{x}_n| = (2/\pi)^{1/2}\sqrt{\operatorname{Var}\bar{x}_n}$ if $E\bar{x}_n = 0$ (as it is in our case). Now, $\bar{x}_n = \int_0^1 X_n(s_i, p_{n-1})\,di = a_n(\varepsilon - p_{n-1})$. We have then $\operatorname{Var}\bar{x}_n = a_n^2 \operatorname{Var}(v - p_{n-1})$ and it is easily checked that $\operatorname{Var}(v - p_{n-1}) = \sigma_v^2 - \operatorname{Var}(p_{n-1}) = \operatorname{Var}(v \mid p_{n-1})$. The result follows then from (i) and (ii). $\square$

Proposition 5.2. *The market price as an estimator of v is*

(i) *biased (in the sense of regression toward the mean: $\operatorname{Sign}\{E\{(v - p_n) \mid v\}\} = \operatorname{Sign}\{v - \bar{v}\})$*

(ii) *strongly consistent (that is, $p_n \underset{n}{\to} v$ a.s.)*

(iii) *normal with asymptotic variance $(A\tau_\infty)^{-1} = \sigma_u^2\rho^2\sigma_\varepsilon^4$ and convergence rate $1/\sqrt{n}$ (that is, $\sqrt{n}(p_n - v) \overset{L}{\to} N(0, \sigma_u^2\rho^2\sigma_\varepsilon^4)$.*

Proof. (i) From $E(p_n \mid v) = (1 - (\tau_v/\tau_n))v + (\tau_v/\tau_n)\bar{v}$, it is immediate that $E\{(v - p_n) \mid v\} = (\tau_v/\tau_n)(v - \bar{v})$.

(ii) From Claim 2 in Section 4 we know that $p_n = (\tau_v\bar{v} + \tau_a \sum_{t=1}^n a_t z_t)/\tau_n$. Therefore $p_n = (\tau_v\bar{v} + \tau_u A_n y_n)/\tau_n$, where $y_n \equiv A_n^{-1} \sum_{t=1}^n a_t z_t$ is the OLS estimator of v based on $z_t = a_t v + u_t$, $t = 1, \ldots, n$. Recalling that $n^{-1}A_n \underset{n}{\to} (\rho\sigma_\varepsilon^2)^{-2}$ (since $a_n \underset{n}{\to} (\rho\sigma_\varepsilon^2)^{-1}$), it is a standard result (see White [38, pp. 17–18]) that $y_n \underset{n}{\to} v$ (a.s.). Therefore, $P_n \underset{n}{\to} v$ a.s. since $\tau_v/\tau_n \underset{n}{\to} 0$ and $\tau_u A_n/\tau_n = (1 - (\tau_v/\tau_n)) \underset{n}{\to} 1$.

(iii) It is immediate that $p_n - v = y_n - v + (\tau_v/\tau_n)(\bar{v} - y_n)$. It follows (see, for example, Amemiya [2, Theorem 3.5.3]) that $\sqrt{n}(y_n - v) \overset{L}{\to} N(0, \sigma_u^2\rho^2\sigma_\varepsilon^4)$ since

$n^{-1}a_n \to (\rho\sigma_\varepsilon^2)^{-2}$ and $\{a_t\}$ is bounded. Furthermore, $\sqrt{n}(\tau_v/\tau_n)(\bar{v} - y_n) \xrightarrow{n} 0$ a.s. since $\sqrt{n}(\tau_v/\tau_n) \xrightarrow{n} 0$ and $y_n \xrightarrow{n} v$ a.s. The result follows. □

Remark. As n tends to infinity, the tâtonnement equilibrium approaches the full information equilibrium where price equals the fundamental value almost surely. This limit equilibrium is obviously degenerate since then v is public information and there is no information asymmetry between informed agents and market makers. It is worth to remark that the limit intensity of trade of informed agents a is exactly the same as in the standard large market rational expectations model (as in Hellwig [14], for example, when the number of traders tends to infinity) in which informed agents submit limit orders to an auctioneer who clears the market in the presence of noise traders.[14]

As the number of rounds of the information tâtonnement grows, prices become more informative (τ_n increases). Competitive market makers increase the (national) liquidity of the market, λ_n^{-1} tends to infinity with n, and the market price is less sensitive to the current order flow. The conditional variance of prices decreases and induces each informed agent i to respond more to his information summarized by the sufficient statistic $(s_i - p_{n-1})$: a_n grows with n. At the same time the volatility of price quotations increases, since they incorporate more information, and the desired volume of trade of informed agents tends to zero since their information advantage with respect to the market makers is vanishing.

Competitive market makers aggregate all the information available in the history of order flows (or prices) into the current market price. This market price eventually coincides (a.s.) with the underlying value of the asset. That is, the market price p_n becomes fully revealing of v. In statistical terms, p_n is a strongly consistent estimator of v, although biased for any finite n (it overestimates v if v is small and underestimates it if v is large).

Price quotations converge to v fast, at the rate $1/\sqrt{n}$, and the asymptotic precision of p_n is decreasing in ρ, σ_n^2, and σ_ε^2. That is, convergence is slower if agents are more risk averse, agents have less precise private information, or noise is larger. A larger ρ or σ_ε^2 makes informed agents respond less to information (this is checked formally in Proposition 7.1 below). Further, this same effect follows from increased noise if n is as large as the simulations reported in Section 7 show (see Figure 1).

In summary, the information tâtonnement only needs a few rounds to get close to the value of the asset since the precision of prices τ_n grows linearly with the number of rounds n. The 'slope' of τ_n with respect to n decreases with ρ, σ_u^2, and σ_ε^2. This can be taken as an indication, perhaps, of the efficiency in aggregating information of the tâtonnement in the opening batch auction in some continuous trading systems. Indeed, the public announcement of theoretical prices proves effective in resolving the uncertainty about the value of the asset. We will see now the need for competitive agents using limit orders (market makers) to obtain fast convergence.

---

[14] This is the approach to rational expectations taken by Kyle [22] and Jackson [16].

6. MARKET MAKERS, LIMIT ORDERS AND
SPEED OF CONVERGENCE

When informed agents use market orders as strategies, market makers play a key role in the speed of convergence by making the market increasingly deep as the number of periods grows and forcing risk averse informed agents to respond increasingly to their information. In fact, in our financial market, the presence of competitive agents using limit orders, and therefore providing liquidity to the market, seems to be a necessary condition to obtain a 'fast' convergence (at the rate $n^{-1/2}$).

We illustrate the possibility of slow convergence when informed agents use market orders by removing the competitive market making sector from the previous model. In this case market depth is fixed *exogenously* by the price sensitive noise traders. A constant or a changing market depth (according to competitive market making) will have important dynamic consequences. This is so since as we have pointed out, ceteris paribus, an increase in the depth of the market induces informed agents to respond more to their information.

Consider then the previous model but without market makers: Informed agents submit market orders and noise traders submit a fixed price elastic demand for the asset $u_n - p_n$ to an auctioneer. The price sensitivity of noise traders has been normalized to $\alpha_n = 1$ for all n. (The asymptotic results obtained below would hold for any sequence of α_n bounded above.) The auctioneer quotes a price to clear the market: $p_n = u_n + \bar{x}_n$. The price function is now exogenous, with depth $\lambda_n = 1$. In this case as time evolves the depth of the market is fixed as the noise traders 'hold' the market. As before at stage n the value v and trade are only realized with probability γ_n.

Agents will have to form a price statistic to estimate v with their past observations of price quotations and knowledge of strategies. At period n, the price sequence p^{n-1} can be summarized in an OLS statistic y_{n-1} analogous to the OLS estimator of v that we have used in the proof of Proposition 5.2(ii): $y_n \equiv A_n^{-1} \sum_{t=1}^{n} a_t z_t$, with $z_t = a_t v + u_t$, where a_t is the response coefficient to private information. Equilibrium strategies will be of the form $X_n(s_i, y_{n-1}) = b_n + a_n s_i + d_n y_{n-1}$. It is worth to remark that now p_{n-1} (the last period price) is no longer a sufficient statistic for the information in the sequence of past prices. Using methods similar to Vives [34] it can be shown (the proof is omitted):

Proposition 6.1. *With no competitive market making sector, linear symmetric equilibria exist and are characterized by*

$$X_n(s_i, y_{n-1}) = b_n + a_n s_i + d_n y_{n-1},$$

where

$$a_n = \frac{\tau_\varepsilon \tau_u (1 - a_n)}{\rho((1 - a_n)^2 \tau_u + \tau_\varepsilon + \tau_{n-1})},$$

yielding a recursive cubic equation with solution in the interval $(0, 1)$

$$G_n(a) \equiv (1 - a)(\rho a(\tau_\varepsilon)^{-1}(1 - a) - 1)\tau_u\tau_\varepsilon + \rho a(\tau_\varepsilon + \tau_{n-1}) = 0,$$

and

$$d_n = \frac{\tau_{n-1} - \tau_n}{a_n^{-1}\tau_v + (\tau_v + \tau_{n-1})(1 - a_n)^{-1}}, \qquad b_n = \frac{\tau_v\bar{v}}{a_n^{-1}\tau_\varepsilon + (\tau_\varepsilon + \tau_{n-1})(1 - a_n)^{-1}}.$$

Remark. The equation $G_n(a) = 0$ may have three positive solutions. Nevertheless for n large it can be checked that the solution is unique.

As n tends to infinity, the price precision τ_n grows without bound but it does so at a rate substantially slower than linear, yielding an order of magnitude of τ_n of $n^{1/3}$. The reason is that without market makers the responsiveness to private information a_n converges to zero as n grows since Bayesian agents decrease the weight they put on their private signals as public information (the price statistic y_{n-1}) becomes better and better. The consequence is that the new information in the current price, represented by z_n $(= a_n v + u_n)$, asymptotically is independent of p (because a_n converges to zero as n grows). Similarly as in Vives [34] the information revealed through prices is a victim of its own success. Precisely because prices become more informative agents put less weight on their private signals; this, in turn, makes the current price less informative and slows down convergence. This can be interpreted as a dynamic analog of the Grossman–Stiglitz [13] paradox on the impossibility of informationally efficient markets. Indeed, in the dynamic model the information in prices eventually reveals the value of the asset but slowly. The final result is that convergence to the shared-information equilibrium (where agents pool their information, learn v, and trade an amount $X(v) = v(1 + \rho\sigma_u^2)^{-1}$) is not precluded but it is slowed down to the rate $1/\sqrt{n^{1/3}}$. The following lemma and proposition state the results formally.

Lemma. *For any linear equilibrium sequence:*

(a) *The response to private information a_n tends to 0, $d_n \xrightarrow{n} (\rho\sigma_u^2 + 1)^{-1}$ and $b_n \xrightarrow{n} 0$, as $n \to \infty$.*

(b) *The informativeness of the price statistic y_n, τ_n, is on the order of $n^{1/3}$ and a_n is on the order of $n^{-1/3}$. The asymptotic precision $A\tau_\infty (\equiv \lim_{n\to\infty} n^{-1/3}\tau_n)$ is given by $\tau_u 3^{1/3}(\tau_\varepsilon/\rho)^{2/3}$.*

Proof. (a) follows from the analyis of the recursive cubic equation $G_n(a) = 0$ and the expressions for d_n and b_n in Proposition 6.2.

(b) follows from the fact that $a_n A_{n-1} \xrightarrow{n} (\rho\sigma_\varepsilon^2)^{-1}$ and $n^{-1/3}A_n \xrightarrow{n} 3^{1/3}(\rho\sigma_\varepsilon^2)^{-2/3}$ (similarly as in the proofs of Claims 1 and 2 in Lemma 5.1 in Vives [34], the proof is omitted). $\qquad\square$

Proposition 6.2 *With no competitive market makers, given any (symmetric) equilibrium sequence:*

(i) *The price statistic y_n converges almost surely to v as n goes to infinity.*
(ii) *The rate of convergence is $1/\sqrt{n^{1/3}}$. More precisely.*

$$\sqrt{n^{1/3}}(y_n - v) \xrightarrow{L} N\left(0, \left(\frac{(\rho\sigma_\varepsilon^2)^2}{3}\right)^{1/3}\sigma_u^2\right).$$

Proof. Results (i) and (ii) follow immediately from Lemma 3.2 in Vives [34]. $\square$

In contrast, in the endogenous depth model (with competitive market makers), strategies of informed agents are of the form $X_n(s_i, p_{n-1}) = a_n(s_i - p_{n-1})$, and a_n increases with n and converges to a positive constant. This is so since then the market depth is endogenous and increasing, through the activity of market makers, as more tâtonnement rounds accumulate, and a risk averse agent responds more to the deviations of p_{n-1} from the private signal s_i the deeper is the market. The current price p_n is a linear transformation of the OLS statistic y_n, and the new information p_n contains, as represented by the variable z_n ($= a_n v + u_n$), does not diminish for n large. The order of a magnitude of the precision of price τ_u is then n.

Further, it is interesting to note that in the exogenous depth case the effects of risk aversion and private information are diminished since the asymptotic variance of $\sqrt{n^{1/3}}(y_n - v)$ is $3^{1/3}(\rho^2\sigma_\varepsilon^4)^{1/3}\sigma_u^2$ versus $\rho^2\sigma_\varepsilon^4\sigma_u^2$ for the asymptotic variance of $\sqrt{n}(p_n - v)$ in the case with market makers. In other words, the presence of market makers compounds the effect of the degree of risk aversion and the precision of private information.

7. COMPARATIVE DYNAMICS OF INFORMATION ADJUSTMENT

In this section, the effect of basic parameters on the information adjustment process is studied and some simulations provided. The first proposition deals with comparative dynamic properties of the equilibrium which hold for all n while the second restricts attention to properties which hold for large n. In both the hatted and unhatted variables refer to different markets.

Proposition 7.1. *Comparative dynamics of equilibrium sequences.*

(i) *If either $\hat{\rho} > \rho$, or $\hat{\sigma}_\varepsilon > \sigma_\varepsilon$, or $\hat{\sigma}_v > \sigma_v$, then $\hat{a}_t < a_t$ for all t.*
(ii) *If either $\hat{\rho} > \rho$, or $\hat{\sigma}_\varepsilon > \sigma_\varepsilon$, or $\hat{\sigma}_\varepsilon > \sigma_\varepsilon$, then $\hat{\tau}_t < \tau_t$ for all t.*
(iii) *If either $\hat{\rho} > \rho$, or $\hat{\sigma}_\varepsilon > \sigma_\varepsilon$, then $\text{Var } \hat{p}_t < \text{Var } p_t$ for all t.*

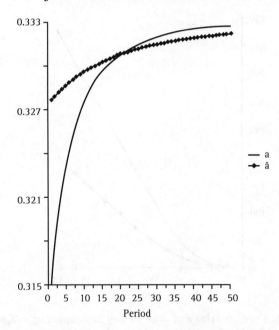

Figure 1. *Responsiveness to information and noise trading. Simulation:* $\sigma_v^2 - 1, \sigma_u^2 - 4$. *Fixed parameters:* $\sigma_t^2 = 1, \sigma_\epsilon^2 = 1.5, \rho = 2$.

Proof. From the proof of Proposition 5.1(i) the response coefficient a_n is increasing with $A_{n-1} = \sum_{t=1}^{n-1} a_t^2$. We show now that, fixing a history $a^{n-1} \equiv (a_1, \ldots, a_{n-1})$, a_n, τ_n, and $\text{Var } p_n$ move appropriately with the parameters ρ, σ_ϵ^2, and σ_v^2. Fix A_{n-1} and consider stage n, note then that: (a) a_n decreases with ρ, σ_ϵ^2, and σ_t^2, (b) τ_n decreases with ρ, σ_ϵ^2, and σ_v^2, and (c) $\text{Var } p_n$ decreases with ρ and σ_ϵ^2.

To prove this claim check that in equilibrium $(F_n(a) = 0) \, \partial F_n/\partial \rho, \, \partial F_n/\partial \sigma_\epsilon^2$, and $\partial F_n/\partial \sigma_v^2$ are all positive. Therefore, $\partial a_n/\partial \rho, \, \partial a_n/\partial \sigma_\epsilon^2$, and $\partial a_n/\partial \sigma_v^2$ are all negative for any n and fixed A_{n-1}. (b) and (c) follow immediately from the expressions for τ_n and $\text{Var } p_n$. The results follow. $\quad\square$

Proposition 7.1 states that comparing two economies, one with either a larger degree of risk aversion or a lower precision of information, or more diffuse priors, agents respond less to the information they have and prices reveal less information, both phenomena uniformly in time. Further, except in the case of the higher prior variance of the value of the asset price, variability is also uniformly lower. This should come as no surprise since prices reflect less information.

How is a_t affected by changes in noise?

We have seen that in the one-shot market that a_1 increases with the level of noise. Nevertheless, for $n \geq 2$ the sufficient statistic that agents use is $(s_i - p_{n-1})$, and increase in noise will decrease the informativeness of prices when n is large

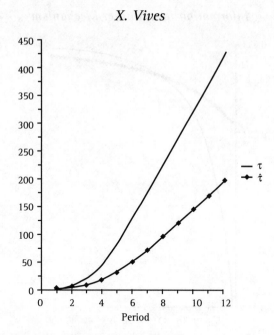

Figure 2. *Price precision and noise trading Simulation:* $\sigma_v^2 = 2, \hat{\sigma}_u^2 = 4$.
Fixed parameters: $\sigma_t^2 = 1, \sigma_\epsilon^2 - 0.1, \rho = 1$.

enough. Informed agents, then, respond less to information.[15] Simulations indicate that the typical pattern, if $\hat{\sigma}_u > \sigma_u$, is that there is a critical n for which $\hat{a}_1 \gtrless \alpha_\tau$ if $t \gtrless v$ (see Figure 1). As we know, for $t = I, \hat{a}_1 > a_1$, but this is revised as time goes on.

Proposition 7.2. *Asymptotic comparative dynamics. For n large enough:*

(i) *If $\hat{\sigma}_u > \sigma_u$, then $\hat{\tau}_n < \tau_n$.*
(ii) *If either $\hat{\rho} > \rho$, or $\hat{\sigma}_\epsilon > \sigma_\epsilon$, then $\hat{\lambda}_n^{-1} < \lambda_n^{-1}$.*
(iii) *If $\hat{\sigma}_u > \sigma_u$, then Var $\hat{p}_n <$ Var p_n.*
(iv) *If $\hat{\sigma}_u > \sigma_u$, then Var $(\tilde{\bar{x}}_n) >$ Var $\bar{x}_n$.*

Proof. (i) $\tau_n = \tau_v + \tau_u A_n$ and $n^{-1}A_n \xrightarrow{n} fa^2$. For n large, therefore, $\tau_n \approx \tau_v + \tau_u a^2 n$. If $\hat{\sigma}_u > \sigma_u$ then $\hat{\tau}_n < \tau_n$, since a is independent of σ_u^2 and a larger σ_u^2 decreases the slope of the approximation to τ_n.

(ii) $\lambda_n^{-1} = (\tau_u a_n)^{-1} \tau_n$. For n large, $\hat{\lambda}_n^{-1} \approx \tau_v (\tau_a a_n)^{-1} + an$. If $\hat{\rho} > \rho$ or $\hat{\sigma}_\epsilon > \sigma_\epsilon$ then $\hat{a} < a$ and we obtain the desired result.

(iii) Var $p_n = \sigma_r^2 - \tau_n^{-1}$. Therefore Var $p_n \approx \sigma_r^2 - (\tau_r + \tau_n \sigma^2 n)^{-1}$ for n large and the result follows as in (i).

---

[15] For n large, and fixing a history A_{n-1}, a_n is decreasing in σ_u^2. This follows similarly as in the claim proof of Proposition 7.1: $\partial F_n/\partial \sigma_u^2 > 0$ for n large. Consequently $\partial a_n/\sigma_\epsilon^2 < 0$.

(iv) $\text{Var}\,\bar{x}_n = a_n^2 \tau_{n-1}^{-1}$. Therefore, $\text{Var}\,\bar{x}_n \approx (\tau_n a^{-2} + \tau_u n)^{-1}$ for n large and the results follows similarly. □

Using simulations[16] it is possible to illustrate some of the results and uncover some interesting patterns. Figure 2 illustrates Provision 7.2(i) and represents the typical patterns found for the price precision. In fact, when $\hat{\sigma}_u > \sigma_u$, $\hat{\tau}_n < \tau_n$ starting from $n = 1$. The price precision, as we know, grows linearly with n (i.e., τ_n is a linear function of n) but the slope of growth asymptotically approaches $\tau_u a^2 = (\rho^2 \sigma_n^4 \sigma_u^2)^{-1}$. We see clearly here the role of the parameters ρ, σ_ε^2, and σ_u^2 in determining the speed of convergence. An increase in any of them decreases the slope of τ_n with respect to n.

With regard to Proposition 7.2(ii) note that the depth of the market, for a given informativeness of prices, increases with the amount of noise and decreases with the responsiveness of informed agents to information (competitive market makers respond to more active insiders by reducing the liquidity of the market). A larger response to information (coming from a decrease in ρ, σ_n^2, or σ_u^2, for n large) has a negative direct effect on λ_n^{-1} but a positive indirect effect through an increase in the informativeness of prices (τ_n). For n large the direct effect dominates for changes in ρ or σ_u^2. In some instances for n small, $\hat{\lambda}_n^{-1} < \lambda_n^{-1}$, while in others the reverse inequality holds for all n. The simulations also show that for n small $\hat{\lambda}_n^{-1} > \lambda_n^{-1}$ if $\hat{\sigma}_u > \sigma_u$, due to the positive initial impact of the increase in noise in market depth. For n large the inequality may be reversed since the increased noise will induce a lower price precision and market makers will respond by decreasing the liquidity of the market.

With regard to Proposition 7.2(iv) the simulations show that the typical pattern is for the (squared) traded volume inequality to hold for all n. Further, it is uncovered that it is possible that for n large we have that $\text{Var}(\bar{x}_n) < \text{Var}(\hat{\bar{x}}_n)$ when $\rho < \hat{\rho}$. A decrease in risk aversion brings more responsiveness to information (a_t goes up) but also increases the informativeness of price (τ_t^{-1} goes down). The first effect tends to increase the desired volume of trade while the second tends to decrease it. The total effect is ambiguous.

8. CONCLUDING REMARKS

The paper has characterized the speed at which privately held information is incorporated into market prices in an information adjustment mechanism with a value discovery purpose. The mechanism aggregates the information of risk averse agents who use market orders as trading strategies. The speed of information revelation has been seen to depend crucially on the presence of a competitive risk neutral market making sector. In its presence convergence occurs at

---

[16] Simulations have been made systematically in the following ranges of parameter values: ρ in $[1, 4]$, σ_r^2 in $[0.5, 5]$, σ_r^2 in $[0.1, 4.6]$ and σ_r^2 in $[0.5, 2.5]$.

a rate of $n^{-1/2}$, where n is the number of tâtonnement rounds. In its absence, convergence is slow, at the rate of $n^{-1/6}$.

A natural question to ask is how robust the results are to changes in the specification of the model. Generalizations within the linear-normal framework are feasible. Among them, the consideration of heterogeneity in terms of risk tolerance and precision of private signals as well as, perhaps more interestingly, the consideration of autocorrelated noise trading. Further, the case of risk averse market makers could be easily accommodated. Indeed, the conjecture is that the results are not driven by the risk neutrality of the market sector. With risk averse market makers, there would be a tendency toward a decreased market depth and decreased trade intensity by risk averse informed agents. Nevertheless, the speed of convergence of prices to the fundamental value should be unaffected (at the rate $n^{-1/2}$) since market depth would increase without bound and the informed agents' trading intensity would converge to a positive constant as in the case of risk neutral market makers. What is crucial to obtain the 'fast' convergence rate of $n^{-1/2}$ is the existence of a mass of agents providing liquidity (depth) to the market with limit orders.

How important is the linear-normal specification for the results to hold? This is an open question which needs further research and, although general results may be hard to obtain, we should be hopeful of the robustness of the results given that the principles isolated in the present paper (in contrast to the techniques used) do not seem to depend crucially on the details of the linear-normal structure. In essence, the presence of a competitive market making sector speeds up convergence because it dynamically increases the depth of the market and prevents risk averse informed agents from responding less to their private information, making in turn prices more informative.

Another potential avenue of research is to study situations of real dynamic trading (as apposed to notional trading in an information tâtonnement). In a financial market model of the same family as that considered in the present paper but with a finite horizon and real trading up to the realization of the fundamental value v, it is easy to see that the precision of prices is bounded above no matter how long the horizon is (see Section 5.1 in Vives [35]). In other words, there is no convergence of prices to the fundamental value as the horizon lengthens. The reason is that the precision incorporated in prices depends on the *net* trading intensities of informed agents (that is, the incremental trading at any period), which in the aggregate across periods is necessarily bounded if information is received only once. This highlights the importance of information tâtonnement mechanisms for value discovery purposes like the above-mentioned opening batch auction in continuous trading systems.

The role of market makers could also be explored in an infinite horizon model with a risky asset paying dividends every period. Traders would receive information and trade also every period. The issue would be then how the presence of market makers affects the steady state precision of prices in the estimation of the dividend flow.

REFERENCES

1. A. R. Admati, A noisy rational expectations equilibrium for multi-asset securities markets. *Econometrica* 53 (1985), 629–657.
2. T. Amemiya, 'Advanced Econometrics.' Basil Blackwell. Oxford. 1985.
3. Y. Amihud and H. Mendelson, Trading mechanisms and stock returns: An empirical investigation. *J. Finance* 42 (1987), 533–553.
4. Y. Amihud and H. Mendelson, Call auction and continuous auction: Effects on market volatility and liquidity, mimeo. Graduate School of Business Administration. 1989.
5. Y. Amihud and H. Mendelson, Market microstructure and price discovery on the Tokyo Stock Exchange. *Japan World Econ.* 1 (1989), 341–370.
6. Y. Amihud, H. Mendelson, and M. Murgia, Stock market microstructure and return volatility: Evidence from Italy, mimeo, 1989.
7. L. Ausurel, Insider trading in a rational expectations economy. *Antcr. Econ. Rev.* 80 (1990), 1022–1041.
8. Compagnie des Agents de Change, Cotation Assistóe en Continu, *Le Marchè Continu de la Bourse de Paris*, January 1988.
9. J. Dennert, Insider trading and the cost of capital in a multi-period economy. Discussion Paper 128, LSE Financial Markets Group. 1992.
10. J. Gennotte and A. Kyle, Intertemporal insider trading with a smooth order flow, mimeo. 1992.
11. J. Gould and R. Verrpchia, The information content of specialist pricing. *J. Polit. Econ.* 93 (1985), 66–83.
12. S. Grossman, On the efficiency of competitive stock markets where trades have diverse information. *J. Finance* 31 (1976), 573–585.
13. S. Grossman and J. Stiglitz, On the impossibility of informationally efficient markets. *Amer. Econ. Rev.* 70 (1980), 393–408.
14. M. F. Hellwig, On the aggregation of information in competitive markets. *J. Econ. Theory* 22 (1980), 477–498.
15. M. Feldman and C. Giles, An expository note on individual risk without aggregate uncertainty. *J. Econ. Theory* 35 (1985), 26–32.
16. M. O. Jackson, Equilibrium, price information and the value of private information. *Rev. Finan. Stud.* 4 (1991), 1–16.
17. J. S. Jordan, A dynamic model of expectations equilibrium. *J. Econ. Theory* 28 (1982), 235–254.
18. J. S. Jordan, Learning rational expectations: The finite state case. *J. Econ. Theory* 36 (1985), 257–276.
19. R. Kuhlstrom and L. Mirman, Information and market equilibrium. *Bell J. Econ.* 6 (1975).
20. T. Kobayashi, A convergence theorem on rational expectations equilibrium with price information. Working Paper 79, The Economics Series, Institute for Mathematical Studies in the Social Sciences, Stanford University, 1977.
21. A. S. Kyle, Continuous auction and insider trading. *Econometrica* 53 (1985), 1315–1335.
22. A. S. Kyle, Informed speculation with imperfect competition. *Rev. Econ. Stud.* 56 (1989), 317–356.
23. J. C. Leach and A. N. Madhavan, Intertemporal price discovery by market makers: Active versus passive learning. *J. Finan. Intermed.* 2 (1992), 207–235.

172   *X. Vives*

24. J. C. Leach and A. N. Madhavan, Price experimentation and security market structure. *Rev. Finan. Stud.* 2 (1993), 375–404.
25. H. Leland, Insider trading: Should it be prohibited? *J. Polit. Econ.* 4 (1992), 859–887.
26. M. Pagano, Endogenous market thinness and stock price volatility. *Rev. Econ. Stud.* 56 (1989), 269–288.
27. M. Pagano and A. Roell, Auction and dealership markets: What is the difference? *Europ. Econ. Rev.* 36 (1992), Papers and Proceedings.
28. M. Pagano and A. Roell, Shifting gears: An economic evaluation of the reform of the Paris Bourse. Discussion Paper 103. LSE Financial Markets Group, 1990: forthcoming in 'Financial Market Liberalisation and the Role and Banks' (V. Conti and R. Hamani Eds.), Cambridge Univ. Press, Cambridge, 1992.
29. R. Ortega, El mercado de renta variable las perspectivas de la bolsa española. *Popeles de Economia Española* 49 (1991).
30. J. C. Rochet and J. L. Vila, Insider trading without normality. *Rev. Econ. Stud.* 61 (1994), 131–152.
31. K. J. Singleton, Asset prices in a time-series model with disparately informed, competitive traders, *in* 'New Approaches to Monetary Economics,' Cambridge Univ. Press, Cambridge, 1987.
32. J. L. Vila, Simple games of market manipulations. *Econ. Lett.* 29 (1989), 21–26.
33. X. Vives, Information aggregation in large Cournot markets. *Econometrica* 56 (1988), 851–876.
34. X. Vives, How fast do rational agents learn? *Rev. Econ. Stud.* 60 (1993), 329–347.
35. X. Vives, Short-term investment and the informational efficiency of the market. *Rev. Finan. Stud.* 8 (1995), 125–160.
36. J. Wang, A model of intertemporal asset prices under asymmetric information. *Rev. Econ. Stud.* 60 (1993), 249–282.
37. D. K. Withcomb, An international comparison of stock exchange trading structures, *in* 'Market Making and the Changing Structure of the Securities Industry' (Y. Amihud, T. S. Y. Ho, and R. A. Schwartz Eds.), Lexington Books, Lexington, MA, 1985.
38. H. White, 'Asymptotic Theory for Econometricians,' Academic Press, New York, 1984.

PART III

SPECULATION

6

Arbitrage Chains

JAMES DOW AND GARY GORTON

The efficiency of security prices depends upon arbitrage, that is, trading based upon knowledge that the price of an asset is different from its fundamental value. (Although the term 'arbitrage,' strictly speaking, refers to an entirely riskless speculation, we use the term in the broader sense common among practitioners.) For example, suppose an agent has private information about a high future dividend to be paid by a firm. If the current stock price does not reflect this information, then the agent can profit by buying the stock, if his purchase does not instantly raise the price, and holding it until the dividend is paid.

The argument depends on two assumptions. First, the arbitrageur's information cannot be instantly reflected in the price he pays upon submission of the order. Second, the arbitrageur must be able to hold the security until the dividend is paid (in order to realize the profit).

The first assumption has been widely studied (Ausubel (1990), Diamond and Verrechia (1981), Grossman and Stiglitz (1976), Kyle (1985)). The second assumption, that the arbitrageur's horizons span the event date (i.e., the date at which the dividend arrives in the example) has received less attention (the relevant literature is discussed below). But this second assumption is also crucial for the argument. There are several reasons why the informed trader's trading horizons may not span the event date. A portfolio manager may have to liquidate his portfolio to make large distributions to pensioners. Alternatively, he may need to show good performance over a short horizon at the end of which his performance is assessed. A third explanation, which we explore in detail below, is that the cost-of-carry of an arbitrage portfolio may make long-term arbitrage prohibitively costly.

Although the second assumption is often not satisfied, arbitrage may still be profitable if the price adjusts to reflect the information by the time the arbitrageur must close out his position. On the one hand, an informed trader with a limited horizon will not trade on his information (if arbitrage is costly) if he believes that tomorrow's price, when he must sell the stock, will not reflect the information. Since he does not buy the stock to start with, the price cannot reflect his information. On the other hand, he may believe that tomorrow another informed

We thank Bruno Biais, Sam Orez, Jean-Charles Rochet, and José Scheinkman for helpful discussions.

trader will arrive and buy the stock, pushing the price up so as to make the arbitrage profitable. In this case, he trades on his information, and this may have the effect of making the price more informative immediately. Of course, the complication is that if the next informed trader does not believe that by the end of his horizon yet another informed trader will push up the price, then *he* will not buy and the chain of arbitrages will unravel.

With limited trading horizons arbitrageurs' decisions to trade are influenced by their beliefs about the distribution of the private information across other (future) arbitrageurs with different, perhaps overlapping, trading horizons. If there is the possibility of a sequence of arbitrageurs with overlapping trading horizons that span the event date, then the decision of the first arbitrageur in the sequence depends on his beliefs about the subsequent chain of arbitrageurs and their decisions. The question we address is whether the actions of arbitrageurs in the chain can replicate the behavior of a single long-lived arbitrageur, or whether it is possible that there could be private information that is not acted upon.

The conventional wisdom is that short horizons, in themselves, will not cause assets to be mispriced. The reasoning is as follows. Suppose that a cash flow in twenty periods is not correctly priced currently. It will certainly be priced correctly in period twenty. Then in the nineteenth period an agent with a one-period horizon will insure that the asset is priced correctly. Since the asset will be priced in the nineteenth period, an agent with a one period horizon in the eighteenth period will insure that it is also correctly priced then. By backward induction, the asset must be correctly priced today. Our article questions this conventional wisdom by examining this argument in more detail. In particular, while this argument certainly applies to cases in which information is public, we argue that it does not extend to the case of private information.

Examples of situations where private information is too long-term relative to traders' horizons include the following. Foreign exchange traders may be unwilling to speculate on anticipated exchange-rate movements in two years' time. Government-bond arbitrageurs may be unwilling to speculate on perceived mispricings that are not corrected within days. Equity portfolio managers may pay little attention to information concerning the prospects of companies twenty years from now unless they believe it will be reflected in the price within a year or two.

We study a general equilibrium model where informed traders (arbitrageurs) have limited horizons and in which there are no exogenous 'noise' traders. The model is one of overlapping generations where prices are formed by a market-maker. Arbitrage is costly (either because of a brokerage fee or because of a borrowing cost). In the model risk-averse uninformed traders choose an amount to trade based on hedging motives. Each period there is a probability of an informed trader (arbitrageur) arriving who may choose to trade. Informed traders have private information about a future dividend that, for the first such trader, will arrive beyond his lifetime. Since arbitrageurs profit at the expense of the hedgers, the amount the hedgers trade can change depending on whether they believe there are informed traders operating or not.

The main result of the article is that informed agents will *not* engage in arbitrage a long time in advance of the event. In particular, only if the probability of another arbitrageur arriving next period is high enough will an informed agent trade this period. Consequently, information can arrive privately that has no chance of being impounded in prices because the arbitrageur finds it too costly to trade.

We then develop a variant of the basic model with long horizons and use this to compare equilibria with long and short horizons. The fact that arbitrage can only be accomplished via a chain of traders dramatically reduces arbitrage profitability, compared to the case where arbitrage does not require the asset to be resold because the arbitrageur's lifetime spans the event date. One reason is that for arbitrage to be profitable, the market must be relatively 'deep' so that the arbitrageur can buy without simultaneously pushing up the price. With a chain, however, profitable arbitrage also requires selling the asset when a subsequent arbitrageur pushes up the price in the next period. This requires that the market not be too deep.

Another reason for the reduced profitability of short-term arbitrage is that profits also depend on the likelihood that another trader will soon receive the same information. That is, the chain must be unbroken.

We have assumed that there is a transaction cost for trading the risky security. The transaction cost may be interpreted as a brokerage fee, as a bid-ask spread, or as a borrowing cost (cost-of-carry). In any model transaction costs are likely to cause price inefficiencies. In our model, however, we show that the effect of the transaction cost is multiplied by the two factors discussed above: the need to carry out arbitrage via a chain, and the possibility that the chain may be broken. This causes a given transaction cost to have a larger impact on the efficiency of asset prices. This conclusion is based on a comparison of arbitrage profits for an investor with a short horizon and an investor with a long horizon.

While we have given several reasons why traders' horizons may be limited, the model allows us to explore one explanation in more detail. Interpreting the transaction cost as a cost-of-carry, we show that a trader with a long horizon may optimally choose to conduct only short-term arbitrages because the cost-of-carry makes long-term arbitrages unprofitable.

The article proceeds as follows. In Section I we set out the model. Section II describes equilibrium order flows, while Section III describes price formation. Section IV describes the trading strategies of the arbitrageurs and proves our main result: informed agents will not engage in arbitrage a long time in advance of the event. Section V derives the quantities traded by the hedgers; Section VI discusses out-of-equilibrium beliefs. Section VII discusses the results and the related literature. In Section VIII we modify the model so that arbitrageurs have long-term horizons. We first show how short horizons reduce arbitrage profitability compared to long horizons. We then show how the cost-of-carry can make long-term arbitrage unprofitable. Section IX concludes.

I. THE MODEL

A. Definitions and Notation

We consider an economy with an infinite sequence of periods $t = -\infty, \ldots, \infty$. There is a stock that pays a dividend of 1 or 0 every period, with probabilities π and $1 - \pi$, respectively. Dividend realizations are serially independent. The other available asset is a riskless asset which earns r. We will focus on the periods preceding the period distinguished as $t = T$. The dividend realization at T may become known in advance to some agents, as described below.

Agents live for only two periods. Thus there are overlapping generations of young and old agents. Consumption occurs in old age. In each generation there are 0, 1, or 2 people. Agents may or may not receive a private piece of information. The probability that there is one uninformed hedger is $\frac{1}{2}$; the probability that there is no uninformed hedger is $\frac{1}{2}$. The probability that there is one informed arbitrageur in generation t is δ_t; with probability $1 - \delta_t$ there is no arbitrageur. These realizations are independent of each other, and serially. Thus, a generation may contain nobody (probability $\frac{1}{2}(1 - \delta_t)$), one informed arbitrageur and no uninformed hedger (probability $\frac{1}{2}\delta_t$), one uninformed hedger and no informed arbitrageur (probability $\frac{1}{2}(1 - \delta_t)$), or one arbitrageur and one hedger (probability $\frac{1}{2}\delta_t$).

Uninformed hedgers have initial wealth W. They also receive a wage income in old age of either 0 or 1 that is perfectly negatively correlated with that period's dividend. Thus the uninformed start life by buying a portfolio that they will liquidate in old age. However, we emphasize that they are not forced to participate in the stock market at all. If they want, they can simply invest at the riskless return r.

Uninformed agents are risk averse and so will have an incentive to buy stock to hedge their income. The reader may wish to read the first part of the article assuming that they are *infinitely* risk averse to simplify the analysis: in this case, they hedge perfectly by buying 1 unit of stock. In Section V, we explain how the quantity traded is determined for the case of finite risk aversion; this is quite straightforward and separate from the rest of the model. In particular, we stress that the equilibrium prices and the period at which information starts to be revealed in equilibrium are not affected.

For technical reasons, an uninformed agent should be viewed as representing a mass of infinitely small, identical, uninformed agents. This assumption will be needed in the derivation of the equilibrium quantities traded by the uninformed in Sections V and VI, and plays no role in the rest of the article. To avoid lengthy circumlocutions, elsewhere in the article we will simply refer to 'an uninformed agent' or 'a hedger' rather than 'a mass of uninformed agents,' etc.

Informed arbitrageurs are risk neutral. Like the uninformed, they receive an endowment W when young (since they are risk neutral, we assume for simplicity that they receive no wage income as this will not affect their decisions). An arbitrageur, if there is one, receives private information about the dividend to be received at the fixed date T. 'Good news' means that he learns it will be high (equal to 1); 'bad news' means it will be zero. As time approaches date T, the probability δ_t that there is an informed agent is increasing. The reader may find it convenient to think of δ_t as following the relation:

$$\delta_t = \epsilon \delta_{t+1} = \epsilon^{(T-t)}, \tag{1}$$

which converges smoothly to 1 at date T, though the analysis does not require us to use any specific process.

Apart from these agents, there is an institution for pricing and trading stocks. In the stock market, prices are set by a risk-neutral marketmaker who faces Bertrand competition and who has an inventory of stocks and cash (see Kyle (1985)). He observes all the (market) orders for the stock, and then posts a price and meets the net order out of his inventory. Because of competition, the price in each period is equal to his expected value of the asset. (His inventory is discussed further below.) We assume that the marketmaker observes all buy and sell orders separately (as will be seen below, in this model it would be equivalent to assume the marketmaker could only observe the net aggregate order).

Notice that when we refer to 'agents,' we do not include the marketmaker in this terminology.

There is a per-share transaction cost, c, to trading the stock. For notational simplicity c is the cost for a round-trip transaction (since all stocks bought when young will be sold the next period in old age).

The timing of events within each period may be summarized thus:

Start of period t
1. Dividends, old wage income, and young endowment arrive.
2. Information arrives (if there is an informed trader).
3. Orders are submitted.
4. Marketmaker sets the price.
5. Trades are executed.
6. Consumption occurs.
End of period t

B. Comments on Assumptions

Here we comment briefly on several aspects of the assumptions that may be questioned by the reader:

1. Why are informed arbitrageurs risk neutral and the uninformed, risk averse?

The risk aversion of uninformed agents makes them want to trade so as to hedge their wage income shock. If they were risk neutral they would simply invest at the risk-free rate and there would be no 'liquidity' trades for the arbitrageurs to hide behind. Arbitrageurs are risk neutral for simplicity (it will be clear that the results do not depend on this).

2. Why not have a lump-sum, rather than proportional, transactions cost? Why is the proportional transactions cost per share, not per dollar?

A lump-sum transaction cost seems less realistic and would complicate matters. The per-share assumption is made for analytical tractability. We have solved the model with proportional costs per dollar, but the closed-form solutions of the model are much more complex. The results are unchanged except that the formula in Proposition 3 is modified appropriately.

Although a proportional cost per dollar might seem more plausible a priori, there is empirical evidence to the contrary. Dimson and Marsh's (1989) data indicate that the bid-ask spread on the London Stock Exchange is approximately six pence regardless of the share price. Brennan and Hughes (1991) argue that brokerage commissions in the United States, expressed as a percentage of the value of the transaction, fall for shares with higher prices ('big' shares).

In Section VII we show that the cost may be interpreted as a borrowing cost, since the per-dollar version of the transaction cost is exactly equivalent to an interest charge on a loan.

3. Why is δ_t increasing over time?

Our model does not require that δ_t increase over time, but it is more plausible and simplifies the exposition to assume that it does. If it is not increasing, it is extremely easy to derive equilibria where long-term information is ignored. For example, if there is always an informed arbitrageur at $T-2$ but never in any other period, there will be such a nonrevealing equilibrium. The harder question is whether information may be ignored even when it is increasingly likely to arrive as we approach the event. Not only is this question harder, but it is more important since increasing δ_t seems more plausible.

4. Does the model depend on all agents having short horizons?

The answer is no. While both the uninformed hedgers and the informed arbitrageurs have limited horizons, the marketmaker is infinitely lived. Thus, as we discuss in Section VII, the results cannot be due to all agents having short horizons. What matters is that the privately informed arbitrageurs have short horizons and that there may be periods in which the arbitrage chain will be broken.

5. Why construct the hedging demand rather than simply adding a 'noise' term to demand (as in Kyle (1985))?

Trading profitably on the basis of private information requires that other agents trade and lose money on average. The standard device in the literature has been to model these 'noise traders' as a random exogenous component of asset demand that prevents asset prices from being fully revealing. The exact motivation of these noise traders, or liquidity traders, is not fully specified and they are sometimes interpreted as irrational (e.g., De Long et al. (1990)). This article is about short-term biases in asset pricing, but it is not about irrationality in asset pricing. On the contrary, we investigate the possibility of short-term biases in a fully rational setting. We therefore consider it important to explicitly model the origin of the 'liquidity' trade.

The model endogenizes the 'liquidity' trade in an attractive way. In our multi-period framework, agents start without assets and do not have to participate in the stock market if they do not want to. If they do participate, however, in order to hedge, then in the second period of their lives they must unwind their positions, i.e., sell their holdings. This distinguishes our model from Biais and Hillion (1992). They interpret the liquidity trade as coming from rational agents who hedge shocks to nontradeable assets, similar to our wage-income shocks. However, theirs is a one-period model where agents start with an endowment of assets, trade once, then the assets pay liquidating dividends and the agents consume.

Models based on multiperiod versions of Kyle (1985) contain a serially independent demand shock representing the liquidity trade. One benefit of our approach is that we impose the restriction that every security bought must be sold later. Thus, we derive the appropriate negatively serially correlated liquidity demand.

Another important aspect of the liquidity trade is the responsiveness of these traders to the amount lost (on average) to the informed traders. In our model the uninformed traders will trade a decreasing amount over time in response to the progressive increase in the profitability of arbitrage activity.

II. ORDER FLOW IN EQUILIBRIUM

We will now describe the equilibrium order flow and stock prices. The equilibrium has the property that arbitrageurs who receive good news act on the information starting a fixed number of periods from the end (date T), but not before. We call this date at which arbitrageurs start to act 'date K.' Subsequently we will show that this is indeed an equilibrium, determine K, and show that this is the unique equilibrium of the model.

It is possible that, after K, the arbitrageur's actions will completely reveal the news to the marketmaker and the price will immediately jump to the full information price from then on. In that case, subsequent arbitrageurs will not act. But unless this happens, in our model arbitrageurs with good news will always act after K for all other price histories.

Let x_t be the amount of stock bought in equilibrium by an uninformed (risk-averse) agent arriving at date t. Because of the transaction cost, the agent will only choose to hedge fully ($x_t = 1$) if he is infinitely risk averse. The determination of x_t is discussed in Section V below. However, the prices and other properties of equilibrium, including the determination of date K, will not be affected by x_t.

What are the possible orders after period K? If no agents arrive in period t, no orders will be submitted. If there is an uninformed hedger, he will buy x_t. We will show in Section VI below that, in order to disguise himself, an arbitrageur who receives good news will also buy x_t. Thus the possible buy orders are $0, x_t$, or $2x_t$. In other words, at all dates orders will be in multiples 0, 1, or 2 of x_t. (Notice that this implies that the total stockholding of the traders in equilibrium is therefore either $0, x_t$, or $2x_t$ shares.)

Arbitrageurs who receive bad news do not act because they would immediately be identified by the marketmaker. They do not sell the asset short. This is because in equilibrium the sell orders at date t will be the same as the buy orders from date $t - 1$. If an arbitrageur with bad news did sell short, sell orders at date t would exceed buys in $t - 1$, so the information would be completely revealed, and he would have incurred the transaction cost. (The model could easily be extended slightly to allow for short sales by arbitrageurs, but we do not pursue that.)

How could these multiples 0, 1, or 2 occur, and what are their probabilities?

Buy = 0

This can occur in two ways: either no agents arrive (probability $\frac{1}{2}(1 - \delta_t)$), or an arbitrageur arrives and receives bad news $(\frac{1}{2}\delta_t(1 - \pi))$:

$$\frac{1}{2}(1 - \delta_t) + \frac{1}{2}\delta_t(1 - \pi) = \frac{1}{2}(1 - \delta_t\pi). \tag{2}$$

Buy = 1

This can occur in three ways: only an uniformed hedger arrives $(\frac{1}{2}(1 - \delta_t))$; only an arbitrageur arrives and he receives good news $(\frac{1}{2}\delta_t\pi)$; both a hedger and an arbitrageur arrive, and the arbitrageur receives bad news $(\frac{1}{2}\delta_t(1 - \pi))$

$$\frac{1}{2}(1 - \delta_t) + \frac{1}{2}\delta_t\pi + 1\frac{1}{2}\delta_t(1 - \pi) = \frac{1}{2}. \tag{3}$$

Buy = 2

This occurs if both an arbitrageur and a hedger arrive, and the arbitrageur receives good news

$$\frac{1}{2}\delta_t\pi. \tag{4}$$

This description of the order flows now allows us to derive the marketmaker's beliefs and hence prices.

III. STOCK PRICES

If we are more than $T - K$ periods from T, by hypothesis, arbitrageurs do *not* act on their information. In that case there is no information in a buy order (there will be either 0 or 1 orders) and the price is given by

$$p = \pi/r, \tag{5}$$

which is the marketmaker's expected valuation.

We now consider prices less than $T - K$ periods from T. Suppose first that the marketmaker knows for sure that the dividend at time T will be 1. Then the price is

$$p_t = \pi/r + (1/(1 + r))^{T-t}(1 - \pi). \tag{6}$$

If the dividend is known to be zero, the price is

$$p_t = \pi/r - (1/(1 + r))^{T-t}\pi. \tag{7}$$

The former case will happen in equilibrium if the marketmaker observes two buy orders—which can only arise when both an uninformed hedger and an informed arbitrageur with good news arrive. The latter case will not arise in equilibrium, since arbitrageurs do not act on bad news.

If the marketmaker observes 0 or 1 buy orders, he does not know the date T dividend for sure. However, the order flow is informative and will be used to update the marketmaker's belief. For example, an order flow 0 could arise if there is an arbitrageur with bad news or no arbitrageur, but not if there is an arbitrageur with good news. So 0 orders will cause the belief to be revised downwards.

Let β_t be the marketmaker's belief at date t, that the date T dividend will be 1. This belief is formed at date t having observed the order flow at date t and is used to set price p_t. The stock price will be a weighted average of the above prices,

$$p_t = \beta_t[\pi/r + (1/(1 + r))^{T-t}(1 - \pi)] + (1 - \beta_t)[\pi/r - (1/(1 + r))^{T-t}\pi]$$
$$= \pi/r + (1/(1 + r))^{T-t}(\beta_t - \pi) \tag{8}$$

for $t \geq T - K$. Note that $\beta_{T-K-1} = \pi$. We now derive the updating rule for subsequent beliefs.

Note that many of the formulas for the probabilities derived below are similar to those in Section II above, but those were marginal probabilities (i.e., not conditional on the realized history of orders in previous periods), while these are the marketmaker's beliefs. So these formulas have β_t where the previous ones had π.

If There Are 0 Buy Orders
As explained in Section II above, this can occur either if no agents arrive, or if only an arbitrageur arrives and he receives bad news. The probability that no agents arrive is $\frac{1}{2}(1 - \delta_t)$. The probability that only an arbitrageur arrives and he receives bad news is $\frac{1}{2}\delta_t(1 - \beta_{t-1})$. So the probability that the dividend is high and that there is a buy order of 0 is $\frac{1}{2}(1 - \delta_t)\beta_{t-1}$. The probability of 0 buy orders is

$$\tfrac{1}{2}(1 - \delta_t) + \tfrac{1}{2}\delta_t(1 - \beta_{t-1}) = \tfrac{1}{2}(1 - \delta_t\beta_{t-1}). \tag{9}$$

So

$$\beta_t = [\tfrac{1}{2}(1 - \delta_t)\beta_{t-1}]/[\tfrac{1}{2}(1 - \delta_t\beta_{t-1})] = (1 - \delta_t)\beta_{t-1}/(1 - \delta_t\beta_{t-1}). \tag{10}$$

If There Is 1 *Buy Order*
This can occur in three ways: if only a hedger arrives (probability $\frac{1}{2}(1 - \delta_t)$), if only an arbitrageur arrives and he receives good news (probability $\frac{1}{2}\delta_t\beta_{t-1}$), or both an arbitrageur and a hedger arrive, but the arbitrageur receives bad news (probability $\frac{1}{2}\delta_t(1 - \beta_{t-1})$). The probability that there is 1 buy order and the dividend is high is

$$\frac{1}{2}(1 - \delta_t)\beta_{t-1} + \frac{1}{2}\delta_t\beta_{t-1} = \frac{1}{2}\beta_{t-1}. \tag{11}$$

The probability of 1 buy order is

$$\frac{1}{2}(1 - \delta_t) + \frac{1}{2}\delta_t\beta_{t-1} + \frac{1}{2}\delta_t(1 - \beta_{t-1}) = \frac{1}{2}. \tag{12}$$

So

$$\beta_t = (\tfrac{1}{2}\beta_{t-1})/\tfrac{1}{2} = \beta_{t-1}. \tag{13}$$

If There Are 2 *Buy Orders*
As discussed above, this can occur only if there are both a hedger and an arbitrageur with good news present. This event, therefore, reveals that the date T dividend is high so $\beta_t = 1$.

This completes the description of beliefs and, hence, describes the evolution of stock prices as a function of the history of information arrival. It remains to determine K.

IV. ARBITRAGEURS' TRADING STRATEGIES

We now consider the decision problem of an arbitrageur. First, if in the next period an arbitrageur (if there is one) would not act, then an arbitrageur this period will not act. Because the next period's price cannot reflect more information than today's, he would simply incur the transaction cost without any benefit. This is Proposition 1.

On the other hand, if in the next period an arbitrageur *would* act, then an arbitrageur this period may or may not act, depending on the likelihood of next period's price reflecting more information than today's and on the size of the capital gain in that event, balanced against the transaction cost.

It may be that the price already completely reflects the information. Clearly in this case the arbitrageur will not trade. But if the price does not already completely reflect the information, then we show in Proposition 2 that if an arbitrageur in the *last* period would have decided to act (because the expected capital gain outweighed the transaction cost), then an arbitrageur this period will also decide to act. In other words, the expected capital gain increasingly outweighs the transaction cost.

Combining Propositions 1 and 2, the equilibrium must have the property that there exists a critical date K before which arbitrageurs never act and after which they always act, except in the event that the price is fully revealing. It remains to show in Proposition 3 how date K is determined.

Proposition 1. *Suppose that the probability of an arbitrageur arriving and acting on his good news next period $(t + 1)$ is zero. Then an arbitrageur will not act on his good news this period (t).*

Proof. Since, by hypothesis, an arbitrageur at date $t + 1$ will not act, $E\beta_{t+1} = \beta_t$. Note that β_t may or may not be updated from date $t - 1$. So

$$p_t = \pi/r + (1/(1 + r))^{T-t}(\beta_t - \pi), \tag{14}$$

and p_{t+1} is nonrandom:

$$p_{t+1} = \pi/r + (1/(1 + r))^{T-(t+1)}(\beta_t - \pi). \tag{15}$$

It follows that

$$p_t(1 + r) = (1 + r)\pi/r + (1/(1 + r))^{T-(t+1)}(\beta_t - \pi) = \pi + p_{t+1}, \tag{16}$$

so if the agent acts, his expected wealth at $t + 1$ is

$$\pi[(W - p_t x_t)(1 + r) + x_t(p_{t+1} - c + 1)]$$
$$+ (1 - \pi)[(W - p_t x_t)(1 + r) + x_t(p_{t+1} - c)] = W(1 + r) - x_t c. \tag{17}$$

This is less than his wealth if he simply invests in the riskless asset, $W(1 + r)$. In other words, the expected return on the share (including the expected dividend) is the same as on the riskless asset (r), but ignoring the transactions cost. When the transaction cost is included, the return on the share is less. □

We next consider the arbitrageur's wealth in case he acts or does not act at time t, assuming that an arbitrageur next period would act. It he does not act, his wealth is simply $W(1 + r)$. If he acts and buys x_t shares, his wealth depends on whether there is also a hedge present at time t. With probability $\frac{1}{2}$, there is a hedger present at time t. In this case, the arbitrageur's order will reveal the information and the marketmaker's belief will jump to 1 and remain there, so the arbitrageur will earn the safe rate of return r, but will also incur a transaction cost $x_t c$. His wealth will be

$$W(1 + r) - x_t c.$$

With probability $\frac{1}{2}$ there is no hedger present. The price at time t will not reveal the information. We will use the notation*, to denote conditioning on the event that there is no hedger present at time t. The marketmaker's current belief, and the corresponding price, are not random, conditional on this event. We denote them $\overset{*}{\beta_t}$ and p_t^* (as shown in Section III, the marketmaker's belief in this event is the same as last period's belief β_{t-1}). The marketmaker's belief next period, and the corresponding price, conditional on this event, are random and we denote their expectations as $E^*\beta_{t+1}$ and E^*p_{t+1}.

With this notation we can now write the arbitrageur's expected wealth (in the event there is no hedger present at t) as:

$$(W - p_t^* x_t)(1 + r) + x_t[E^* p_{t+1} - c + \pi]$$
$$= W(1 + r) + x_t[E^* p_{t+1} - p_t^*(1 + r) - c + \pi]. \tag{18}$$

Averaging over the two events, the arbitrageur's expected wealth if he acts is

$$\tfrac{1}{2}[W(1 + r) - x_t c] + \tfrac{1}{2}[W(1 + r) + x_t[E^* p_{t+1} - p_t^*(1 + r) - c + \pi]. \tag{19}$$

If he does not act on his information he receives $W(1 + r)$. Comparing these, the arbitrageur will act if

$$E^* p_{t+1} + \pi - p_t^*(1 + r) > 2c. \tag{20}$$

This decision rule will enable us to characterize the equilibrium.

Proposition 2. *Suppose that there is an initial date K at which an arbitrageur will act an good news. Then an arbitrageur will act on good news at all subsequent dates, if the price is not already fully revealing.*

Proof. An arbitrageur with good news at date $t \geq K$ will act if

$$E^* p_{t+1} + \pi - p_t^*(1 + r) > 2c, \tag{21}$$

i.e.,

$$(\pi/r)(1 + r) + (1/(1 + r))^{T-(t-1)}(E^*\beta_{t+1} - \pi)$$
$$(1 + r)[(\pi/r) + (1/(1 + r))^{T-t}(\beta_i^* - \pi)] > 2c, \tag{22}$$

or

$$(1/(1 + r))^{T-(t+1)}(E^*\beta_{t+1} - \pi - \beta_t^* + \pi) > 2c$$
$$E^*\beta_{t+1} - \beta_t^* > 2c(1 + r)^{T-(t+1)}. \tag{23}$$

By definition of K this expression holds for $t = K$. Note that the right-hand side of this inequality falls with time. We will show that the left-hand side increases over time regardless of how β_t evolves (so long as it does not reach 1).

Suppose first that an arbitrageur acting at date K is followed by an uninterrupted sequence of single buy orders until date $t > K$. We now consider the decision problem of an arbitrageur at date t. The updating rule for β_t implies that

$\beta_t^* = \beta_K = \pi$. Note that from the expression given above for the value of $E^*\beta_{t+1}$,

$$E^*\beta_{t+1} - \beta_t^* = \delta_{t+1}(1 - \beta_t^*)^2/[2(1 - \delta_{t+1}\beta_t^*)]. \tag{24}$$

Thus,

$$\partial[E^*\beta_{t+1} - \beta_t^*]/\partial\delta = (1 - \beta_t^*)^2/[2(1 - \delta_{t+1}\beta_t^*)^2] > 0. \tag{25}$$

It follows immediately that

$$E^*\beta_{t+1} - \beta_t^* > E^*\beta_{K+1} - \beta_K > 2c(1 + r)^{T-(K+1)} > 2c(1 + r)^{T-(t+1)}, \tag{26}$$

and therefore an arbitrageur at date t will act.

If the sequence of buy orders between date K and date t include some dates at which there were no buys, then $\beta_t^* < \beta_K$. The reason is that a buy of 0 causes the marketmaker to revise his beliefs downward, while a buy of 1 causes beliefs to remain unchanged. (Note that a buy of 2 reveals the information, so beliefs reach 1, but we are not describing this case here.) However, when beliefs are revised downward this simply increases $E^*\beta_{t+1} - \beta_t^*$ and the result remains true:

$$\partial[E^*\beta_{t+1} - \beta_t^*]/\partial\beta_t^*$$
$$= \delta_{t+1}(1 - \beta_t^*)(\delta_{t+1} + \delta_{t+1}\beta_t^* - 2)/[2(1 - \delta_{t+1}\beta_t^*)^2] < 0, \tag{27}$$

since

$$\delta_{t+1} + \delta_{t+1}\beta_t^* < 2. \qquad\qquad\qquad\square$$

By Proposition 1 arbitrageurs will not act on good news before date K, and by Proposition 2 they will act afterward, except if the price is fully revealing. Note that Proposition 2 implies there are no mixed strategy equilibria (except possibly in the negligible case that the agent is indifferent at date K).

We will now find the largest δ_t (and hence the last date t) at which an arbitrageur who receives good news is unwilling to act, assuming that at date $t + 1$ an arbitrageur will act. This determines date K.

Proposition 3. *K is the first date t for which*:

$$\tfrac{1}{4}\delta_{t+1}(1 - \pi)^2/(1 - \delta_{t+1}\pi) > c(1 + r)^{T-(t+1)}. \tag{28}$$

Proof. Since by hypothesis the arbitrageur is not supposed to act on his information in $t - 1$, the marketmaker will not update his beliefs when he sees a buy order of 1, unless there is also a hedger at $t - 1$. So long as there is no hedger at $t - 1$, the hedger will therefore purchase the share at price:

$$p_{t-1} = \pi/r. \tag{29}$$

(Of course, if there is a hedger at $t - 1$ then there will be two buy orders and the good news will be revealed.)

An arbitrageur will choose *not* to act if:

$$E^*p_{t+1} + \pi - p_t^*(1 + r) < 2c, \tag{30}$$

or, substituting for E^*p_{t+1} using the formula for p_{t+1},

$$(1/(1 + r))^{T-(t+1)}[E^*\beta_{t+1} - \pi] < 2c \tag{31}$$

since prices are linear in beliefs. We now compute $E^*\beta_{t+1}$.

Period $t + 1$ is, by hypothesis, the first date at which an arbitrageur with good news will act. Therefore, depending on whether trading volume at $t + 1$ is 0, 1 or 2 (times x_{t+1}), the marketmaker's belief will be:

$$\beta_{t+1} = (1 - \delta_{t+1})\pi/(1 - \delta_{t+1}\pi),$$

$$\beta_{t+1} = \pi,$$

or

$$\beta_{t+1} = 1, \tag{32}$$

respectively. Since the arbitrageur is informed (he knows the dividend at date T will be 1) the probabilities he attaches to each of these three beliefs (and corresponding prices) occurring are different from the probabilities attached to these events by the uninformed marketmaker. From the point of view of the arbitrageur their chances of occurrence are as follows:

Buy $= 0$: No agents arrive, $\frac{1}{2}(1 - \delta_{t+1})$.
Buy $= 1$: Only one agent arrives and he is informed, $\frac{1}{2}\delta_{t+1}$, or only one agent arrives and he is uninformed, $\frac{1}{2}(1 - \delta_{t+1})$. Total probability $= \frac{1}{2}$.
Buy $= 2$: Two agents, one uninformed and one informed, $\frac{1}{2}\delta_{t+1}$.

Thus

$$E^*\beta_{t+1} = \frac{1}{2}(1 - \delta_{t+1})[(1 - \delta_{t+1})\pi/(1 - \delta_{t+1}\pi)] + \frac{1}{2}\pi + \frac{1}{2}\delta_{t+1} \tag{33}$$

So

$$E^*\beta_{t+1} - \pi = \frac{1}{2}(1 - \delta_{t+1})[(1 - \delta_{t+1})\pi/(1 - \delta_{t+1}\pi)] - \frac{1}{2}\pi + \frac{1}{2}\delta_{t+1}$$

$$= \frac{1}{2}\delta_{t+1}(1 - \pi)^2/(1 - \delta_{t+1}\pi). \tag{34}$$

K is therefore defined as the first time index t for which:

$$[\frac{1}{2}\delta_{t+1}(1 - \pi)^2/(1 - \delta_{t+1}\pi)]/(1 + r)^{T-(t+1)} > 2c. \tag{35}$$

□

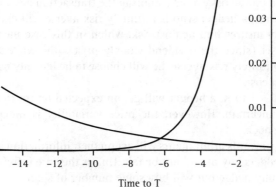

Figure 1. *Inequality relationship to determine K.*

Figure 1 illustrates the determination of K. Viewing times as a continuous variable, it graphs the left-hand side and right-hand side of the inequality defining K:

$$\tfrac{1}{4}\delta_{t+1}(1 - \pi^2)/(1 - \delta_{t+1}\pi) > c(1 + r)^{T-(t+1)}, \tag{36}$$

for $c = 0.001$, $\pi = 0.01$, $r = 0.01$, and $\delta_t = 0.5^{T-1}$. Note that the (uninformative) price for the asset is $\pi/r = 1$, so c is approximately 0.1 percent of the asset price. The information cannot be revealed more than 6 periods from the event date T.

Date K is essentially determined by the tradeoff between the chance of another arbitrageur arriving next period (the left-hand side) and the transation cost (the right-hand side). To see this, note that the left-hand side is almost equal to a constant times δ_{t+1} (because the denominator rapidly approaches 1). On the other hand, the solution is not very sensitive to the interest growth term on the right-hand side. By ignoring this term we get a lower bound for K (the true date K happens *later*).

V. UNINFORMED HEDGERS' TRADING STRATEGIES: DETERMINATION OF x_t

To this point, the amount traded by the hedgers, x_t, has been taken as given. In this section the amount these risk-averse agents will trade each period will be determined. As was seen above, x_t does not affect the equilibrium prices and strategies so long as it is positive. But if the uninformed agents are only slightly risk averse, they might choose not to hedge at all Therefore, we also provide conditions on their utility function that guarantee that they are sufficiently risk averse to hedge.

In periods before $K - 1$, hedgers buy and sell at the same price, π/r. Their expected return on the risky asset (ignoring the transaction cost) is r, the same as on the bond. Thus, a hedger who is infinitely risk averse will choose a portfolio that completely insures him against risk, which in this case means buying one unit of the asset (since the dividend exactly offsets the wage income). If the hedger is not infinitely risk averse, he will choose to hedge only partly because of the transaction cost.

From date $K - 1$ to K, a hedger will get an expected return to r, but this time the return is uncertain. However, the price variability is independent of the wage-income shock.

From date K onwards arbitrageurs will act on their information so that the price uninformed hedgers buy at will not be fair. Unless they are infinitely risk averse, they will not fully hedge but will buy some number of shares $x_t < 1$ even if the transaction cost is zero.

In summary, there are three cases:

1. Before date $K - 1$.
2. At date $K - 1$.
3. From date K onwards.

The details of the derivations of x_t in the three cases, and the conditions for x_t to be strictly positive, are given in the Appendix.

VI. OUT-OF-EQUILIBRIUM BELIEFS

To this point we have only considered the possibility that all agents trade a multiple 0, 1, or 2 of x_t. To complete the construction of the equilibrium, it remains to verify that no agent has an incentive to deviate by trading other quantities. Recall that the belief maps β_{t-1} to β_t as a function of the total quantity traded at time t. We proceed, as usual, by specifying beliefs for the marketmaker at other quantities, as follows:

1. For trading volume less than or equal to 0, the marketmaker has the same beliefs as he does at 0: $\beta_t = (1 - \delta_t)\beta_{t-1}/(1 - \delta_t\beta_{t-1})$.
2. For trading volume greater than 0, but less than or equal to x_t, the marketmaker has the same beliefs as he does at x_t, so $\beta_t = \beta_{t-1}$.
3. For trading volume greater than x_t, the marketmaker believes the asset is of high value, $\beta_t = 1$.

There are two possible deviations an arbitrageur can make. He can trade more than x_t, in which case the price will immediately become fully revealing, and he will earn the riskless return r less the transaction cost. This is clearly not a profitable deviation.

He can trade less than x_t, in which case the price will be unchanged and he will earn the same percentage return on a smaller quantity. Again, this is clearly suboptimal.

Finally, the hedgers have no incentive to deviate by definition of x_t. Since the hedgers are a continuum of infinitesimal agents (see Section I.A), an individual cannot affect the aggregate trading volume and so cannot change the market-maker's beliefs. The quantity x_t was derived under precisely this assumption.

VII. DISCUSSION OF THE RESULTS

A. Pricing of Public Information and Horizon Length

Our analysis has investigated the formation of asset prices in a model where agents with private information have short horizons. However, our analysis does not assume, or require, that all agents have short horizons. It should be stressed that the risk-neutral marketmaker does not have a limited horizon; he is infinitely lived. The price is determined by the information set of the marketmaker; public information is 'properly' priced. The marketmaker may be viewed as a 'sea' of uninformed, risk-neutral traders (this interpretation is given by Kyle (1985)). Our analysis only requires that the privately informed agents have limited horizons.

B. The Marketmaker's Inventory

The total stockholding of the traders in equilibrium is either 0, 1, or 2 shares. Hence the number of shares in existence could be as few as 2, in which case the marketmaker would hold 2, 1, or 0 shares (respectively) in inventory. In parti-cular, it is not necessary for the marketmaker to hold an infinite inventory, as in Kyle (1985) and Glosten and Milgrom (1985). A more important difference is that in those models the marketmaker's inventory has no mean reversion because it follows a random walk. The reason for this difference is that our uninformed hedgers 'unwind' their positions, whereas in the above models the 'liquidity' trade each period is an independent random variable.

C. Interpretation of the Transaction Cost

In the model we interpreted the transaction cost essentially as a brokerage fee for trading, but this is not essential. The cost could also be interpreted as a borrowing cost, i.e., c is the interest rate premium on a loan (above r). In other words, an arbitrageur who borrowed $x_t p_t$ would repay $x_t p_t (1 + r + c)$. This could arise because of transaction costs or, possibly, because of default risk. In any case, this would be equivalent to making the transaction cost proportional to the value of the shares rather than the number of shares. As discussed above in Section I.B.2, we have solved the model for this case and the results are qualitatively unchanged, although the algebra is considerably more complicated.

D. Path Dependence of the Hedgers' Trades

The arbitrageurs' decisions on whether to act is path dependent only in the following, limited, sense. If a previous arbitrageur has already pushed up the price, then subsequent arbitrageurs will not act. In general, the decision on whether to act would have more complicated path dependencies, but the structure of our model has been chosen to avoid these complications.

However, the quantity, x_t, traded by the hedgers will, in general, be path dependent in our model after date K, depending on whether the sequence of past orders was 0 in every period, 1 in every period, or any of the other possible combinations. Note, however, that the magnitude of x_t does not affect the arbitrageurs' decisions on whether to act; nor does it affect the price.

E. Speculation on Bad News

In our model arbitrageurs do not sell short upon receiving bad news. This is because the hedgers never sell short, so that the marketmaker could always infer that a short sale originated with an arbitrageur. This is a pure modelling feature that would be different if hedgers' demand did not have the simplified form we have assumed here.

F. Interpretation of the Information Event

We took the information to be knowledge of the dividend at date T. The results would not be significantly changed if we assumed any form of uncertainty in which 'news' became public at the event date T. For example, it could be that the probability of the dividend being 1 could increase at every date starting with date T. Alternatively, the dividend growth rate could change at date T.

In our model, the uncertainty relates to the dividend at a single fixed date, T. One could imagine a variant of the model in which information could arrive about dividends in different periods. This scenario is more realistic, but agents' inferences in such a model would be considerably more complex. However, there is no reason to believe that the properties of the model would be fundamentally altered.

G. Related Literature

A number of articles have, explicitly or implicitly, analyzed asset pricing with short horizons. These include Allen and Gorton (1993), Hart and Kreps (1986), and Froot et al. (1992). Allen and Gorton (1993) show that asset price bubbles can occur when there are short horizons and contracting problems with professional money managers. Hart and Kreps (1986) show that introducing long-horizon arbitrageurs with a commodity storage technology can actually increase price volatility. Froot et al. (1992) show that if traders have short horizons then they will coordinate on producing the same piece of information so that it will be impounded in the price when they unwind their position. In other words, they ask whether some types of information are more valuable, and hence more worthwhile to produce, than others. The same question could be asked in the different setting of our model: is short-term information more valuable than long-term information? We have not addressed this question since it would be quite easy to argue that agents should prefer to produce short-term rather than long-term information. For example, it is plausible that time spent producing short-term information is more productive: short-term information may be easier to produce than long-term information. Instead, we sought to obtain the stronger result that information may actually be worthless to an agent if it is too long term.

Other articles emphasize the effects of the presence of irrational traders interacting with rational traders who have short horizons. In these articles the question is whether informed traders can profit from the mispricing of assets in the presence of irrational traders. In the model of De Long et al. (1990) prices can deviate from fundamentals because irrational traders trade on incorrect beliefs. In one equilibrium of the model two identical assets trade at different prices. Rational traders, who are risk averse, do not engage in arbitrage because the irrational traders may drive the price even further from fundamentals within their horizons. This would be impossible in our setting where prices are set by a risk-neutral, long-lived marketmaker.

Shleifer and Vishny (1990) consider a model in which noise traders drive initial prices away from fundamental values because they are either 'optimistic' or 'pessimistic.' Arbitrageurs, who borrow in order to trade, prefer short-term assets because the loan can be paid off sooner, both because the interest cost of carrying the arbitrage position is lower and because they face rationing in their borrowing of funds for arbitrage (we model a similar argument about the cost-of-carry in Section VIII, below). As in De Long et al. (1990), the mispricing of the assets depends on the noise traders' beliefs being exogenously wrong.

Our intention is somewhat different. We wish to investigate the possibility of short-term mispricing in a model where all agents are rational. We show that irrationality is not necessary for assets to be mispriced in the short term. Short-term mispricing of private information can plausibly occur when all agents are fully rational.

VIII. LIMITED HORIZONS

In this section we discuss two modifications to the above model to address the following two questions. The first question concerns the effects of introducing transaction costs into an environment with short-term horizons. At first sight, it might be argued that transaction costs alone explain the inefficiency that we have analyzed. We show that the effect of transaction costs on short-term speculators is greatly multiplied compared to the effect on speculators with long horizons. Thus, our result is not simply a description of the effect of a transaction cost. It describes the effect of limited horizons, rather than long horizons, in an environment with transaction costs.

Second, we have assumed that horizons are limited. In the introduction we mentioned that short horizons may emanate from monitoring portfolio managers in the presence of agency problems. In this section we provide another explanation for why horizons are limited: the cost-of-carry of an arbitrage portfolio will rapidly accumulate, making longer-term arbitrages inherently less profitable. Arbitrageurs prefer short-term arbitrages to long-term ones. This provides a justification for our assumption of short horizons.

To address the first question, we compare the short-lived agent of our model to a long-lived agent who also faces a fixed round-trip transaction cost. To address the second question, we compare our short-lived agent to a long-lived agent who incurs a per-period transaction cost. Both of these comparisons are based on a version of the model modified to include long-lived agents.

A. Introducing Long Horizon Arbitrageurs

To derive the long-term model, suppose that arbitrageurs live forever rather than for two periods. Each period there is a probability, δ_t, of an arbitrageur arriving (as before—so the marketmaker's beliefs are the same). If the arbitrageur arrives he will mimic a liquidity trader by buying x_t shares. However, since he has no incentive to sell the shares next period, δ_t has no effect on his decision.

The details for modifying the model so that the equilibrium prices, and the inferences of the marketmaker, will be exactly the same as in the short-term model are as follows. Hedgers are also long lived. They consume at date T. When a hedger arrives, at date t, he will buy some shares to hedge the wage-income shock that will occur at date T. Hedgers are assumed to have preferences displaying constant absolute risk aversion. Since CARA preferences have no income effects, hedgers will not adjust their positions even though their wealth evolves over the interval from date t to date T.

The modification to the hedgers' utility functions is necessary because otherwise a marketmaker observing the mismatch between buy orders one period and sell orders the next period could infer the presence of an arbitrageur. The equilibrium of the model would then be completely different and not directly comparable to our basic model. Note that in the long-term model the hedgers will choose different x_t, but as will be seen below, this does not affect either the prices or the arbitrageurs' decision concerning whether to act on information.

B. Transaction Costs and Speculative Horizons

The point of this subsection is to show that our above results are not simply due to the presence of transaction costs. In any model transaction costs may prevent arbitrageurs from acting on their information a long time in advance (because the present value of a mispriced dividend in the distant future is small). However, we will show that the effect of transaction costs in our model is magnified because of short horizons.

The short horizons of the arbitrageurs makes the chain of future arbitrageurs important for arbitrage. An additional factor concerns the likelihood of future arbitrageurs arriving. Each of these factors is important for the result that prices are inefficient prior to K. Moreover, each factor is important in delaying trading by arbitrageurs with short horizons, relative to the decision that would be made by an arbitrageur facing the same transaction cost, but without a short horizon.

We analyze these issues by comparing the long-term model, defined above, to the short-term model. In this subsection long-term arbitrageurs will face the same round-trip transaction cost, cx_t, as in the short-term model. We will denote by K^* the date at which the arbitrageur starts to act in the long-term model.

There are two differences between the two models. First, in the short-term model arbitrage must be carried out via a chain. Second, there is a positive probability, $(1 - \delta_t)$, that the next link in the chain may be missing. We can separate these two effects by analyzing the short-term model in the case where the probability of an arbitrageur arriving next period is 1 (i.e., $\delta t = 1$, for all t).

Consider the arbitrageur's decision problem. If he buys at time t, then with probability $\frac{1}{2}$ he submits an order at the same time that an uninformed hedger submits a buy order. In this case, he loses cx_t (because the marketmaker will price the asset to give a return, r, conditional on the information having been revealed); the value of his wealth at $t + 1$ is $W(1 + r) - cx_t$. With probability $\frac{1}{2}$ he is the only trader, and he buys at price p_t. Then he holds the shares until the date T dividend; the value of his wealth at $t + 1$ is:

$$W(1 + r) + x_t[\pi/r + 1/(1 + r)^{(T-(t+1))}(1 - \pi) - p_t(1 + r) - c + \pi]. \quad (37)$$

Therefore, he buys if

$$\frac{1}{2}[W(1 + r) - cx_t] + \frac{1}{2}[W(1 + r) + x_t(\pi/r + (1 + r))^{(T-(t+1))}(1 - \pi)$$
$$-(p_t(1 + r) - c + \pi)] > W(1 + r), \quad (38)$$

or

$$\pi/r + 1/(1 + r)^{(T-(t+1))}(1 - \pi) - p_t(1 + r) + \pi > 2c. \quad (39)$$

K^* is determined by the previous expression with $p_t = \pi/r$; it is the first period t for which

$$\frac{1}{2}(1 - \pi)/1 + r)^{T-(t+1)} > c. \quad (40)$$

Note that the left-hand side, representing the benefit of the arbitrage, has the term '$\frac{1}{2}$' in it because half the time the arbitrageur reveals the information when he buys the shares at the same time as a hedger.

To clarify the comparison between the short-term and long-term models, consider the decision rule of an arbitrageur in the short-term model when $\delta_t = 1$, for all t. In other words, assume that an arbitrageur *will* always arrive next period, but the arbitrageurs have short horizons, and their profits depend on reselling the asset. K is determined by setting $\delta_{t+1} = 1$ in the expression in Proposition 3; it is the first period t for which

$$\tfrac{1}{4}(1 - \pi)/(1 + r)^{T-(t+1)} > c. \tag{41}$$

Comparing the two inequalities, we can see the effect of the arbitrageurs' short horizons that make profit depend on the chain of future arbitrageurs. Since we are examining the case where $\delta_t = 1$ at all t, the chain is certain to be unbroken. However, the profitability of the arbitrage depends not only on buying the asset cheaply at time t (which happens half the time) but also on selling it at a high price at time $t + 1$ (which happens only half the time, conditional on having bought cheaply at t). This will only happen if the arbitrageur next period coincides with the arrival of an uninformed hedger who buys (in which case the information is revealed). Thus the dependence on the chain reduces the profitability of arbitrage by 50 percent, relative to the long-term model, even when the chain is certain to be unbroken. This is why $\tfrac{1}{4}$ appears in the determination of K, rather than $\tfrac{1}{2}$ in the determination of K^*.

When $\delta_t < 1$ the date K at which information may first be revealed is delayed even further. The reason is clear: the short-term arbitrage cannot succeed unless the next arbitrageur is present to push up the price. When $\delta_t = 1$, the problem for the arbitrageur is that next period's arbitrageur may not push up the price because there may be no hedging demand. When $\delta_t < 1$, there is the additional problem that there may be no arbitrageur next period. Thus, we have shown:

Proposition 4. *When the transaction cost is charged per stock purchase, and $\delta_t = 1$, then the profitability of short-term arbitrage is one-half the profitability of long-term arbitrage. When $\delta_t < 1$, the profitability of short-term arbitrage is further reduced. Thus, the effect of a given transaction cost implies a later date for the beginning of information revelation with short-term arbitrage than with long-term arbitrage.*

We can illustrate this effect using the numerical example given in Section IV. Recall that date K was six periods before date T in that example, i.e., with short-term horizons information cannot be revealed more than six periods before the event. Using the same parameter values, K^*, the date at which the long-term arbitrageur is willing to act on his information is determined by

$$\tfrac{1}{2}(1 - 0.99) = 0.001(1.01)^{T-(K+1)}. \tag{42}$$

Or, in other words, $K = 624$. The information may be revealed as early as 624 periods before the event, rather than six periods. This illustrates how short horizons may affect the efficient pricing of information. Of course, this example is only an illustration, it is sensitive to the parameters.

A different specification of the model might have a greater chance of revealing the information at $t + 1$. We have taken the probability of a hedger arriving to be $\tfrac{1}{2}$. If this probability were higher, increasing the likelihood of next period's price being fully revealing, then the chance of the arbitrageur being able to buy the asset cheaply at time t would be reduced. A short-term arbitrageur, like a long-term arbitrageur, wants to buy in a deep market so that his purchase does not push up the price too much. But, unlike a long-term arbitrageur, he cannot profit if the market is too deep, because there is a smaller likelihood that a subsequent arbitrageur's purchase will push up the price by the time he needs to sell. In other words, the presence of short horizons has the effect of reducing the profitability of arbitrage and thereby multiplying the effect of the transaction cost on the revelation of information.

C. Cost-of-Carry and the Origin of Limited Horizons

One reason for short horizons concerns the cost of financing an arbitrage position for a long period of time. In this subsection we argue that this cost will rapidly mount up, making longer-term arbitrage unprofitable. This motivates our assumption of exogenous fixed horizons. In order to compare the borrowing costs of long-term and short-term horizons we need to interpret our transaction cost, c, as a borrowing cost. The difference when c is interpreted as a borrowing cost is that the costs should accumulate every period, rather than once per transaction. As discussed above in Section VII.A, it is possible to perform the analysis when the transaction cost is proportional to the cost of the shares rather than the quantity alone, but the closed-form expressions are more complicated without fundamentally changing any insights. For this reason we shall maintain the assumption that the cost is proportional to the number of shares, but not to the price paid for them.

We now develop a 'cost-of-carry' model in which arbitrageurs can choose their horizon, but face a cost of financing their portfolios. Strictly speaking, a portfolio costing $p_t x_t$ at time t, held until t', financed at a premium, c, above the interest rate, r, should accumulate debt of $(1 + r + c)^{t'-t} p_t x_t$. However, to maintain comparability with the rest of the article, we will instead assume that an arbitrageur who holds x_t shares for n periods incurs transaction costs of $c x_t$ in each of the n successive periods. The main simplification is that the interest is not compounding every period. However, this simplified form of transaction cost captures the principal feature of cost-of-carry, namely that the cost accumulates every period.

We will calculate the arbitrage profits accruing to a long-term trader who borrows to finance his trade. A long-term trader is a trader whose horizon spans the events date, T. To make the cost-of-carry interpretation more natural, we will assume that he has zero initial wealth, but unlimited liability. (Consideration of arbitrage with the option to default is beyond the scope of this article.)

We compare the arbitrage profits of the long-term trader to the profit earned by a short-term trader (as given in Proposition 3). (Although we did not assume, in Proposition 3, that the arbitrageur had zero initial wealth, it can easily be seen that the level of initial wealth was simply a constant in the risk-neutral arbitrageur's decision problem.)

Suppose that the long-term trader with cost-of-carry buys the asset at date t when the marketmaker's belief is π. One-half the time he will buy the asset without revealing his information; otherwise he will buy the shares when there is a buying hedger present, fully revealing his information and pushing up the price. (These features are exactly the same as in the short-term model worked out above.)

If he is able to buy the asset at the uninformative price, $p_t = \pi/r$, he will gain/lose the following amounts of money per share: at time t he pays π/r; from $t+1$ onwards he gains the dividend stream, π, in perpetuity, except at date T when the dividend will be 1; finally, from date $t+1$ to T he loses a transaction cost, c, each period. The present value of these cash flows sums to

$$-(\pi/r)(1+r) + \pi + \pi/r + (1-\pi)/(1+r)^{T-(t+1)} - c(1 + A(t+1, T))$$
(43)

where $A(t+1, T)$ is the present value at date $t+1$ of an annuity of \$1 starting the following period and continuing until date T

$$A(t+1, T) = (1/r)[1 - (1/(1+r))^{T-(t+2)}].$$
(44)

The other half of the time the agent will buy the asset at the fully revealing price. Clearly, it is better in this eventuality to liquidate the position the following period incurring only a single period's borrowing cost, c. Averaging across both cases, the agent's expected arbitrage profits (as of time $t+1$) are

$$\tfrac{1}{2}\{-(\pi/r)(1+r) + \pi + \pi/r + (1-\pi)/(1+r)^{T-(t+1)}$$
$$- c(1 + A(t+1, T))\} + \tfrac{1}{2}\{-c\}$$
$$= \tfrac{1}{2}(1-\pi)/(1+r)^{T-(t+1)} - c - \tfrac{1}{2}cA(t+1, T).$$
(45)

Compare this to the arbitrage profits per share of the short-term trader (given in Proposition 3)

$$= \tfrac{1}{4}(1-\pi)/(1+r)^{T-(t+1)} - c.$$
(46)

There are two differences. The first, as discussed above, is that the arbitrage is successful twice as often in the case of a long-term trader. Second, the borrowing costs born by the long-term trader have been repeated every period between $t+1$ and T. Clearly, if T is distant from t, then the long-term arbitrage is inherently unprofitable compared to one period arbitrage, relying on the chain. Thus, we have shown:

Proposition 5. *If T is sufficiently distant that*

$$A(t+1, T) > \tfrac{1}{2}(1-\pi)/(1+r)^{T-(t+1)}c,$$
(47)

then the arbitrageur will unwind his position after one period rather than waiting till T.

In other words, with cost-of-carry that accumulate every period, only short-term arbitrages will be profitable. This provides a justification for the exogenous short-term horizons assumed in the main model above.

For expositional purposes, Proposition 5, and the above analysis, only allow the arbitrageur to choose between holding the position until date T and unwinding the position after one period. In fact, the arbitrageur will sometimes choose to unwind the position at an intervening date, i.e., if and when a subsequent arbitrageur has pushed the price up. If that happens, the asset will be priced to give the fair return, r, conditional on the information, so there is no point in continuing to incur the cost of carry. We now give the details of the actual expected cost-of-carry taking this into account.

In the analysis above the probability that the transaction cost, cx_t, was paid at date $t + n$ was given as

$$1 \quad for \ n = 1;$$
$$\tfrac{1}{2} \quad for \ 1 < n \le T - t. \tag{48}$$

In fact, the probability that an uninformed hedger and an arbitrageur simultaneously buy in one of the intervening periods, i, is $\frac{1}{2}(1 - \delta_t)$. When this first happens the price will be fully revealing, and in the following period our original arbitrageur will close out his position. Thus, the probability of incurring the transaction cost at period $t + n$ is

$$\frac{1}{2}\left[\left(\frac{1}{2}\right)^{n-1} \prod_{i=t+1}^{n-1} (1 - \delta_t)\right]. \tag{49}$$

Clearly, the expected transaction cost will be larger than in the short-term model but it will not be as large as in the discussion preceding Proposition 5.

IX. FINAL REMARKS

The conventional wisdom is that short-term horizons do not cause short-term biases in the kind of information that is incorporated in asset prices. This reasoning is based on the principle that a chain of arbitrageurs with short horizons should, by backward induction, replicate the actions of long-term arbitrageurs.

This conventional wisdom implies that short-term biases in asset pricing are incompatible with rationality. Thus, some analyses have attempted to explain short-term biases by describing the effects of irrational traders, while others have asserted that the sophistication of financial market participants is such as to make short-term biases unlikely.

By examining the backward induction argument in greater detail, we have shown that private information, in the presence of transaction costs, will prevent short-term arbitrageurs from acting like long-term traders. Prices may not be informative about events that are too far distant. Our article does not explicitly endogenize the trading horizons of arbitrageurs, but we show how the cost-of-carry of an arbitrage portfolio can make long-term arbitrage unprofitable. Contracting problems with portfolio managers may also lead them to focus on short-term profit opportunities.

Appendix

This appendix gives the details of the derivation of x_t and the condition for x_t to be strictly positive, as described in Section V. Note that since the hedgers are a continuum of small agents they take prices as given.

Case 1. The agent buys and sells a quantity, x, at $p = \pi/r$. There is no uncertainty in the price. If the dividend is high, his wealth is

$$(W - px)(1 + r) + x + px - cx = W(1 + r) + x - pxr - cx$$
$$= W(1 + r) + x - x\pi - cx.$$

If the dividend is low, his wealth is

$$(W - px)(1 + r) + 1 + px - cx = W(1 + r) + 1 - pxr - cx$$
$$= W(1 + r) + 1 - x\pi - cx.$$

Thus, his expected utility is

$$\pi U[W(1 + r) + x - x(\pi + c)] + (1 - \pi)U[W(1 + r) + 1 - x(\pi + c)].$$

So for t prior to $K - 1$, x_t is defined to be the maximizer of this function. Taking the derivative with respect to x

$$\pi U'[W(1 + r) + x - x(\pi + c)](1 - \pi - c)$$
$$+ (1 - \pi)U'[W(1 + r) + 1 - x(\pi + c)](-\pi - c).$$

Note that the transaction cost will prevent the agent from hedging completely. If $c = 0$, it is easy to verify that the derivative is zero when wealth is equal in the two states, hence $x = 1$. This is the usual local risk neutrality argument.

On the other hand, if $c > 0$, the derivative at $x = 1$ is

$$\pi(1 - \pi - c)U'[W(1 + r) + 1 - (\pi + c)]$$
$$+ (1 - \pi)(-\pi - c)U'[W(1 + r) + 1 - (\pi + c)]$$
$$= [\pi(1 - \pi - c) - (1 - \pi)(\pi + c)]U'[W(1 + r) + 1 - (\pi + c)]$$
$$= -cU'[W(1 + r) + 1 - (\pi + c)] < 0$$

showing that the agent does not completely hedge.

Next we derive the condition for the agent to hedge when $c > 0$. The derivative at $x = 0$ will be positive and the agent will hedge if:

$$\pi(1 - \pi - c)U'[W(1 + r)] > (1 - \pi)(\pi + c)U'[W(1 + r) + 1]$$

i.e.,

$$U'[W(1+r)]/U'[W(1+r)+1] > [(1-\pi)(\pi+c)]/[\pi(1-\pi-c)].$$

Our analysis therefore requires that agents be sufficiently risk-averse for this condition to hold. Otherwise there will be no trading.

Case 2. The agent buys at price $p_{K-1} = \pi/r$ and sells at a price that will depend on the number of traders in period K.

In every period, the return earned by agents in aggregate is r. Since the marketmaker earns an expected return of r, so do the other agents combined. Since there are no arbitrageurs active from $K-1$ to K, the uninformed hedgers earn an expected return of r over this period. Recall also that the variation in the expected price at period K is independent of the dividend and the uninformed agent's wage-income shock.

In period K, the trading volume may be a multiple 0, 1, or 2 of x_K. In each case there will be a different price, which we denote p_K^i, for $i = 0, 1, 2$. The corresponding probabilities are denoted Pr_K^i. (The formulas for these prices and probabilities were computed in Sections II and III.)

The expected utility of a hedger is therefore

$$\pi \sum_i Pr_K^i U[W(1+r) + x_{K-1}(p_K^i - \pi/r - \pi - c + 1)]$$

$$+ (1-\pi) \sum_i Pr_K^i U[W(1+r) + x_{K-1}(p_K^i - \pi/r - \pi - c) + 1].$$

x_{K-1} is therefore defined to be the maximizer of this function. The derivative is

$$\pi \sum_i Pr_K^i U'[W(1+r) + x_{K-1}(p_K^i - \pi/r - \pi - c + 1)](p_K^i - \pi/r - \pi - c + 1)$$

$$+ (1-\pi) \sum_i Pr_K^i U'[W(1+r) + x_{K-1}(p_K^i - \pi/r - \pi - c) + 1]$$

$$\times (p_K^i - \pi/r - \pi - c).$$

By evaluating at $x_{K-1} = 0$, we obtain that the agent will hedge a positive amount if

$$\pi U'[W(1+r)](Ep_K^i - \pi/r - \pi - c + 1)$$

$$> (1-\pi)U'[W(1+r)+1](c + \pi + \pi/r - Ep_K^i),$$

because of the independence of dividends and trader arrivals. Furthermore, since (as explained above) $Ep_K^i = \pi/r$, this condition becomes

$$\pi(1 - \pi - c)U'[W(1+r)] > (1-\pi)(\pi + c)U'[W(1+r)+1]$$

as in Case 1.

Case 3. There are two subcases. First, when the hedger buys at time t, an arbitrageur may also submit an order. In this case, the purchase is made at the fully revealing price, and in the next period the shares are sold at the fully revealing price. The second subcase occurs when only the hedger submits an order at time t. Then when he sells the share at time $t + 1$ there are three possible prices.

We start by computing expected utility conditional on each of these subcases. If good news is revealed at time t, the asset earns an expected return of r thereafter. The expected utility conditional on this subcase is, as in Case 1 above,

$$\pi U[W(1 + r) + x_t - x_t(\pi + c)] + (1 - \pi)U[w(1 + r) + 1 - x_t(\pi + c)],$$

where we have used the fact that, since the return on the stock is r, $p_t(1 + r) = p_{t+1} + \pi$. In this subcase, x_t will therefore be the same as in periods before $K - 1$.

If there is no other trade at time t (the other subcase), then the hedger buys at price p_t and sells at one of three prices at time $t + 1$. As before we use p^i_{t+1}, $i = 0, 1, 2$, to denote the three prices corresponding to the trading volume multiples of 0, 1, or 2 of x_t. The corresponding probabilities are denoted Pr^i_{t+1}. The expected utility conditional on this subcase is

$$\pi \sum_i Pr^i_{t+1} U[W(1 + r) + x_t(p^i_{t+1} - p_t(1 + r) - c + 1)]$$

$$+ (1 - \pi) \sum_i Pr^i_{t+1} U[W(1 + r) + x_t(p^i_{t+1} - p(1 + r) - c) + 1].$$

The first subcase, where there is an arbitrageur submitting an order in addition to the uninformed, occurs with probability $\delta_t \beta_t$. The second subcase, where there is no other agent submitting an order, therefore has probability $1 - \delta_t \beta_t$. The overall expected utility is therefore the expectation, using these two probabilities, of the above conditional expected utilities. x_t is defined to be the maximizer of this expected utility; note that the actual quantity x_t will be sample-path dependent because Pr^i_{t+1} and p^i_{t+1} depend on the marketmaker's beliefs (we give the formulas for these below).

The derivative with respect to x_t is

$$\delta_t \beta_t \{ \pi U'[W(1 + r) + x_t - x_t(\pi + c)](1 - \pi - c)$$

$$+ (1 - \pi)U'[W(1 + r) + 1 - x_t(\pi + c)](-\pi - c) \}$$

$$+ (1 - \delta_t \beta_t) \Big\{ \pi \sum_i Pr^i_{t+1} U'[W(1 + r) + x_t(p^i_{t+1} - p_t(1 + r) - c + 1)] x$$

$$\times (p^i_{t+1} - p_t(1 + r) - c + 1) + (1 - \pi) \sum_i Pr^i_{t+1} U'[W(1 + r)$$

$$+ x_t(p^i_{t+1} - p_t(1 + r) - c) + 1](p^i_{t+1} - p_t(1 + r) - c) \Big\}.$$

We now derive the condition for x_t to be positive. Evaluated at $x_t = 0$, the derivative becomes

$$\delta_t \beta_t \{\pi U'[W(1+r)](1-\pi-c) + (1-\pi)U'[W(1+r)+1](-\pi-c)\}$$
$$+ (1 - \delta_t \beta_t)\{\pi U'[W(1+r)](E^\# p_{t+1} - p_t(1+r) - c + 1)$$
$$+ (1-\pi)U'[W(1+r)+1](E^\# p_{t+1} - p_t(1+r) - c)$$
$$= [(E^\# p_{t+1} - p_t(1+r))(1 - \delta_t \beta_t) - c - \pi \delta_t \beta_t][\pi U'[W(1+r)]$$
$$+ (1-\pi)U'[W(1+r)+1]] + \pi U'[W(1+r)],$$

where

$$E^\# p_{t+1} = \sum_i Pr^i_{t+1} p^i_{t+1}$$

denotes the expectation of p_{t+1}, conditional on the event that there was no arbitrageur acting at t. This expectation is analogous to $E^* p_{t+1}$ discussed above, but here expectations are from the point of view of the hedger.

Therefore, the uninformed trader will choose to hedge a positive amount if

$$\pi \delta_t \beta_t - (1 - \delta_t \beta t)(E^\# p_{t+1} - p_t(1+r))$$
$$< \pi U'[W(1+r)]/[(1-\pi)U'[W(1+r)+1] + \pi U'[W(1+r)]] - c.$$

We can show that this is stronger than the corresponding condition for dates prior to K (case 1):

$$\pi < \pi U'[W(1+r)/[(1-\pi)U'[W(1+r)+1] + \pi U'[W(1+r)]] - c,$$

since the expected return to the hedger after date K is less than the market return, $1 + r$

$$(E^\# p_{t+1} - p_t + \pi)/p_t < r,$$

or, equivalently

$$E^\# p_{t+1} - p_t(1+r) < -\pi.$$

Thus,

$$\pi \delta_t \beta_t - (1 - \delta_t \beta_t)(E^\# p_{t+1} - p_t(1+r)) > \pi.$$

We can derive an explicit expression for the derivative by computing an expression for $E^\# p_{t+1} - p_t(1+r)$ in terms of $E^\# \beta_{t+1}$

$$p_{t+1} = \pi/r + (1/(1+r))^{T-(t+1)}(\beta_{t+1} - \pi)$$
$$p_t(1+r) = \pi/r + (1/(1+r))^{T-(t+1)}(\beta_t - \pi).$$

So

$$E^{\#}p_{t+1} - p_t(1 + r) = (1/(1 + r))^{T-(t+1)}(E^{\#}\beta_{t+1} - \beta_t).$$

We now compute $E^{\#}\beta_{t+1}$. At time $t + 1$, there may be 0, 1, or 2 buy orders and corresponding values of β_{t+1}. The conditional probabilities of these events are

Buy = 0:

$$Pr_{t+1}^0 = \tfrac{1}{2}\{(1 - \delta_{t+1}) + \delta_{t+1}[1 - \beta_t(1 - \delta_t)/[1 - \delta_t) + \delta_t(1 - \beta_t)]]\}$$
$$= \tfrac{1}{2}[1 - \delta_{t+1}\beta_t(1 - \delta_t)/(1 - \delta_t\beta_t).$$

Buy = 1:

$$Pr_{t+1}^1 = \tfrac{1}{2}(1 - \delta_{t+1}) + \tfrac{1}{2}\{\delta_{t+1}[1 - \beta_t(1 - \delta_t)/[(1 - \delta_t) + \delta_t(1 - \beta_t)]]\}$$
$$+ \tfrac{1}{2}\delta_{t+1}\beta_t(1 - \delta_t)/[1 - \delta_t) + \delta_t(1 - \beta_t)]$$
$$= \tfrac{1}{2}.$$

Buy = 2:

$$Pr_{t+1}^2 = \tfrac{1}{2}\delta_{t+1}\beta_t(1 - \delta_t)/[(1 - \delta_t) + \delta_t(1 - \beta_t)]$$
$$= \tfrac{1}{2}\delta_{t+1}\beta_t(1 - \delta_t/1 - \delta_t\beta_t).$$

The marketmaker's beliefs in these three events are:

Buy $= 0:\quad \beta_{t+1} = (1 - \delta_{t+1})\beta_t/(1 - \delta_{t+1}\beta_t).$
Buy $= 1:\quad \beta_{t+1} = \beta_t.$
Buy $= 2:\quad \beta_{t+1} = 1.$

So the expected belief from the hedger's viewpoint is

$$E^{\#}\beta_{t+1} = [(1 - \delta_{t+1})\beta_t/(1 - \delta_{t+1}\beta_t)] \times \tfrac{1}{2}[1 - \delta_{t+1}\beta_t(1 - \delta_t)/(1 - \delta_t\beta_t)]$$
$$+ \beta_t \times \tfrac{1}{2} + 1 \times \tfrac{1}{2}[1 - \delta_{t+1}\beta_t(1 - \delta_t)/(1 - \delta_t\beta_t).$$
$$= \tfrac{1}{2}\beta_t[1 + (1 - \delta_{t+1})\beta_t/(1 - \delta_{t+1}\beta_t)][1 + \delta_{t+1}(1 - \delta_t)/(1 - \delta_t\beta_t)].$$

Using this expression, $E^{\#}p_{t+1} - p_t(1 + r)$ may be evaluated to verify the condition that uninformed agents choose to hedge a positive amount. We therefore require that the hedgers are sufficiently risk averse that this condition holds for all $t > K$ for all possible nonrevealing price paths. Of course, if the information has already been revealed prior to t, the prices are set to ensure the riskless return r and the hedging conditions for the uninformed is ensured by the analysis in Case 1.

REFERENCES

Allen, Franklin, and Gary Gorton, 1993, Churning Bubbles, *Review of Economic Studies* 60, 813–836.

Ausubel, Lawrence, 1990, Partially-revealing Rational Expectations Equilibrium in a Competitive Economy, *Journal of Economic Theory* 50, 1022–1041.

Biais, Bruno, and Pierre Hillion, 1992, Insider Trading and Stock Options Markets, Working paper, Groupe HEC.

Brennan, Michael, and Patricia Hughes, 1991, Stock Prices and the Supply of Information, *Journal of Finance* 46, 1665–1691.

De Long, Bradford, Andrei Shleifer, Lawrence Summers, and Robert Waldman, 1990, Noise Trader Risk in Financial Markets, *Journal of Political Economy* 98, 703–738.

Diamond, Douglas, and Robert Verrechia, 1981, Information Aggregation in a Noisy Rational Expectations Economy, *Journal of Financial Economics* 9, 221–235.

Dimson, Elroy, and Paul Marsh, 1989, The Marketability of Smaller Companies in the UK, Working paper, London Business School.

Dow, James, and Gary Gorton, 1993, Noise Trading, Professional Portfolio Management and Economic Welfare, Working paper, London Business School.

Froot, Kenneth, David Scharfstein, and Jeremy Stein, 1992, Herd on the Street: Informational Inefficiencies in a Market with Short-Term Speculation, *Journal of Finance* 47, 1461–1484.

Glosten, Lawrence, and Paul Milgrom, 1985, Bid, Ask, and Transaction Prices in a Specialist Market with Heterogeneously Informed Traders, *Journal of Financial Economics* 14, 71–100.

Grossman, Sanford, and Joseph Stiglitz, 1976, Information and Competitive Price Systems, *American Economic Review* 66, 246–253.

Hart, Oliver, and David Kreps, 1986, Price Destabilizing Speculation, *Journal of Political Economy* 94, 393–408.

Kyle, Albert, 1985, Continuous Auctions and Insider Trading, *Econometrica* 53, 1315–1335.

Shleifer, Andrei, and Robert Vishny, 1990, Equilibrium Short Horizons of Investors and Firms, *American Economic Review* 80, 148–153.

Vives, Xavier, 1992, Short-term Investment and the Informational Efficiency of the Market, Working paper, Institut d'Analisi Economica, Universidad Autonoma de Barcelona.

7

Asset Price Dynamics and Infrequent Feedback Trades

PIERLUIGI BALDUZZI, GIUSEPPE BERTOLA, AND SILVERIO FORESI

Investors routinely rebalance their portfolios in response to changes in prices. In order to hold portfolio weights constant, for example, investors would buy losers and sell winners, a typical negative-feedback or contrarian strategy.[1] Alternatively, investors may implement positive-feedback strategies: buy stocks when their prices rise, and sell them when their prices fall. These strategies include portfolio choice based on extrapolative expectations (trend-chasing), the use of stop-loss orders, and portfolio insurance. Positive-feedback strategies may be optimal for investors who do not tolerate falls in wealth below a given fraction of the original wealth (Grossman and Zhou (1994)) or declines in consumption (Dybvig (1995)), or for rational investors who, in turn, exploit the positive-feedback trading of noise traders (De Long, Shleifer, Summers, and Waldmann (1990)).[2]

This article combines the continuous arrival of information with the infrequency of trades, and investigates the effects on asset price dynamics of positive and negative-feedback trading. In the presence of transactions costs, investors

Valuable comments on earlier drafts were made by Dave Backus, Kobi Boudoukh, Ned Elton, Marty Gruber, Anthony Lynch, Dilip Madan, René Stulz (the editor), Ian Werner, Robert Whitelaw, David Yermack, two anonymous referees, and seminar participants at Princeton University, New York University, an NBER Asset Pricing Program meeting, an ESF-CEPR Network on Financial Markets meeting, the 1993 Meetings of the Western Finance Association, INSEAD, the 1994 Meetings of the Econometric Society, the Atlanta Finance Forum, and the 1994 conference on 'Recent developments in asset pricing' at Rutgers University. A previous version of the article circulated with the title 'Nonlinearities in Asset Prices and Infrequent Noise Trading,' and appeared as CEPR-ESF Working Paper of the Network in Financial Markets No. 33. Bertola gratefully acknowledges financial support from the National Science Foundation. Balduzzi and Foresi gratefully acknowledge financial support from New York University summer grants.

[1] Chan (1988), and more recently Lo and McKinley (1990) investigate the origin and extent of profits deriving from such strategies.

[2] The positive or negative response of traders to price changes may take elaborate forms, when it is the past pattern of price changes and transactions volume to determine the direction of trade. This is the case of trading based on technical analysis. This type of strategy can be rationalized in the context of a model with informational asymmetries, as shown by Blume, Easley, and O'Hara (1994). Recent articles that investigate the empirical performance of technical analysis in the stock market are Neftci (1991) and Brock, Lakonishok, and LeBaron (1992).

may find it optimal to rebalance their portfolios only occasionally, and by discrete amounts. In fact, if transactions costs are proportional, trades would occur only when the portfolio is sufficiently far 'out of line,' as shown in Constantinides (1986) and Davis and Norman (1991). And if part of the transactions costs is fixed, as in Duffie and Sun (1990), it becomes optimal to trade discrete amounts of assets. While some investors may trade infrequently and only in response to price changes, other investors are always ready to take the opposite side of such trades. Examples of these are 'value' investors who purchase assets when offered to them at the 'right' prices. Also, the market makers of an exchange have an institutional responsibility to provide liquidity by absorbing sudden changes in supply and demand.

We examine the interaction of the two types of investors described above and its implications for asset price dynamics. We model an economy where stocks and bonds are exchanged by speculators, defined as expected-utility maximizers, who are always present in the market, and feedback traders, who trade infrequently and in discrete amounts. The infrequency of trades is not only realistic in light of the existence of transactions costs, but it is also analytically quite convenient, in that it allows us to isolate effects of trade that would be much harder to investigate in more complicated settings.

Our analysis focuses on the relation between stock prices and 'fundamentals,' i.e., dividends. We show that the presence of positive-feedback trading increases stocks' price responses to dividend news, while negative-feedback trading reduces such responses relative to the no-trade case. Across scenarios, speculators' expectations of stock sales *depress* stock prices, while expectations of stock purchases tend to *inflate* them. Both the depression and the inflation of stock prices induce heteroskedasticity and predictability of stock returns, even though dividend growth rates are assumed i.i.d. We also find that the presence of positive-feedback traders *increases* the volatility of stock returns, while negative-feedback trading *reduces* stock-return volatility relative to the no-trade case.

To see the intuition for these results, consider the effects of *positive* feedback traders who sell stocks when stock prices reach a *lower* threshold. Rational anticipation of such trade on the part of speculators leads to prices being depressed relative to the no-trade case. In fact, the trade is welfare-improving from the speculators' point of view, and their expectations of higher future utility reduce their incentives to save; this translates into a 'softer' demand for assets, and lower stock prices. This effect also makes stock prices more sensitive to dividend news and more volatile: when dividends fall, the intrinsic value of a stock decreases, and a wave of sales on the part of feedback traders becomes more likely.

Our article is related to a substantial stream of research that studies price reactions in the presence of portfolio insurance and of other positive-feedback strategies, and *extends* this literature by explicitly considering negative-feedback strategies. Our model resembles the treatment of portfolio insurance by Brennan and Schwartz (1989) in that we also identify the economy's pricing kernel with the speculators' marginal utility; and we find that the presence of portfolio insurers depresses stock prices and increases their volatility. Unlike their portfolio insurers, though, our feedback traders' are only allowed to trade *infrequently*, and the horizon of our economy is *infinite*, rather than finite. Basak (1993) develops a model where portfolio insurance schemes are derived endogenously from a constraint on wealth that may bind prior to the last date of trading. Since both speculators' and portfolio insurers' marginal rates of substitution determine prices, he finds the implications of portfolio insurance to be the opposite of Brennan and Schwartz's (1989): stock prices are *higher* and *less* volatile relative to prices in an economy with no portfolio insurers. In a similar spirit, Grossman and Zhou (1994) investigate the equilibrium implications of portfolio insurance, where the portfolio insurers' behavior is also derived endogenously from a 'floor' on the value of their wealth at any time. Similar to positive-feedback traders in our model, Grossman and Zhou's (1994) insurers sell stocks when prices fall, and this depresses stock prices, increases their volatility, and causes negative serial correlation of returns.

A related model introduced by Campbell and Kyle (1993) shares with ours the formal decomposition of asset prices into fundamental value and 'noise,' where the noise component is induced by current and future expected trade on the part of noise traders. Their empirical findings show that in order to contribute to stock price behavior, noise trading must be correlated with the dividend process. This feature is captured by the examples in our article that assume dividends to trigger trades, through prices.

Section I presents the model. We identify a component of asset prices that reflects the value of having the opportunity to trade the asset at some point in the future. This decomposition of prices becomes the basis of a solution technique for equilibrium prices developed in Section II, in the context of a first example of positive-feedback trading. Section III discusses the relevance of the example for actual stock price behavior. Section IV looks at alternative positive and negative-feedback trading strategies, and at the role of risk aversion. Section V concludes, suggesting extensions of our framework to more realistic trade scenarios.

I. TRADE AND PRICES

We begin our analysis with a description of the structure of the economy.

Assumption 1. The economy is populated by two groups of investors: speculators and feedback traders. Speculators are identical, maximize their utility from consumption, and have rational expectations about the dynamics of future cash flows generated by available assets, and about the structure of possible trades. Feedback traders submit infrequent and discrete market orders. The determinants of these trades are not modeled.

Assumption 2. Two assets exist in positive net supply: stocks, which entitle their owner to a stochastic flow of dividends $\{\xi\}$, and bonds, which entitle their owner to a certain and constant coupon flow $\{r\}$. The time horizon is infinite. We

P. Balduzzi, G. Bertola, and S. Foresi

abstract from issues of physical investment and economic growth, and assume that no storage technology is available.

Assumption 3. The state of the economy is summarized by a vector of state variables $[\xi, S, B, Y]$, where ξ is the dividend flow of stocks, and S and B denote per-capita holdings of stocks and bonds, respectively, among speculators. The probabilistic structure of trade is summarized by the state vector Y, which contains information relevant to the speculators' assessment of the likelihood and size of market orders at every point in the economy's state space.

Speculators' Optimum. Let c denote the speculators' consumption flow, $U(\cdot)$ an increasing and concave utility function, and ρ the rate of time preference. Also, let P_s and P_b denote the prices of stocks and bonds. The following first-order conditions link optimal speculator's consumption to asset prices (these conditions follow directly from the Bellman equation, as shown in Appendix A):

$$\rho U'(c)P_s = U'(c)\xi + \frac{1}{dt}E_t\{d[U'(c)P_s]\}, \tag{1}$$

$$\rho U'(c)P_b = U'(c)r + \frac{1}{dt}E_t\{d[U'(c)P_b]\}. \tag{2}$$

After adjusting prices and payoffs by the marginal utility of consumption, all assets should yield the same expected rate of return, ρ. Also, speculators' consumption need satisfy the following transversality conditions

$$\lim_{\tau \to \infty} E_t[U'(c(\tau))P_i(\tau)]e^{-\rho(t-\tau)} = 0, \quad i = s, b. \tag{3}$$

Equilibrium. As we have assumed away storage or physical investment, speculators consume dividends and coupons generated by the stocks and bonds they own:

$$c = S\xi + Br.$$

Consider next the prices supporting the equilibrium. We define risk-adjusted asset prices p_i and cash-flows f_i,

$$p_s \equiv U'(c)P_s, \ f_s \equiv U'(c)\xi, \ p_b \equiv U'(c)P_b, \ f_b \equiv U'(c)r,$$

and rewrite equations (1) and (2) as:

$$\rho p_i = f_i + \frac{1}{dt}E_t(dp_i), \quad i = s, b. \tag{4}$$

The differential equations (4) must be satisfied at all points in the economy's state space, regardless of the likelihood of trade.

No-expected-jump Conditions. Given equation (4), $E_t(dp_i)$ cannot be of order larger than dt, and this rules out expected jumps in risk-adjusted price paths. It follows that

$$E_t(\Delta p_i) = 0, \quad i = s, b, \tag{5}$$

at trading times. Hence, when trade takes place, the discrete change in asset prices is 'compensated' by a discrete change in the marginal utility of consumption so that expected risk-adjusted price paths remain continuous.

Trade and prices. Note that unlike in Lucas (1978), consumption and risk-adjusted payoffs $f_i(\tau)$ are affected by trade as well as by dividends. Hence it is useful to decompose risk-adjusted prices in the form

$$p_i(\xi, S, B, Y) = g_i(\xi, S, B) + h_i(\xi, S, B, Y), \quad i = s, b, \tag{6}$$

for

$$g_i = \int_t^\infty E_t[f_i(\tau) \,|\, \text{no trade}] e^{-\rho(t-\tau)} \, d\tau, \quad i = s, b, \tag{7}$$

where $[f_s(\tau) \,|\, \text{no trade}] \equiv U'(S_t\xi_\tau + B_t r)\xi_\tau$, and $[f_b(\tau) \,|\, \text{no trade}] \equiv U'(S_t\xi_\tau + B_t r)r$. The functioning g_i takes the speculators' portfolio composition as given, and would be the asset's equilibrium value if trade could be disregarded. Hence, h_i reflects the effects of trade on the asset's price, and can be viewed as the value of trading the asset at some point in the future.

Campbell and Kyle (1993) obtain a similar decomposition of asset prices. They identify the 'fundamental value,' which depends on current and expected future cash flows only, and the 'noise,' which is induced by current and future expected trade on the part of noise traders.

II. A SPECIALIZED FRAMEWORK

We now specialize our framework in terms of preferences, cash-flow dynamics, and structure of trade. We confine ourselves to situations where the stock price is a monotonic function of the dividend flow.

Assumption 4. The speculators' instantaneous utility function has the form

$$U(c) = \frac{c^{1-\gamma}}{1-\gamma},$$

where γ is the relative risk aversion parameter.

Assumption 5. Dividends follow a geometric random walk

$$d\xi = \mu\xi\, dt + \sigma\xi\, dw,$$

with μ and σ positive constants.

Expanding $E_t(dp_i)$ in equation (4) by the usual stochastic calculus arguments, we find that in the interior of no-trade regions the p_i functions satisfy the valuation equations

$$\rho p_i = f_i + \mu\xi p_i' + \frac{\sigma^2\xi^2}{2} p_i'', \quad i = s, b. \tag{8}$$

No-trade Solutions. When either $B = 0$ or $S = 0$, the solution for the no-trade component g_i in equation (6) is obtained from evaluation of the integral in equation (7). We have

$$B = 0 \Rightarrow g_s = \frac{\xi}{(S\xi)^r d_s}, \quad g_b = \frac{r}{(S\xi)^r d_b}, \tag{9}$$

where $d_s \equiv [\rho + (\gamma - 1)\mu - (\gamma - 1)\gamma\sigma^2/2]$, $d_b \equiv [\rho + \gamma\mu - \gamma(\gamma + 1)\sigma^2/2]$; and

$$S = 0 \Rightarrow g_s = \frac{\xi}{(\rho - \mu)(Br)^\gamma}, \quad g_b = \frac{r}{\rho(Br)^\gamma}. \tag{10}$$

Goods-denominated prices P_i are computed from the risk-adjusted prices p_i by the relation $P_i = p_i c^\gamma$, with $c = S\xi$ in the $B = 0$ case, and $c = Br$ in the $S = 0$ case. To ensure that prices are positive and finite, parameter values must be such that $d_s > 0$, $d_b > 0$, and $\rho > \mu$.

Homogeneous Solutions. The second component of asset prices in equation (6), h_i, can be found as the homogeneous solution of equation (8). The solution has the form

$$h_i = Q_i(S, B, Y)\xi^{\lambda_1} + N_i(S, B, Y)\xi^{\lambda_2}, \quad i = s, b, \tag{11}$$

where λ_1 and λ_2 solve the characteristic equation associated with equation (8) (see Appendix B), and Q_i and N_i are constants of integration.

In the following we consider a positive-feedback trade scenario: feedback traders sell off stocks, in exchange for all the bonds held by the speculators, when stock prices reach a *lower* threshold.

Assumption 6. Initially speculators do not hold stocks: $B = B_0 > 0, S = 0$. Feedback traders buy all of the speculators' bonds, selling S_1 shares of stocks when P_s hits a lower threshold P_{sl}. After the barrier is hit, it disappears and no more trades take place at P_{sl} or any other price.

Similar positive-feedback strategies may be optimal for the investors described in Grossman and Zhou (1994), who do not tolerate falls in wealth below a given fraction of the original wealth, or for the consumers of Dybvig (1995), who do not tolerate declines in consumption.

We do not model feedback traders' motives and constraints, but we take as given their demand of stocks (and bonds) as a function of stock prices. The infrequent and discrete trades postulated in Assumption 6 can be rationalized by considering realistic frictions. With transactions costs, for example, it is not optimal to trade unless the portfolio composition is sufficiently far out of line. The optimal no-trade region when transactions costs are proportional to the amounts traded has been studied by Constantinides (1986) and Davis and Norman (1991) in a continuous-time setting similar to ours. When trade can take place continuously, however, traded amounts will not be discrete unless part of the costs is fixed, as in the framework considered by Duffie and Sun (1990).

While the initial and final asset allocations assumed here are extreme, this allows us to use the formulas in equations (9) and (10) to compute explicit solutions for before and after-trade prices. Also, trade occurs only once. This need not be taken literally: we may think that after one trade takes place, other trades are expected in the future, but that the likelihood of their occurring soon is *low*.

In equilibrium there is a unique level of dividends ξ_l at which trade takes place. This level is implicitly defined by the condition $P_{sl} \equiv P_s(\xi_l, 0, B_0, Y_0)$. The state variable $Y = Y_0$ summarizes the information in Assumption 6 on the possible future trade at ξ_l, and $Y = Y_1$ indicates that no trade is expected to ever take place after the barrier is hit.

At $\xi = \xi_l$ the no-jump conditions (5) reduce to

$$p_i(\xi_l, 0, B_0, Y_0) = p_i(\xi_l, S_1, 0, Y_1), \quad i = s, b. \tag{12}$$

As trade occurs with certainty at ξ_l, (12) implies that the risk-adjusted price of each asset cannot jump at the time of trade.

Trade and Asset Allocation. Since no trade takes place after the barrier is hit, the amount of stocks held by speculators after the trade is endogenously determined by the budget constraint:

$$
\begin{aligned}
S_1 &= \frac{P_b(\xi_l, S_1, 0, Y_1)}{P_s(\xi_l, S_1, 0, Y_1)} B_0 = \frac{p_b(\xi_l, S_1, 0, Y_1)c^{-\gamma}}{p_s(\xi_l, S_1, 0, Y_1)c^{-\gamma}} B_0 \\
&= \frac{p_b(\xi_l, S_1, 0, Y_1)}{p_s(\xi_l, S_1, 0, Y_1)} B_0 = \frac{rd_s}{\xi_l d_b} B_0.
\end{aligned}
\tag{13}
$$

Note that because of the boundary conditions in equation (12), the relative price at which trade takes place can be obtained as the ratio between after-trade prices. Equation (13) illustrates how traded quantities are endogenous, and how trade events are not the same as endowment shocks in a modified Lucas (1978) 'tree' economy: the number of stocks received by speculators in exchange for bonds is determined by endogenous prices.

As shown in Appendix C, the transversality conditions (3) require $Q_i = N_i = 0$ after trade takes place, and $Q_i = 0$ before trade takes place. Moreover, the

P. Balduzzi, G. Bertola, and S. Foresi

constants N_i in the before-trade price functions must satisfy the following version of equation (12)

$$\frac{\xi_l}{(\rho - \mu)(B_0 r)^\gamma} + N_s \xi_l^{\lambda_2} = \frac{\xi_l}{d_s(S_1 \xi_l)^\gamma}, \quad \frac{r}{\rho(B_0 r)^\gamma} + N_b \xi_l^{\lambda_2} = \frac{r}{d_b(S_1 \xi_l)^\gamma}, \quad (14)$$

where the after-trade allocation S_1 can be obtained from equation (13).

In the rest of the article we shall focus our discussion on the behavior of stock prices for explicit choices of parameter values. The behavior of bond prices is similar, but less interesting, due to the absence of fluctuations in the coupon flow.

Risk-adjusted versus goods-denominated prices. Figure 1 illustrates the before-trade, after-trade, and no-trade risk-adjusted stock pricing functions p_s, for the

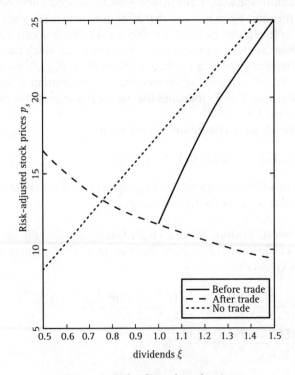

Figure 1. *Risk-adjusted stock prices*

Note: This figure shows the risk-adjusted pricing function for stocks p_s as a function of dividends ξ, before and after infrequent traders sell stocks at low prices, and compares it to the pricing function without trade opportunities. The speculators' initial endowment of bonds is $B_0 = 1$ and of stocks is $S_0 = 0$; we set the relative risk aversion parameter $\gamma = 1.5$, the rate of time preference $\rho = 0.075$, the instantaneous expected rate of growth of dividends $\mu = 0.018$, and the instantaneous variance of the rate of growth of dividends $\sigma^2 = 0.015$.

choice of parameter values: $\gamma = 1.5, \rho = .075, \mu = .018$, and $\sigma^2 = 0.015$. We further set $\xi_l = 1$ and $B_0 = 1$, and normalize $r = 1$.

Figure 1 shows that trade cannot induce discrete changes in the risk-adjusted price p_s. On the other hand, Figure 2 shows that actual prices jump because the speculators' marginal utility of consumption changes at trade times.

For our choice of parameter values, stock prices *rebound* promptly after the trade.

The next section further discusses the implications of the example above, and relates them to actual price behavior.

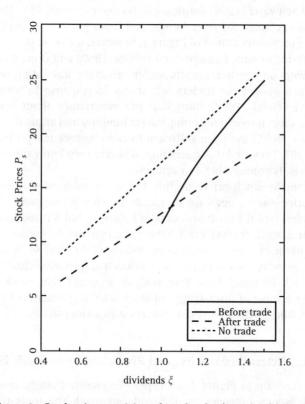

Figure 2. *Stock prices: anticipated stock sales (positive feedback)*

Note: This figure shows the pricing function for stocks P_s as a function of dividends ξ, before and after infrequent traders sell stocks at low prices, and compares it to the pricing function without trade opportunities. The speculators' initial endowment of bonds is $B_0 = 1$ and of stocks is $S_0 = 0$; we set the relative risk aversion parameter $\gamma = 1.5$, the rate of time preference $\rho = 0.075$, the instantaneous expected rate of growth of dividends $\mu = 0.018$, and the instantaneous variance of the rate of growth of dividends $\sigma^2 = 0.015$.

III. IMPLICATIONS FOR STOCK PRICE BEHAVIOR

A. About Crashes and Rebounds

Our Assumption 6 postulates a demand function for stocks on the part of feedback traders that is positively related to stock prices; this demand resembles that of the 'hedgers, rebalancers, and others who use dynamic strategies akin to portfolio insurance' considered by Gennotte and Leland (1990) (p. 1003). The trade situation described in the previous section can be viewed as a stop-loss sale by which feedback traders try to protect the value of their portfolio.

The strategy implemented by feedback traders may not ensure that their portfolio value is a 'convex function of some underlying [...] reference portfolio,' as Brennan and Schwartz (1989) define portfolio insurance, pp. 455–456, since they sell stocks in exchange for risky bonds, and bond prices may decline after the trade. For the parameter values of Figure 1, however, the bond price does not fall.

In work related to ours, Gennotte and Leland (1990) and Donaldson and Uhlig (1991) develop one-period models which generate discontinuities in prices (crashes) when exogenous traders sell stocks in response to price decreases. Gennotte and Leland (1990) show that the uncertainty about price-triggered trades plays a crucial role in reducing market liquidity and argue that even mildly negative news could have been sufficient to cause a stock market crash like that of October 1987. They find that a rebound, which in their context is a 'melt-up' to precrash levels, is conceivable, but unlikely.

In our example, stock prices decline *before* the trade as dividends fall. The decline in price due to news on dividends is more pronounced than without feedback traders (see the no-trade curve of Figure 2), but it is too smooth to have the flavor of a stock-market crash. The price increase in Figure 2, instead, is reminiscent of the increase of stock prices following the 1987 stock-market crash, when, by Wednesday, October 21st, stock prices had recovered close to half of the previous 'Black Monday' loss. Our analysis suggests that stock prices may rebound after a wave of price-triggered stock sales if speculators try to increase their stock holdings when portfolio insurers stop selling stocks.

B. Volatility, Heteroskedasticity, and Predictability of Stock Returns

The pricing function in Figure 2 is steeper everywhere than its no-trade counterpart, and becomes steeper as dividends approach the trade-trigger point; expectations of trade increase the sensitivity of stock prices to current dividends, and hence the volatility of stock returns. If no trade is expected in the future, the sensitivity of stock prices to dividends is $\partial P_s/\partial \xi = 1/(\rho - \mu)$. When dividends carry information on the likelihood of trade in the future we have

$$\frac{\partial P_s}{\partial \xi} = \frac{1}{\rho - \mu} + N_s \lambda_2 (B_0 r)^\gamma \xi^{\lambda_2 - 1}.$$

In fact, one can decompose the elasticity of prices with respect to dividends as in Lucas (1978),

$$\frac{\xi \, \partial P_s/\partial \xi}{P_s} \equiv -\frac{\xi \, \partial U'/\partial \xi}{U'} + \frac{\xi \, \partial p_s/\partial \xi}{p_s},$$

thus making it explicit that a larger dividend has both an income and an 'information' effect. The income effect (the first term) is always positive, as rational investors attempt to pass part of a positive windfall over to future dates through purchases of securities. This effect drives securities prices up. In our example, however, before-trade utility does not depend on dividends ($S_0 = 0$) and the income effect is nil. We can then focus exclusively on the second term, which reflects *two* types of information carried by decreasing dividends. First, since dividends are autocorrelated, lower dividends signal lower future cash flows, lowering stock prices. Second, the current size of dividends relative to the trigger level affects the likelihood and timing of future trade.

Moreover, in the no-trade case the rate of return on stocks is given by

$$\frac{dP_s + \xi \, dt}{P_s} = \rho \, dt + \sigma \, dw.$$

Absent trade, rates of return on stocks are i.i.d. normal variates, with mean $\rho\tau$ and variance $\sigma^2\tau$ over nonoverlapping time-segments of length τ. Thus, rates of return on stocks are as volatile as dividend growth rates and homoskedastic, and current dividends provide no information as to future rates of return.

Conversely, the possibility of trade increases the volatility of rates of return on stocks, and makes them heteroskedastic and predictable. Since $P_s = \xi/(\rho - \mu) + N_s(B_0 r)^\gamma \xi^{\lambda_2}$, the instantaneous return on stocks is

$$dP_s + \xi \, dt = \left[\frac{\mu\xi}{\rho - \mu} + \mu N_s\lambda_2(B_0 r)^\gamma \xi^{\lambda_2} + \xi + \frac{1}{2}N_s\lambda_2(\lambda_2 - 1)(B_0 r)^\gamma \xi^{\lambda_2}\sigma^2\right] dt$$
$$+ \left[\frac{\sigma\xi}{\rho - \mu} + \sigma N_s\lambda_2(B_0 r)^\gamma \xi^{\lambda_2}\right] dw.$$

The diffusion term for the instantaneous before-trade return on stocks (the term in the second square brackets) exceeds its no-trade counterpart by the quantity

$$\sigma N_s\lambda_2(B_0 r)^\gamma \xi^{\lambda_2}$$

whose sign is positive, since $N_s < 0$ (see equation (14)) and $\lambda_2 < 0$ (see Appendix B). Also, the before-trade stock price is lower than its no-trade counterpart (again, $N_s < 0$). As in Brennan and Schwartz (1989), the conditional volatility of rates of return on stocks is *higher* than in the no-trade case. The conditional volatility also *changes over time*, since it depends on the level of dividends.

Also, unlike in the no-trade case, the conditional expectation of rates of return on stocks is a function of the dividend level. Hence, stock returns are *predictable*, since dividends are serially correlated. These results are similar to those of Grossman and Zhou (1994), who find that stock prices are more volatile, and stock returns are serially correlated, in the presence of portfolio insurers.

The price depression and increased volatility of stock prices are apparent in Figure 2, where the before-trade pricing function is everywhere lower and steeper than the no-trade one.

IV. ALTERNATIVE TRADE SCENARIOS

The example of Section II suggests that the presence of positive-feedback traders may lead to a *depression* of stock prices and an increase in their *volatility* relative to the no-trade case. Here, we discuss the implications of alternative positive and negative-feedback strategies, and the role of risk aversion.

A. Positive and Negative-Feedback Trading

For concreteness, we frame our discussion in the context of the four specific trade scenarios illustrated in Figure 3.

We assume that feedback traders buy all the bonds in the hands of the speculators in exchange for stocks (top two panels), or buy all the stocks in the hands of the speculators in exchange for bonds (bottom two panels). Also, trade may occur at a *lower* price threshold (left two panels), or at an *upper* price threshold (right two panels). The solution technique is analogous to that of Section III, and parameter values are the same as in Figures 1 and 2. The constant of integration Q_s has been set to satisfy the transversality condition (left two panels), or to ensure no jumps in risk-adjusted prices (right two panels). Similarly, the constant of integration N_s has been set to satisfy the no-jump conditions in equation (5) (left two panels), or to ensure that stock prices do not diverge to $\pm\infty$ as dividends tend to zero (right two panels).

The main message from Figure 3 is that stock prices are *depressed*, relative to the no-trade case, when a *sale* of stocks is anticipated; they are *inflated* when a *purchase* of stocks is anticipated. Both price depression and price inflation become stronger as the market gets closer to the price threshold. Hence, both the conditional volatility and the conditional mean of stock returns depend on the dividend flow, and stock returns are heteroskedastic and predictable.

Moreover, when before-trade stock prices are depressed relative to their no-trade counterparts, they are likely to jump *upwards* after the occurrence of trade, as in the top two panels of Figure 3. On the other hand, when before-trade stock prices are inflated, they are likely to jump *downwards* after the occurrence of trade, as in the bottom two panels of Figure 3.

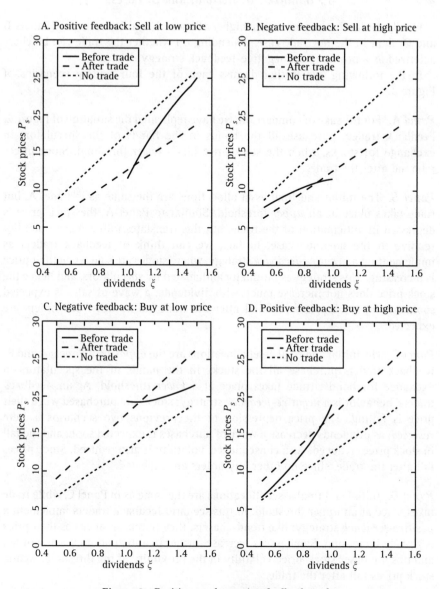

Figure 3. *Positive- and negative-feedback trade*

Note: For different trade scenarios, this figure shows the stock price P_s as a function of dividends ξ, before and after trade, and compares it to the pricing function without trade opportunities. The speculators' initial endowment of bonds and stocks is $B_0 = 1$ and $S_0 = 0$ (top two panels), and $B_0 = 0$ and $S_0 = 1$ (bottom two panels). The price threshold is either lower (left two panels), or higher (right two panels) than the before-trade price. We set the relative risk aversion parameter $\gamma = 1.5$, the rate of time preference $\rho = 0.075$, the instantaneous expected rate of growth of dividends $\mu = 0.018$, and the instantaneous variance of the rate of growth of dividends $\sigma^2 = 0.015$.

Finally, volatility can be either higher (Panels A and D) or lower (Panels B and C) than in the no-trade case, depending on whether the trade can be characterized as a positive or a negative-feedback strategy.

In the following, we further discuss each of the four trading scenarios of Figure 3:

Panel A. For the sake of comparison, we have replicated the situation of Figure 2. Feedback traders purchase all the bonds in the hands of the speculators in exchange for stocks, when the stock price hits a *lower* threshold. Stock prices rebound after the trade.

Panel B. The initial and final asset allocations are the same as in Panel A, but trade takes place at an *upper* threshold. Similar to Panel A, the stock price is depressed in anticipation of the trade, but this translates into a *lower* volatility relative to the no-trade case. In fact, we can think of feedback traders as implementing a *negative-feedback* strategy, where stocks are sold when their price is increasing. This strategy is rationally anticipated by speculators, and hence the stock price does not increase much with dividends: a wave of sales is expected soon. Again, stock prices rebound after the trade, as no other sell orders are expected.

Panel C. The initial and final asset allocations are the *opposite* of Panels A and B: feedback traders purchase all the stocks in the hands of the speculators in exchange for bonds; trade takes place at a *lower* threshold. Again, feedback traders' behavior is a *negative-feedback* strategy: stocks are purchased when their price is falling. The price depression of the previous two scenarios is here *reversed*: as dividends decrease a wave of purchases is expected soon, and the fall in stock prices reduced. As a consequence, volatility is also reduced. Stock prices fall after the trade, since no other buy orders are expected.

Panel D. Initial and final asset allocations are the same as in Panel C, while trade takes place at an *upper* threshold. In this scenario feedback traders implement a *positive-feedback* strategy: like trend-chasers, they purchase stocks as their price is already increasing. Stock prices increase further in anticipation of a buy order, and this increases stock-price volatility in the proximity of the threshold. Again, stock prices fall after the trade.

In summary, the effects of trade on prices and price volatility depend on the specific trade scenario under scrutiny. Stock prices are depressed if stock sales are expected soon, whereas they are inflated if stock purchases are expected. The implications for volatility crucially depend on the relative position of the price threshold, that is, on the type of strategy followed by feedback traders. Stop-loss and trend-chasing strategies exacerbate the trend in stock prices, leading to an increase in volatility. Contrarian strategies, on the other hand, dampen the trend in prices and reduce volatility.

B. Risk Aversion, Price Effects, and Welfare

Experimenting with different values of the speculators' relative risk aversion parameter γ, we found both the price-depression and the price-inflation effect to be stronger the higher γ. In fact the two effects can be so strong that in the scenarios of Panels B and C, the monotonicity of the before-trade pricing function can be lost. This is not a problem in general, but it prevents the inversion of the price-dividend correspondence, and the intuition of a *price* threshold (rather than a dividend threshold) triggering the trade would be lost.

The mechanisms driving the price effects above go as follows: Consider, the example, the trade scenario of Panel A in Figure 3, which replicates the scenario discussed in Section III. Before trade we have $p_s = g_s + N_s \xi^{\lambda_2}$, whereas, if trade were ruled out, we would have $p_s = g_s$. Since $P_s = p_s U'(c)$, the difference between before- and no-trade stock prices is given by the quantity

$$N_s \xi^{\lambda_2} (B_0 r)^{\gamma}. \tag{15}$$

It can be shown that N_s is always negative and decreasing in γ, and hence the quantity in equation (15) is more negative the higher γ. A similar argument holds for the trade scenario of Panel B. Here, the difference between before-and no-trade stock prices is given by $Q_s \xi^{\lambda_1} (B_0 r)^{\gamma}$, which is also negative and decreasing in γ. Hence, the higher γ, the stronger the price-depression effect.

In Panels C and D, the difference between before- and no-trade stock prices is given by $N_s \xi^{\lambda_2} (S_0 \xi)^{\gamma}$ and $Q_s \xi^{\lambda_1} (S_0 \xi)^{\gamma}$, respectively. It can be shown that both N_s and Q_s are here positive, and increasing in γ. Hence, the higher γ, the stronger the price-inflation effect.

The economics behind the price effects of anticipated trade has to do with welfare effects. In Appendix D we show how to calculate the speculators' expected lifetime utility before trade, after trade, and in the no-trade case, for the four trade scenarios of Figure 3. We find that when feedback traders buy bonds in exchange for stocks (top two panels) speculators' expected lifetime utility is *higher* than in the absence of trade, and more so the closer the trade. Hence, stock prices are depressed because speculators look forward to higher welfare, are less willing to save, and have weaker demand for stocks. When feedback traders buy stocks in exchange for bonds (bottom two panels) the opposite holds true: speculators' expected lifetime utility is *lower* than in the absence of trade, and this effect is more pronounced the closer the trade. Stock prices are inflated because speculators expect lower welfare, are more willing to save, and have stronger demand for stocks.

Whether trade has a positive or a negative effect on welfare depends, in turn, on the relative price at which stocks and bonds are exchanged. Risk-adjusted prices at the time of trade must equal (in expectation) their after-trade counterparts (see equation (5)): equilibrium conditions fix the rate at which the two assets are exchanged. A welfare-decreasing trade, at these prices, will be accepted by speculators only if they are somehow 'committed' to trade, much like market makers on the floor of an exchange.

The parameter γ regulates the degree of intertemporal substitution as well as risk aversion. Hence, the higher γ, the more speculators try to hedge future changes in welfare and the stronger are the price effects discussed above.

V. CONCLUSIONS

This article investigates the effects on asset price dynamics of positive and negative-feedback trading. Specifically, we model an economy where stocks and bonds are traded by two types of agents: speculators who maximize expected utility, and feedback traders who mechanically respond to price changes and infrequently submit market orders. We find that stock prices are depressed in anticipation of a wave of price-triggered sales, while they are inflated in anticipation of a wave of price-triggered purchases. We show that positive-feedback strategies increase the volatility of stock returns, and the response of stock prices to dividend news. Conversely, the presence of negative-feedback traders makes stock returns less volatile, and prices less responsive to dividends. Both positive- and negative-feedback strategies bring about heteroskedasticity and predictability of stock returns, even though dividend growth rates are assumed independent and identically distributed (i.i.d.).

Appendix

A. First-Order Conditions

Let $W \equiv SP_s + BP_b$ be the speculator's wealth, and $I \equiv I(W, \xi, S, B, Y)$ denote the value function:

$$Ie^{-\rho t} = \max_{c(\tau), s(\tau), b(\tau)} \int_t^\infty E_t\{U[c(\tau)]\}e^{-\rho\tau}\,d\tau.$$

The speculator's optimal program obeys the relations

$$0 = \max_{c(\tau), s(\tau), b(\tau)} \left\{ e^{-\rho t} U(c) + E_t \left[\frac{1}{dt} d(Ie^{-\rho t}) \right] \right\} \text{ s.t.}$$

$$-c\,dt = \Delta s(P_s + \Delta P_s) + \Delta b(P_s + \Delta P_b) - (s\xi + br)\,dt. \tag{16}$$

The first order condition for optimal equity holdings is given by

$$e^{-\rho t} U'(c)\xi + \frac{\partial}{\partial s} E_t \left[\frac{1}{dt} d(Ie^{-\rho t}) \right] = 0.$$

Hence, we obtain

$$U'(c)\xi + \frac{\partial}{\partial s} E_t \left[\frac{1}{dt} (-\rho I \, dt + dI) \right] = 0,$$

and thus

$$U'(c)\xi - \rho \frac{\partial I}{\partial W} \frac{\partial W}{\partial s} + E_t \left[\frac{1}{dt} d \left(\frac{\partial I}{\partial W} \frac{\partial W}{\partial s} \right) \right] = 0.$$

Using the envelope condition $\partial I / \partial W = U'(c)$ and the definition of wealth, yields equation (1). A similar argument yields equation (2).

B. Homogeneous Solutions

The homogeneous solutions of equation (8) have the form

$$h_i(\xi) = Q_i \xi^{\lambda_1} + N_i \xi^{\lambda_2},$$

where Q_i and N_i are constants of integration and λ_1, λ_2 are the roots of the characteristic equation associated with (8):

$$\lambda_1 = \frac{-(\mu - \sigma^2/2) + \sqrt{(\mu - \sigma^2/2)^2 + 2\rho\sigma^2}}{\sigma^2} > 0,$$

$$\lambda_2 = \frac{-(\mu - \sigma^2/2) - \sqrt{(\mu - \sigma^2/2)^2 + 2\rho\sigma^2}}{\sigma^2} < 0.$$

C. Prices and Transversality Conditions

Consider again the transversality conditions

$$\lim_{\tau \to \infty} E_t[p_i(\xi, s, b, Y)]e^{-\rho(\tau - t)} = 0, \quad i = s, b.$$

Writing $p_i = g_i + h_i$ as in equation (6), we note that the particular solution satisfies the transversality condition by construction. As to h_i, we compute

$$E_t(\xi^\lambda)e^{-\rho(\tau - t)} = \xi_t^\lambda e^{[(\sigma^2/2)\lambda^2 + (\mu - \sigma^2/2)\lambda - \rho](\tau - t)},$$

and since λ_1 and λ_2 solve $(\sigma^2/2)\lambda^2 + (\mu - \sigma^2/2)\lambda - \rho = 0$, we have

$$\lim_{\tau \to \infty} E_t[h_i(\xi_\tau)]e^{-\rho(\tau - t)} = Q_i \xi_t^{\lambda_1} + N_i \xi_t^{\lambda_2}, \quad i = s, b.$$

Hence, homogeneous solutions h_i satisfy the transversality conditions only if $Q_i = N_i = 0$.

D. Welfare and Price Effects of Trade

Here, we demonstrate the correspondence between welfare and price effects of anticipated trades.

From equation (16) we have

$$\rho I = U(c) + \frac{1}{dt} E_t(dI). \tag{17}$$

Given equation (17), $E_t(dI)$ cannot be of order larger than dt, and this rules out expected jumps in the value function I,

$$E_t(\Delta I) = 0,$$

at trading times.

It is useful to decompose the value function I, in equilibrium, in the form

$$I(\xi, S, B, Y) = \max_{c(\tau),s(\tau),b(\tau)} \int_t^\infty E_t\{U[c(\tau)]\}e^{-\rho(t-\tau)}d\tau = \max_{c(\tau),s(\tau),b(\tau)}$$

$$\times \int_t^\infty E_t\{U[c(\tau) \mid \text{no trade}]\}e^{-\rho(\tau-t)}d\tau + V(\xi, S, B, Y),$$

where $V(\xi, S, B, Y)$ summarizes the effects of trade on expected-lifetime utility.

Expanding $E_t(I)$ in equation (17) by the usual stochastic calculus arguments, we find that in the interior of no-trade regions the value function I satisfies

$$\rho I = U(c) + \mu\xi I' + \frac{\sigma^2\xi^2}{2}I''.$$

When either $B = 0$ or $S = 0$, the solution for the no-trade component of the value function is obtained as follows. When $B = 0$ we have

$$\max_{c(\tau),\,s(\tau),\,b(\tau)} \int_t^\infty E_t\{U[c(\tau) \mid \text{no trade}]\}e^{-\rho(\tau-t)}d\tau$$

$$= \frac{S}{1-\gamma}\int_t^\infty E_t\{[S\xi(\tau)]^{-\gamma}\xi(\tau)\}e^{-\rho(\tau-t)}d\tau = \frac{S}{1-\gamma}\frac{\xi_t}{(S\xi_t)^\gamma d_s},$$

where it is useful to recognize that the integrand function corresponds to $f_s \equiv (S\xi)^{-\gamma}\xi$. When $S = 0$, we have

$$\max_{c(\tau),s(\tau),b(\tau)} \int_t^\infty E_t\{U[c(\tau) \mid \text{no trade}]\}e^{-\rho(\tau-t)}d\tau$$

$$= \frac{B}{1-\gamma}\int_t^\infty E_t\{(Br)^{-\gamma}r\}e^{-\rho(\tau-t)}d\tau = \frac{B}{1-\gamma}\frac{r}{\rho(Br)^\gamma},$$

where the integrand function corresponds to $f_b \equiv (Br)^{-\gamma}r$.

The function V is thus analogous to the homogeneous solutions of equation (11), and has the form

$$V = Q_\nu(S, B, Y)\xi^{\lambda_1} + N_\nu(S, B, Y)\xi^{\lambda_2}.$$

The constants of integration Q_ν and N_ν are chosen so as to ensure no-expected jumps of the value function at trading times. Moreover, depending on the trade scenario, we impose the before-trade value function to be finite as $\xi \to 0$, and to converge to its no-trade counterpart as $\xi \to \infty$.

It can be shown that the function V is always positive for the trade scenarios illustrated in the two top panels of Figure 3: feedback traders buy bonds in exchange for stocks. The opposite holds true when feedback traders buy stocks in exchange for bonds (Figure 3, bottom two panels): the function V is always negative. These findings are stronger the higher γ, and are robust to different values of ξ triggering the trade.

REFERENCES

Basak, S., 1993, A General equilibrium model of portfolio insurance, Working paper, University of Pennsylvania.

Blume, L., D. Easley, and M. O'Hara, 1994, Market statistics and technical analysis: The role of volume, *Journal of Finance* 49, 153–181.

Brennan, M. J., and E. S. Schwartz, 1989, Portfolio insurance and financial market equilibrium, *Journal of Business* 62, 455–472.

Brock, W., J. Lakonishok, and B. LeBaron, 1992, Simple technical trading rules and the stochastic properties of stock returns, *Journal of Finance* 47, 1731–1764.

Chan, K. C., 1988, On the contrarian investment strategy, *Journal of Business* 61, 147–163.

Campbell, J. Y., and A. S. Kyle, 1993, Smart money, noise trading and stock price behavior, *Review of Economic Studies* 60, 1–34.

Constantinides, G. M., 1986, Capital market equilibrium with transactions costs, *Journal of Political Economy* 94, 842–862.

Davis, M. H. A., and A. R. Norman, 1990, Portfolio selection with transactions costs, *Mathematics of Operations Research* 15, 677–713.

De Long, J. B., A. Shleifer, L. H. Summers, and R. J. Waldmann, 1990, Positive feedback investment strategies and destabilizing rational speculation, *Journal of Finance* 45, 379–395.

Donaldson, G. R., and H. Uhlig, 1991, Portfolio insurance and asset prices, *Journal of Finance* 48, 1943–1955.

Duffie, D., and T. Sun, 1990, Transaction costs and portfolio choice in a discrete-continuous-time setting, *Journal of Economic Dynamics and Control* 14, 35–41.

Dybvig, P. H., 1995, Ratcheting, Consumption and Portfolios, *Review of Economic Studies* forthcoming.

Gennotte, G., and H. Leland, 1990, Market liquidity, hedging, and crashes, *American Economic Review* 80, 999–1021.

Grossman, S. J., and Z. Zhou, 1994, Equilibrium analysis of portfolio insurance, Working paper, University of Pennsylvania.

Lo, A. W., and C. A. MacKinlay, 1990, When are contrarian profits due to stock market overreaction? *Review of Financial Studies* 3, 175–205.

Lucas, R. E. Jr., 1978, Asset prices in an exchange economy, *Econometrica* 46, 1429–1445.

Neftci, S. N., 1991, Naive trading rules in financial markets and Wiener-Kolmogorov prediction theory: A study of 'technical analysis,' *Journal of Business* 64, 549–571.

8

Asset Prices and Trading Volume in a Beauty Contest

BRUNO BIAIS AND PETER BOSSAERTS

1. INTRODUCTION

Consider an asset market where investors have different private valuations for an asset. For example, in the art market, different persons have different tastes for a given painting. These differences may generate speculation in the sense of Harrison and Kreps (1978, p. 323).

An investor may buy the stock now, so as to sell it later for more than what he thinks it is actually worth, thereby reaping capital gains.

When the private valuations of potential future buyers are unknown, speculators ought to form beliefs about them in order to assess the resale potential of the asset. They should also anticipate that future buyers will speculate as well, on the basis of their own beliefs. When these beliefs are unknown, beliefs about them have to be formed. One can easily see how beliefs over those beliefs will be necessary to evaluate the resale worth. Iterating, a beliefs hierarchy results. Keynes (1958, p. 156) described this situation in his metaphor of the beauty contest:

... each competitor has to pick, not those faces which he himself finds prettiest, but those which he thinks likeliest to catch the fancy of the other competitors, all of whom are looking at the problem from the same point of view. It is not the case of choosing those which, to the best of one's judgement, are really the prettiest, nor even those the average opinion genuinely thinks the prettiest. We have reached the third degree where we devote our intelligences to anticipating what average opinion expects the average opinion to be. And there are some I believe, who practise the fourth, fifth and higher degrees.

The authors are grateful for helpful comments from the editors Ian Jewitt and Hyun Shin and three referees as well as from Mahmoud El Gamal, Jean Pierre Florens, Tom Palfrey, Eric Renault, Jean Charles Rochet, Jean Marie Rolin, Jean Tirole, Jean Luc Vila and Jiang Wang, and from participants at the Caltech, Carnegie Mellon University, HEC, Universitat Autonoma de Barcelona-BBV, University of British Columbia, and Wharton School seminars, at the Fédération Francaise des Sociétés d'Assurances seminar at the Université de Toulouse, at the 1993 Summer Meetings of the Econometric Society in Boston and the 1994 Meetings of the American Finance Association.

Keynes' quote characterizes only the first steps in what is generally an infinite beliefs hierarchy. Because of their dimensionality, beliefs hierarchies are quite complicated to analyse. Mertens and Zamir (1985) proved that they are nevertheless well behaved, in the sense that they do converage to a well-defined set, called the "universal beliefs space." Unfortunately, this universal beliefs space is a very complicated mathematical object. In practice one needs to make sufficient common knowledge assumptions to reduce this set to a manageable dimension.

The need for simplification is one of the reasons why Harsanyi (1967) introduced the *common prior assumption*. In his words (Harsanyi (1967, p. 164)):

The main purpose of this paper is to describe an alternative approach to the analysis of games within complete information, which completely avoids the difficulties associated with sequences of higher and higher-order reciprocal expectations.

Harsanyi (1967) imposes the following restrictions on first-order beliefs, i.e. on the beliefs of each agent about the private valuations of the others: there must exist a joint prior, common to all agents and common knowledge, such that the first-order beliefs of each agent can be interpreted as the Bayesian update of this prior, given his own private valuation. This ensures that there is a common knowledge link between an agent's private valuation and his first-order beliefs. This implies that higher-order beliefs of each agent are also a common knowledge function of his private valuation. This simplifies dramatically beliefs hierarchies.

Unfortunately, the common prior assumption has a major drawback. It implies that agents will not agree to disagree (see Aumann (1976)). In a financial markets context, this means that there will be no trading after reallocation for risk sharing has taken place. Subsequent bids, no matter how attractive, will always be viewed with suspicion: they will be interpreted as reflecting superior information in the hands of the bidder. In other words, investors will refrain from speculating (see Milgrom and Stokey (1981) and Tirole (1982)). Genuine disagreement seems to be a plausible description of the actual situation in certain speculative markets, however. Shiller (1995), for instance, reports results from opinion polls among Japanese and U.S. investors about likely price developments on Japanese equity markets. From his study emerges a clear picture of mutually recognized disagreement.[1]

The methodological contribution of the present paper is to show that tractability can also be obtained without assuming common priors, provided there is a common knowledge link between an agent's private valuation and his first-order belief. This common knowledge link is hereafter referred to as the "*common knowledge beliefs formation rule*".

Under the assumption that the beliefs formation rules are common knowledge, we study speculation in markets where agents may disagree. While other common knowledge beliefs formation rules are possible, this paper will work with a particularly intuitive one, to be called the "*average opinion rule*". It specifies that,

---

[1] Also see Morris (1993) and (1994) for an interesting discussion of why differences in priors is an attractive assumption.

prior to the game, agents consider their own private valuations to be average. In other words, an agent's private valuation anchors what she thinks other investors' private valuations are on average. The average opinion rule is consistent with Muth's original description of rational expectations. In particular, it implies the following which is taken from Muth (1961, p. 316):

Averages of expectations [...] are more accurate than naive models and as accurate as elaborate equation systems, although there are considerable cross-sectional differences of opinion.

We analyse the following trading game. There are an infinite number of trading rounds. In each trading round, the holder of the single unit of the asset meets two randomly chosen investors with identical private valuations. The latter compete *à la* Bertrand for the asset, and, therefore, offer to pay their reservation values. The holder then decides to hand over the asset in exchange of the bid price, or to keep it. Whoever holds the asset at the end moves on to the next trading round. The other investors leave the market. After a certain number of rounds, trading halts and the asset pays its dividend to the holder. When the true distribution of private valuations is unknown, investors update their beliefs using Bayes' law and the *entire* history of quotes and trades, to reflect the fact that the track record of financial markets is usually readily available.

The paper investigates three different specifications for the beliefs of the investors:

- In the first one, every investor knows the distribution of private valuations, and this is common knowledge.
- In the second specification, the agents share a common prior about the distribution of private valuations, and hence cannot agree to disagree. This will be referred to as the common prior case.
- In the third specification, Harsanyi's common prior assumption does not hold. There is genuine disagreement. This case will be referred to as the disagreement case.

The speculative value of the asset (the value of the right to resell before maturity) depends on the distribution of private values. It is impossible for the agents to agree to disagree on the distribution of private values in the case where the parameter of the distribution of private values is common knowledge or where the agents have a common prior on it. Hence, the agents must agree on the speculative value of the asset. This implies that newly arrived agents value the asset more than the current holder (and therefore purchase it) if and only if they have a larger private valuation. In the third specification, agents may disagree on the speculative value of the asset. This disagreement may lead to trades in which agents with low private valuations buy the asset from agents with higher valuations, because of optimism about the resale potential of the asset. To reflect that they originate in disagreement, this paper refers to such trades as *controversial trades*. Controversial trades lead to trading patterns which do not arise in the case where the parameter of the distribution of private values is common knowledge or when the agents have a common prior about it. For example, in the disagreement case, investors with low private valuations but high speculative valuations often buy the asset in the early stages of the trading game hoping to sell it later at a premium. If they eventually are unable to do so, these speculators unload their holdings.

From the analysis of the trading game, the paper attempts to distill those characteristics that allow one to empirically distinguish between the three beliefs specifications. It turns out that the case where the parameter of the distribution of private values is common knowledge can easily be differentiated: it displays features that are typical in standard rational expectations asset pricing models, such as constant expected returns and volatility. In contrast, when there is learning about this parameter, expected returns and volatility are time-varying. In the absence of information on investors' private valuations, however, it is difficult to differentiate the disagreement and the common prior cases. Among many statistics, the projection of changes in best offers (i.e. the highest among the valuations of the agents in the market place) onto volume and the projection of transaction price volatility onto volume generate the greatest discrimination. The key role of volume in these statistics reflects the above discussion on controversial trades.

Our results are obtained with the aid of a tightly parametrized model, which could lead one to question external validity. The differences between the Harsanyian and disagreement cases hinges on the presence of controversial trades. The impact of such trades on readily available statistics is likely to be qualitatively the same across parameterizations. In contrast, their quantitative impact will depend on the parameterization and its effect on the frequency with which controversial trades are observed.

The simplicity of the trading game and its clear empirical implications could inspire experimental work. Within a laboratory environment, it would be possible to gauge the importance of disagreement, and thus shed light on the empirical relevance of the common prior assumption in theoretical modelling of economic phenomena.

The paper is organized as follows. In the next section, it is shown how common knowledge of the beliefs formation rule facilitates the analysis of beliefs hierarchies in Bayesian games, in analogy with Harsanyi's common prior assumption. In Section 3, the trading game is presented. Section 4 provides analytical results. Section 5 offers simulation results. Some concluding comments are in section 6. The proofs are in the appendix.

2. BELIEFS

Consider the strategic interaction between agents bargaining over an asset. The agents are rational, i.e. they maximize expected utility, use Bayes' law to form expectations, and rationally anticipate the strategies of their opponents (we will consider perfect Bayesian equilibria). The novelty is that agents may have different priors, and, therefore, agree to disagree. If these priors are not common knowledge an infinite beliefs hierarchy arises. This section presents a methodological framework to study infinite beliefs hierarchies.

2.1. Private Valuations

Consider one asset and two agents i and j with private valuations for this asset equal to μ_i and μ_j. For simplicity, and without consequences for the qualitative nature of the results, assume that valuations are positive reals $\mu_i \in R^+, \mu_j \in R^+$.

The interpretation for the differences in private valuations is the following: if the asset is a work of art, a house or a bottle of fine wine, the agents have different tastes for it and enjoy different consumption values from it. In the case of a financial asset, different private valuations can reflect differential tax treatments.[2]

2.2. First-Order Beliefs

Agents i and j play a game of incomplete information (see Harsanyi (1967)), because each of them is uncertain about certain aspects of the game such as the preferences and beliefs of the other. Now, the larger the private valuation of j, the larger the price i can ask for the asset. Hence each agent needs to form beliefs about the private valuations of the other. We refer to these beliefs as first-order beliefs. To determine first-order beliefs, we first specify agent's joint priors over the pair (μ_i, μ_j). We will then use Bayes' law to compute the first-order belief as the conditional distribution of the private valuation of the other, given one's own private valuation. For any set X, denote $\Delta(X)$ the set of densities with respect to the Lebesgue measure over X. The joint prior of i over (μ_i, μ_j) is $\pi^i(\mu_i, \mu_j) \in \Delta(R^{+2})$.[3] The joint prior of j over (μ_i, μ_j) is $\pi^j(\mu_i, \mu_j) \in \Delta(R^{+2})$. Denote the first-order beliefs of i over μ_j.

$$\lambda_1^i(\cdot \mid \mu_i) = \lambda_1^i \in \Delta(R^+),$$

and the first-order belief of j over μ_i

$$\lambda_1^j(\cdot \mid \mu_j) = \lambda_1^j \in \Delta(R^+).$$

By Bayes' law

$$\lambda_1^i(\mu_j / \mu_i) = \frac{\pi^i(\mu_i, \mu_j)}{\int_{m \in R^+} \pi^i(\mu_i, m) dm}.$$

---

[2] Michaely and Vila (1994) analyse a model of financial markets where gains from trade are generated by differential tax treatments, and describe real-world situations where this is a reasonable assumption.

[3] To avoid technicalities, we do not consider other distributions than densities with respect to the Lebesgue measure. More general assumptions, allowing in particular for discrete types, could have been made, without altering the qualitative results, but at the cost of some complications.

Similarly,

$$\lambda_1^j(\mu_i/\mu_j) = \frac{\pi^j(\mu_i, \mu_j)}{\int_{m \in R^+} \pi^j(m, \mu_j)\, dm}.$$

2.3. Beliefs Hierarchies

In addition to first-order beliefs over μ_j, i must form beliefs over the first-order belief of j, λ_1^j, that is, he must form *second-order beliefs*. Indeed, if j has a relatively pessimistic first-order belief (λ_1^j) then j will not be too demanding in the bargaining and, consequently i will be quoted a favourable price. Denote the second-order belief of i over the first-order belief of j $\lambda_2^i \in \Delta(\Delta(R^+)) = \Delta^2(R^+)$, and the second-order belief of j over the first-order belief of i $\lambda_2^j \in \Delta(\Delta(R^+)) = \Delta^2(R^+)$.

Note that i's belief about λ_1^j (i.e. the second-order beliefs of i) cannot be computed using only λ_1^i and μ_i. This is because λ_1^i gives information about μ_j while λ_1^j depends on μ_j *and* π^j. Hence the formation of the second-order beliefs of i about λ_1^j also requires beliefs about π^j. Consequently, as the second-order beliefs come into play, an additional degree of freedom (and element of complexity) is added in the model.

In the same way, second-order beliefs are generally not common knowledge, which implies that *third-order beliefs* are necessary as well. Continuing, fourth-order, fifth-order, and higher-order beliefs must be specified. Iterating, an infinite hierarchy of beliefs unfolds. The nth-order beliefs of i, i.e. his beliefs about the $(n-1)$st-order beliefs of j are denoted $\lambda_n^i \in \Delta^n(R^+)$. Since each level in the hierarchy cannot in general be obtained from the previous one using Bayes' law, each level in the hierarchy brings an additional level of freedom into the model. That is why beliefs hierarchies are large-dimensional objects (and infinite beliefs hierarchies are in general infinite-dimensional) and thus difficult to deal with.

Mertens and Zamir (1985) have shown that all games of incomplete information can be defined as Bayesian games, where each player is characterized by a type, which summarizes the player's preferences and beliefs. As illustrated in the above example, these types can be infinite-dimensional, if the agents need to form infinite beliefs hierarchies. Mertens and Zamir (1985) have shown that, in spite of this infinite dimensionality, under regularity conditions, Bayesian games are well defined and can be analysed. But, because of the complexity of infinite belief hierarchies, applied work on incomplete information games with differences of opinion is relatively scarce.

2.4. Common Knowledge of a Common Prior

The "Harsanyi doctrine" offers a powerful way to cut through beliefs hierarchies, and thus restore tractability, by assuming that agents share a common prior and that it is common knowledge. In our model this amounts to assuming that $\pi^i = \pi^j = \pi$, and that this is common knowledge.

In such a case, the first-order belief of i

$$\lambda_1^i(\cdot \mid \mu_i) \underline{\qquad} = \frac{\pi(\mu_i, \cdot)}{\int_{m \in R^+} \pi(\mu_i, m) \, dm},$$

is a common knowledge function of μ_i. Let ϕ_i denote this function (it maps the private valuation of agent i into a density function, namely, his first-order belief)

$$\phi_i : R^+ \rightarrow \Delta(R^+),$$

$$\mu_i \mapsto \lambda_1^i.$$

Since ϕ_i reflects the link between i's private value and his first-order belief, we will hereafter refer to it as i's *beliefs formation rule.*

Similarly, the first-order belief of j

$$\lambda_1^j(\cdot \mid \mu_j) = \frac{\pi(\cdot, \mu_j)}{\int_{m \in R^+} \pi(m, \mu_j) \, dm},$$

is a common knowledge function of μ_j denoted ϕ_j. ϕ_j is the beliefs formation rule of j.

Once ϕ_j is known, λ_2^i can readily be obtained from λ_1^i through a change of variables

$$\lambda_2^i(\lambda_1^j(\cdot \mid \mu_j) \mid \mu_i) = \lambda_2^i \left(\left. \frac{(\pi(\cdot, \mu_j)}{\int_{m \in R^+} \pi(m, \mu_j) \, dm} \right| \mu_i \right) = \lambda_2^i(\phi_j(\mu_j) \mid \mu_i).$$

Hence, i's first-order belief λ_1^i and j's beliefs formation rule $\phi_j(\cdot)$ suffice to determine i's second-order beliefs.

If ϕ_j is differentiable and invertible, this can be expressed more formally as follows. Let Φ denote a realization of the (transformed) random variable $\phi_j(\mu_j)$ (Φ is a density) and ϕ_j^{-1} the inverse of ϕ_j. Then

$$\lambda_2^i(\Phi \mid \mu_i) = \lambda_1^i(\phi_j^{-1}(\Phi) \mid \mu_i) \frac{d\phi_j^{-1}}{d\Phi}.$$

One can iterate the above construction. At each level of the beliefs hierarchy, the beliefs of i and j are common knowledge functions of their private values μ_i and μ_j. Therefore, the entire belief hierarchies and i and j are common knowledge functions of μ_i and μ_j respectively. Consequently, the complexity induced by the infinite dimensionality, that arose in the general case (discussed in the previous subsection), does not arise under the Harsanyi doctrine.

2.5. Common Knowledge of Different Priors

Now assume that agents have different priors, i.e. $\pi^i \neq \pi^j$, but *these* (*different*) *priors are common knowledge.*[4] Since π^i is common knowledge, the first-order belief of i

$$\lambda_1^i(\cdot \mid \mu_i) = \frac{\pi^i(\mu_i, \cdot)}{\int_{m \in R^+} \pi^i(\mu_i, m) \, dm},$$

is still a common knowledge function of μ_i, denoted (as in the previous subsection) ϕ_i. Similarly, since π^j is common knowledge, the first-order belief of j

$$\lambda_1^j(\cdot \mid \mu_j) = \frac{\pi^j(\cdot, \mu_j)}{\int_{m \in R^+} \pi^j(m, \mu_j) \, dm},$$

is a common knowledge function (ϕ_j) of μ_j. Using the same arguments as in the common knowledge, common prior case, the entire beliefs hierarchies of i and j are common knowledge functions of μ_i and μ_j, and the infinite dimensionality problem does not arise.

2.6. Common Knowledge of the Belief Formation Rules Only

In the two above cases the fact the entire (conditional) beliefs hierarchy of each agent was a common knowledge function of his private value was implied simply by the common knowledge of the beliefs formation rules ϕ_i and ϕ_j. Building on this remark, consider now the case where the priors π^i and π^j are *not* common knowledge while *the beliefs formation rules ϕ_i and ϕ_j are common knowledge.* Although i does not know π^j, his knowledge of ϕ^i is enough to enable him to construct his second-order beliefs. As in the common prior case

$$\lambda_2^i(\lambda_1^j(\cdot \mid \mu_j) \mid \mu_i) = \lambda_2^i(\phi_j(\mu_j) \mid \mu_i).$$

Again, since ϕ^i and ϕ^j are common knowledge, the link between i's second-order belief and his private valuation μ_i, is common knowledge. Iterating, the entire beliefs hierarchies of i and j become common knowledge functions of μ_i and μ_j, and the infinite dimensionality problem does not arise.

For this route to resolving the infinite beliefs hierarchy to be viable, one should be in a case where it is not logically inconsistent to start with a specification of the first-order beliefs (λ_1^i and λ_1^j), which are conditional densities, and beliefs formation rules (ϕ^i and ϕ^j), while leaving the priors of the agents (π^i and ϕ^j), which are *unconditional* densities, unspecified. The following lemma states that it will always be possible to find (unconditional) joint priors which are consistent with

---

[4] Allen, Morris and Postlewaite (1993), and Morris (1994) analyse trading games where agents have different priors and these priors are common knowledge.

the specification of the (conditional) first-order beliefs and the beliefs formation rules.

Lemma 1. *Consider, as a candidate (conditional) first-order belief, any density $l^i \in \Delta(R^+)$. There exists an (unconditional) joint prior over μ_i and μ_j, $\pi^i \in \Delta(R^+ \times R^+)$ such that l_i is the Bayesian update of π^i, over μ_j, conditional on μ_i.*

The proof of the lemma has an important by-product. While the specification of the (unconditional) priors uniquely determines (conditional) first-order beliefs and beliefs formation rules, the converse is not true. Indeed, for each beliefs formation rule, there exist a multiplicity of (unconditional) priors from which the posited first-order beliefs can be obtained. Hence the informational requirements in our solution technique are less than those needed under the assumption of common knowledge of the (unconditional) priors.

In brief: while the common knowledge of priors is sufficient to simplify the infinite beliefs hierarchy, it is not necessary. One can work under the *weaker* assumption that the beliefs formation rule is common knowledge.

2.7. The Average Opinion Rule

The first-order belief of i, λ_1^i, is a density. Suppose that the first moment of this distribution exists

$$E_i(\mu_j|\mu_i) = \int_{m \in R^+} m\lambda_1^i(m \mid \mu_i)\, dm.$$

Although not mandated by probability theory, the requirement that $E_i(\mu_j \mid \mu_i) = \mu_i$, i.e. that each player, before observing the others, thinks of himself as average, is very reasonable. We hereafter refer to this requirement as "average opinion rule". Although it can be justified only by common sense, the average opinion rule puts structure on otherwise rather flexible beliefs structures.

Suppose that it is common knowledge that the beliefs of each player obey the average opinion rule, i.e. it is common knowledge that $E_i(\mu_j \mid \mu_i) = \mu_i$ and $E_j(\mu_i \mid \mu_j) = \mu_j$. In that case, agent i (she) expects agent j (he) to expect μ_i to be (on average) equal to μ_j. This is also common knowledge, since there is common knowledge of the average opinion rule. Iterating, it is common knowledge that she expects him to expect that she expects that he expects... to be average. Hence, the entire hierarchy of expectations is common knowledge. Note that this obtains under common knowledge of the average opinion rule, a weaker requirement than common knowledge of the beliefs formation rule.

2.8. Learning

Let us now analyse learning in the context of our procedure to model different priors. Until now, we needed only two agents to develop our ideas. To clarify learning, however, we want to introduce more agents. As the game proceeds, agent i observes his own private valuation, as well as the private valuations of others. He uses these to update his beliefs over the likely private values of future opponents. To facilitate the study of learning, we introduce a parameter, θ, and assume that each agent believes that the private values of the others are i.i.d. draws from a distribution indexed by θ, with density[5] $f(\cdot \mid \theta) \in \Delta(R^+)$. Agents know the functional form of $f(\cdot \mid \theta)$ but are uncertain about θ. Agent i will infer θ, first of all, from i's own private valuation and subsequently from observation of others' private valuations.

To update beliefs using his own valuation, i posits a joint prior over θ and μ_i, denoted $p^i(\theta, \mu_i)$. Bayes' law implies the following posterior

$$p^i(\theta \mid \mu_i) = \frac{p^i(\theta, \mu_i)}{\int_{t \in \Theta} p^i(t, \mu_i)\, dt}.$$

$p^i(\theta \mid \mu_i)$ fixes agent i's first-order belief in a particular realization of the game. In other words, it determines the conditional belief λ_1^i, as follows

$$\lambda_1^i(\cdot \mid \mu_i) = \int_{t \in \Theta} f(\cdot \mid t)p^i(t \mid \mu_i)\, dt.$$

When interpreted as a function of μ_i taking its values in $\Delta(R^+)$, $\lambda_1^i(\cdot \mid \mu_i)$ gives rise to the beliefs formation rule, $\phi_i(\mu_i)$. Since it is determined by $f(\cdot \mid \cdot)$ and $p^i(\cdot \mid \mu_i)$, common knowledge of those functions implies common knowledge of the beliefs formation rule ϕ_i. Most importantly, the unconditional prior over θ and μ_i, $p^i(\theta, \mu_i)$, is *not* necessary to determine the (conditional) first-order belief λ_1^i, and hence, the beliefs formation rule ϕ_i. In other words, the unconditional prior need not be common knowledge, confirming the claims of the previous subsection.

Subsequently, i observes the private valuation of other agents. Say that he observes the private valuation of agent k, μ_k. Then i updates his beliefs about θ using Bayes' law generating the posterior $p^i(\theta \mid \mu_i, \mu_k)$

$$p^i(\theta \mid \mu_i, \mu_k) = \frac{f(\mu_k \mid \theta)p^i(\theta \mid \mu_i)}{\int_{t \in \Theta} f(\mu_k \mid t)p^i(t \mid \mu_i)\, dt}.$$

This leads to a revision in the first-order belief of i over other agents' private valuations. For instance, the first-order belief over j's private valuation becomes

$$\lambda_1^i(\mu_j \mid \mu_i, \mu_k) = \int_{t \in \Theta} f(\mu_j \mid t)p^i(t \mid \mu_i, \mu_k)\, dt.$$

Inspection of these updating rules again reveals that the unconditional prior over θ and μ_i, $p^i(\theta, \mu_i)$, is *not needed* to determine agents' first-order beliefs conditional

---

[5] We could have considered different densities for different agents. Similarly, we could have assumed dependence of private valuations across agents, and even dependence of other agents' private valuation of i's private valuation beyond θ. All this does not lead to new insights, yet does add substantial notational burden.

on their own valuation and those of others which they already observed. Agents only use their beliefs formation rule, ϕ_i, composed of $f(\cdot \mid \cdot)$ and $p^i(\cdot \mid \mu_i)$, to infer the distribution of the private valuation of others.

It follows that, to assess how their *opponents* conduct inferences, agents only need to use their own beliefs formation rule, and the (common knowledge) beliefs formation rules of others. In other words, the second-order beliefs can be obtained from one's own beliefs formation rule and those of others. Since the former is a function of one's private valuation, it follows that second-order beliefs are functions of own private valuations. For instance, agent i's second-order belief over the first-order belief of j, after having observed μ_i and μ_k, when j also observed μ_k, is

$$\lambda_2^i(\lambda_1^j(\cdot \mid \mu_j, \mu_k) \mid \mu_i, \mu_k) = \int_{m \in R^+} \left(\int_{t \in \Theta} f(\cdot \mid t) p^j(t \mid m, \mu_k) dt \right) \lambda_1^i(m \mid \mu_i, \mu_k) dm.$$

Since the functional forms in the above are common knowledge, second-order beliefs are common knowledge functions of own private valuations. Iterating, we conclude that higher-order beliefs are common knowledge functions of own private valuations, and, to assess the beliefs hierarchy of others, agents merely refer to their own first-order beliefs.

2.9. A Parametric Example

Suppose each player believes that the private values of opponents are i.i.d. draws from an exponential distribution with parameter θ

$$f(\mu_j \mid \theta) = \frac{1}{\theta} \exp\left(-\frac{\mu_j}{\theta}\right).$$

Note that this implies $E(\mu_j \mid \theta) = \theta$. We will consider 3 different cases. In the first case *all* private values are i.i.d. exponentially distributed, with parameter θ^*, and this is common knowledge. We will refer to it as the "common knowledge of θ^*" case. In the second case, it is common knowledge that the agents believe that *all* private values are drawn from an exponential distribution; they are uncertain about its parameter (θ), but have a common prior on it. We will refer to this case as the "common prior" case. In the third case, the agents believe that the private values *of the others* are i.i.d. draws from an exponential with parameter θ; they don't know θ and have different priors over the joint distribution of their own private value and θ. We will refer to this case as the "disagreement" case.

2.9.1. *The Common Prior Case*
Suppose it is common knowledge that all agents have the same inverse gamma prior over θ. Consider the case of the diffuse prior, with parameters $\alpha = 1, \beta = \infty$.

Suppose it is common knowledge that agents believe that all private values (including their own) are i.i.d. exponential with parameter θ. After observing his own private value, μ_i, agent i will have inverse gamma posteriors about θ, with parameters

$$\alpha_{i,1} = 2, \qquad \beta_{i,1} = \frac{1}{\mu_i}.$$

This implies that

$$E_i(\theta \mid \mu_i) = \frac{1}{(\alpha_{i,1} - 1)\beta_{i,1}} = \mu_i,$$

which in turn implies that

$$E_i(\mu_j \mid \mu_i) = E_i(E_i(\mu_j \mid \theta) \mid \mu_i) = E_i(\theta \mid \mu_i) = \mu_i.$$

Hence, the *average opinion rule* holds.

2.9.2. *The Disagreement Case*

Agent i believes that the distribution $f(\cdot \mid \theta)$ from which the private values of the others are i.i.d. draws is the expotential distribution with parameter θ. His conditional first-order belief (λ_i^1) results from f and his belief over θ: $p^i(\theta \mid \mu_i)$. Suppose that, conditional on μ_i, agent i believes that the distribution of θ is inverse gamma distribution with parameters: $\alpha_{i,1} = \mu_i + 1$, and $\beta_{i,1} = 1/\mu_i^2$. The beliefs formation rule (ϕ_i) is obtained from $p^i(\cdot \mid \cdot)$ and $f(\cdot \mid \cdot)$.

Note that the beliefs thus specified satisfy the average opinion rule. Indeed

$$E_i(\mu_j \mid \mu_i) = E_i(\theta \mid \mu_i) = \frac{1}{(\alpha_{i,1} - 1)\beta_{i,1}} = \frac{\mu_i^2}{(\mu_i + 1 - 1)} = \mu_i.$$

Can these beliefs be obtained as the Bayesian updates formed by the agents once they have observed their type, based on some unconditional, prior, distribution? Lemma 1, states that it is always possible. The next corollary illustrates this property by exhibiting a class of distributions which do, indeed, lead to $p^i(\cdot \mid \cdot)$:

Corollary 1. *Consider any density on $R^+ : m^i \in \Delta(R^+)$. If the joint prior of i over (θ, μ_i) equals*

$$p^i(\theta, \mu_i) = \frac{1}{\theta} \frac{1}{\theta^{\mu_i+1}} e^{-(\mu_i^2/\theta)} \frac{m^i(\mu_i)}{(1/\mu_i^2)^{\mu_i+1}\mu_i!},$$

then the conditional first-order belief of i over θ is the inverse gamma density with parameters

$$\alpha_{i,1} = \mu_i + 1, \qquad \beta_{i,1} = 1\mu_i^2.$$

The prior defined in equation (2) is somewhat complicated and does not lend itself readily to interpretations. It should be noted, however, that Corollary 1 does not impose restrictions on the prior m_i. In that sense the class of priors giving rise to the parametric example is generic.

3. THE TRADING GAME

Consider the market for an asset. This asset could be a bottle of wine, a house, a painting or a financial asset. At the end of the trading game, at time $T+1$, the agent who holds the asset derives a private consumption value from it. In the case of the bottle of wine, $T+1$ corresponds to the wine's right drinking age. In the case of a financial contract such as a futures contract, it would be the expiration date. For simplicity assume there is only one unit of the asset, and that it is indivisible. Before maturity, there are $T+1$ trading rounds, indexed $t = 0, \ldots, T$. For simplicity, assume agents are infinitely patient, i.e. there is no discounting.

There is a continuum of risk neutral and infinitely patient investors, identified by their positive private valuation for the asset, $\mu \in R^+$. At each trading round t, two investors with identical private valuation (μ_t) and identical beliefs enter the market. The two investors compete *à la* Bertrand. This drives their bids for the asset up to their reservation value. In computing their reservation values, investors take into account the resale option. The latter's value will be determined in equilibrium.

When the final bids are in, the holder can decide to sell the asset or to wait for a subsequent trading opportunity. If the holder sells the asset, he exits the market, and obtains utility equal to the selling price. One of the two bidders pays the price and becomes the owner, while the other exits the market.[6] Each bidder has equal probability to be selected as the owner. If the holder decides not to take the bids, the two bidders exit the market and the holder goes to the next trading round.

Speculation (in the sense of Harrison and Kreps (1978)) ensues because the asset has resale value. The determination of the value of the resale option involves the formation of higher-order beliefs. To see this, consider the following. Investors entering the market at time T have reservation values of equal to their private valuation, because there is no further resale opportunity. In contrast, the asset has speculative value for the investors entering the market at time $T - 1$: they may want to sell to investors bidding for the asset at time T. To compute the speculative value, time $T - 1$ investors need to form beliefs over the distribution of private valuations (which will determine time T bids), i.e. first order beliefs. Now consider time $T - 2$ investors. They anticipate the opportunity to resell the asset to bidders at time $T - 1$ and T. They know that the bids will depend on

---

[6] At time $t = 0$, Nature is assumed to be the owner, and always sells the asset to one of the bidders. Because of Bertrand competition between identical agents, the decision rule of the owner, which determines whether he sells or not, does not affect the bids. Hence time 0 bids are determined in the same fashion as subsequent ones.

private valuations and first-order beliefs. Hence, they need first-order and second-order beliefs to determine the speculative value of the asset. And so forth for investors at time $T - 3, \ldots, 0$.

Because of Bertrand competition, bids are reservation values. This substantially simplifies the analysis. In particular, only the solution of a one-sided beliefs hierarchy is required. It is not necessary for the holder to form beliefs over what bidders think that his higher-order beliefs are. In a more realistic bargaining situation, however, two-sided beliefs hierarchies would have to be contemplated, which would greatly increase the complexity of the analysis.

As time passes, quotes and trades are observed. When agents are uncertain about the distribution of private valuations (and, hence, about the distribution of higher-order beliefs), investors use the quotes and trades to update their beliefs using Bayes' law.

The specification of beliefs is as in the previous section, where it served as a framework to study beliefs hierarchies and learning. There are three cases. In the first case, (i) each agent believes that private valuations are i.i.d. draws from an exponential density with parameter θ, and (ii) θ is (correctly) known to have the value θ^*. In the second case, (i) is the same, but (ii) differs: the value of θ is unknown, but investors have a common inverse gamma prior over it. In the third case, (i) each agent believes that private valuations *of opponents only* are i.i.d. draws from an exponential density with parameter θ, and (ii) agent i's first-order belief over θ, conditional on his μ_i, is inverse gamma with parameters determined by μ_i.

Beliefs are parametrized such that quotes are invertible in private valuations.[7] Investors use this invertibility property. In the second and third cases, the history of implied private valuations is used (along with Bayes' law) to update beliefs about the distribution of θ, and, hence, of future opponents' private valuations. Because of the common knowledge link between higher-order beliefs and private valuations, the revision of first-order beliefs simultaneously updates higher-order beliefs.

4. ANALYTICAL RESULTS

4.1. The General Case

In equilibrium, investors obtain their reservation values by backward recursion from time T on. In order to illustrate the computation, consider a two-period case, where $T = 2$. There are three trading rounds ($t = 0, 1, 2$). The possible decision sequences can be represented in the form of a tree, as in Diagram 1.

- At time 2, two investors with equal private valuation for the final dividend, μ_2, enter the market. Their reservation value is determined only by μ_2 as they will not have any resale opportunity. The current holder will transfer the asset to

---

[7] If quotes were not made to be perfectly revealing, complexity would be added to the analysis, without much change in substance.

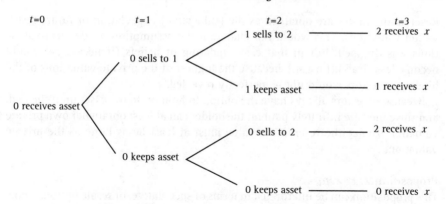

Diagram 1. *Event tree with three trading rounds (T=2; x denotes the dividend)*

one of the two investors only if her private valuation is lower than μ_2. If the holder is one of the investors entering the market at time 1, one of the entering investors at time 2 is allocated the asset whenever $\mu_2 > \mu_1$. If the holder is the initial (time-0) investor, she will sell if $\mu_2 > \mu_0$.

- At time 1, the entering investors know that they can either sell the asset at time 2, and obtain μ_2, or keep it and obtain μ_1. So, their time-1 reservation value (denoted r_1^1), and, hence, their offer, is

$$r_1^1 = E_1(\max[\mu_1, \mu_2] \mid H_1),\qquad(3)$$

where, in general, $E_i(\cdot \mid H_t)$ denotes the expectations operator from the point of view of an agent i at time t, formed using his own beliefs, updated with the history of revealed private valuations, H_t. Similarly, the time-1 reservation value of the initial holder ("she") of the asset equals $r_0^1 = E_0(\max[\mu_0, \mu_2] \mid H_1)$. She sells the asset whenever $r_1^1 > r_0^1$.

- At time 0, anticipating choices at later times, her reservation value equals

$$r_0^0 = E_0(\max[r_0^1, r_1^1] \mid H_0)$$
$$= E_0(\max[E_0(\max[\mu_0, \mu_2] \mid H_1), E_1(\max[\mu_1, \mu_2] \mid H_1)] \mid H_0).$$

One can generalize the two-period example in a straightforward way. It leads to the following recursive formula.

Proposition 1. *The reservation value of investor i at time t equals*

$$r_i^t = E_i(\max[r_i^{t+1}, r_{t+1}^{t+1}] \mid H_t).$$

This proposition should also clarify the role of the Bertrand competition and the assumption of identical private valuations of new arrivals to the marketplace.

Reservation values are obtained as the (subjective) expectation of future reservation valuations. This would not change if the assumption of identical valuations was dropped. But in that case, updating of beliefs (if necessary) would become less straightforward, because the highest of the private valuations of the bidding investors would not be perfectly revealed.[8]

Because investors always have the option to hold on to the asset until the end, and since they are infinitely patient, the holder can at least obtain her own private valuation. Hence the reservation value must at least be as large as the private valuation.

Proposition 2. $r_i^t \geq \mu_i$.

This proposition can be interpreted in terms of speculative, or resale option, value. If agents did not have the possibility to resell the asset, the value they would attach it would simply equal their private valuation. In the speculative game, however, the agents also attach a speculative or resale option value to the asset.

$$W_t^i = r_i^t - \mu_i \geq 0.$$

One of the goals of this paper is to study the consequences of differences in beliefs and beliefs hierarchies on this speculative value and their implications for asset prices, volatility and volume dynamics.

Now consider the *best offer* in the marketplace at time t, which will be denoted b_t. The best offer is defined as the maximum of the reservation values of the holder of the asset and the investors who enter the market at time t

$$b_t = \max[r_t^t, r_{(t-1)^*}^t],$$

where $(t-1)^*$ identifies the holder at the end of the $t-1$st trading round.

At t, the holder expects to be able to sell the asset at time $t+1$ at the reservation value of the new entrants r_{t+1}^{t+1} or to keep the asset because his own (future) reservation value is higher. The maximum of the two is the best offer in the market, b_{t+1}. Since the agents are risk-neutral, a martingale result immediately follows.

Proposition 3. *From the point of the holder, the best offer in the market is a martingale:*

$$b_t = E_{t^*}(b_{t+1} \mid H_t).$$

Proposition 3 is simply a rationality condition, as in Samuelson (1965). Note, however, that the martingale property only holds *from the perspective of the holder.* Under other beliefs, the best offer may not be a martingale.

---

[8] If we considered more complex bargaining mechanisms we would encounter additional problems, associated with equilibrium multiplicity and two-sided beliefs hierarchies.

4.2. The Case where θ^* is Common Knowledge

If the correct value of θ, θ^*, is common knowledge, the martingale property obtains under the true probability measure. This is stated in the next corollary, where E_{θ^*} denotes the expectation where $\theta = \theta^*$.

Corollary 2. *If θ^* is common knowledge, $b_t = E_{\theta^*}(b_{t+1} \mid H_t)$.*

Consequently, if θ^* is common knowledge, changes in best offers are on average zero: $E_{\theta^*}(b_{t+1} - b_t | H_t) = 0$. Provided the econometrician has long times series, this martingale difference result should be readily verifiable. The next section will illustrate this.

4.3. The Common Prior Case

Now consider the second case, where agents start from a common prior, as in Harsanyi (1968). From Aumann's (1976) analysis, we know that investors will not disagree in any fundamental way. However, there is learning, because the value of θ, and, hence, the true distribution of private valuations, is unknown.

Using the characterization of reservation values of Proposition 1, the following can be obtained.

Proposition 4. *In the common prior case, investor i's reservation value at time t equals*

$$r_i^t = E(\max[\mu_i, \mu_{t+1}, \mu_{t+2}, \ldots, \mu_T] \mid H_t),$$

where E denotes the expectation over $\mu_{t+1}, \mu_{t+2}, \ldots, \mu_T$ taken with respect to the common prior.

Proposition 4 immediately implies that reservation values are increasing in private valuations. This is started as a corollary.

Corollary 3. *In the common prior case, $r_i^t > r_j^t \Leftrightarrow \mu_i > \mu_j$.*

As a result of Corollary 3, trade occurs only when the newly arrived investors have a higher private valuation than the current holder of the asset. This implies that, at time t, the current holder of the asset is the investor with the (historically) highest private valuation.[9]

Proposition 4 and, hence, Corollary 3, holds in particular when the prior on θ is concentrated on the true value θ^*. Hence, uncertainty over θ does not *per se* affect trading volume.

---

[9] Corollary 3 also implies that reservation values are invertible in private valuations. Since quotes equal reservation values, because of Bertrand competition and the assumption that investors arriving to the marketplace have identical private valuations, other investors can infer the private valuation of the bidder from her quote. This simplifies the learning of the distribution of private valuations.

The speculative, or resale option, value can be more precisely analysed by studying the expectation in Proposition 4.

Corollary 4. *In the common prior case, investor i's resale option value at time t equals*

$$W_i^t = \int_\Theta \left(\int_{\mu_i}^\infty P(\max[\mu_{t+1}, \ldots, \mu_T] > s/t)ds \right) p(t/H_t)\, dt,$$

(where P is the multivariate probability distribution corresponding to the density $f(\mu/\theta)$ and $p(\theta/H_t)$ is the posterior density derived from the common prior p, the history of revealed private valuations H_t and Bayes' law).

In the exponential-inverse gamma parametrization, the resale option value can be computed explicitly.

Corollary 5. *Assume p is the inverse gamma prior with parameter $\alpha = 1$ and $\beta = \infty$, then*

$$W_i^t = \mu_i + \sum_{j=1}^{T-t} C_{T-t}^j \frac{(-1)^{j+1}}{j} \frac{\bar\mu_t + j\mu_i}{t+1}\left[1 + j\frac{\mu_i}{\bar\mu_t}\right]^{-(t+2)},$$

where $\hat\mu_t \equiv \Sigma_{j=0}^t \mu_j$.

The above results enable one to discuss the role of the resale option (or speculative) value in the common prior case. Consider two agents, with private values μ_i and μ_j, meeting in the marketplace at time t. From Corollary 4

$$W_t^i < W_t^j \Leftrightarrow \mu_i > \mu_j,$$

i.e. the agent with the highest private value has the lowest option value. On the other hand, Corollary 3 stated that

$$r_t^i > r_t^j \Leftrightarrow \mu_i > \mu_j,$$

i.e. the agent with the highest private value has the highest reservation value for the asset. Hence, differences in option value are not sufficient to overcome differences in private values and to generate trades where the agent with the lowest private value would buy from the agent with the largest private value. In other words, there is no disagreement. Of course, this confirms Aumann's (1976) result. When priors differ, however, there is genuine disagreement. In this case differences in option value can overcome the difference in private valuation. This generates trades where agents with low private valuations purchase from agents with larger private valuations. These are *controversial* trades since each party of the trade thinks the other is making a bad deal. The existence of consequences of controversial trades is studied in the next section.[10]

---

[10] The next section relies on simulations. In a three trading periods case and in the context of our exponential inverse gamma parametrization we proved analytically that controversial trades can arise.

Corollary 4 implies a further characterization of the process of the reservation values. In particular:

Corollary 6. *In the common prior case, r_i^t is a submartingale from the point of view of the market participants*

$$r_i^t \geq E(r_i^{t+1} \mid H_t).$$

This result reflects the decrease in the speculative value of the asset as the horizon gets closer. The decline is due to the loss of resale opportunities and the decrease in uncertainty about the distribution of beliefs. Corollary 6 does not contradict Proposition 3 (which stated that the best offer is a martingale from the point of view of the holder). There, the decrease in the option value is offset by the fact that the new entrants might have a higher private valuation for the asset than the current holder, so that the latter would sell and earn capital gains.

Again, when taking p to be concentrated on the true value, θ^*, one concludes that the submartingale property holds equally well when there is no uncertainty over θ. The decline in reservation value, however, is then entirely due to the decreasing resale opportunities.

Using Proposition 4 and Corollary 3, the following proposition about the best offer in the marketplace (b_t) obtains.

Proposition 5. *In the common prior case*

$$b_t = E(\max[\mu_0, \ldots, \mu_T] \mid H_t).$$

Proposition 5 reflects the (rational) expectation by the market participants that, after each round, the asset will be owned by the investor with the maximum private valuation. Since investors are risk-neutral, their reservation value for the asset is equal to their conditional expectation of this maximum.

The best offer in the market at time t can be expressed analytically.

Corollary 7. *In the common prior case*

$$b_t = \mu_t^* + \int_\Theta \left(\int_{\mu_t^*}^\infty P(\max[\mu_{t+1}, \ldots, \mu_T] > s \mid \theta) \, ds \right) p(\theta \mid H_t) \, d\theta,$$

where $\mu_t^* = \max[\mu_0, \ldots, \mu_t]$.

5. SIMULATION ANALYSIS

In this section, simulations are used to study and compare the dynamics of prices and trades when there is common knowledge of the correct θ^*, or common priors over θ or disagreement.

Since the proof is rather long and tedious we have not included it in the paper. It is available from the authors upon request.

The simulations were conducted as follows:

1. The number of trading rounds $(T+1)$ was set equal to 20;
2. Three possible values of θ^* were used, namely 0.6, 0.8 and 1.0;
3. Reservation values were calculated using numerical integration with a mesh equal to 0.1;
4. 1000 sample paths of $T+1$ private valuations were drawn, discretized over intervals of size 0.1 (i.e. matching the mesh in the numerical calculations);
5. At each point in time, and for each sample path, reservation values were calculated for the holder and for the newly arriving investors, thus determining quotes, and whether there was a trade and at what price;
6. Several statistics, such as the average change in the best offer or the volatility of returns, were computed on the basis of the 1000 simulations.

Note that our specification of the disagreement case is biased in favour of the existence of controversial trades. Indeed investors with high private valuations (μ_i) have very precise first-order beliefs.[11] This reduces the value attached to the resale option, and makes it possible that an agent with a relatively large private value has a relatively low resale option value. This creates the potential for controversial trades. In addition, the three values of θ^* used in the simulations (0.6, 0.8 and 1.0) were chosen in order to generate a reasonable frequency of controversial trades. Virtually all controversial trades are generated when an investor with $\mu < 1$ meets another investor with higher private valuations. This is because for $\mu < 1$, first-order beliefs have zero precision, and, hence, the resale option is valued highly. When setting θ^* equal to some value substantially above one, however, there is only a relatively small probability of finding an investor with $\mu < 1$. Correspondingly, there are fewer controversial trades, and the descriptive statistics look more like those obtained in the common prior case.

5.1. A First Look at the Simulations

The simulations were run in order to find descriptive statistics that allow one to empirically distinguish between the three versions of the model. The statistics may not be computed from variables that an econometrician is unlikely to observe, such as private valuations. Instead, they should be cast in terms of readily available data, such as quotes, returns and volume.

The task is not easy. In particular, the difference between the Harsanyian cases (where θ^* is common knowledge or the agents share a common prior), on the one hand, and disagreement, on the other, hinges on the importance of controversial trades. Such trades are absent in the former. If one could observe private valuations, controversial trades and hence, the relevance of disagreement, would

---

[11] For example, the precision of i's (conditional) first-order belief over $\theta = (\mu_i - 1)^{-1}$, which is a decreasing function of μ_i.

immediately be recognizable. This could be achieved in an experimental setting, but not in field data from actual markets. Hence it is a much more difficult task to establish the presence of disagreement when attention must be limited to standard data from asset markets.

To get a feel for the problem, Figure 1 plots quotes (reservation values of bidders and holder), transaction prices and trades for ten (independent) realizations of 20 trading rounds. Figure 1 should provide an idea of the type of data that were used to compute the descriptive statistics soon to be discussed.

One could cite the increased volatility and the substantially higher average price level as features that distinguish the case where θ^* is common knowledge, from the common prior case, but these are difficult yardsticks to employ in any practical situation, as it is almost always impossible to determine what the "right" level of volatility and prices should be.

From Figure 1, it is difficult to discriminate the second and third cases. As a matter of fact, the histories for both models seem almost identical in all respects. Controversial trades should provide the distinguishing characteristic. Unfortunately, such trades are not easily discernible in the plots. The subsequent subsections discuss descriptive statistics that one could compute from replications of simulations like the ones plotted in Figure 1. Some of them provide ways to discriminate the common prior case from the disagreement case.[12]

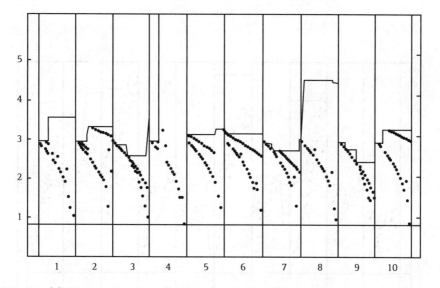

Figure 1 (a). *Transaction prices (solid line), bid quotes (reservation values of the arriving agent) and ask quotes (reservation values of the holder whenever there is no transaction) for ten independent periods of twenty trading rounds with common knowledge of θ^**

---

[12] In our model we do not allow sellers to re-enter the market after they have exited it. Notice that, even if re-entry was allowed for, it would never occur in equilibrium in the common knowledge of θ^*

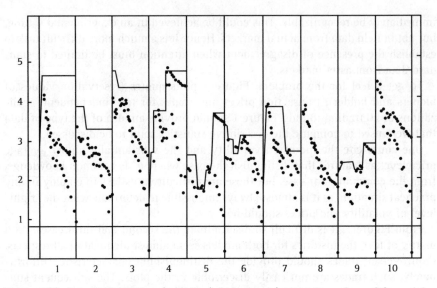

Figure 1(b). *Transaction prices (solid line), bid quotes (reservation values of the arriving agent) and ask quotes (reservation values of the holder whenever there is no transaction) for ten independent periods of twenty trading rounds with common prior*

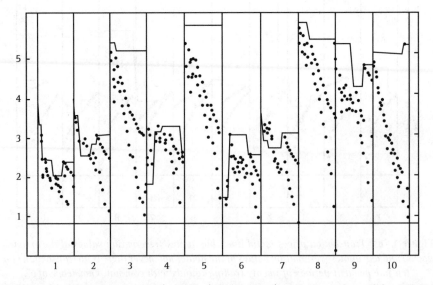

Figure 1 (c). *Transaction prices (solid line), bid quotes (reservation values of the arriving agent) and ask quotes (reservation values of the holder whenever there is no transaction) for ten independent periods of twenty trading rounds with disagreement*

5.2. The Identity of the Holder

Were it easily observable, the private valuation of the holder would be the best variable by which to distinguish the common prior and disagreement cases. As mentioned before, with common knowledge of θ^* or with common priors, trading occurs whenever the private valuation of the bidders is higher than that of the holder. In contrast, with different priors, controversial trades are possible, whereby holders with a lower (or higher) private valuation decline trades (or do trade) with investors with a higher (or lower) private valuation.

Table 1 illustrates this. It lists, for each trading round, the average private valuation of the holder. The averages are strictly increasing only in the Harsanyian cases (where there is common knowledge of θ^* or common priors).[13] The numerical differences with the disagreement case reveal the importance of controversial trades. They are most pronounced for low values of θ^*, when there are relatively more investors with low precision first-order beliefs all of whom initially assign extremely high values to the resale option.

Figure 2 highlights those difference. It plots, as a function of the trading rounds, the average change in the private valuation of the holder in the disagreement case *in excess of* that in the case where θ^* is common knowledge. The dots delineate two-standard deviation confidence intervals. The effect of controversial trades is most pronounced when $\theta^* = 0.6$, but is still evident in the other cases: in early trading rounds, the average change in the private valuation of the holder is much lower in the disagreement case; in later rounds, it is significantly higher. The intuition is the following:

- In the common prior case trades occur when the agents entering the market have a larger private valuation than the current holder. This is rather frequent early on in the game, and, therefore, generates substantial average changes in the private value of the holder. On the other hand, this tends to be infrequent towards the end of the game, where the average increase is minimal.
- With disagreement, agents with low private valuations may buy or keep early on, because they value the resale option. This slows down the increase in the private value of the holder. Towards the end of the game, in contrast, as the option value becomes negligible, speculators who could not sell before unload their inventory to agents with larger private values. This leads to late increases in the private value of the holder.

and common prior cases. In contrast, with disagreement, re-entry is a possibility. Hence, data on individual retrading would provide a way to recognize disagreement. Since data on the identity of the traders are sometimes available, this route could provide additional information, certainly in an experimental setting, where private valuations can be strictly controlled.

[13] The simulations for the cases where θ^* is common knowledge and for the common prior case were pooled to increase power (as a consequence, there were 2000 observations). Pooling is allowed because the identity (private valuation) of the holders does not differ in those two cases.

Table 1. Average private valuations

θ^*		Trading Rounds																				
		0	1	2	3	4	5	6	7	8	9	10	11	12	13	14	15	16	17	18	19	20
0.6	Common knowledge of θ^* or common prior	0.65	0.95	1.15	1.31	1.41	1.53	1.62	1.69	1.74	1.80	1.86	1.91	1.96	2.00	2.05	2.08	2.12	2.15	2.19	2.23	2.25
		(0.02)	(0.02)	(0.02)	(0.02)	(0.02)	(0.02)	(0.02)	(0.02)	(0.02)	(0.02)	(0.02)	(0.02)	(0.02)	(0.02)	(0.02)	(0.02)	(0.02)	(0.02)	(0.02)	(0.02)	(0.02)
	Disagreement	0.66	0.60	0.66	0.74	0.84	0.95	1.08	1.21	1.31	1.43	1.55	1.64	1.74	1.83	1.90	1.98	2.03	2.08	2.13	2.16	2.19
		(0.02)	(0.02)	(0.03)	(0.03)	(0.03)	(0.03)	(0.03)	(0.03)	(0.03)	(0.03)	(0.03)	(0.03)	(0.03)	(0.03)	(0.03)	(0.03)	(0.03)	(0.03)	(0.03)	(0.02)	(0.02)
0.8	Common knowledge of θ^* or common prior	0.86	1.27	1.52	1.73	1.88	2.02	2.14	2.22	2.30	2.39	2.45	2.51	2.57	2.63	2.68	2.73	2.78	2.82	2.87	2.90	2.95
		(0.02)	(0.02)	(0.02)	(0.02)	(0.02)	(0.02)	(0.02)	(0.02)	(0.02)	(0.02)	(0.02)	(0.02)	(0.02)	(0.02)	(0.02)	(0.02)	(0.02)	(0.02)	(0.02)	(0.02)	(0.02)
	Disagreement	0.84	0.94	1.08	1.24	1.47	1.67	1.84	1.99	2.11	2.22	2.30	2.41	2.49	2.55	2.60	2.67	2.74	2.81	2.85	2.90	2.93
		(0.02)	(0.03)	(0.04)	(0.04)	(0.04)	(0.04)	(0.04)	(0.04)	(0.04)	(0.04)	(0.04)	(0.04)	(0.03)	(0.03)	(0.03)	(0.03)	(0.03)	(0.03)	(0.03)	(0.03)	(0.03)
1.0	Common knowledge of θ^* or common prior	1.00	1.50	1.84	2.10	2.32	2.46	2.62	2.75	2.87	2.98	3.08	3.15	3.22	3.28	3.34	3.40	3.44	3.49	3.53	3.59	3.64
		(0.03)	(0.03)	(0.04)	(0.04)	(0.04)	(0.04)	(0.04)	(0.04)	(0.04)	(0.04)	(0.04)	(0.04)	(0.04)	(0.04)	(0.04)	(0.04)	(0.04)	(0.04)	(0.04)	(0.04)	(0.04)
	Disagreement	1.06	1.25	1.55	1.80	2.05	2.24	2.42	2.59	2.73	2.86	2.98	3.08	3.19	3.27	3.35	3.42	3.49	3.55	3.60	3.64	3.68
		(0.03)	(0.04)	(0.04)	(0.05)	(0.05)	(0.05)	(0.05)	(0.04)	(0.04)	(0.04)	(0.04)	(0.04)	(0.04)	(0.04)	(0.04)	(0.04)	(0.04)	(0.04)	(0.04)	(0.04)	(0.04)

Note: Average private valuations of the holder of the asset at each of 20 trading rounds. Based on 1000 (disagreement) or 2000 (common prior or common knowledge of θ^*) simulations. Standard errors in parentheses.

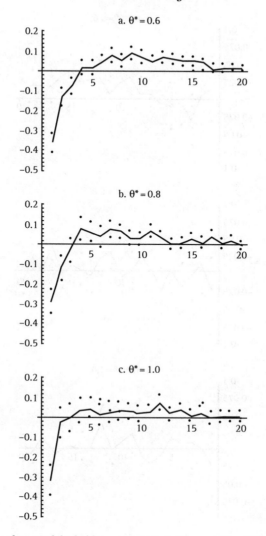

Figure 2. *Average change of the holder over twenty trading rounds; difference between the disagreement and common prior cases. Holders are identified by their private valuations. Based on 1000 simulations (dots indicate two-standard-error confidence intervals)*

5.3. Volume

One would expect the presence of controversial trades to have an impact on volume. In particular, the phenomenon mentioned above (where holders with a low private valuation yet initially high resale option valuation unload the asset towards the end of the game) should be reflected in volume figures. Figure 3 illustrates that this is the case, but the effect is only marginal. In fact, significantly

B. Biais and P. Bossaerts

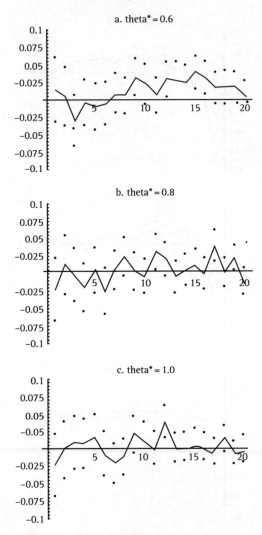

Figure 3. *Average volume over twenty trading rounds; difference between the disagreement and common prior cases. Based on 1000 simulations (dots indicate two-standard-error confidence intervals)*

higher volume in later trading rounds is found only when $\theta^* = 0.6$. Consequently, volume statistics do not provide good power to discriminate disagreement from the other cases. Also, there is no effect of controversial trades on volume in early rounds. Certain trades that would occur under a common prior or common knowledge of θ^* do not happen and vice versa. The net impact is not significant.

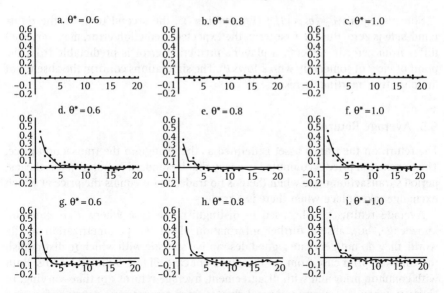

Figure 4. *Average change in the highest reservation values (bidders' or holder's) over twenty trading rounds. Based on 1000 simulations (dots indicate two-standard-error confidence intervals). The top row corresponds to the case where there is common knowledge of θ^*, the second row corresponds to the common prior case, the bottom row corresponds to the disagreement case*

5.4. Best Offers

Figure 4 illustrates how the average change in the best offer (highest of the reservations values of the holder or the bidders; hitherto denoted b_t) provides an unambiguous way to distinguish the case where θ^* is common knowledge. Corollary 2 characterized the best offer as a martingale in this case. Consequently, the change in the best offer should be a martingale difference sequence. This is verified in Figure 4.

Learning generates predictability in the best offers. One might conclude that, at least in the common prior case, investors should realize that their valuations are biased (after all, they as well can perform the simulations of this paper), and therefore revise their bids accordingly. However, this line of reasoning is incorrect. Figure 4 plots estimates of $E_{\theta^*}(b_{t+1} - b_t)$. The holder after round t (who must have had the highest reservation value in that round), however, was setting her reservation value, b_t, to equal $E_{t*}(b_{t+1} \mid H_t)$ (see Proposition 3). Consequently, $E_{t*}(b_{t+1} - b_t) = 0$. This subjective martingale difference property cannot be used to derive an 'objective' martingale difference result. To see this, consider the following

$$E_{\theta^*}(b_{t+1} - b_t) = E_{\theta^*}[b_{t+1} - E_{t*}(b_{t+1} \mid H_t)]$$

$$+ E_{\theta^*}[E_{t*}(b_{t+1} \mid H_t) - b_t].$$

Since b_t equals $E_{\theta^*}(b_{t+1} \mid H_t)$ (Proposition 3), the second term on the right-hand-side is zero. But the first term, the expected prediction error, may very well differ from zero: in general, a player's prediction error is predictable from the point of view of somebody who knows θ^*. The simulations confirm the absence of an 'objective' martingale result.

5.5. Average Returns

The return on the traded asset is defined as the change in the transaction price. The transaction price is computed in a way that is standard in finance: it is the last period's transaction price when there is no trade, and it equals the price at which exchange takes place when there is a trade.

Average returns can be used to distinguish the case where θ^* is common knowledge, but, absent further information about the parametrization of the world, they do not generate a good descriptive statistic with which to distinguish the common prior case from the disagreement case. Figure 5 illustrates this. Both with common prior and with disagreement, average returns are time-varying. In contrast, when θ^* is common knowledge, average returns are a constant function of time.

Incidentally, notice how average returns are a constant, yet (significantly) positive function of time. this means that an econometrician who ignores other

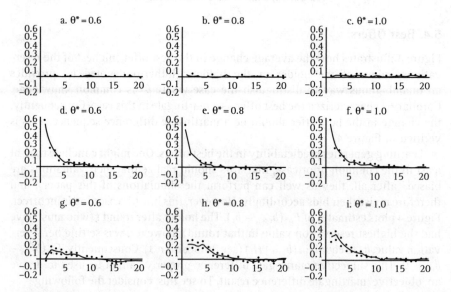

Figure 5. *Average asset return over twenty trading rounds. Based on 1000 simulations (dots indicate two-standard-error confidence intervals). The top row corresponds to the case where there is common knowledge of θ^*, the second row corresponds to the common prior case, the bottom row corresponds to the disagreement case*

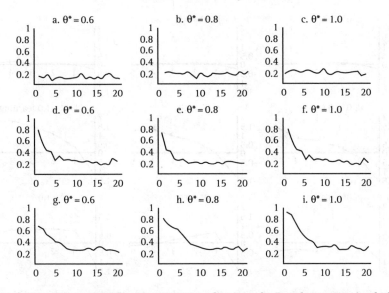

Figure 6. *Asset return volatility over twenty trading rounds. Based on 1000 simulations. The top row corresponds to the case where there is common knowledge of θ^*, the second row corresponds to the common prior case, the bottom row corresponds to the disagreement case*

features of the data, including specifics of the model such as the risk neutrality of the investors, may erroneously conclude that returns have been generated in a standard, static (constant risk premium) rational expectations asset pricing model. This impression is reinforced when looking at return volatility.

5.6. Return Volatility

Figure 6 plots the return volatility (standard deviation) as a function of time. It is constant when θ^* is common knowledge. As mentioned at the end of the previous subsection, this may give one the impression to be in the standard financial world of static asset pricing models without speculation, at least if, as is often the case in empirical work, other aspects of the data such as volume are ignored.

In contrast, volatility is decreasing over time both with a common prior and with disagreement. There is no way, however, to distinguish these two cases by focusing on volatility only. A distinction can be made empirically only if one looks at the *relationship* between volume and quote changes or return volatility. This is discussed next.

5.7. The Relation Between Volume and Best Offers

Figure 7 plots the relation between the average change in the best offer (previously denoted b_t) from $t=0$ till $t=10$ against the total volume over the

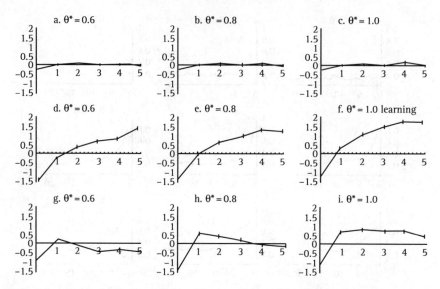

Figure 7. *Average change in the best offer over the first ten trading rounds conditional on total volume over the same period. Based on 1000 simulations (dots indicate two-standard-error confidence intervals). The top row corresponds to the case where there is common knowledge of θ^*, the second row corresponds to the common prior case, the bottom row corresponds to the disagreement case*

same period (the volume at $t = 0$ is not counted; it always equals 1). The picture is similar over periods that end at alternative points in time. Dots again delineate confidence intervals of a size equal to two standard errors. The X axis only shows volume up to 5 units; the relationship is subject to substantially larger error for a total volume of 6 or more, because events with such a high level of volume occur only rarely.

First consider the case where θ^* is common knowledge. Because of the martingale property of best offers (Corollary 2), one would expect the average change in the best offer to be zero for a mean level of volume (which was estimated to be about 2). This is confirmed in the plot. Likewise, one would expect a significantly positive average change in the best offer for a volume above the mean. Conversely, low volume should give rise to decreases in the best offers. These conjectures are confirmed in Figure 7.

The positive impact of volume on best offers is more pronounced when there is learning with a common prior. Trades occur whenever an investor with a higher private valuation than historically observed enters the market. These surprises lead to optimistic forecasts of the resale value, pushing up the best offer. The phenomenon is very clear in the plots of Figure 7.

The relationship between volume and best offers is less clear in the disagreement case. Trades not only occur when investors with historically high private valuations enter the marketplace, but also as "controversial trades" (which includes those events where a trade does not take place which would go through in the other cases). In particular, high volume may now be an indication of the presence of investors who originally took a controversial position, unloading the asset later on, reluctant to keep the asset for the dividend. These investors' disappointment with the actual resale potential is reflected in low reservation values, and hence, low best offers. The result is a nonmonotonic (inverted-U shaped) relation between volume and changes in best offers. This is confirmed in the plots of Figure 7.

Some may object to plots like the ones in Figure 7, where a variable is regressed onto another, pointing to the endogeneity of the regressor (volume in the case of Figure 7). Problems of simultaneity are an issue, however, only if one is interpreting the regression coefficients as structural parameters. In the present paper, the focus is on descriptive statistics, including the (potentially nonlinear) relation between two endogenous variables. The results make sense as long as the estimation can be done consistently.[14]

5.8. The Relation between Volume and Volatility

Measuring the volatility as the difference between the highest and lowest transaction price over the twenty-round trading game, Table 2 displays the results from a regression of volatility onto total volume (measured over the same twenty trading rounds, excluding the first round, where volume always equals 1). To add realism to the regressions, zero-volume cases were not included in the estimation. Weighted least squares (WLS) is used, to correct for the number of observations for each volume level. In particular, the variance of the regression error is assumed to be inversely proportional to the number of observations.

Notice how there is a strong positive relationship between volume and volatility in the Harsanyian cases. Its cause is essentially the same as for the positive relation between volume and best offers, discussed in the previous subsection. In contrast, there is no relation between volume and volatility in the disagreement case. Plots (not reported) suggest that there is no pattern, unlike with the relation between volume and best offers documented in the previous subsection. It is conjectured that the lack of relationship is mainly due to the fact that low (but positive) volume already generates substantial volatility when it reflects dumping by investors with controversial positions. This conjecture is supported by the fact that for the three parameter values, the volatility for low volume (volume $= 1$) is about two times larger than in the common prior case, and more than three times as large as in the case where θ^* is common knowledge.

Some may wonder whether these results reflect a different distribution of the regressor, total volume. It would indeed be hard to interpret the regression results

---

[14] The focus on simple regressions between endogenous variables instead of often intractable structural relations is also at the heart of *indirect inference* (Gouriéroux, Monfort and Renault (1993)).

Table 2. Relation between volume and volatility

θ^*	α		β	
	Estimate	t-stat	Estimate	t-stat
0.6				
Common knowledge of θ^*	0.198	2.687	0.104	4.034
Common prior	0.624	7.064	0.126	4.102
Disagreement	1.293	14.580	0.034	1.162
0.8				
Common knowledge of θ^*	0.397	5.956	0.091	4.024
Common prior	0.597	7.956	0.192	7.312
Disagreement	1.514	13.751	0.038	1.000
1.0				
Common knowledge of θ^*	0.364	8.863	0.148	10.753
Common prior	0.578	4.264	0.285	6.154
Disagreement	1.481	11.745	0.086	2.061

Note: Intercept (α) and slope coefficient (β) in a WLS regression of the difference between highest and lowest transaction prices over twenty trading rounds onto total volume (if positive).

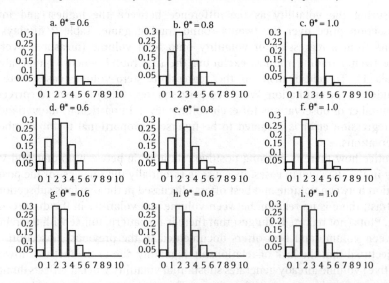

Figure 8. Histograms of total volume over twenty trading rounds. Based on
1000 simulations. The top row corresponds to the case where there is
common knowledge of θ^*, the second row corresponds to the common
prior case, the bottom row corresponds to the disagreement case

in Table 2 if the distribution of volume would be concentrated, say, around 2 in
the case where θ^* is common knowledge, and around 4 for the other models.
Figure 8 proves that no such interpretative difficulties exist: the distribution of
total volume hardly differs across models. Incidentally, Figure 8 also falsifies

(within the present model) the conjecture that disagreement generates additional trading.[15]

6. CONCLUDING REMARKS

This paper provides a framework to theoretically analyse economic interactions, in particular speculation, in the presence of differences of opinion.

In the context of a simple trading game, we show that it is possible to discriminate empirically between genuine disagreement and mere Bayesian learning with agreeing agents. Within the framework of this paper, it suffices to look at the relation between volume and quotes (best offers), and between volume and volatility (highest minus lowest transaction prices).

Admittedly, our simulation results reflect in part the particular nature of the common knowledge beliefs formation rule entertained in that section, as well as our parametric assumptions. But, more fundamentally, our results hinge on one of the distinguishing features of the different priors case: the presence of controversial trades. Consequently we believe that our qualitative results should be reasonably robust to alterations in the parametrization of the model.

Our analysis could also enable one to verify the relevance of disagreement in an experimental setting. One possible experimental approach could hinge on the remark that in our trading game, under Harsanyi's (1967) assumption, agents do not wish to buy back the asset after having sold it, while, with differences of opinion, they might wish to repurchase the asset having sold it in a controversial trade.

The possibility of genuine disagreement has been the subject of substantial controversy. Opponents have elevated Harsanyi's common prior assumption (where, as shown by Aumann (1976), it is impossible to agree to disagree) to the level of doctrine. The possibility of disagreement seems, however, to be an empirical issue. The present paper is a first attempt at proposing a methodology that would enable empirical arguments to replace philosophical ones in the debate about the possibility of disagreement.

Appendix

Proof of Lemma 1. To prove the lemma, we construct the joint prior from which l^i is the Bayesian update. Take *any* marginal density $m^i \in \Delta(R^+)$. m^i will play the role of the marginal prior of i over μ_i. Then construct the prior π^i as $\pi^i(\mu_i, \mu_j) = l^i(\mu_j)m^i(\mu_i)$. By construction, π^i is a proper density

$$\int_{x \in R^+} \int_{y \in R^+} \pi^i(x, y)\, dx\, dy = 1.$$

---

[15] See, e.g. Harris and Raviv (1993).

Also, by construction, the three densities, l^i, m^i and π^i, are consistent with Bayes' law

$$\int_{x \in R^+} \pi^i(\mu_i, x) \, dx = \int_{x \in R^+} l^i(x) m^i(\mu_i) \, dx = m^i(\mu_i),$$

and

$$l_i(\mu_j) = \frac{\pi^i(\mu_i, \mu_j)}{m^i(\mu_i)} = \frac{\pi^i(\mu_i, \mu_j)}{\int_{x \in R^+} \pi^i(\mu_i, x) \, dx}. \qquad \Box$$

Proof of Corollary 1. Following Lemma 1, we take as *marginal* prior over μ_i any density on $R^+ m^i(\cdot) \in \Delta(R^+)$. Now consider the following candidate (joint) prior over θ and μ_i

$$p^i(\theta, \mu_i) = \frac{1}{\theta} \frac{1}{\theta \mu_i + 1} e^{(\mu_i^2/\theta)} G_i(\mu_i), \tag{4}$$

where

$$G_i(\theta) = \frac{m^i(\mu_i)}{(1/\mu_i^2)^{\mu_i+1} \mu_i!}. \tag{5}$$

The proof follows from the next two lemmas.

Lemma 2. $p^i(\theta, \mu_i)$ (*as defined by equations* (4) *and* (5)) *has the properties of a density, and its relation with* $m^i(\mu_i)$ *obeys Bayes' rule.*

Proof. First of all, $p^i(\theta, \mu_i) \geq 0$. Moreover,

$$\int_0^\infty p^i(t, \mu_i) dt = \left[\int_0^\infty \frac{1}{t^{\mu_i+2}} e^{-\mu_i^2/t} \, dt \right] G_i(\mu_i).$$

After a change-of-variables, $X = 1/t$, with

$$\frac{dt}{dX} = -\frac{1}{X^2},$$

we obtain

$$\int_0^\infty p^i(t, \mu_i) dt = \left[\int_0^\infty X^{\mu_i} e^{-\mu_i^2 X} \, dX \right] G_i(\mu_i)$$

$$= \left[\frac{\int_0^\infty X^{\mu_i} e^{-\mu_i^2 X} \, dX}{(1/\mu_i^2)^{\mu_i+1} \mu_i!} \right] \left(\frac{1}{\mu_i^2} \right)^{\mu_i+1} \mu_i! G_i(\mu_i).$$

The term within brackets is the integral over the entire domain of a gamma density with parameters $\alpha_i = \mu_i + 1$, $\beta_i = 1/\mu_i^2$. Hence

$$\int_0^\infty p^i(t, \mu_i)dt = \left(\frac{1}{\mu_i^2}\right)^{\mu_i+1} \mu_i! G_i(\mu_i)$$

$$= \left(\frac{1}{\mu_i^2}\right)^{\mu_i+1} \mu_i!$$

$$= m^i(\mu_i). \qquad \square$$

Lemma 3. *For the joint prior $p^i(\theta, \mu_i)$, defined in (4) and (5), the first-order belief of i over θ conditional on μ_i is inverse gamma with parameters $\alpha_{i,1} = \mu_i + 1, \beta_{i,1} = 1/\mu_i^2$.*

Proof.

$$p^i(\theta \mid \mu_i) = \frac{p^i(\theta, \mu_i)}{\int_0^\infty p^i(t, \mu_i)dt}$$

$$= \frac{p^i(\theta, \mu_i)}{m^i(\mu_i)}$$

$$= \frac{(1/\theta)(1/\theta^{\mu_i+1})e^{-(\mu_i^2/\theta)}G_i(\mu_i)}{(1/\mu_1^2)^{\mu_i+1}\mu_i! G_i(\mu_i)}$$

$$= (1/\theta)(\mu_i^2/\theta)^{\mu_i+1}(e^{-(\mu_i^2/\theta)}/\mu_i!),$$

which is the density mentioned in the Lemma. $\qquad \square$

Proof of Proposition 4. The proof is by induction.
At time $T - 1$, the reservation value of investor i is $E_i(\max[\mu_i, \mu_T] \mid H_{T-1})$. Hence, at that time, the property holds. Assume that at $t + 1$ the property holds, i.e., the reservation value of investor i at $t + 1$ is

$$r_i^{t+1} = E_i(\max[\mu_i, \mu_{t+2}, \ldots, \mu_T] \mid H_{t+1}).$$

It is now shown that the property holds at time t. At time $t + 1$, the investor can keep the asset, and obtain his reservation value. Alternatively, he can sell the asset to investor $t + 1$ at the reservation value of the latter, which equals

$$r_{t+1}^{t+1} = E_{t+1}(\max[\mu_{t+1}, \mu_{t+2}, \ldots, \mu_T] \mid H_{t+1}).$$

Because of the common prior assumption,

$$r_{t+1}^{t+1} = E_i(\max[\mu_{t+1}, \mu_{t+2}, \ldots, \mu_T] \mid H_{t+1}).$$

If $\mu_i > \mu_{t+1}$, investor i sells the asset and obtains

$$r_{t+1}^{t+1} = E_i(\max[\mu_{t+1}, \dots, \mu_T] \mid H_{t+1}) = E_i(\max[\mu_i, \mu_{t+1}, \dots, \mu_T] \mid H_{t+1}).$$

If instead $\mu_i > \mu_{t+1}$, investor i keeps the asset and obtains

$$
\begin{aligned}
r_i^{t+1} &= E_i(\max[\mu_i, \mu_{t+2}, \dots, \mu_t] \mid H_{t+1}) \\
&= E_i(\max[\mu_i, \mu_{t+1}, \mu_{t+2}, \dots, \mu_T] \mid H_{t+1}).
\end{aligned}
$$

So, in both cases he obtains $E_i(\max[\mu_i, \mu_{t+1}, \dots, \mu_T] \mid H_{t+1})$.

At time t, investor i anticipates that, so his reservation value for the asset equals

$$r_i^t = E_i[E_i(\max[\mu_i, \mu_{t+1}, \dots, \mu_T] \mid H_{t+1}) \mid H_t].$$

Since both expectations operators are taken from the perspective of investor i, the law of iterated expectations can be applied. Hence, the reservation value of the asset for investor i at time t is

$$r_i^t = E_i(\max[\mu_i, \mu_{t+1}, \dots, \mu_T] \mid H_t). \qquad \square$$

Proof of Corollary 3.

$$r_i^t > r_j^t \Leftrightarrow E_i(\max[\mu_i, \mu_{t+2}, \dots, \mu_T] \mid H_t) > E_j(\max[\mu_j, \mu_{t+2}, \dots, \mu_T] \mid H_t).$$

However, under the common prior assumption, $E_i(\cdot \mid H_t) = E_j(\cdot \mid H_t)$. Hence

$$r_i^t > r_j^t \Leftrightarrow E_i(\max[\mu_i, \mu_{t+2}, \dots, \mu_T] \mid H_t) > E_i(\max[\mu_j, \mu_{t+2}, \dots, \mu_T] \mid H_t).$$

So, $r_i^t > r_j^t \Leftrightarrow \mu_i > \mu_j$. $\qquad \square$

Proof of Corollary 4. From Proposition 4, $r_i^t = E_i(\max[\mu_i, \mu_{t+1}, \dots, \mu_T] \mid H_t)$. This can be rewritten ($\Theta = (0, \infty)$, the set in which θ lives)

$$r_i^t = \mu_i + \int_\Theta \int_{\mu_i}^\infty (m - \mu_i) \, dP(\max[\mu_{t+1}, \dots, \mu_T] < m) p(t \mid H_t) \, dt,$$

where P is the multivariate probability distribution corresponding to the density $f(\mu \mid \theta)$ and $p(\theta \mid H_t)$ is the posterior density derived from the common prior p, the history of revealed private valuations H_t, and Bayes' law. Note that

$$\int_{\mu_i}^\infty (m - \mu_i) \, dP(\max[\mu_{t+1}, \dots, \mu_T] < m),$$

can be rewritten

$$\int_{\mu_i}^\infty m \, dP(\max[\mu_{t+1}, \dots, \mu_T] < m) - \mu_i \int_{\mu_i}^\infty dP(\max[\mu_{t+1}, \dots, \mu_T] < m).$$

Now

$$\int_{\mu_i}^{\infty} dP(\max[\mu_{t+1}, \ldots, \mu_T] < m) = 1 - P(\max[\mu_{t+1}, \ldots, \mu_T] < \mu_i),$$

and

$$\int_{\mu_i}^{\infty} m \, dP(\max[\mu_{t+1}, \ldots, \mu_T] < m)$$

$$= -\int_{\mu_i}^{\infty} m d(1 - P(\max[\mu_{t+1}, \ldots, \mu_T] < m)).$$

Integrating by parts, one obtains

$$[-m(1 - P(\max[\mu_{t+1}, \ldots, \mu_T] < m))]_{\mu_i}^{\infty}$$
$$+ \int_{\mu_i}^{\infty} (1 - P(\max[\mu_{t+1}, \ldots, \mu_T] < m)) \, dm.$$

Simplifying

$$r_i^t = \mu_i + \int_{\Theta} \int_{\mu_i}^{\infty} (1 - P(\max[\mu_{t+1}, \ldots, \mu_T] < m) dm p(t \mid H_t) \, dt.$$

$\square$

Proof of Corollary 6. From Corollary 4 $r_i^t = \mu_i + E_i[\Psi(\mu_i, \theta, t)|H_t]$, where

$$\Psi(\mu_i, \theta, t) \equiv \int_{\mu_i}^{\infty} P(\max[m_{t+1}, \ldots, \mu_T] > m) \, dm,$$

(note that Ψ is non-increasing in its third argument), and, E_i is taken over θ. Consequently

$$r_i^t \geq E_i(r_i^{t+1}|H_i) \Leftrightarrow E_i[\Psi(\mu_i, \theta, t)|H_t] \geq E_i(E_i[(\Psi(\mu_i, \theta, t))|H_{t+1}] \mid H_t).$$

This holds because $\Psi(\mu_i, \theta, t) \geq \Psi(\mu_i, \theta, t+1)$. $\square$

Proof of Proposition 5. Let i be the investor who holds the asset after the tth round of trade. Hence, $\mu_i = \max[\mu_0, \ldots, \mu_t]$. The proof is completed when combining this with Proposition 4. $\square$

Proof of Corollary 7. Combine Proposition 5 with Corollary 4. $\square$

Proof of Corollary 5.
From Corollary 4, the reservation value of investor i at time t is $(\Theta = (0, \infty)$, the set in which θ lives)

$$r_i^t = \mu_i + \int_{\Theta} \left(\int_{\mu_i}^{\infty} P(\max[\mu_{t+1}, \ldots, \mu_T] > m) \, dm \right) p(t|H_t) \, dt.$$

To compute this more explicitly, first analyse $\int_{\mu_i}^{\infty} P(\max[\mu_{t+1}, \ldots, \mu_T] > m)dm$, then integrate over θ.

Analyse $\int_{\mu_i}^{\infty} P(\max[\mu_{t+1}, \ldots, \mu_T] > m)dm$ first. The probability that one exponential variable with parameter θ is smaller than m equals

$$1 - e^{-m/\theta}.$$

The probability that $T - t$ exponential variables are smaller than m equals

$$[1 - e^{-m/\theta}]^{T-t} = \sum_{j=0}^{T-t} C_{T-t}^j (-1)^j e^{-jm/\theta},$$

or

$$1 + \sum_{j=1}^{T-t} C_{T-t}^j (-1)^j e^{-jm/\theta}.$$

So, the probability that $T - t$ exponential variables are larger than m equals

$$P(\max[\mu_{t+1}, \ldots, \mu_T] > m) = \sum_{j=1}^{T-t} C_{T-t}^j (-1)^{j+1} e^{-jm/\theta}.$$

Now integrate over $m \in [\mu_i, \infty]$

$$\int_{\mu_i}^{\infty} \Sigma_{j=1}^{T-t} C_{T-t}^j (-1)^{j+1} e^{-jm/\theta} \, dm = \sum_{j=1}^{T-t} C_{T-t}^j (-1)^{j+1} \int_{\mu_i}^{\infty} e^{-jm/\theta} \, dm.$$

This can be rewritten

$$\sum_{j=1}^{T-t} C_{T-t}^j (-1)^{j+1} (\theta/j) e^{-j\mu_i/\theta}.$$

Integrate over θ

$$r_i^t = \mu_i + \int_{\Theta} \sum_{j=1}^{T-t} C_{T-t}^j (-1)^{j+1} (s/j) e^{-j\mu_i/s} p(s \mid H_t) \, ds$$

or

$$r_i^t = \mu_i + \sum_{j=1}^{T-t} C_{T-t}^j (-1)^{j+1} /j \int_{\Theta} \theta e^{-j\mu_i/s} p(s \mid H_t) \, ds.$$

The latter integral can be written more explicitly

$$\int_{\Theta} \theta e^{-j\mu_i/s} \left(\frac{1}{s} \frac{e^{-1/(\beta_t s)}}{(\alpha_t - 1)!} \left(\frac{1}{\beta_t s} \right)^{\alpha_t} \right) ds,$$

where

$$\beta_t = \left(\sum_{s=0}^{t} \mu_s \right)^{-1} \equiv (\bar{\mu}_t)^{-1},$$

and

$$\alpha_t = t + 2,$$

are the parameters of the inverse gamma distribution (the posterior beliefs about θ of the investors in the market at time t). The integral can be rewritten

$$\int_{\Theta} s \left(\frac{1}{s} \frac{e^{-j\mu_i + \bar{\mu}_t / s}}{(t+1)!} \left(\frac{\bar{\mu}_t^{t+2}}{s} \right) \right) ds,$$

or

$$\left(\frac{\bar{\mu}_t}{j\mu_i + \bar{\mu}_t} \right)^{t+2} \int_{\Theta} s \left(\frac{1}{s} \frac{e^{-j\mu_i + \bar{\mu}_t / s}}{(t+1)!} \left(\frac{j\mu_i + \hat{\mu}_t^{t+2}}{s} \right) \right) ds.$$

The integral is the expectation of an inverse gamma variable with parameters $(t + 2, (j\mu_i + \bar{\mu}_t)^{-1})$, i.e.

$$\frac{j\mu_i + \bar{\mu}_t}{t + 1}$$

Substituting this in the formula for the reservation value, the proposition obtains. □

REFERENCES

Allen, F., Morris, S. and Postlewaite, A. (1993), "Finite Bubbles With Short-Sale Constraints and Asymmetric Information", *Journal of Economic Theory*, 61, 206–229.

Aumann R. J. (1976), "Agreeing to Disagree", *Annals of Statistics*, 4, 1236–39.

Gouriéroux, C., Monfort, A. and Renault, E. (1993), "Indirect Inference", *Journal of Applied Econometrics*, 8, 85–118.

Harris, M. and Raviv, A. (1993), "Differences of Opinion Make a Horse Race", *Review of Financial Studies*, 6, 473–506.

Harrison, J. M. and Kreps, D. M. (1978), "Speculative Investor Behavior in a Stock Market with Heterogeneous Expectations", *Quarterly Journal of Economics*, 92, 323–36.

Harsanyi, J. C. (1967), "Games with Incomplete Information Played by 'Bayesian' Players, I: The Basic Model", *Management Science*, 14, 159–82.

Keynes, J. M. (1921), *A Treatise on Probability* (London: Macmillan).

—(1958), *The general Theory of Employment, Interest and Money* (New York: Harcourt Brace).

Kurz, M. (1994), "On the Structure and Diversity of Rational Beliefs", *Economic Theory*, 4, 1–24.

Mertens, J.-F. and Zamir, S. (1985), "Formulation of Bayesian Analysis for Games with Incomplete Information", *International Journal of Game Theory*, 14, 1–29.

Michaely, R. and Vila, J. L. (1994), "Trading Volume with Private Valuations: Evidence from the Ex-Dividend Day" (Working paper, MIT).

Milgrom, P. and Stokey, N. (1982), "Information, Trade and Common–Knowledge", *Journal of Economic Theory*, 26, 17–27.

Morris, S. (1993), "The Common Prior Assumption in Economic Theory", *Economics and Philosophy*, 33, 1–27.

— (1994), "Trade with heterogeneous prior beliefs and asymmetric information", *Econometrica*, 62, 1327–1348.

Muth, J. F. (1961), "Rational Expectations and the Theory of Price Movements", *Econometrica*, 29, 315–35

Samuelson, P. A. (1965), "Proof that Properly Anticipated Prices Fluctuate Randomly", *Industrial Management Review*, 6, 41–50.

Shiller, R. (1995), "Speculative Behavior and the Functioning of Credit Markets", *Proceedings of the 7th Symposium of Moneda y Credito*.

Tirole, J. (1982), "On the Possibility of Speculation under Rational Expectations", *Econometrica*, 50, 1163–81.

9

Unique Equilibrium in a Model of Self-Fulfilling Currency Attacks

STEPHEN MORRIS AND HYUN SONG SHIN

Speculative attacks are sometimes triggered without warning, and without any apparent change in the economic fundamentals. Commentators who have attempted to explain episodes of speculative crises have pointed to the self-fulfilling nature of the belief in an imminent speculative attack. If speculators believe that a currency will come under attack, their actions in anticipation of this precipitate the crisis itself, while if they believe that a currency is not in danger of imminent attack, their inaction spares the currency from attack, thereby vindicating their initial beliefs.[1]

However, merely pointing to the self-fulfilling nature of beliefs leaves open a number of crucial questions. First, such an account leaves unexplained the actual *onset* of an attack when it occurs. By most accounts, both the European Exchange Rate Mechanism (ERM) and the Mexican peso were 'ripe' for attack for some time before the crises that brought them down in the early 1990s—at least two years in Europe and perhaps a year in Mexico (Barry Eichengreen and Charles Wyplosz, 1993; Rudiger Dornbusch and Alejandro M. Werner, 1994). At any point in those periods, concerted selling by speculators would have raised the costs of maintaining the exchange rate sufficiently high that the monetary authorities would have been forced to abandon the parity. Why did the attacks happen when they did? Conventional accounts resort to forces that operate outside the theoretical model in trying to explain the shift of expectations that precipitated the attack. Some of these informal accounts are more persuasive than others, but none can be fully compelling as a theoretical model of the onset of a currency crisis.

We are grateful to Marcus Miller for encouraging us to pursue this topic and to Stephen Coate and John Driffill for advice during the preparation of this paper. We thank Anne Sibert for her comments as discussant at the CEPR conference on "Origins and Management of Financial Crises." The first author acknowledges the support of the Alfred P. Sloan Foundation. The second author acknowledges the support of the U.K. Economic and Social Research Council under Grant No. R000221556. Finally, we thank two anonymous referees for comments on an earlier version.

[1] This theme is explored in Robert P. Flood and Peter M. Garber (1984) and Maurice Obstfeld (1986, 1994, 1996). A closely related literature explores self-fulfilling debt crises; see Guillermo A. Calvo (1988), Jonathan Eaton and Raquel Fernandez (1995), and Harold L. Cole and Timothy J. Kehoe (1996).

Secondly, merely pointing to the self-fulfilling nature of beliefs leaves open the policy issues associated with curbing speculative attacks. For example, it is often argued that increased capital mobility induced by lower transaction costs increases the likelihood of currency crises, and that judicious 'throwing of sand' into the excessively well-oiled wheels of international finance will play a role in curbing speculative attacks (Eichengreen et al., 1995). However, an account that merely points to the self-fulfilling nature of beliefs cannot contribute to this debate, since the question of how the beliefs are determined is beyond the scope of such an account. Any argument for or against the proposal has to resort to forces outside the formal theory.

We argue here that the apparent multiplicity of equilibria associated with self-fulfilling beliefs is the consequence of assuming too simple a picture of the role played by information in a speculative episode. Although market participants each have a window on to the world, the imperfect nature of such a vantage point generates a failure of common knowledge of the fundamentals. Thus, everyone may know that the fundamentals are sound, but it may not be that everyone knows that everyone knows this. Still higher orders of such uncertainty may be relevant. Uncertainty about other participants' beliefs is crucial to a speculative episode, since the onset of a speculative attack relies to a large extent on coordinated behavior of speculators. We propose a more realistic modelling of the information structure underlying speculative situations that enables us to pinpoint the forces which determine the onset of a speculative attack. When speculators observe an independent noisy signal of the state of fundamentals, common knowledge of the fundamentals no longer holds. This is enough to induce a unique equilibrium of the model, in which there is a critical state below which attack always occurs and above which attack never occurs.[2] The value of this critical state depends on financial variables such as the mass of speculators and the transaction costs associated with attacking the currency. As a consequence, we can say something about how this unique outcome depends on the parameters of the problem, such as the costs of speculation, the underlying strength of the economy, and the size of the pool of hot money in circulation.

Information plays a subtle role in speculative crises. What is important is not the amount of information, per se, but rather how public and transparent this information is. If market participants are well informed about the fundamentals, but they are unsure of the information received by other participants, and hence unsure of the beliefs held by others, speculative attacks may be triggered even though everyone knows that the fundamentals are sound. Our analysis highlights the importance of the transparency of the conduct of monetary policy and its dissemination to the public.

---

[2] Andrew Postlewaite and Xavier Vives (1987) discuss the role of information in selecting among multiple equilibria in the closely related context of bank runs. Our analysis builds on and extends the earlier incomplete information game analysis of Hans Carlsson and Eric E. van Damme (1993) and Morris et al. (1995).

I. MODEL

Our model is concerned with the strategic interaction between the government and a group of speculators in the foreign exchange market that takes place against the backdrop of a competitive market for foreign exchange. The economy is characterized by a state of fundamentals θ, which we assume to be uniformly distributed over the unit interval $[0, 1]$. The exchange rate in the absence of government intervention is a function of θ, and is given by $f(\theta)$. We assume that f is strictly increasing in θ, so that higher values of θ correspond to 'stronger fundamentals.'

The exchange rate is initially pegged by the government at e^*, where $e^* \geq f(\theta)$ for all θ. Facing the government is a continuum of speculators who may take one of two actions. A speculator may either attack the currency by selling short one unit of the currency, or refrain from doing so. There is a cost $t > 0$ associated with short-selling. If a speculator short-sells the currency and the government abandons the exchange rate peg, then the payoff at state θ by attacking the currency is given by the fall in the exchange rate minus the transaction cost. Thus the speculator's payoff is $e^* - f(\theta) - t$. If the government defends the peg, then the speculator pays the transaction cost, but has no capital gain. Thus his payoff is $-t$. If the speculator chooses not to attack the currency, his payoff is zero.

The government derives a value $v > 0$ from defending the exchange rate at the pegged level, but also faces costs of doing so. The cost of defending the peg depends on the state of the fundamentals, as well as the proportion of speculators who attack the currency. We denote by $c(\alpha, \theta)$ the cost of defending the peg if proportion α of the speculators attack the currency at the state θ. The government's payoff to abandoning the exchange rate is thus zero while the payoff to defending the exchange rate is

$$v - c(\alpha, \theta).$$

We assume that c is continuous and is increasing in α while decreasing in θ. In particular, to make the problem economically interesting we will impose the following assumptions on the cost function and the floating exchange rate $f(\theta)$.

- $c(0, 0) > v$. In the worst state of fundamentals, the cost of defending the currency is so high that it exceeds the value v even if no speculators attack.
- $c(1, 1) > v$. If all the speculators attack the currency, then even in the best state of the fundamentals, the cost of defending the currency exceeds the value.
- $e^* - f(1) < t$. In the best state of the fundamentals, the floating exchange rate $f(1)$ is sufficiently close to the pegged level e^* such that any profit from the depreciation of the currency is outweighed by the transactions cost t.

Let us denote by $\underline{\theta}$ the value of θ which solves $c(0, \theta) = v$. In other words, $\underline{\theta}$ is the value of θ at which the government is indifferent between defending the peg and abandoning it in the absence of any speculative selling. When $\theta < \underline{\theta}$, the cost of

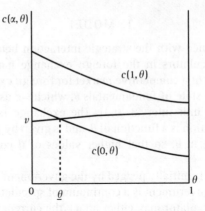

Figure 1. *Cost and benefit to the government in maintaining the currency peg*

defending the currency exceeds the value, even if no speculators attack the currency (see Figure 1). At the other end, denote by $\bar{\theta}$ the value of θ at which $f(\theta) = e^* - t$, so that the floating exchange rate is below the peg by the amount of the cost of attack. When $\theta > \bar{\theta}$, then the floating exchange rate is sufficiently close to the peg that a speculator cannot obtain a positive payoff by attacking the currency (see Figure 2). Using the two benchmark levels of the state of fundamentals $\underline{\theta}$ and $\bar{\theta}$, we can classify the state of fundamentals under three headings, according to the underlying strategic situation.

A. Tripartite Classification of Fundamentals

Assuming that $\underline{\theta} < \bar{\theta}$, we can partition the space of fundamentals into three intervals,[3] emphasized by Maurice Obstfeld (1996).

- In the interval $[0, \underline{\theta}]$, the value of defending the peg is outweighed by its cost irrespective of the actions of the speculators. The government then has no reason to defend the currency. For this reason, we say that the currency is *unstable* if $\theta \in [0, \underline{\theta}]$.
- In the interval $(\underline{\theta}, \bar{\theta})$, the value of defending the currency is greater than the cost, provided that sufficiently few speculators attack the currency. In particular, if none of the speculators attacks, then the value of defending the currency is greater than the cost, and so the government will maintain the peg, which in turn justifies the decision not to attack. However, it is also the case that if all the speculators attack the currency, then the cost of defending the currency is too high, and the government will abandon the peg. Moreover, since $\bar{\theta}$ is the right end point of this interval, a speculator will make a positive profit if the government were to abandon the peg at any state θ in the

---

[3] This assumption will hold if v is large and t is small.

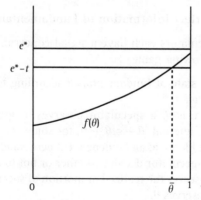

Figure 2. *The managed exchange rate and the exchange rate in the absence of intervention as a function of the state of fundamentals*

interval $(\underline{\theta}, \bar{\theta})$, so that if a speculator believes that the currency peg will be abandoned, then attacking the currency is the rational action. For this reason, we say that the currency is *ripe for attack* if $\theta \in (\underline{\theta}, \bar{\theta})$.

- Finally, in the interval $[\bar{\theta}, 1]$, although the speculators can force the government to abandon the peg, the resulting depreciation of the currency is so small that they cannot recoup the cost of attacking the currency. Thus, even if a speculator were to believe that the currency will fall, the rational action is to refrain from attacking it. In other words, it is a dominant action not to attack. For this reason, we say that the currency is *stable* if $\theta \in [\bar{\theta}, 1]$.

The interesting range is the 'ripe for attack' region. Suppose that the government's decision on whether or not to defend the currency is determined purely by weighing up the costs and benefits, and that it makes its decision once all the speculators have made their decisions. Then, if all the speculators have perfect information concerning the realization of θ, the 'ripe for attack' region gives rise to the standard case of multiple equilibria due to the self-fulfilling nature of the speculators' beliefs. If the speculators believe that the currency peg will be maintained, then it is optimal not to attack, which in turn induces the government to defend the currency, thereby vindicating the speculators' decisions not to attack the currency. On the other hand, if the speculators believe that the currency peg will be abandoned, the rational action is to attack the currency, which in turn induces the government to abandon the peg, vindicating the decision to attack. Given this multiplicity of equilibria, no definitive prediction can be made as to whether the currency will come under attack or not. We will now see, however, that the situation is very different when the speculators face a small amount of uncertainty concerning the fundamentals. Each state of fundamentals gives rise to a unique outcome.

B. Game with Imperfect Information of Fundamentals

Suppose that the speculators each have a signal concerning the state of fundamentals, as in the following game.

- Nature chooses the state of fundamentals θ according to the uniform density
  over the unit interval.
- When the true state is θ, a speculator observes a signal x which is drawn
  uniformly from the interval $[\theta - \varepsilon, \theta + \varepsilon]$, for some small[4] $\varepsilon > 0$. Conditional
  on θ, the signals are identical and independent across individuals. Based on the
  signal observed, a speculator decides whether or not to attack the currency.
- The government observes the realized proportion of speculators who attack the
  currency, α, and observes θ.

The payoffs of the game follow from the description of the model above. We
assume that if a speculator is indifferent between attacking and not attacking, he
will refrain from attacking and that if the government is indifferent between
defending the peg and abandoning it, it will choose to abandon it.[5]

An equilibrium for this game consists of strategies for government and for the
continuum of speculators such that no player has an incentive to deviate. We can
solve out the government's strategy at the final stage of the game, to define a
reduced-form game between the speculators only. To do this, consider the critical
proportion of speculators needed to trigger the government to abandon the peg at
state θ. Let $a(\theta)$ denote this critical mass. In the 'unstable' region $a(\theta) = 0$, while
elsewhere $a(\theta)$ is the value of α which solves $c(\alpha, \theta) = v$. Figure 3 depicts this

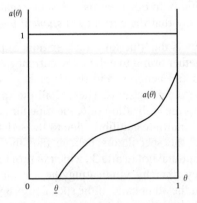

Figure 3. *The Proportion of speculators whose short sales are sufficient to induce
depreciation, expressed as a function of the fundamentals*

---

[4] In particular, we assume that $2\varepsilon < \min\{\theta, 1 - \bar{\theta}\}$.
[5] Nothing substantial hinges on these assumptions, which are made for purposes of simplifying the
statement of our results.

function, which is continuous and strictly increasing in θ where it takes a positive value, and is bounded above by 1.

The unique optimal strategy for the government is then to abandon the exchange rate only if the observed fraction of deviators, α, is greater than or equal to the critical mass $a(\theta)$ in the prevailing state θ.

Taking as given this optimal strategy for the government, we can characterize the payoffs in the reduced-form game between the speculators. For a given profile of strategies of the speculators, we denote by

$$\pi(x)$$

the proportion of speculators who attack the currency when the value of the signal is x. We denote by $s(\theta, \pi)$ the proportion of speculators who end up attacking the currency when the state of fundamentals is θ, given aggregate selling strategy π. Since signals are uniformly distributed over $[\theta - \varepsilon, \theta + \varepsilon]$ at θ, we have[6]

$$s(\theta, \pi) = \frac{1}{2\varepsilon} \int_{\theta - \varepsilon}^{\theta + \varepsilon} \pi(x) dx. \tag{1}$$

Denote by $A(\pi)$ the event where the government abandons the currency peg if the speculators follow strategy π:

$$A(\pi) = \{\theta | s(\theta, \pi) \geq a(\theta)\}. \tag{2}$$

We can then define the payoffs of a reduced-form game between the speculators. The payoff to a speculator of attacking the currency at state θ when aggregate short sales are given by π is

$$h(\theta, \pi) \equiv \begin{cases} e^* - f(\theta) - t & \text{if } \theta \in A(\pi) \\ -t & \text{if } \theta \notin A(\pi). \end{cases} \tag{3}$$

However, a speculator does not observe θ directly. The payoff to attacking the currency must be calculated from the posterior distribution over the states conditional on the signal x. The expected payoff to attacking the currency conditional on the signal x is given by the expectation of (3) conditional on x. Denoting this by $u(x, \pi)$, we have

$$u(x, \pi) = \frac{1}{2\varepsilon} \int_{x - \varepsilon}^{x + \varepsilon} h(\theta, \pi) d\theta = \frac{1}{2\varepsilon} \left[\int_{A(\pi) \cap [x - \varepsilon, x + \varepsilon]} (e^* - f(\theta)) d\theta \right] - t. \tag{4}$$

Since a speculator can guarantee a payoff of zero by refraining from attacking the currency, the rational decision conditional on signal x depends on whether $u(x, \pi)$

---

[6] The following formula is for $\theta \in [\varepsilon, 1 - \varepsilon]$; for θ close to 0 or 1, the limits of the integration must be adjusted accordingly.

is positive or negative. Thus if the government follows its unique optimal strategy, π is an equilibrium of the first period game if $\pi(x) = 1$ whenever $u(x, \pi) > 0$ and $\pi(x) = 0$ whenever $u(x, \pi) \leq 0$.

II. UNIQUE EQUILIBRIUM

We now state the main result of our paper, noting the contrast between the multiplicity of possible outcomes when there is perfect information of the fundamentals against the uniqueness of outcome when there is a small amount of noise.

Theorem 1. *There is a unique θ^* such that, in any equilibrium of the game with imperfect information, the government abandons the currency peg if and only if $\theta \leq \theta^*$.*

The argument for our result can be presented in three steps.

Lemma 1. *If $\pi(x) \geq \pi'(x)$ for all x, then $u(x, \pi) \geq u(x, \pi')$ for all x.*

In other words, if we compare two strategy profiles π and π', where π entails a greater proportion of speculators who attack for any message x, then the payoff to attacking the currency is greater given π than when it is given by π'. Thus speculators' decisions to attack the currency are strategic complements.

Proof of lemma 1. Since $\pi(x) \geq \pi'(x)$, we have $s(\theta, \pi) \geq s(\theta, \pi')$ for every θ, from the definition of s given by (1). Thus, from (2),

$$A(\pi) \supseteq A(\pi').$$

In other words, the event in which the currency peg is abandoned is strictly larger under π. Then, from (4) and the fact that $e^* - f(\theta)$ is nonnegative,

$$u(x, \pi) = \frac{1}{2\varepsilon} \left[\int_{A(\pi)\cap[x-\varepsilon, x+\varepsilon]} (e^* - f(\theta))d\theta \right] - t$$

$$\geq \frac{1}{2\varepsilon} \left[\int_{A(\pi')\cap[x-\varepsilon, x+\varepsilon]} (e^* - f(\theta))d\theta \right] - t$$

$$= u(x, \pi'),$$

which proves the lemma.

For the next step, consider the strategy profile where every speculator attacks the currency if and only if the message x is less than some fixed number k. Then, aggregate short sales π will be given by the indicator function I_k, defined as

$$I_k(x) = \begin{cases} 1 & \text{if } x < k \\ 0 & \text{if } x \geq k. \end{cases} \tag{5}$$

When speculators follow this simple rule of action, the expected payoff to attacking the currency satisfies the following property. $\square$

Lemma 2. $u(k, I_k)$ *is continuous and strictly decreasing in* k.

In other words, when aggregate short sales are governed by I_k, and we consider the payoff to attacking the currency given the marginal message k, this payoff is decreasing as the fundamentals of the economy become stronger. Put another way, when the fundamentals of the economy are stronger, the payoff to attacking the currency is lower for a speculator on the margin of switching from attacking to not attacking. Such a property would be a reasonable feature of any model of currency attacks where the government is able to resist speculators better when the fundamentals are stronger.

The proof of Lemma 2 is simple but involves some algebraic manipulation, and hence is presented separately in the Appendix. Taking Lemma 2 as given, we can then prove the following result.

Lemma 3. *There is a unique* x^* *such that, in any equilibrium of the game with imperfect information of the fundamentals, a speculator with signal x attacks the currency if and only if $x < x^*$.*

To prove this, we begin by establishing that there is a unique value of k at which

$$u(k, I_k) = 0.$$

From Lemma 2, we know that $u(k, I_k)$ is continuous and strictly decreasing in k. If we can show that it is positive for small values of k and negative for large values, then we can guarantee that $u(k, I_k) = 0$ for some k. When k is sufficiently small (i.e., $k \leq \underline{\theta} - \varepsilon$), the marginal speculator with message k knows that the true state of fundamentals is in the 'unstable' region, since such a message is consistent only with a realization of θ in the interval $[0, \underline{\theta}]$. Since the payoff to attacking the currency is positive at any θ in this interval, we have $u(k, I_k) > 0$. Similarly, when k is sufficiently large (i.e., $k \geq \bar{\theta} + \varepsilon$), the marginal speculator with message k knows that the true state of fundamentals is in the 'stable' region. Since the payoff to attacking is negative at every state in this region, we have $u(k, I_k) < 0$. Hence, there is a unique value of k for which $u(k, I_k) = 0$, and we define the value x^* as this unique solution to $u(k, I_k) = 0$.

Now, consider any equilibrium of the game, and denote by $\pi(x)$ the proportion of speculators who attack the currency given message x. Define the numbers $\underline{x}$ and $\bar{x}$ as

$$\underline{x} = \inf\{x | \pi(x) < 1\}$$

$$\text{and } \bar{x} = \sup\{x | \pi(x) > 0\}.$$

Since $\bar{x} \geq \sup\{x|0 < \pi(x) < 1\} \geq \inf\{x|0 < \pi(x) < 1\} \geq \underline{x}$,

$$\underline{x} \leq \bar{x}. \tag{6}$$

When $\pi(x) < 1$, there are some speculators who are not attacking the currency. This is only consistent with equilibrium behavior if the payoff to not attacking is at least as high as the payoff to attacking given message x. By continuity, this is true at $\underline{x}$ also. In other words,

$$u(\underline{x}, \pi) \leq 0. \tag{7}$$

Now, consider the payoff $u(\underline{x}, I_{\underline{x}})$. Clearly, $I_{\underline{x}} \leq \pi$, so that Lemma 1 and (7) imply $u(\underline{x}, I_{\underline{x}}) \leq u(\underline{x}, \pi) \leq 0$. Thus, $u(\underline{x}, I_{\underline{x}}) \leq 0$. Since we know from Lemma 2 that $u(k, I_k)$ is decreasing in k and x^* is the unique value of k which solves $u(k, I_k) = 0$, we have

$$\underline{x} \geq x^*. \tag{8}$$

A symmetric argument establishes that

$$\bar{x} \leq x^*. \tag{9}$$

Thus, from (8) and (9), we have $\underline{x} \geq x^* \geq \bar{x}$. However, we know from (6) that this implies

$$\underline{x} = x^* = \bar{x}.$$

Thus, the equilibrium π is given by the step function I_{x^*}, which is what Lemma 3 states. Hence, this proves Lemma 3.

From this, it is a short step to the proof of our main theorem itself. Given that equilibrium π is given by the step function I_{x^*}, the aggregate short sales at the state θ are given by

$$s(\theta, I_{x^*}) = \begin{cases} 1 & \text{if } \theta < x^* - \varepsilon \\ \frac{1}{2} - \frac{1}{2\varepsilon}(\theta - x^*) & \text{if } x^* - \varepsilon \leq \theta < x^* + \varepsilon \\ 0 & \text{if } \theta \geq x^* + \varepsilon. \end{cases}$$

Aggregate short sales $s(\theta, I_{x^*})$ are decreasing in θ when its value is strictly between 0 and 1, while $a(\theta)$ is increasing in θ for this range. See Figure 4, which illustrates the derivation of the cutoff point for the state of fundamentals at which the equilibrium short sales are equal to the short sales which induce depreciation.

We know that $x^* > \underline{\theta} - \varepsilon$, since otherwise attacking the currency is a strictly better action, contradicting the fact that x^* is a switching point. Thus, $s(\theta, I_{x^*})$ and $a(\theta)$ cross precisely once. Define θ^* to be the value of θ at which these two curves cross. Then, $s(\theta, I_{x^*}) \geq a(\theta)$ if and only if $\theta \leq \theta^*$, so that the government abandons the currency peg if and only if $\theta \leq \theta^*$. This is the claim of our main theorem.

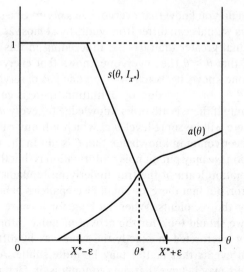

Figure 4. *The derivation of the cutoff point for the state of fundamentals at which the equilibrium short sales are equal to the short sales which induce depreciation*

III. COMPARATIVE STATICS AND POLICY IMPLICATIONS

A. Changes in the Information Structure

When there is no noise, there are multiple equilibria throughout the 'ripe for attack' region of fundamentals. But when there is positive noise, there is a unique equilibrium with critical value θ^*. The value of θ^* in the limit as ε tends to zero has a particularly simple characterization.

Theorem 2. *In the limit as ε tends to zero, θ^* is given by the unique solution to the equation $f(\theta^*) = e^* - 2t$.*

The proof is in the Appendix. Intuition is gained by considering the marginal speculator who observes message $x = \theta^*$. With ε small, this tells the speculator that the true θ is close to θ^*. Since the government abandons the peg if and only if θ is less than θ^*, he attaches equal probability to the currency being abandoned and defended. So, the expected payoff to attacking is $1/2(e^* - f(\theta^*))$, while the cost is t. For the marginal speculator, these are equal, leading to the equation in Theorem 2.

Information plays a subtle role in the model. What matters is not the amount of information, per se, but whether there is common knowledge. With noise, it is never common knowledge that the fundamentals are consistent with the government maintaining the currency peg, i.e., that $\theta \geq \underline{\theta}$. If you observe a signal greater than $\underline{\theta} + \varepsilon$, then you can claim to *know* that $\theta \geq \underline{\theta}$, since your message has the margin of error of ε. When do you know that *everyone* knows that $\theta \geq \underline{\theta}$? In other words, when do you know that everyone has observed a signal greater than $\theta + \varepsilon$? Since others' signals can differ from yours by at most 2ε, this will be true if you observe a signal greater than $\underline{\theta} + 3\varepsilon$. Proceeding in this way, there is 'nth order knowledge' that $\theta \geq \underline{\theta}$ (i.e., everyone knows that everyone knows ... (n times) that everyone knows it) exactly if everyone has observed a signal greater than or equal to $\underline{\theta} + (2n - 1)\varepsilon$. But, by definition, there is common knowledge that $\theta \geq \underline{\theta}$ if and only if there is nth order knowledge for every n. But for any fixed ε and signal x, there will be some level n at which nth order iterated knowledge fails. Thus it is never common knowledge that θ is not in the unstable region.

One interpretation we may put on noisy information is that the recipients of the differential information learn of the true underlying fundamentals of the economy with little error, but that there are small discrepancies in how these messages are interpreted by the recipients. When looking for a cause or a trigger for a currency attack, we should look for the arrival of noisy information, i.e., news events that are not interpreted in exactly the same way by different speculators. The informational events that matter may be quite subtle. A 'grain of doubt,' allowing that others may believe that the economy is, in fact, unstable, will lead to a currency crisis even if everyone knows that the economy is not unstable. In predicting when crises will occur, average opinion or even extreme opinion need not precipitate a crisis. Rather, what matters is the higher order beliefs of some participants who are apprehensive about the beliefs of others, concerning the beliefs of yet further individuals, on these extreme opinions. This interpretation may shed light on some accounts of recent currency crises. Rumors of political trouble in Chiapas Province were widely cited as a cause of the 1994 Mexico crisis (*New York Times*, 1994); uncertainty about Maastricht, German unification, and Bundesbank pronouncements were argued to be important in the 1992 European Monetary System crises. Our analysis suggests that such 'informational events' might precipitate a crisis even if no investor thought they conveyed real information about fundamentals themselves. It is enough that the announcements remove common knowledge that the fundamentals were sustainable.

Above all, our analysis suggests an important role for public announcements by the monetary authorities, and more generally, the transparency of the conduct of monetary policy and its dissemination to the public. If it is the case that the onset of currency crises may be precipitated by higher-order beliefs, even though participants believe that the fundamentals are sound, then the policy instruments which will stabilize the market are those which aim to restore transparency to the situation, in an attempt to restore common knowledge of the fundamentals. The most effective means towards this would be a prominent public announcement which is commonly known to convey information to all relevant participants. The canonical case of a communication arrangement which would be conducive to achieving common knowledge is the 'town hall meeting' in which an announcement is made to an audience gathered in a single room, where everyone can observe that all other participants are in an identical position. In contrast, if the audience is fragmented, and must communicate in small groups, common knowledge is extremely difficult to achieve.[7] The Clinton administration's announcement of the $40 billion dollar rescue package for the Mexican peso can be seen as an attempt to restore the sort of transparency referred to above. Its effectiveness derived more from its very public nature, rather than the actual sum of money involved. This suggests a crucial role for the timely and effective dissemination of information on the part of policy makers, and the smooth functioning of a reliable and transparent set of communication channels between market participants and the policy makers, as well as between the market participants themselves.

B. Changes in Transaction Costs

We next examine shifts in t. Drawing on Theorem 2, which determines θ^* in the limit as ε becomes small, we can totally differentiate the equation $f(\theta^*) = e^* - 2t$ to obtain

$$\frac{d\theta^*}{dt} = -\frac{2}{f\prime(\theta^*)}.$$

Thus increasing transaction costs prevents currency crises, since it reduces the range of fundamentals where an attack occurs. The size of this effect depends on the slope of f: when the $f\prime$ is small, an increase in the cost of speculation has a large effect on the switching point θ^*. This suggests that the imposition of small transactions costs as advocated by several commentators will have a large impact on the prevalence of speculation precisely when the *consequences* of such speculative attacks are small. If speculative attacks are predicted to lead to drastic effects (i.e., when $f(\theta)$ is a steep function of θ), then the imposition of a small additional cost is unlikely to have a large effect on the incidence of currency attacks.

C. Changes in Aggregate Wealth

Now consider how our analysis is affected when aggregate wealth varies. The international flow of so-called 'hot money' would be one factor in determining this aggregate wealth, as well as changes in the numbers of speculators themselves. The main effect of a change in aggregate wealth of the speculators is a change in the function $a(\theta)$, which indicates the critical proportion of speculators needed to attack the currency in order to induce the government to abandon the currency peg. When the aggregate wealth of the speculators increases, then this critical proportion of speculators falls, since the government's decision is based on the absolute *level* of short sales.

---

[7] Ariel Rubinstein's (1989) e-mail game is a case in point, and Michael S.-Y. Chwe (1996) has suggested some of the relevant factors which would allow us to address this issue in a more general context.

As can be seen from Figure 4, a downward shift in the $a(\theta)$ function has the effect of enlarging the set of states at which the government abandons the exchange rate peg. In other words the event $A(\pi) = \{\theta | s(\theta, \pi) > a(\theta)\}$ is strictly larger with a lower $a(\cdot)$ function. Since the payoff to speculation is given by

$$\int_{A(\pi) \cap [x-\varepsilon, x+\varepsilon]} (e^* - f(\theta))d\theta - t,$$

the enlargement of the event $A(\pi)$ has an unambiguous effect in increasing the payoff to attacking the currency at any value of the signal x. Thus, the benchmark value θ^* is shifted to the right, and the incidence of speculative attacks increases.

Note, however, from Figure 4 that the effect of an increase in the $a(\cdot)$ function depends on the size of the noise ε. The effect is largest when ε is also large. In the limiting case when ε tends to zero, the equilibrium $s(\theta, I_{x^*})$ becomes the step function I_{x^*}, so that a shift in the $a(\cdot)$ function has no effect on the switching point θ^*. Thus, our analysis suggests that changes in the aggregate wealth of speculators need not have a large impact on the incidence of currency attacks when the speculators have fairly precise information concerning the fundamentals. It is when the noise is large that shifts in wealth have a big impact.

This suggests that the imposition of direct capital controls work best when there is a lack of 'transparency' of the economic fundamentals, in the sense that observers differ widely in their interpretation of the economic fundamentals. When the fundamentals are relatively transparent to all (corresponding to a small ε), direct capital controls seem far less effective. Under such circumstances, strategic considerations dominate any uncertainty concerning the fundamentals.

IV. CONCLUSION

Existing models of currency attacks that focus on fundamentals ignore the role of speculators' beliefs about other speculators' behavior. Existing self-fulfilling beliefs models of currency attacks assume that speculators *know* (in equilibrium) exactly what other speculators will do. Neither feature is realistic. Our model takes neither extreme. Because there is some uncertainty about equilibrium, speculators are uncertain as to exactly what other speculators will do; but their behavior depends nontrivially on what they believe they will do. Because our model of self-fulfilling currency attacks is consistent with unique equilibrium, we are able to analyze the impact of alternative policies.

Appendix

Proof of Lemma 2. Consider the function $s(\theta, I_k)$, which gives the proportion of speculators who attack the currency at θ when the aggregate short sales is given by the step function I_k. Since x is uniformly distributed over $[\theta - \varepsilon, \theta + \varepsilon]$, we have

$$
s(\theta, I_k) = \begin{cases} 1 & \text{if } \theta \leq k - \varepsilon \\ \frac{1}{2} - \frac{1}{2\varepsilon}(\theta - k) & \text{if } k - \varepsilon \leq \theta \leq k + \varepsilon \\ 0 & \text{if } \theta \geq k + \varepsilon. \end{cases} \tag{A1}
$$

If aggregate short sales are given by I_k, there is a unique θ (which depends on k) where the mass of speculators attacking equals the mass of speculators necessary to cause the government to abandon the exchange rate [where $s(\theta, I_k) = a(\theta)$]. Write $\psi(k)$ for the amount that θ must exceed k in order for this to be true. In other words, $\psi(k)$ is the unique value of ψ solving $s(k + \psi, I_k) = a(k + \psi)$. Observe that $\psi(k) = \varepsilon$ if $k \leq \underline{\theta} - \varepsilon$, while if $k > \underline{\theta} - \varepsilon$, then $-\varepsilon < \psi(k) < \varepsilon$ and is the value of ψ solving $(1/2 - \psi/2\varepsilon) = a(k + \psi)$.

Since the government abandons the currency peg if and only if θ lies in the interval $[0, k + \psi(k)]$, the payoff function $u(k, I_k)$ is given by

$$
\frac{1}{2\varepsilon} \int_{k-\varepsilon}^{k+\psi(k)} (e^* - f(\theta))d\theta - t. \tag{A2}
$$

Since $e^* - f(\theta)$ is strictly decreasing in θ, if we can show that $\psi(k)$ is weakly decreasing in k, this will be sufficient to show that $u(k, I_k)$ is strictly decreasing in k. To see that $\psi(k)$ is weakly decreasing in k, totally differentiate the equation $(1/2 - \psi/2\varepsilon) = a(k + \psi)$ with respect to k, to obtain $-(1/2\varepsilon)\psi'(k) = a'(\theta)(1 + \psi'(k))$. Hence,

$$
\psi'(k) = -\frac{a'(\theta)}{a'(\theta) + (1/2\varepsilon)} \leq 0,
$$

which is sufficient for $u(k, I_k)$ to be strictly decreasing in k. Finally, the continuity of $u(k, I_k)$ follows immediately from the fact that it is an integral in which the limits of integration are themselves continuous in k. This completes the proof of Lemma 2. ☐

Proof of Theorem 2. Consider the switching point x^*, which is the solution to the equation $u(x^*, I_{x^*}) = 0$. Then, writing $F(\varepsilon) = \int_{A(I_{x_*}) \cap [x^* - \varepsilon, x^* + \varepsilon]} (e^* - f(\theta))d\theta$, we can express this equation as $(F(\varepsilon)/2\varepsilon) - t = 0$. By using L'Hôpital's rule,

$$
\lim_{\varepsilon \to 0} \frac{F(\varepsilon)}{2\varepsilon} = \frac{F'(0)}{2} = \frac{e^* - f(x^*)}{2}.
$$

Thus, in the limit as $\varepsilon \to 0$, equation (A3) yields $f(x^*) = e^* - 2t$. Finally, we note that x^* converges to θ^* when ε tends to zero, since in the limit, $s(\theta, I_{x^*}) = I_{x^*}$. ☐

REFERENCES

Calvo, Guillermo A. 'Servicing the Public Debt: The Role of Expectations.' *American Economic Review*, September 1988, 78(4), pp. 647–61.

Carlsson, Hans and van Damme, Eric E. 'Global Games and Equilibrium Selection.' *Econometrica*, September 1993, 61(5), pp. 989–1018.

Chwe, Michael S.-Y. 'Structure and Strategy in Collective Action: Communication and Coordination in Social Networks.' Mimeo, University of Chicago, 1996.

Cole, Harold L. and Kehoe, Timothy J. 'Self-Fulfilling Debt Crises.' Federal Reserve Bank of Minneapolis Research Department Staff Report No. 211, 1996.

Dornbusch, Rudiger and Werner, Alejandro M. 'Mexico: Stabilization, Reform and No Growth.' *Brookings Papers on Economic Activity*, 1994, (1), pp. 253–315.

Eaton, Jonathan, and Fernandez, Raquel. 'Sovereign Debt,' in Gene M. Grossman and Kenneth Rogoff, eds., *Handbook of international economics*, Vol. III. Amsterdam: North-Holland, 1995, pp. 2031–71.

Eichengreen, Barry; Tobin, James and Wyplosz, Charles. 'Two Cases for Sand in the Wheels of International Finance.' *Economic Journal*, January 1995, 105(428), pp. 162–72.

Eichengreen, Barry and Wyplosz, Charles. 'The Unstable EMS.' *Brookings Papers on Economic Activity*, 1993, (1), pp. 51–143.

Flood, Robert P. and Garber, Peter M. 'Gold Monetization and Gold Discipline.' *Journal of Political Economy*, February 1984, 92(1), pp. 90–107.

Morris, Stephen; Rob, Rafael and Shin, Hyun Song. '*p*-Dominance and Belief Potential.' *Econometrica*, January 1995, 63(1), pp. 145–57.

New York Times, The. December 20–23, 1994, various articles.

Obstfeld, Maurice. 'Rational and Self-Fulfilling Balance-of-Payments Crises.' *American Economic Review*, March 1986, 76(1), pp. 72–81.

—— 'The Logic of Currency Crises.' *Cahiers Economiques et Monetaires (Banque de France)*, 1994, 43, pp. 189–213.

—— 'Models of Currency Crises with Self-Fulfilling Features.' *European Economic Review*, April 1996, 40(3–5), pp. 1037–47.

Postlewaite, Andrew and Vives, Xavier. 'Bank runs as an Equilibrium Phenomenon.' *Journal of Political Economy*, June 1987, 95(3), pp. 485–91.

Rubinstein, Ariel. 'The Electronic Mail Game: Strategic Behavior Under 'Almost Common Knowledge.'' *American Economic Review*, June 1989, 79(3), pp. 385–91.

PART IV

ASSET PRICING AND CORPORATE FINANCE

10

Design and Valuation of Debt Contracts

RONALD W. ANDERSON AND SURESH SUNDARESAN

This article studies the design and valuation of debt contracts in a general dynamic setting under uncertainty. In doing so we draw together two strands of the finance literature that have developed significantly in recent years, but have done so in large part independently of one another. By incorporating some insights of the recent corporate finance literature into a valuation framework, we obtain a model that seems promising for the empirical study of pricing of risky debt claims and which gives insights into the question of why certain contractual provisions are selected in some situations but not in others. Beyond this we believe our framework suggests a general approach incorporating strategic considerations in valuation setting which can be usefully explored in future work.

DEBT VALUATION THEORY

Merton (1974) was the first to apply the valuation insights of Black and Scholes (1973) to the pricing of corporate debt contracts. He takes two key contractual provisions exogenously: first, the lower reorganization boundary (which is the threshold value of the firm at which the control of the firm transfers from the stockholders to the bondholders) is specified. Second, the compensation to be received by creditors upon reaching the lower reorganization boundary is taken as given. Jones et al. (1984) extended the Merton model to coupon and callable debt, however, maintaining the assumption that the lower reorganization boundary is the minimum of the firm's value at maturity and the promised face amount. This implies that there are no enforcements of indentures prior to maturity. When applied to a sample of 305 bonds of various ratings, their model resulted in prices systematically in excess of those observed in the market, that is, their model underestimated observed yield spreads. They interpreted their results

We have benefited from the comments of seminar participants at the Stockholm School of Economics, ECARE, IGIER, Baruch College, Carnegie-Mellon University, and the ESF Finance Network Symposium in Gerzensee, Switzerland, and from discussion with Hayne Leland, John Parsons, and William Perraudin. We thank Yonghua Pan and Pierre Tychon for computational assistance and comments. This article has been improved by the comments of the referee and the editor, Franklin Allen. This research has been supported through an ESF Network in Financial Markets travel grant. Responsibility for views expressed and for errors is our own.

as 'establishing research priorities in what will be a large and complex task' of applying contingent claims pricing models to risky debt. Kim, Ramaswamy and Sundaresan (1993) pursued this agenda by extending the continent claims pricing model to incorporate (1) enforcement of bond covenants on intermediate coupon payments and (2) a stochastic term structure. Their results indicated that yield spreads were sensitive to imposing cash flow checks prior to maturity and that they are an increasing function of the bankruptcy costs (parameterized in their model as the recovery rate). Surprisingly, yield spreads were found to be relatively insensitive to the volatility of interest rates. Maloney (1992) has recently extended this approach to allow for more general stochastic processes for the firm cash flows and interest rates.

All these studies take as exogenously given the firm's lower reorganization boundary as well as the payoffs when that boundary is met. These models are also not consistent with the empirical regularities reported in recent studies on financial distress by Asquith, Gertner, and Scharfstein (1991), Franks and Torous (1989, 1993), and Weiss (1990). These regularities are (1) bankruptcies are costly both because of direct costs and because of disruptions of the firm's activities; (2) bankruptcy procedures give considerable scope for opportunistic behavior by the various parties involved; (3) deviations from absolute priority of claims are common; and (4) despite the incentives to do so, in practice it often proves impossible to renegotiate claims so that formal bankruptcy and liquidation often result. Thus costly liquidations represent a possible source of inefficiency associated with debt contracts.

CORPORATE FINANCE AND DEBT DESIGN

Historically, corporate finance has been concerned with other possible inefficiencies. Jensen and Meckling (1976) emphasized the agency costs of equity finance in the face of managerial moral hazard. In another vein, Myers (1977) identified the agency costs of debt by pointing out the underinvestment problem, that is, the possibility that firms will forego positive net present value investment opportunities because benefits are likely to accrue to debtholders rather than shareholders. Recent theory has reexamined these issues from the perspective of security design. This approach considers how both control rights and cash flow claims may be structured so as to minimize contracting inefficiencies. Aghion and Bolton (1992) and Zender (1991) emphasize that contracts that grant control to one class of agents exclusively may not be efficient because either they fail to give the controlling agent the incentives to make first-best decisions or because contracts sold to outsiders will not be sufficiently valuable to permit raising the required outside finance. They show that contracts with *contingent transfer of control rights* may minimize inefficiencies; this provides a rationale for debt contracts.

The properties of debt contracts have been studied recently in a number of theoretical models. For example, Hart and Moore (1991) examine the problem of designing optimal debt contracts in a dynamic setting under certainty. Bolton and Scharfstein (1993) study the trade-offs involved in making debt more or less easy to renegotiate. A number of other models examine the consequences of alternative bankruptcy models.[1]

SYNTHESIS OF VALUATION AND CORPORATE FINANCE

These corporate finance models tend to be very stylized and not truly dynamic. Furthermore, they have *no* valuation consequences or direct testable implications for corporate bond yield spreads. On the other hand, the valuation theory is truly dynamic but fails to endogenize contractual provisions.

Our article attempts to fill the gap by integrating these two strands of research. The basics of our approach are summarized as follows. For us, the terms of a debt contract and bankruptcy law establish the extensive form game in which debt-holders and equityholders interact. The allocation of cash flows and the firm's reorganization boundary are determined *endogenously* as the noncooperative equilibrium in this game. Given this solution, we are then able to address the question of the design and the valuation of multiperiod debt contracts under uncertainty.

Two additional recent studies address some of the questions that we do and obtain results that are in some ways similar to our own. Leland (1993) reconsiders the contingent claims framework in continuous time. By assuming that all debt service must be met by issuing new equity he endogenizes the firm's bankruptcy point. Specifically, it is the point where the value of equity is zero. He restricts his study to the case of perpetual debt essentially in order to obtain closed-form solutions permitting the calculation of a variety of interesting comparative statics. His approach is similar to ours in that it endogenizes the lower reorganization boundary of the firm. Otherwise the approaches are quite different. In particular, there is no modeling of the process for resolving financial distress and there is no scope for strategic debt service. Furthermore, since the framework is constrained to using perceptual coupon bonds, it cannot be used to address issues of financial contract design.

Like Leland, Mella-Barral and Perraudin (1993) also work in continuous time and confine their attention to perpetual coupon bonds. They explicitly model the shutdown decision of a firm operating with constant flow costs but with a stochastically varying output price. In this way they are able to study the effect of leverage on the operations of the firm. Their analysis allows for strategic debt service, and in this sense is closer to our model than is any other. However, they do not explicitly model the bankruptcy game. Their analysis is simplified considerably by the fact that they work with perpetual debt. This reduces its relevance to pricing actual bonds with finite maturities and specific (sometimes

---

[1] Other recent papers concerned with debt include Bergman and Callen (1991), Dewatripont and Tirole (1992), and Franks and Nyborg (1993).

complicated) contractual features. Furthermore, this means that they cannot address the question of the design of debt contracts.

In the next section we set out our model and derive the equilibrium values of corporate liabilities. Using a simple model of the bankruptcy process, we find the equilibrium often will result in renegotiations with deviations of priority in the favor of equity. In Section 2, we compare our results to Merton (1974) and subsequent applications of the contingent claims approach to pricing risky debt. We find our model produces risk premia more in line with levels observed in the market for reasonable parameter values. Section 3 is devoted to the design of debt contracts. We show how high cash payout rates, low leverage, and low liquidation costs lead to higher coupon debt, in general. Sinking fund provisions are generally used to trade off the tax advantages of interest payments with risks of costly liquidations. Section 4 states our conclusions and suggests avenues for future work.

1. THE MODEL

1.1. Preliminaries

The setting we consider is simple: there is one owner-manager who has 'access' to a technology and is endowed with a technology-specific human capital. His human capital is imbedded in a project which, if undertaken, will give rise to a stream of rents indefinitely into the future. The project requires financing in the amount of capital D which the owner-manager does not have. We assume that the financing is to be arranged through the issue of a debt contract, which we take to be characterized by the priority of claims and contingent transfer of control.[2]

We restrict attention to a single homogeneous group of creditors to abstract from holdout problems. The terms of the contract call for a payment of CS_t in period t up to the maturity date T. It is assumed that debt service is met out of cash flows and that asset sales or the issue of new securities would require the explicit agreement of creditors. Finally, we assume that all contracting parties have full information about the states of the nature.

1.2. The Technology

The ongoing project is represented as a stochastic process for the value V_t, which is the present value of current and all future cash flows. The value is assumed to

---

[2] This assumption is also used by Aghion and Bolton (1992) and Hart and Moore (1991) among others to study capital structure and security design. In this context, contingent transfer of control through a debt contract is preferred to outside equity since the latter would incur an agency cost from the outset. Later, we will see that the tax deductibility of debt service would provide an additional reason for issuing debt.

follow a simple binomial process as illustrated[3]

where $d = 1/u$. V_t may be interpreted as the cum dividend value of the firm were it to be financed entirely by equity. This is also the value of assets of the firm under alternative financing arrangements. This specification allows us to nest as a special case of Merton's (1974) analysis of zero coupon debt. Cash flows are assumed to be proportional to the value of the project; thus $f_t = \beta V_t$, where β is the payout ratio.

The mapping between the cash flows and value processes is based on martingale probabilities p which are time and state invariant and which are given by $(r(1 - \beta) - d)/(u - d)$.[4] We assume $u > r(1 - \beta) > d$. It will be noticed that the cash payout ratio β enters the martingale probability of an 'up move' with a negative sign. This allows us to model within the same framework 'growth firms' (low β projects for which a large proportion of current value is accounted for by expected future growth) and 'cash cows' (high β projects for which a large proportion of current value is accounted for by near-term cash flows). Our main restriction is that in taking the cash flow process as exogenous we are not able to study explicitly the possible feedback of the financial contracting onto future production decisions.

Once underway, control of the project can be transferred only at a cost. This may in part take a direct form, such as legal costs, that reflect costly verification of collateral values. In part this may reflect a loss of project-specific human capital: after the transfer of control, it takes time and effort for the creditor to find another management team that will be able to produce the cash flows from the technology at its full efficiency. In what follows we assume these costs are all summarized in constant liquidation cost of K so that the collateral value equals $V - K$. The model could easily accommodate other functional forms for collateral values possibly at the cost of greater complexity. In other respects the markets are assumed to be frictionless. We examine later a variant of the model that allows for corporate income taxation.

All cash flows from the project are paid out in the form of dividends, debt service, or to cover bankruptcy costs. Thus the model satisfies the value preservation property, $V = E + B + L$, where E is the value of equity, B is the value

---

[3] Our approach is easily applied to more general two-state branching processes with state-dependent probabilities. For expositional clarity, we are illustrating the model with a simple binomial lattice.

[4] This can be derived by solving for p such that V_t is the sum of the current cash flow plus the expected discounted value of V_{t+1}. This solution is unique. The Appendix provides a proof of these assertions.

of debt, and L is the present expected value of future bankruptcy costs. Thus the value of the levered firm V_t, given by the value of its financial claims, is the asset value of the firm less the expected bankruptcy costs, $V_t = V - L$. We now proceed to discuss the interaction of the owner-manager and the creditor taking the financial contract as given. The optimal design of financial contracts is discussed below.

1.3. The Game

The technology, the provisions of the debt contract, and the law establish the environment within which the owner and the creditor interact. We represent this with an extensive form game which, though very simple, has interesting dynamic implications. Our general approach can readily accommodate modifications to this game form.

At any given time while the project is ongoing, there will be a realization of the cash flow, f_t. Given this, the owner chooses a level of debt service, $S_t \in [0, f_t]$. If the debt service is equal to or greater than the contracted amount, CS_t, the game continues to the next period. If it is less than the contracted amount, the creditor has the choice of not initiating legal action (i.e., accepting the service) or initiating legal action (i.e., rejecting the debt service). If the debt service is accepted the project continues to the next date. If the debt service is rejected, the project is liquidated, leaving the creditor with the cum dividend value of the project less the liquidation cost.

The subgame originating from a state V_{t-1} is depicted in Figure 1.

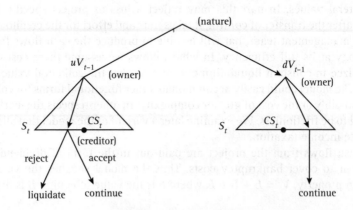

Figure 1. *The subgame at t*

Note: The arrows in Figure 1 indicate a decision. The event illustrated is a 'down move' to dV_{t-1}. From that point the owner chooses a debt service that lies within the range indicated by the base of the triangle. Here he is shown as offering a debt service greater than the contracted service CS_t which leads to a continuation to date $t + 1$.

At each node the player taking the action is indicated in parentheses. (A random variable is viewed as an action taken by nature.) The arrows indicate a decision. Thus in the figure the event is a 'down move' to dV_{t-1}. From that point the owner chooses a debt service that lies within the range indicated by the base of the triangle. Here he is shown as offering a debt service greater than the contracted service CS_t, which leads to a continuation to date $t + 1$. Had there been an 'up move' to uV_{t-1} the owner is shown as offering a debt service below the contracted amount. Since a covenant of the debt contract is violated, this creates a decision node for the creditor. The figure indicates that he accepts the service rather than electing to liquidate the project. In Figure 1 the indicated actions of the owner and creditor are not necessarily their best responses. Below we will discuss the *equilibrium* in the game.

In our formulation we have modified the modeling of the firm bankruptcy process fundamentally as compared to the approach of Merton where bankruptcy is determined simply by the state of the nature and the contract, leaving no scope for either the owner or the creditor to take any initiative. Our model gives the owner the scope for choosing to underperform his debt contract, even when the health of the project would enable him to fully meet his obligations. We will see that the costliness of liquidation means that the owner can exploit this opportunity to his own advantage. At the same time our model gives the creditor the scope for choosing how to approach a potential bankruptcy. He need not force bankruptcy when it is not in his interests to do so. This can be viewed as a simple representation of a negotiation between the owner and the creditor that arises whenever a contractual provision is violated. Admittedly this is very stylized and gives a first-mover advantage to the owner. Other ways of modeling bankruptcies could be considered that might allow more elaborate interactions, possibly to the creditor's advantage.

In our formulation an important loan indenture is meeting the currently scheduled payment of interest and principal. This is a basic and widespread feature of debt contracts. It should be noted, however, that violating this does not automatically throw the firm into bankruptcy. It merely creates a decision node for the creditor in which he must decide whether or not to initiate legal action against the owner-manager.

Requiring debt service to lie in the interval $[0, f_t)$ is important and requires some comment. First, it implicitly assumes that the owner cannot issue additional debt once the project is underway. Loan indentures very frequently do forbid the issue of additional debt with priority equal or superior to that of the original issue. Here we also exclude the issue of junior debt since the incorporation of subordinated debt valuation is a complication best approached after our basic model is fully understood. Similarly, we do not allow debt service to be funded through asset sales or equity issues. Loan indentures commonly do restrict asset liquidation since this might be exploited by owner-managers as a means of extracting value at the expense of undermining collateral values. Furthermore, the assets in place may be discrete.

The assumption that no new securities are issued to service existing debt simplifies our analysis and arguably comes close to reality in many circumstances. There may be fixed costs associated with security issues that may be higher for a firm in financial distress than for a healthy firm. Furthermore, adding new classes of claimants may make subsequent renegotiations more difficult so that the firm liquidation may simply be delayed but not prevented. Therefore, we believe working with a model where new security issues are excluded is a good starting point for the analysis of strategic debt service. Nevertheless, we would view enriching the game form to allow for securities issues in *some* circumstances to be an interesting avenue for future work.

1.4. Equilibrium

We assume that, once the debt contract has been established, the owner and the creditor each choose actions in their own self-interest. We assume complete information in the sense that the game as just described, as well as the payoffs to the two sides, are both common knowledge. As a result our attention is restricted to the subgame perfect equilibria of the game. That is to say that an equilibrium is constructed under the assumption that at each possible decision point, including those that are never actually observed in equilibrium, the agent makes a maximizing decision. As is typical in such settings, we construct the equilibrium recursively.

At maturity T, V_T is observed, and the owner selects a debt service S_T. If this is not less than the contracted amount, $S_T \geq CS_T$, the game ends. Otherwise, $S_T < CS_T$, the creditor must decide whether to accept or reject. If debt service fulfills the contract or if the creditor accepts, the payoffs to the debtholder and the owner, respectively, are

$$(S_T, V_T - S_T),$$

whereas if a debt service is rejected the payoffs are

$$(\max(V_T - K, 0), 0).$$

The assumption that the liquidation value of the firm cannot be negative reflects the fact that liquidation costs are deducted from remaining firm value.

Equilibrium in this subgame is formed by the decisions rules of the creditor and owner that constitute the best responses in light of the payoffs. Given underperformance, $S_T < CS_T$, the best response of the creditor is to accept if $S_T \geq \max(V_T - K, 0)$ and to reject otherwise. The best response of the owner is to set $S_T = CS_T$ if $V_T - K > CS_T$. Otherwise he sets $S_T = \max(V_T - K, 0)$. Thus if the value of the firm is relatively high so that the liquidation value exceeds the contracted debt service, the owner is best off simply honoring the contract. For relatively low values of the firm, the owner is best off by making the minimum debt service payment which just leaves the creditor indifferent between accepting or liquidating the firm.

The payoffs for the creditor and owner conditional on the realization of V_T are given by the equilibrium values which are

$$B(V_T) = \min(CS_T, \max(V_T - K, 0)) \tag{1}$$

for debt, while the value of the equity is

$$E(V_T) = V_T - B(V_T). \tag{2}$$

Notice that these payoffs reflect the possibility of strategic debt service: in terminal states where contracted payment is less than the project value but greater than its liquidation value, the owner-manager underperforms the debt contract, but by an amount insufficient to provoke the creditor to take legal action.

For periods prior to the term of the debt contract, the best responses of the agents will be based on similar reasoning. That is, the owner-manager in some states will try to reduce debt service to the point where the creditor is just indifferent between accepting the service and taking legal action. The important complication in these earlier periods is that, in calculating payoffs, the agents must take into account the values of the continuation subgames. Since these depend on the future realizations of the project values, they are uncertain. Under the assumption that the markets are dynamically complete, both the debtholder and the owner-manager will evaluate the continuation payoffs using the same martingale probabilities [see Harrison and Kreps (1978)]. This preserves the complete information character of the game.

Suppose at time t the project is ongoing, and there has been a realization V_t. The owner selects a debt service S_t. If this at least equals the contracted amount, CS_t the game continues. If this underperforms the contract, the creditor can reject the payment, which results in the liquidation value

$$\max(V_t - K, 0).$$

Alternatively, the creditor can accept, which results in the payoff

$$S_t + \frac{pB(uV_t) + (1 - p)B(dV_t)}{r}$$

where r is one plus the risk-free interest rate per period. Thus, in the face of underperformance, the best response of the creditor amounts to selecting the greater of these two values. The owner determines his best action in light of this. For relatively high realized values of the firm, $(V_t - K) > CS_t$, the owner simply meets the contractual debt service. For relatively lower values of the firm, he elects to underperform the contract to the point that leaves the creditor indifferent between liquidating or not.

To find the equilibrium value of the debt contract, note that the owner will try to reduce the debt service but seeks to avoid provoking the creditor to liquidate the firm. If liquidation does not occur, then in state V_t^j the level of debt service is

$$S(V_t) = \min\left(CS_t, \max\left(0, \max(V_t - K, 0)\right.\right.$$
$$\left.\left. - \frac{pB(uV_t) + (1 - p)B(dV_t)}{r}\right)\right). \tag{3}$$

The value of debt thus is

$$B(V_t) = S(V_t) + \frac{pB(uV_t) + (1 - p)B(dV_t)}{r}. \tag{4}$$

The corresponding value of equity is

$$E(V_t) = f_t - S(V_t) + \frac{pE(uV_t) + (1 - p)E(dV_t)}{r}. \tag{5}$$

In some states, however, cash flows will be insufficient to pay an amount acceptable to the creditor. Since in this framework asset sales and new security issues are excluded, liquidation will result. Thus, forced liquidation occurs if

$$S(V_t) > f_t.$$

In the case of forced liquidation, the value of debt is

$$B(V_t) = \max(0, \min(V_t - K, CS_t + P_t)), \tag{6}$$

where P_t is the principal of loan outstanding at time t. The value of equity is

$$E(V_t) = V_t - K - B(V_t). \tag{7}$$

This completes the construction of a subgame perfect equilibrium. This is a unique equilibrium if the liquidation costs are strictly positive. For in that case, even though S_t is chosen to leave the creditor indifferent between accepting and rejecting the service, rejecting never occurs in equilibrium. The owner's best action in anticipation of rejection is to slightly raise S_t, which would make the creditor strictly prefer acceptance.

This equilibrium merits a few comments. First, in contrast with the traditional approach in contingent claims valuation, the states in which contract default occurs have been determined endogenously from the primitives of the model. Furthermore, control of the project is transferred to creditors only in a subset of default states where the firm is illiquid. Second, the equilibrium may involve strategic debt service, which is consistent with the observed opportunism of contracting parties under many bankruptcy procedures. Our strategic debt service can be interpreted as the outcome of a negotiation process with a deviation from absolute priority in favor of equity. The size of the deviation depends on the health of the asset in place and the costliness of liquidation. Third, costly forced liquidations can occur in equilibrium since asset sales are infeasible. This kind of *ex post* inefficiency implies that the debt capacity of the project, that is, the maximum amount that can be raised to finance the project may be less than its full asset value. This implies a possible *ex ante* inefficiency as well: positive net present value projects may not be undertaken if the debt capacity is less than the financing requirement of the owner-manager. Thus the model reflects an underinvestment problem that can be interpreted as an agency cost of debt. However, it should be recognized that since we do not allow feedback onto future investment decisions we do not incorporate the form of agency cost originally identified by Myers (1977).[5] Fourth, our model has been set out in discrete time. This has the advantage of making the modeling of the bankruptcy process transparent. Our particular model has the feature of giving a first-mover advantage to the owner-manager. A number of alternative models of the bankruptcy process that have been suggested in the literature could be incorporated as rather direct extensions of our framework. In contrast, modeling noncooperative games in continuous time can present subtle difficulties. Indeed, Fudenberg and Tirole [1985] have convincingly argued that for continuous time games it is preferable to find the equilibrium in a discretized version of the game and then take limits as the time interval goes to zero. Fifth, the equilibrium holds for quite general stochastic processes. Furthermore, it is consistent with risk averse utility maximizing owners and creditors.

2. VALUATION

In this section we use our model to evaluate straight debt contracts, that is, contracts offering nominally a fixed coupon and full principal reimbursement at maturity. This involves a promised payment of a coupon interest rate of c per period and a principal P to be reimbursed at the maturity date T. Thus we have $CS_t = cP$ for $t < T$ and $CS_T = (c + 1)P$. We first consider the case of a zero coupon (pure discount) debt to serve as a benchmark for comparison with Merton (1974). Later we consider the more important case of coupon bonds.

2.1. Discount Debt

A useful benchmark for our model is Merton's (1974) analysis of zero coupon, risky bonds. Our model in the special case of a zero coupon ($c = 0$) and zero cost of liquidation ($K = 0$) is a discretized version of Merton's. Strategic considerations in the bankruptcy decision only enter into play for strictly positive bankruptcy costs ($K > 0$). Table 1 presents the risk premium of debt (i.e., the difference between the internal rate of return on the risky bond, R, and the

---

[5] See Mello and Parsons (1992) for an attempt to measure debt agency costs arising both from lack of investment commitment by shareholders and from bankruptcy costs. However, this study does not endogenize the lower reorganization boundary of the firm, nor does it accommodate strategic behavior in bankruptcy.

Table 1. *Discount debt* $(V = 1, \beta = 0.00, c = 0.00, r = 1.05^{1})$

σ^2	d	Risk premium, $R - r$ $(\%)^2$		
		$K = 0$	$K = 0.1$	$K = 0.2$
(a) Time to maturity $(T) = 2.00$ **years**				
0.030	0.200	0.000	0.000	0.000
0.030	0.500	0.012	0.106	0.513
0.030	1.000	5.129	8.396	12.734
0.030	1.500	20.578	25.556	31.429
0.100	0.200	0.002	0.050	0.378
0.100	0.500	0.817	2.031	4.138
0.100	1.000	9.738	13.365	17.779
0.100	1.500	23.022	27.581	32.845
0.200	0.200	0.118	0.796	2.702
0.200	0.500	3.087	5.682	9.358
0.200	1.000	14.266	18.404	23.310
0.200	1.500	26.601	31.232	36.345
(b) Time to maturity $(T) = 10.00$ **years**				
0.030	0.200	0.004	0.031	0.113
0.030	0.500	0.376	0.629	0.994
0.030	1.000	2.430	2.988	3.680
0.030	1.500	4.969	5.678	6.568
0.100	0.200	0.474	1.049	1.956
0.100	0.500	2.113	2.860	3.799
0.100	1.000	4.826	5.622	6.568
0.100	1.500	7.116	7.919	8.869
0.200	0.200	1.872	3.435	5.522
0.200	0.500	4.379	5.695	7.356
0.200	1.000	7.351	8.494	9.878
0.200	1.500	9.546	10.609	11.867

[1] V refers to the initial value of the firm, d is the quasi debt to value ratio, c is the coupon, β is the cash payout ratio (cash flow divided by the value of the firm), r is the riskless rate, K is the fixed liquidation cost, and T is the time to maturity in years.

[2] $R - r$ is the risk premium. The results are based on discrete time binomial valuation procedure in which the time to maturity is divided into 1,000 time steps.

risk-free rate, r) for zero coupon bonds under a variety of assumptions about the remaining parameters. For ease of comparison we have parameterized our model as in Merton with respect to the volatility of value process, σ^2, the firm's quasi-debt firm value ratio, $d = Pe^{-rT}/V_0$, and have assumed $\beta = 0$.

The results for $K = 0$ correspond to those reported by Merton (1974) in his Table 1. The slight discrepancies between our results and his are due to our working with a discrete version of his continuous time model. Thus we see that, in the case of zero bankruptcy costs, the premium is increasing in the leverage, d, and the volatility of the underlying asset, σ^2. The effect with respect to time to maturity depends crucially on the degree on the firm's leverage. For example, for $d = 0.5$ the premia for $T = 2$ are less than those when $T = 10$, whereas the reverse holds for $d = 1.5$. The interpretation is that, for firms with a low degree of leverage, default will occur only if the firm value declines substantially, a prospect that is more likely for long maturities than for short maturities. For highly leveraged firms, default will be avoided only if the firm value improves significantly, a prospect that is more likely for higher maturities.

The effect of positive bankruptcy costs is indicated in Table 1 by the yield spreads calculated under the assumption that $K = 0.1, 0.2$. For example, for a firm with $\sigma^2 = 0.03$ and $d = 0.5$, 2-year debt requires an insignificant spread (about 1 basis point) if liquidation is costless, whereas it carries spreads of 10 basis points and 51 basis points, respectively, when liquidation costs are 10 percent and 20 percent of value.[6]

Thus Table 1 demonstrates an important property of our model—properly accounting for costly bankruptcy can better explain observed premia on traded risky debt than does the standard contingent claims framework.[7] Much of the increase in calculated spreads is accounted for by strategic debt service in our model. To see this we have also computed the implied spreads if Merton's (1974) model is modified by deducting liquidation costs K whenever the exogenous reorganization boundary $\min(V_T, P)$ is met. For the case of $T = 2, \sigma^2 = 0.03$, $d = 0.5$, and $K = 0.2$ this ad hoc adjustment results in a yield spread of only 8 basis points. Thus most of the 51 basis point spread found in our model reflects strategic debt service in states where $V_T \geq P$. In order to get additional insights on the impact of strategic debt service in our model, we provide Figure 2 in which the liquidation costs are varied from 0 to 0.20 and the default premia implied by our model are compared with those implied by Merton with ad hoc adjustment. Note that for a lower debt level of $d = 0.2$ the possibility of strategic debt service contributes much more to the default premia even when the liquidation costs are relatively low. To see why, note that in the range of states $V_T \in (P, P + K)$ our model involves strategic debt service, whereas the modified Merton model repays debt in full. In the range $V_T < P$, debt payments in the two models are identical. For initially low leverage firms the former range is relatively more likely; therefore, a higher proportion of yield spreads are accounted for by strategic debt service.

Careful inspection of Table 1 reveals that the amount that bankruptcy costs increase the yield spreads depends systematically on the degree of leverage and the volatility of the underlying asset. This is shown clearly in Figures 3 and 4, which plot yield spreads on zero coupon debt in the Merton model $(K = 0)$ and in our model with $K = 0.1$ with respect to d and σ^2.

In Figure 3 we see that yield spreads in the face of costly bankruptcy exceed those with costless bankruptcy for all degrees of leverage. The difference in yield

---

[6] It should be stressed that $K = 0.2$ is used to reflect an upper bound on the direct and indirect costs of liquidation.

[7] Below we make an explicit comparison to observed spreads with reference to coupon bearing debt.

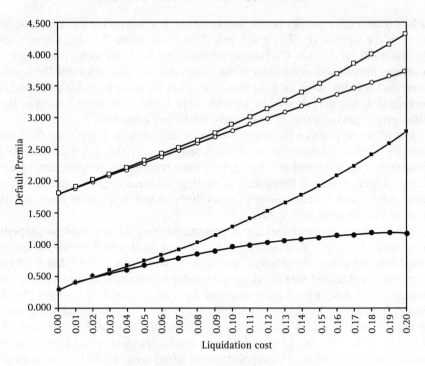

Figure 2. *Effect of strategic debt service on default premia*

Note: Starting firm value is assumed to be 1. The debt has a time to maturity of 10 years. A zero coupon bond, with a firm beta of 0.04 and a variance of 10 percent is considered. Riskless rate is assumed to be 5 percent.

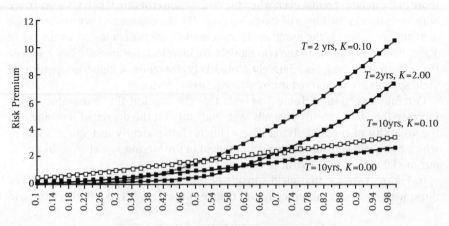

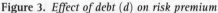

Figure 3. *Effect of debt (d) on risk premium*

Note: This figure shows the effect of debt level on risk premium. A zero coupon bond, with a firm beta of 0 and a variance of 3 percent is considered. Riskless rate is assumed to be 5 percent.

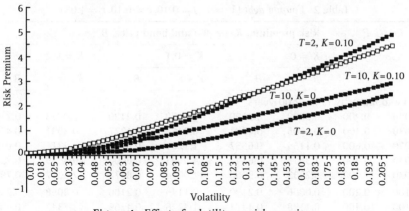

Figure 4. *Effect of volatility on risk premium*

Note: The effect of volatility on risk premium is plotted for debt contracts with 2 years and 10 years maturities. Two liquidation costs (0 and 10 percent) are used. We have assumed a zero coupon bond, with a firm beta of 0. Riskless rate is assumed to be 5 percent.

spreads grows with the degree of leverage, particularly in the case of short-term debt $(T = 2)$. Similarly in Figure 4 we see that the premia for bonds with costly bankruptcy are greater than premia without bankruptcy cost by an amount that is an increasing function of the underlying asset volatility. Increasing the volatility increases the chances that asset values will erode sufficiently after 2 years so that shareholders will default in the payment of principal outstanding either opportunistically or through forced liquidation.

Having established some of the properties of our model for the case of pure discount instruments we now turn to the empirically more important case of coupon paying debt.

2.2. Coupon Paying Debt

A widely observed feature of risky debt contracts such as corporate bonds or syndicated bank loans is that loan indentures specify the regular payment of interest. Violation of this covenant can lead to bankruptcy and possible liquidation of the firm. This common practice reflects the fact that such flow payments are more readily verifiable than are firm values. Our model incorporates this feature when we specify a strictly positive coupon payment $(c > 0)$. When liquidation costs are zero $(K = 0)$, equilibrium debt service involves the payment of the scheduled coupon whenever the firm is able to pay $(\beta V_t \geq cP)$; otherwise, the firm is liquidated. This is a direct extension of the Merton (1974) model.[8] When $K > 0$ equilibrium debt service in our model may fall short of scheduled coupon payment without provoking liquidation.

---

[8] Kim, Ramaswamy, and Sundaresan (1993) extend the Merton model to coupon debt and allow for interest rate uncertainty. Our model with $c > 0$ and $K = 0$ is a discretized version of their model in the case of zero interest rate volatility.

Table 2. *Coupon debt* $(V = 1, \beta = 0.10, c = 0.10, r = 1.05)$

σ^2	P	Risk premium, $R - r$ (%) and bond price, B					
		$K = 0$		$K = 0.1$		$K = 0.2$	
		$R - r$	B	$R - r$	B	$R - r$	B
Time to maturity $(T) = 2.00$ years							
0.030	0.200	0.0000	0.2190	0.0000	0.2190	0.0033	0.2190
0.030	0.400	0.0005	0.4381	0.0467	0.4377	0.3931	0.4349
0.030	0.600	0.1154	0.6557	1.1265	0.6437	3.2311	0.6196
0.030	0.800	1.3613	0.8547	4.9593	0.8006	9.4939	0.7376
0.030	1.000	5.2333	0.9958	11.0074	0.8972	17.5217	0.7983
0.100	0.200	0.0006	0.2190	0.1135	0.2186	0.8058	0.2158
0.100	0.400	0.1188	0.4371	1.4226	0.4269	3.7347	0.4093
0.100	0.600	1.0055	0.6452	4.3400	0.6072	8.4881	0.5633
0.100	0.800	2.5711	0.8361	7.5786	0.7635	13.2828	0.6890
0.100	1.000	5.5684	0.9897	11.3698	0.8913	17.9093	0.7928
0.200	0.200	0.0430	0.2189	1.1839	0.2144	3.9532	0.2038
0.200	0.400	0.4974	0.4341	3.9863	0.4074	8.5708	0.3750
0.200	0.600	1.7529	0.6364	6.8005	0.5807	12.6833	0.5223
0.200	0.800	3.7057	0.8190	9.3993	0.7388	15.8690	0.6578
0.200	1.000	5.8894	0.9840	11.7317	0.8856	18.3205	0.7871
Time to maturity $(T) = 10.00$ years							
0.030	0.200	0.0321	0.2780	0.3602	0.2718	1.1849	0.2569
0.030	0.400	0.5155	0.5378	1.4209	0.5056	2.6057	0.4670
0.030	0.600	1.6407	0.7471	2.9029	0.6868	4.3726	0.6243
0.030	0.800	3.1564	0.9006	4.6492	0.8178	6.3662	0.7344
0.030	1.000	5.0813	0.9946	6.7689	0.8957	8.7301	0.7968
0.100	0.200	0.4765	0.2696	2.1688	0.2404	4.2609	0.2096
0.100	0.400	1.4857	0.5033	3.2769	0.4468	5.4490	0.3887
0.100	0.600	2.7824	0.6923	4.5286	0.6181	6.5894	0.5433
0.100	0.800	4.0296	0.8508	5.7473	0.7631	7.7546	0.6752
0.100	1.000	5.2222	0.9857	6.9302	0.8869	8.9183	0.7881
0.200	0.200	1.1050	0.2582	4.2667	0.2095	7.4505	0.1719
0.200	0.400	2.3809	0.4740	4.8206	0.4045	7.9177	0.3343
0.200	0.600	3.4482	0.6627	5.5296	0.5802	8.0542	0.4975
0.200	0.800	4.1523	0.8442	5.9937	0.7515	8.1684	0.6588
0.200	1.000	5.5106	0.9681	7.2566	0.8696	9.2954	0.7711

Results pertaining to coupon paying debt are presented in Table 2. Here we have taken the face value of the debt, P, to be the indicator of leverage.[9] The table reports results for a 10 percent per annum coupon bond to be paid continuously. The payout ratio, β, is also set at 10 percent per annum. Other parameters are set as in the case of zero coupon debt.

[9] Note that since this differs from the quasi-debt ratio d, Tables 1 and 2 are not directly comparable.

The results are reported with respect to three levels of liquidation costs, $K = 0, 0.1, 0.2$. Required yield spreads are increasing in K, as expected. In fact, the premia appear quite sensitive to changes in liquidation costs. For example, for the parameters $\sigma^2 = 0.03, P = 0.6$, and $T = 2$ the spread ranges from 11 basis points to 323 basis points for $K = 0$ to $K = 0.2$, respectively. The sensitivity of coupon debt is the result of the fact that the frequent cash flow checks implied by coupon debt increase the scope for opportunistic debt service.

The results for coupon debt are more directly comparable to risky debt traded in the market place. In the United States yield spreads on long-term corporate bonds of firms rated AAA or AA have averaged approximately 125 basis points in recent years [see Salomon Brothers (1992)]. The median debt-to-capital ratio for firms in this category is approximately 20 percent [see Standard and Poors (1982)]. For a firm with this degree of leverage an asset variance of 10 percent corresponds to an equity volatility that is consistent with this firm being rated AAA or AA.[10]

From the results for the case of $P = 0.2, \sigma^2 = 0.1$, and $T = 10$, we see that these levels of yield spreads are produced in our model with $K = 0.045$. Thus, with coupon debt observed spreads are consistent with low levels of asset volatility and bankruptcy costs of less than 5 percent of initial values.

The results in Table 2 reveal that the sensitivities with respect to the basic parameters are similar to those found in our model for discount debt. Yield spreads increase with increases of volatility (σ^2). They are almost always increasing in the degree of leverage used. The only exception appears in the case of $T = 10, \sigma^2 = 0.2$, and $K = 0.2$, where an increase in principal from 0.2 to 0.4 entails a decrease in the yield spread. The reason that increasing leverage can at times be beneficial to bondholders in our context is that it can make forced liquidations more frequent, which in turn can result in a higher net payoff to bondholders than if they were exposed to opportunistic debt service subsequently. The sensitivity with respect to time to maturity depends on the degree of leverage. The spread is increasing in T if leverage is low and decreasing if leverage is high.

Figure 5 presents the yield spreads as a function of time to maturity for bonds with face value of 0.3 when the underlying project has a payout rate of 10 percent per year and a volatility of 0.03. Four cases are plotted, corresponding to two values of liquidation costs ($K = 0, 0.1$) and two coupons ($c = 0, 0.1$). In each case the yield spread is increasing in the time to maturity, reflecting the low leverage involved. Furthermore, spreads are higher when the liquidation costs are positive. For the case presented, spreads are higher for the zero coupon bond than for the coupon bearing bond, holding liquidation costs constant. We explore this effect more explicitly in what follows.

---

[10] The volatility of equity as related to the value of the firm is given as

$$\sigma_e = \sigma E_v V / E \leq \sigma V / E,$$

where E_v is the partial derivative of equity with respect to underlying value. Thus $\sigma^2 = 0.1$ and $P = 0.2$ give an upper bound for σ_e of 0.395.

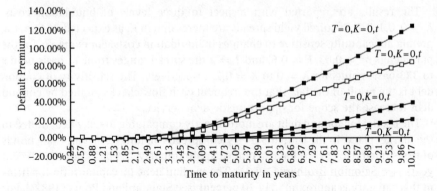

Figure 5. *Risk structure of interest rates*

Note: Starting firm value is assumed to be 1. The risk structure is plotted when the firm beta is 0.1, face is 0.3, and the variance is 3 percent. Riskless rate is assumed to be 5 percent.

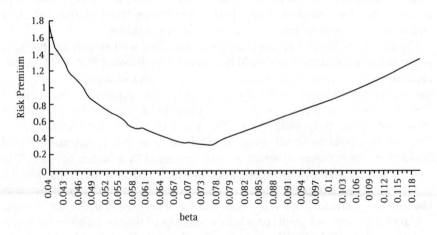

Figure 6. *Effect of beta on risk premium*

Note: The effect of cash payout ratio (beta) on risk premium is illustrated for $T = 10$ years, face = 0.30, and coupon = 10 percent. The liquidation cost is assumed to be 10 percent and the variance is 3 percent. Riskless rate is assumed to be 5 percent.

Further subtleties of bond valuation in the face of opportunistic debt service are illustrated in Figures 6 and 7. Figure 6 depicts the relationship between the yield spread and the cash payout ratio, β. It is striking that yield spreads are initially decreasing and then increasing in this payout rate. Sufficiently low levels of β combined with a positive coupon interest lead to a quick forced liquidation. Even if liquidation costs are not so high as to prevent the bondholder from fully recovering the principal, this means the bond carries a risk premium, since the

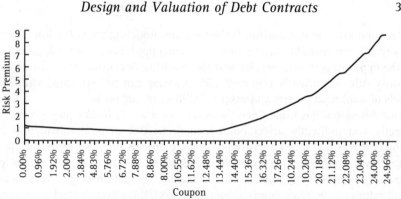

Figure 7. *Coupon effect on risk premium*

Note: This figure examines the effect of increasing the coupon rate on risk premium. We assume that the debt has 10 years to maturity, beta = 0.10, and face = 0.30. The liquidation cost is assumed to be 10 percent and the variance is 3 percent. Riskless rate is assumed to be 5 percent.

risk-free bond would be valued more than its face value when coupons exceed the risk-free rate. Thus an increase in β from low levels reduces the chances of this occurring and thus reduces required yield spreads. However, increases in β also imply that the growth prospects of the project are worsened.[11] Thus a high β project will not be cash constrained initially; however, it has a relatively high possibility of falling in value, pushing the project into the range where owner-managers will engage in opportunistic violation of the terms of the debt contract. In other words, extending high levels of long-term, fixed interest credit to today's cash cows is a risky business that should command a significant yield spread.

Figure 7 represents the relationship between required spreads and coupon level for debt with given principal and maturity. Again yield spreads at first decrease and later increase as the coupon is increased from 0 to 25 percent. This reflects two effects that operate in different directions. First, increasing the coupon increases the range of states in which a violation of an indenture is likely to occur. However, instead of unambiguously working in favor of the bondholder, the violation of the covenant presents the bondholder with a difficult choice. Either he initiates legal action and thereby incurs a deadweight loss, or he accepts the debt service the owner is willing or able to pay. Since accepting is often the better choice, the owner can take advantage of this to default opportunistically, that is, by increasing the range of outcomes where the debt will not be fully serviced. The second, opposite effect is that a positive coupon in some states results in bank-ruptcy for reasons of illiquidity. These forced liquidations in part can help the bondholder in cutting off a possible future of opportunistic debt service by the owner-manager. In effect the positive coupons combined with a no-asset-sale clause serves as a credible commitment by bondholders to require debt service.

[11] The probability of a 'down' move is $1 - p = (u - r(1 - \beta))/(u - d)$ which is increasing in β.

To summarize, in comparison to the previous models in the valuation literature surveyed in the introductory section, our model produces higher risk premia due to the opportunistic debt service and the resulting deviations from the absolute priority rule. Empirically observed yield spreads can be replicated with lower levels of bankruptcy costs and asset volatilities in our model.

Our discussion has underlined the ways that a costly bankruptcy process can directly and indirectly affect bond valuations. One general thread that runs through this is that a more costly bankruptcy process provides greater scope for opportunistic debt service since the bondholder will hesitate to initiate legal action. The corollary of this is that increasing liquidation costs which depress bond values can increase equity values. Of course, this effect depends crucially on the incidence of bankruptcy costs which in our model fall on the bondholder. The effect is also tempered to the extent there is a positive probability of forced liquidation. We explore these issues below in our treatment of the design of contract terms. Before doing so, however, we consider how valuation is affected by the introduction of corporate taxes.

2.3. Corporate Taxes

We have already noted that the framework that we have introduced could be modified without changing the essential valuation methodology. In particular, recent literature on financial distress provides a rich array of one-shot bankruptcy models that could substitute for that in Section 2. We view understanding the dynamic implications of such models a very worthwhile line of inquiry, but we will not attempt this here. Instead, we consider only a slight modification of our model. In particular, we model an extremely simple tax code where corporate earnings are taxed at a flat rate of τ but where all interest payments are tax deductible. In this context, equity valuation in the absence of forced liquidation involves replacing Equation (5) with

$$E(V_t) = (f_t - S(V_t))(1 - \tau) + \frac{pE(uV_t) + (1-p)E(dV_{t+1})}{r} \tag{8}$$

for $t < T$. At maturity, $E_T = (1 - \beta)V_T + (f_T - s_T cP)(1 - \tau) - s_T P$ where $s_T = S(V_T)/(1 + c)P$. In the case of forced liquidation, tax liabilities on current earnings are deducted before calculating liquidation values. This is the only way bond valuations are modified. Since this tax liability $\tau \beta V_t$ is small relative to V_{t_1} introducing taxes will have little effect on equilibrium debt service strategies. Taxes will mean, however, that modifications of the terms of the debt contract can have different impacts on equity values depending on the tax rates applied. Thus taxes change bond valuation little but can be an important consideration in determining optimal contract terms.

3. DESIGN OF DEBT CONTRACTS

A problem of security design emerges when an inappropriate choice of contract features can result in inefficiencies, that is, a loss of aggregate value for the contracting parties. An optimal financial contract minimizes these inefficiencies subject possibly to certain constraints. The literature on security design has considered several alternative sources of contracting inefficiency. Examples include incomplete risk sharing [Allen and Gale (1988)], inefficient information acquisition [Boot and Thakor (1993)], and inefficient allocation of control rights [Aghion and Bolton (1992)].

In our framework, the security design problem originates from inefficiencies in the process for managing financial distress. Specifically, they arise through costly liquidations which we have seen may be possible outcomes in equilibrium. This feature of our model is similar to other treatments emphasizing control rights [see, in particular, Aghion and Bolton (1992) and Hart and Moore (1991)]. In this related literature and in our model, debt is chosen despite its possible inefficiencies because the alternative forms of financial contracting such as all outside equity, will imply inefficiencies or agency costs of their own which may exceed those of debt. However, unlike these models, our framework allows us to explore in detail the choice of the terms of the debt contract, taking into account their full dynamic implications in a stochastic setting. Consequently, we are closer to the practical design problem faced by companies issuing debt.

Formally, a change in the contract specification affects the game form faced by the contracting parties. The problem is to choose the contractual features so as to minimize the inefficiencies that emerge in the associated equilibrium. With many periods and possible states of the world, the design problem is likely to admit a great multiplicity of solutions unless some structure is placed on the set of possible contracts.[12] We consider contracts where contractual debt service is time dependent, but not state dependent, and all control rights remain with the owner-manager unless there is a default on contractual terms that induces the debtholders to proceed with liquidation. Further, we focus on four features: (1) coupon, (2) maturity, (3) face amount, and (4) the amortization schedule. These features allow us to model a large variety of contract forms encountered in practice. However, the treatment of convertible and callable bonds is left for future work.

Contract terms are modeled as follows. Let P_t be the outstanding principal amount of the bond in period t, T be the maturity date of the bond, c be the coupon, A_t be the principal amount that is amortized in period t and g be the grace period in years, that is, the number of years before amortization is included in scheduled debt service. The index t refers to the number of years elapsed since the issue date. Then the contracted payments to the creditors are $CS_t = cP_t + A_t$, where $P_t = P_{t-1} - A_{t-1}$. The amortization is computed as follows: $A_t = 0$,

---

[12] Hart and Moore (1991) working in a certainty setting find multiple solutions, which leads them to introduce some restrictions on contract forms.

if $t \leq g$ and $A_t = P/(T - g)$, otherwise. By setting $g = T - 1$, we get straight coupon debt, which has zero coupon debt as a special case. Generally, this specification permits sinking fund schedules with different grace periods and purely amortizing debt.[13]

In the design problem the owner-manager selects the vector (c, T, P, g) so as to maximize the value of the equity subject to constraint that the value of the debt be at least equal to the funding requirement for undertaking the project. This choice will be guided by the primitives of the firm which are (1) the payout factor β, (2) the liquidation costs K, (3) the amount of money that the firm needs to raise in the debt market D, (4) the volatility of the firm σ^2, and (5) the tax rate τ. Thus the problem is

$$\max_{c,T,P,g} E(V_0; \sigma^2, \beta, r, K, \tau)$$

such that

$$D \leq B(V_0; \sigma^2, \beta, r, K, \tau).$$

Here both E and B are given by the equilibrium values in the game implied by the contract. As seen above, the equilibrium generally will not be first-best efficient because it will typically result in forced liquidations in some future states. The solution to the security design problem may also be *ex ante* inefficient in the sense that positive net present value projects may not be undertaken. This will occur when it is not possible to write a debt issue valuable enough to meet the funding requirement. The solution will be second-best optimal when the corporate tax rate is zero. This is because the model has a basic value preservation property so that the value of equity equals the asset value of the firm less the value of debt less the value of expected future liquidation costs plus the value of future tax shields. Thus absent taxes, the problem reduces to minimizing liquidation costs subject to a funding constraint.

This design problem does not admit of analytical solutions in non-trivial cases, and its numerical solution is itself rather time-consuming.[14] We report here the results of two sets of design experiments. The first restricts the contracts to be nonamortizing bonds and varies the payout rate, β; the liquidation costs, K; and the debt ratio, D. The second focuses on the relationship between the speed of amortization and the remaining parameters.

The results of the first experiment are summarized in Table 3. Each row reports the optimal contract for a given combination of β, K, D, and T. We describe the optimal contract by the contractual interest payment expressed as a percent of the value of debt and report the associated value of equity.

---

[13] A term annuity is taken as the limiting case as principal tends toward zero and coupon is adjusted to maintain cP constant.

[14] Our program written in C produces the results for Table 4 in about 72 hours on a RISC 6000 machine.

Table 3. *Optimal design of debt contracts* ($V = 1, \tau = 0.10, r = 1.05$)

Debt ratio	β	Coupon (%)	Equity
Time to maturity = 5 years			
Liquidation cost = 0.1			
0.250	0.040	3.69	0.66470
0.250	0.060	5.25	0.65648
0.250	0.080	7.69	0.64992
0.250	0.100	7.80	0.64380
0.500	0.040	2.58	0.42695
0.500	0.060	4.44	0.41670
0.500	0.080	5.44	0.41174
0.500	0.100	5.60	0.40583
Liquidation cost = 0.2			
0.250	0.040	3.71	0.61797
0.250	0.060	5.67	0.60799
0.250	0.080	7.71	0.60086
0.250	0.100	9.67	0.59649
0.500	0.040	3.00	0.39859
0.500	0.060	0.43	0.38694
0.500	0.080	5.43	0.38262
0.500	0.100	7.36	0.38149
Time to maturity = 10 years			
Liquidation cost = 0.1			
0.250	0.040	2.55	0.67233
0.250	0.060	3.93	0.66082
0.250	0.080	4.73	0.65229
0.250	0.100	5.94	0.64701
0.500	0.040	4.85	0.43718
0.500	0.060	6.59	0.41544
0.500	0.080	3.17	0.40767
0.500	0.100	8.99	0.39768
Liquidation cost = 0.2			
0.250	0.040	3.32	0.64787
0.250	0.060	5.17	0.63919
0.250	0.080	7.12	0.63675
0.250	0.100	8.85	0.63431
0.500	0.040	2.09	0.41478
0.500	0.060	3.78	0.40842
0.500	0.080	5.24	0.40157
0.500	0.100	8.00	0.35585

The most striking pattern in Table 3 is that as the payout rate β increases, the contractual interest increases and the value of equity decreases. To interpret this it is important to recall that the payout rate determines the expected growth rate of the asset value of the firm: the higher β the slower growth in the asset value of the firm. Fast-growing, that is, low β, firms favor relatively low interest burdens because this reduces the chances of an early forced liquidation that would deny the owner the benefits of future growth. In doing so they forego the tax shield benefits that would be associated with higher contractual interest. As we consider progressively slower growing firms, balancing the trade-off leads to higher and higher interest payments. The cash cow (the high β firm with poor growth prospects) chooses a relatively higher interest burden because the value of the near-term tax shield is substantial and the prospect of a near-term illiquidity default is less daunting because cash is relatively abundant and the future cut off by such a default is less bright. The value of equity with the optimal contract is a decreasing function of β because most of the benefits of a high growth rate accrue to equity.

The effect of leverage on contract design is seen by comparing the cases of $D = 0.25$ and $D = 0.5$, holding other parameters constant. In most cases the firm with the higher leverage selects a lower level of contractual interest. The reason is that higher leverage tends to make forced liquidation in advance of maturity more likely. The firm can offset this by decreasing contractual interest payments. This appears to be the dominant effect, but as is often the case in the comparative statics of bond valuation, other effects are present that can sometimes dominate. In particular, for $T = 10$ and $K = 0.1$ higher leverage is associated with higher interest. By raising interest payments the firm is able to increase the tax shield benefits which are substantial for the highly levered firm. This plus the reduced probability of default at maturity are sufficient to compensate the heightened prospect of an early illiquidity default.

From Table 3 we also see that the value of equity with the optimal design is decreasing the cost of liquidation. This might at first seem surprising because our game form allowed equity holders to extract a surplus by reducing debt service by an amount determined by liquidation costs. Here we see that some of the burden of *realized* liquidation costs falls on equity. The reason is that such liquidations sometimes occur when liquidation values exceed the face value of debt so that equity holders benefit from smaller liquidation costs.

The last point to be made with reference to Table 3 is that equity is higher for $T = 10$ than for $T = 5$ for most of the cases. Here firms tend to prefer to issue longer-term debt rather than shorter-term debt, because with nonamortizing debt there is relatively high chance of liquidation at maturity. The longer this is forestalled the better. Again this is not the only effect at work, as can be seen in the case of higher leverage, higher β firms with lower liquidation costs. For a sufficiently high β the firm is expected to shrink with time. If so, repayment of principal is more problematic with long-term debt than short-term debt.

In this first experiment the sensitivities with respect to several parameters reflected two considerations, namely, the implications for the tax shield and for the probability of liquidation. For example, raising coupon interest brings carry tax benefits, but its effect on default is ambiguous. By reducing the principal needed to produce a debt of given value, higher coupon reduces the chances of difficulties in repaying the loan at maturity. But it raises the chances of provoking an illiquidity default prior to maturity. This suggests that there may be some advantages to considering designs that involve some amortization of principal or of a sinking fund. We explore this in a second design experiment in which we consider various possible values of the grace period before starting a straight-line amortization of principal. Other parameters considered are T, β, and D.

The general result that emerges from this experiment is that optimal debt contracts will typically require partial repayments of principal prior to maturity, but that it is often beneficial to delay the start of repayments of principal. This is depicted clearly in Figure 8. Here, as the grace period is increased, we see the highest value of equity that is attainable by varying coupon and principal so as to produce debt that meets the funding requirement. It can be seen that the equity increases until $g = 7$, beyond which it declines. The reason for this is that by setting grace too low, amortization will start too early, reducing the tax shield that comes exclusively from the payments of interest. On the other hand, by allowing too long a period of grace, the debt service payments toward the end of the life of the bond are relatively heavy. This runs a relatively great risk of provoking a liquidation. The optimal grace period balances these two considerations.

The second experiment is further reported in Table 4, which lists the optimal grace and contractual interest as well as the associated value of equity attained. Making the grace period an object of design choice of course has implications for the optimal contractual interest, and this alters significantly some of the patterns

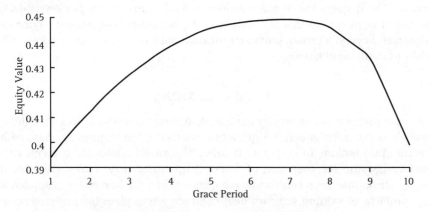

Figure 8. *Optimal design of debt contracts*

Note: This figure examines the effect of sinking fund provisions on equity values. We assume that the debt has 10 years to maturity, beta = 0.10, and the debt level $d = 0.50$. The optimal grace period is 7 years.

Table 4. *Optimal design of debt contracts* $(\tau = 0.1, K = 0.1)$

T	β	D	g	Contractual interest (%)	Equity
5	0.04	0.25	5	3.69	0.66470
5	0.04	0.50	5	2.58	0.42695
5	0.10	0.25	4	3.45	0.64814
5	0.10	0.50	4	0.98	0.44243
10	0.04	0.25	9	2.42	0.67808
10	0.04	0.50	8	1.77	0.45896
10	0.10	0.25	9	0.81	0.66795
10	0.10	0.50	7	3.51	0.44917

seen in Table 3. In particular, in most cases we see that the higher values of β are associated with lower values of contractual interest. This result emerges because in these cases the higher β firms select contracts with shorter grace periods. That is, slower growth firms choose to begin repaying principal earlier in order to reduce the chances of realizing costly bankruptcies as the project matures. This may be desirable even if it implies that coupon levels must be kept moderate so that tax shield benefits are sacrificed.

In our view, our findings on amortizing debt provide a rationale for the widely observed use of sinking funds in corporate bond issues. We see that the optimal sinking fund feature balances off tax shield benefits with potential costs of financial distress that can fall on shareholders. Furthermore, despite the fact that we have not explicitly dealt with monitored financial contracts, our model helps explain the frequent use of grace periods in bank loans. Again, borrowers delay principal payments so that they can reap the tax benefits of interest payments. However, beyond a certain point amortization must begin in order to control the risks of costly liquidations.

4. CONCLUSIONS

We have presented an internally consistent, arbitrage-free framework for valuing risky debt contracts which incorporates a number of the features emphasized in recent contributions to corporate finance. The model allows for strategic debt service because the costliness of formal bankruptcy may induce creditors to accept deviations from contractual payments. When the framework is applied to the problem of valuing standard debt contracts using plausible parameters, we find yield spreads over Treasuries that correspond closely to observed levels even if costs of bankruptcy are relatively low. This suggests that the framework offers promise for the econometric modeling of spreads of corporate bonds and other risky debt contracts.

Our framework is flexible enough to allow altering assumptions about contractual features, bankruptcy procedures, or other aspects of the economic environment. We examined a model variant with corporate taxes. Other bankruptcy games seen in the static theory of corporate finance could be introduced into our dynamic framework at the cost of adding parameters and computational complexity.

The framework is used to address the question of debt contract design, that is, to find the combination of contractual features that minimize the combined tax burden and expected bankruptcy costs. Our results show that high growth (low β) firms in general tend to use a low coupon debt contract. On the other hand, low growth firms tend to use a high coupon debt contract. Although not reported here, as the tax rate increases, firms tend to increase the coupons to take advantage of the tax shield from interest payments. Highly levered firms tend to use low coupon debt. In general, sinking fund provisions are used so as to better match the cash payout from the assets: here the trade-offs are between tax shields and forced liquidations.

In our view, there is considerable opportunity for additional work along the lines of the framework we have developed here. In particular, the extension of the model to callable and convertible debt and the incorporation of a stochastic term structure would be very desirable. Second, it is clear that the modeling of the bankruptcy game could have an important impact on the results. The game form that we have adopted gives a first-mover advantage to the owner-manager with the result that he has the most scope for opportunism. Other models of bankruptcy might alter the distribution of the gains from renegotiation.[15] Changing the bankruptcy model is very likely to have important implications for optimal security design. For example, in our model strategic debt service tends to reduce the frequency of illiquidity default. Models with less scope for renegotiation may result in lower coupons or greater reliance on sinking funds. Finally, we believe that the valuation of subordinated debt and the issue of traded debt versus bank loans could be usefully studied within a framework similar to the one we have used here.

Appendix

This appendix shows that the martingale probability which makes the cash flow process internally consistent with the cum cash flow value process of the firm is given by $p = ((1 - \beta)r - d)/(u - d)$. The proof is provided for two time steps: it is easy to verify that the arguments go through for any number of future time periods.

The cum cash flow value process is specified below. The associated cash flow process is obtained by simply multiplying the cum cash flow values at each node by the factor β.

---

[15] Interesting alternative simplified models can be found in Aghion, Hart, and Moore (1992), Bergman and Callen (1991), Hart and Moore (1991), and Kahn and Huberman (1989).

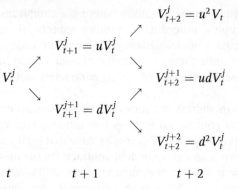

$$V_{t+2}^j = u^2 V_t$$

$$V_{t+1}^j = uV_t^j$$

$$V_t^j$$

$$V_{t+2}^{j+1} = udV_t^j$$

$$V_{t+1}^{j+1} = dV_t^j$$

$$V_{t+2}^{j+2} = d^2 V_t^j$$

$$t \qquad\qquad t+1 \qquad\qquad t+2$$

Let p be martingale probability. Then,

$$V_{t+1}^j = \frac{pV_{t+2}^j + (1-p)V_{t+2}^{j+1}}{r} + \beta V_{t+1}^j.$$

Recognizing that $V_{t+2}^j = uV_{t+1}^j$ and $V_{t+2}^{j+1} = dV_{t+1}^j$ and substituting these relationships in the previous equation we get

$$r(1 - \beta) = pu + (1 - p)d.$$

Solving, we get

$$p = \frac{r(1 - \beta) - d}{u - d}.$$

Note that the same relationship holds for p in each step of the recursion. The martingale probability p is also state independent. It is useful to point out that $\partial p / \partial \beta = -r/(u - d)$. This implies that as the cash payout increases, the martingale probability p falls: this will have the effect of giving greater weight to cash flows in relatively 'poorer' states of the world and lesser weight to 'richer' states of the world in the discounting process. This occurs in our model so as to keep the cum cash flow value of the firm the same, *irrespective of the payout*. Note that this effect becomes less important as σ^2 increases; this is due to the fact that as σ^2 increases $(u - d)$ increases as well, causing p to depend less on the payout factor β. Thus, in our model, as the volatility of the firm increases, the payout factor β becomes less important in affecting the martingale probability. These factors play a role in the valuation of alternate debt contracts.

REFERENCES

Aghion, P., and P. Bolton, 1992, 'An Incomplete Contracts Approach to Financial Contracting,' *Review of Economic Studies*, 59, 473–494.

Aghion, P., O. Hart, and J. Moore, 1992, 'The Economics of Bankruptcy Reform,' Working Paper 148, LSE Financial Markets Group.

Allen, F., and D. Gale, 1988, 'Optimal Security Design,' *Review of Financial Studies*, 1, 229–263.

Asquith, P., R. Gertner, and D. Scharfstein, 1991, 'Anatomy of Financial Distress: An Examination of Junk Bond Issuers,' working paper, Massachusetts Institute of Technology.

Bergman, Y., and J. Callen, 1991, 'Opportunistic Underinvestment in Debt Renegotiation and Capital Structure,' *Journal of Financial Economics*, 29, 137–171.

Black, P., and M. Scholes, 1973, 'The Pricing of Options and Corporate Liabilities,' *Journal of Political Economy*, 81, 637–654.

Bolton, P., and D. Scharfstein, 1993, 'Optimal Debt Structures with Multiple Creditors,' Working Paper 32, ESP Network in Financial Markets.

Boot, A. W. A., and A. V. Thakor, 1993, 'Security Design,' *Journal of Finance*, 48, 1349–1378.

Dewatripont, M., and J. Tirole, 1992, 'A Theory of Debt and Equity: Creditor Diversity and Manager-Shareholder Congruence,' working paper, ECARE.

Franks, J., and K. Nyborg, 1993, Debt Structure and the Loss of Private Benefit: the Case of the UK Insolvency Code,' working paper, London Business School.

—, and W. Torous, 1989, 'An Empirical Investigation of Firms in Reorganization,' *Journal of Finance*, 44, 747–779.

—, —, 1993, 'A Comparison of Financial Recontracting in Workouts and Chapter 11 Reorganizations,' Working paper 26, ESP Finance Network (forthcoming *Journal of Financial Economics*).

Fudenberg, D., and J. Tirole, 1985, Preemption and Rent Equalization in the Adoption of New Technology, *Review of Economic Studies*, 52, 383–401.

Harrison, J. M., and D. M. Kreps, 1978, 'Martingales and Arbitrage in Multiperiod Security Markets,' *Journal of Economic Theory*, 20, 381–408.

Hart, O., and J. Moore, 1991, 'A Theory of Debt Based on the Inalienability of Human Capital,' LSE Financial Markets Group Discussion Paper Series.

Jensen, M. C., and W. Meckling, 1976, 'The Theory of the Firm: Managerial Behavior,' Agency Cost, and Ownership Structure,' *Journal of Financial Economics*, 3, 305–360.

Jones, E. P., S. P. Mason, and E. Rosenfeld, 1984, 'Contingent Claims Analysis of Corporate Capital Structures: An Empirical Analysis,' *Journal of Finance*, 39, 611–625.

Kahn, C., and G. Huberman, 1989, 'Default, Foreclosure, and Strategic Renegotiation,' *Law and Contemporary Problems*, 52, 49–61.

Kim, I. J., K. Ramaswamy, and S. M. Sundaresan, 1993, 'Valuation of Corporate Fixed-Income Securities,' *Financial Management*, Special Issue on Financial Distress, Autumn, 117–131.

Leland, H., 1993, 'Risky Debt, Bond Covenants and Optimal Capital Structure,' working paper, University of California, Berkeley.

Maloney, K. J., 1992, 'A Contingent Claims Model of Corporate Security Valuation using a Realistic Model of Financial Distress,' working paper, Dartmouth University.

Mella-Barral, P., and W. R. M. Perraudin, 1993, 'Strategic Debt Service,' Working Paper No. 39, Center for Economic Policy Research, London.

Mello, A., and J. Parsons, 1992, 'Measuring the Agency Cost of Debt,' *Journal of Finance*, 47, 1887–1904.

Merton, R. C., 1974, 'On the Pricing of Corporate Debt: The Risk Structure of Interest Rates', *Journal of Finance*, 29, 449–470.

Myers, S., 1977, 'Determinants of Corporate Borrowing,' *Journal of Financial Economics*, 5, 147–175.

Salomon Brothers, 1992, *Analytical Record of Yields and Yield Spreads*, Salomon Brothers, New York.

Standard and Poors, 1982, *Credit Overview*, Standard and Poors, New York.

Weiss, L., 1990, 'Bankruptcy Resolution: Direct Costs and Violation of Priority of Claims,' *Journal of Financial Economics*, 27, 285–314.

Zender, J., 1991, 'Optimal Financial Instruments,' *Journal of Finance*, 46, 1645–1663.

11

Foreign Equity Investment Restrictions, Capital Flight, and Shareholder Wealth Maximization: Theory and Evidence

RENÉ M. STULZ AND WALTER WASSERFALLEN

In many countries, foreign investors face restrictions on owning domestic shares.[1] In some countries, such as Japan, these restrictions are imposed by law; in others, such as Switzerland, they are chosen by individual companies. In the United States and a number of other countries, foreign ownership restrictions which are binding only in rare cases in which a control contest is initiated by a foreign bidder exist in some industries. In other countries, such as Switzerland, Finland, or Thailand, ownership restrictions are almost always binding for the firms affected. Whereas legislated restrictions are sometimes motivated by a desire to preserve the independence of local industries, possibly because of national defense concerns, such a motivation cannot explain binding restrictions imposed by individual firms. In this paper, we propose a theory of foreign equity investment restrictions which shows conditions under which the imposition of binding ownership restrictions maximizes firm value. Although we are aware of models that study how foreign equity investment restrictions affect share prices and explain why unrestricted shares generally trade at a premium relative to the restricted shares, we do not know of any theory explaining why such restrictions exist.[2]

In this paper, we test our theory using data from Switzerland. The Swiss case is a promising testing ground because it is a country where one major firm, Nestlé,

We are grateful for comments from Kee-Hong Bae, Warren Bailey, Bhagwan Chowdry, Richard Green (the editor), Jeff Harris, David Hyland, Bong-Chan Kho, Darrell Lee, Claudio Loderer, John McConnell, James Tompkins, and Justin Wood, an anonymous referee, and participants at seminars at Harvard University, the Ohio State University, the University of North Carolina, the University of St.-Gallen, the University of Vienna, the 1992 meetings of the French Finance Association, the 1992 meetings of the American Finance Association, and the Northwestern Conference on Globalization and the Financial Services Industry. Address correspondence to René M. Stulz, Department of Finance, Fisher College of Business, The Ohio State University, 1775 S. College Road, Columbus, OH 43210.

[1] Eun and Janakiramanan (1986) provide a partial list of such restrictions.

[2] See Stulz (1981) for a general model of barriers to international investment. Eun and Janakiramanan (1986) analyze the effect of equity ownership restrictions on the pricing of shares when the fraction of shares that can be held by foreign investors is the same for all shares in a country.

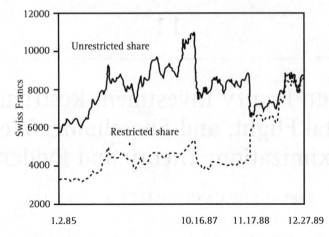

Figure 1. *Prices of Nestlé restricted and unrestricted shares*

Note: Wednesday closing Swiss francs prices of Nestlé unrestricted and restricted shares from 1/2/85 to 12/27/89 are used. Unrestricted shares are bearer shares that can be held by all investors irrespective of their residence or nationality. Restricted shares are registered shares that can only be held by resident investors until 11/17/88 but have the same voting rights and dividend payments as bearer shares. After 11/77/88, Nestlé allows all investors to hold registered shares. The stock market crashed on 10/16/87.

relaxed ownership restrictions during our sample period. Figure 1 shows the main empirical facts that a good theory should explain, using share prices of Nestlé as an example. The facts are (1) firms impose binding ownership restrictions willingly; (2) shares with restrictions trade at a substantially lower price than comparable shares without restrictions; (3) an increase in the supply of unrestricted shares associated with the relaxation of restrictions decreases the price of unrestricted shares; and (4) firms that have ownership restrictions sometimes choose to eliminate them. Our theory is consistent with this empirical evidence. In contrast, alternative theories which focus on the pricing of shares in the presence of ownership restrictions are consistent only with the second empirical fact, namely the premium on unrestricted shares.

Our basic argument is that if the demand functions for domestic shares differ for foreign and domestic investors, a firm seeking financing by issuing shares will find it advantageous to price discriminate between the two classes of buyers by selling shares at different prices to domestic and foreign investors. In our model, demand functions for domestic shares differ between domestic and foreign investors because investors bear deadweight costs for holding risky assets which

Hietala (1989) has a model where domestic investors cannot hold foreign shares and foreign investors can hold a limited quantity of domestic shares. Horner (1986) studies restrictions on foreign equity investment when restrictions can be bypassed at a cost. Errunza and Losq (1985, 1989) have a model where investors can invest in an unrestricted market and some investors can invest in a restricted market.

differ across investors and across countries. Examples of such deadweight costs might be withholding taxes, political risks, transaction costs, or information acquisition costs. If, as a result of these costs, the demand for shares from domestic investors is more price elastic than the demand from foreign investors, the shares available to foreign investors trade at a premium relative to the shares available to domestic investors.[3]

The model we develop differs from existing models with deadweight costs in two important respects. First, we allow deadweight costs to vary across investors within a country. Second, some foreign investors face deadweight costs on assets held in their country of residence. With these two extensions, the domestic country can benefit from capital flight, which is defined in the literature as 'the acquisition . . . of a claim on nonresidents that is motivated by the owner's concern that the value of his asset would be subject to discrete losses if his claim continued to be held' in his country of residence.[4] In other words, some foreign investors may choose to hold more domestic assets in their portfolios than the domestic market's share in the world market portfolio. Such overweighting could be explained by fear of expropriation, a demand for secrecy, advantageous tax treatment, and so on. The literature on international portfolio choice has ignored capital flight, which is surprising given its economic importance and given the attention paid to it in the international economics literature.[5] Our paper is the first paper in the international portfolio choice and asset pricing literature that takes capital flight into account and is consistent with the simultaneous existence of a home bias in asset holdings for most investors and of capital flight from some investors.

We show that our model can explain the empirical evidence when (1) there is a home bias in the asset holdings of foreign investors and only a subset of foreign investors hold domestic shares and (2) the foreign investors who invest in the domestic country face greater deadweight costs in their home country than in the domestic country. There is substantial evidence that the first condition is generally met because relatively few investors take advantage of international diversification.[6] The second condition implies that countries benefiting from capital flight are countries where binding foreign ownership restrictions maximize firm value. With this second condition, capital flight leads some foreign investors to value the payoffs of domestic shares more than domestic investors so that foreign investors are willing to buy domestic shares at a premium. The home bias condition ensures that foreign investors have a demand for domestic shares that is less price elastic than the demand from domestic investors.

---

[3] Whereas it is traditional in finance to assume that the demand for shares by investors is perfectly elastic, it is now recognized that this assumption is not always appropriate. See Bagwell (1991) for a review of some evidence on the imperfect elasticity of demand curves for shares and for a discussion of the implications of the evidence. Loderer and Zimmermann (1988) provide evidence that the demand for Swiss shares is downward sloping by studying the price reaction to stock issues.

[4] See Deppler and Williamson (1987, p. 41). Williamson and Lessard (1987) review some of the definitions used in the literature.   [5] See Williamson and Lessard (1987) for additional references.

[6] See, for instance, French and Poterba (1991) and Cooper and Kaplanis (1994).

Though not all countries benefit from capital flight, Switzerland is surely one that has benefited from it. Historically, investors have been attracted to Switzerland by the lack of political risk, the bank secrecy, the low purchasing power risk, and the fact that tax fraud is not a penal violation so that foreign tax authorities receive limited help in pursuing tax fraud cases involving Swiss bank accounts. Walter (1990, p. 205) argues that 'the amount of flight capital in Swiss banks was around 100 billion SFr in 1984,' but there is wide variation in estimates. For instance, Walter (1990) shows that estimates of French funds invested in Switzerland following the accession of Mitterrand to power range from $3.75 billion to $60 billion and estimates of Ferdinand Marcos' holdings in Switzerland when he left the Philippines have ranged from less than $100 million to $15 billion. Interestingly, one would expect that China does not benefit from capital flight and does not, therefore, meet our conditions for a premium on unrestricted shares. Evidence that shares of Chinese companies that can be held by foreign investors sell at substantial discounts relative to the shares of the same companies that can only be bought by resident investors could therefore also be viewed as evidence supporting our model.[7]

Our theory helps to understand the evolution of share ownership restrictions. As the foreign demand for domestic shares changes, firms find it advantageous to modify the extent to which foreign investors can acquire domestic shares. In particular, if the price elasticity of the demand from foreign investors increases sufficiently, for example, because of greater integration of international financial markets, it may become optimal to remove all restrictions on share ownership. With our model, unexpectedly removing share ownership restrictions can decrease the value of the unrestricted shares substantially. This prediction differs drastically from the prediction obtained from international asset pricing models without deadweight costs, which suggest that the removal of restrictions has only a marginal effect on the price of unrestricted shares. It is consistent, however, with the evidence on Nestlé presented in Figure 1 and discussed further later.[8]

The paper proceeds as follows. In Section 1, we present our model and derive its empirical implications. In Section 2, we present our data for Switzerland. In Section 3, we show how the time-series and cross-sectional properties of the data are consistent with our theory. In Section 4, we demonstrate that the change in the price of Nestlé shares around the announcement concerning the relaxation of its foreign equity restrictions is supportive of our theory. In Section 5, we provide some concluding remarks.

1. A THEORY OF FOREIGN EQUITY INVESTMENT RESTRICTIONS

In Section 1.1, we show how the general results of the literature on price discrimination apply in the context of this paper. In Section 1.2, we provide a

---

[7] See Bailey (1994) for empirical evidence on this issue.

[8] Loderer and Jacobs (1994), in a contemporaneous paper, show that the evidence associated with the Nestlé announcement is consistent with the existence of finite demand elasticities.

detailed analysis of the conditions under which discrimination results in a higher price for shares available to foreign investors for the simple case where there is only one domestic firm. In Section 1.3, the pricing results of Section 1.2 are extended to the case of many domestic firms. Finally, in Section 1.4, we compare the implications of our theory with the implications of the argument that ownership restrictions exist for corporate control reasons.

1.1. Price Discrimination and Ownership Restrictions

It is well known from microeconomics that a firm selling a good to consumers with different demand functions can increase its income through price discrimination.[9] The literature, following Pigou (1920), distinguishes between various types of price discrimination. One type is called *perfect price discrimination* and occurs when the seller can extract the surplus of each consumer. The more relevant type of price discrimination is the one in which consumers differ according to observable characteristics and the seller charges different prices to buyers with different observable characteristics. This type of price discrimination is called *third-degree price discrimination*. If consumer characteristics differ predictably according to their country of origin, discrimination according to country of origin benefits the seller. This is true irrespective of the nature of the good sold, as long as the seller can charge different prices to buyers from different countries. For prices to differ across countries, though, the seller must be able to prevent buyers in countries where the price is high from buying where the price is low and buyers in countries where the price is low from reselling where the price is high. Hence, for discrimination to be implemented for securities, the issuing firm must be able to prevent sales of securities from investors of one country to investors of another country.

There are many reasons to believe that demands for assets differ across countries. For instance, investors from different countries have different tax rates for identical securities and face different degrees of political risk. One would therefore expect to observe cases where price discrimination occurs. What remains to be seen is whether price discrimination can explain the widely observed fact that securities available to foreign investors typically sell at a higher price than those available to domestic investors only.

To derive the conditions under which it is optimal for a domestic firm to discriminate by charging a higher price to foreign investors than to domestic investors, we consider a domestic entrepreneur who wants to maximize the proceeds from selling his firm's shares. There is no other firm in the domestic country and there is only one foreign asset in the simple two-date model. Both the domestic country and the foreign country have the same numeraire, so that there is no exchange rate risk. The firm pays a liquidating dividend Sp at date 1, where

---

[9] See Tirole (1988) for an exposition of the theory of price discrimination.

S is the number of shares and p is the random payoff per share. The entrepreneur must decide how to divide the S shares between S_R restricted R shares available to domestic residents only, and S_U unrestricted U shares available to foreign investors only.[10] The U and R shares differ only in their ownership restrictions and thus receive the same liquidating payoff p. The distribution of p does not depend on how the shares are divided between U and R shares. The foreign asset, asset F, pays a random liquidating dividend at date 1 of p_F per share. There is a risk-free asset which pays interest of r at date 1 per unit invested. P_a denotes the price of asset a, $a = R, U, F$, at date 0. The model is a partial equilibrium model in the sense that P_F, the distribution of p_F, and r are fixed and do not depend on the solution of the entrepreneur's maximization problem. Hence, the entrepreneur's decision to discriminate against foreign investors does not result in price discrimination abroad against domestic investors. We discuss later the implications of relaxing this assumption. The partial equilibrium perspective is the analog of the small country assumption used in international economics where, for small countries, prices abroad are taken as given.

Let $D_a = D_a(P_a)$ be the demand for asset a, and assume that the demand function is differentiable with respect to P_a for $D_a(P_a) > 0$. With this notation, the entrepreneur's proceeds from selling his shares are

$$V = D_R P_R + D_U P_U. \tag{1}$$

To maximize V, the entrepreneur chooses S_R and S_U so that the market for R and U shares is in equilibrium, $D_R(P_R) = S_R$ and $D_U(P_U) = S_U$, the supply of R and U shares equals the supply of shares available, $S_R + S_U = S$, and the asset supplies are nonnegative, $S_R \geq 0$ and $S_U \geq 0$. With our assumptions, the maximization problem of the entrepreneur differs from the problem usually examined in the finance literature. The entrepreneur here is a monopolist in the capital market and faces a downward-sloping demand curve for the firm's shares on a risk-adjusted basis. There are no perfect substitutes for the securities he offers for either domestic or foreign investors. If the entrepreneur supplies strictly positive quantities of R and U shares, share prices that maximize V satisfy

$$\frac{P_U}{P_R} = \left[\frac{\varepsilon_U \varepsilon_R - \varepsilon_U}{\varepsilon_U \varepsilon_R - \varepsilon_R}\right], \tag{2}$$

---

[10] We could allow domestic investors to hold unrestricted shares, but we would have to assume that they cannot sell unrestricted shares short to prevent them from selling short U shares and hedging their short-sales with long positions in R shares. In this case, domestic investors would not hold unrestricted shares in equilibria with price discrimination, since in such equilibria, U shares are dominated by R shares for domestic investors. Consequently, allowing domestic investors to hold unrestricted shares would not change our results. The model could be extended so that some domestic investors hold unrestricted shares in equilibrium by creating a class of domestic investors with deadweight costs similar to those of foreign investors. Such an extension would not affect the results of this article as long as this class of domestic investors is not too large.

where ε_a is the price elasticity of demand for shares of type a.[11] For domestic investors, therefore $\varepsilon_R = -[\partial D_R(P_R)/\partial P_R][P_R/D_R(P_R)]$. It follows from Equation (2) that

Result 1. *It is optimal for the entrepreneur to sell shares at a higher price to foreign investors if the price elasticity of the demand from foreign investors is lower than the price elasticity of the demand from domestic investors.*

In models that assume perfect markets, the price elasticity of the demand for the individual securities is generally considered to be high because of the presumption that there are many close substitutes for each individual security. Thus, the firm is typically assumed to be a price-taker with respect to the market price of risk, and, given the firm's assets, its cost of capital. In an international setting, though, the securities of the domestic country might have few close substitutes for foreign investors. This might be because the foreign investors face unattractive investment opportunities elsewhere, because there are barriers to international investment that lead them to prefer securities from their own country, or finally because domestic shares offer great diversification benefits. In the literature on international investment, deadweight costs are often used to model barriers to international investment. In the next section, we use deadweight costs to derive a model where some foreign investors face barriers to international investment and others face unattractive investment opportunities in their home country.

1.2. Pricing R and U Shares in the Presence of Deadweight Holding Costs

To obtain asset demands which differ across countries, we follow Stulz (1981) and assume that investors bear deadweight costs for holding risky assets which depend on the country of origin of investors and on the country in which an asset is traded. To allow for the simultaneous existence of a home bias in asset holdings and of capital flight, deadweight costs are allowed to differ across investors and investors bear deadweight costs for holding assets in their home country, as well as for holding assets outside their home country. To simplify the analysis, we assume that in each country, there are two classes of investors: one class faces low deadweight costs of investing abroad and the other class faces high deadweight costs of investing abroad. All investors in the same class are identical. We only consider the equilibria where (1) all investors choose to be long in securities from their own country and (2) in each country only one class of investors invests in the foreign country so that there is a home bias similar to the one observed empirically. Deadweight costs are defined as in Stulz (1981) as a fraction of the beginning-of-period investment in a security. Investor k's deadweight cost in the

---

[11] To derive Equation (2), maximize firm value given by Equation (1) with respect to prices subject to the constraints that $S = S_R + S_U, S_R = D_R(P_R), S_U = D_U(P_U), S_R \geq 0, S_U \geq 0$, and rearrange the first-order conditions.

322					R. M. Stulz and W. Wasserfallen

domestic country is C_k, and h_k is her deadweight cost in the foreign country. We assume for simplicity that deadweight costs are prohibitive on short-sales.[12] The liquidating payoffs at the end of the period do not depend on deadweight costs and are jointly normally distributed. There are no other imperfections in capital markets besides those already mentioned. Risk-free borrowing or lending is allowed for all investors at the rate r with no deadweight costs.[13]

All investors maximize

$$E[U_k(w_k)] = E[-\exp[-Aw_k]],\tag{3}$$

where w_k is the end-of-period wealth of investor k and A is her coefficient of absolute risk aversion, which is assumed to be the same for all investors. End-of-period random variables are written in lowercase letters and beginning-of-period variables are written in uppercase letters. The kth investor must satisfy the following budget constraint:

$$W_k = D_{kF}P_F + D_{ka}P_a + L_k,\tag{4}$$

where W_k is investor k's initial wealth, D_{kF} her holdings of F shares, D_{ka} her holdings of a shares, $a = U$ for a foreign investor and $a = R$ for a domestic investor, and L_k her holdings of the riskless asset. The end-of-period wealth of investor k is given by

$$w_k = D_{kF}(p_F - h_kP_F) + D_{ka}(p - c_kP_a) + (1+r)L_k.\tag{5}$$

The asset demands are obtained by maximizing Equation (3) subject to the budget constraint of Equation (4) and to the constraints that holdings of each type of shares must be nonnegative. Note that, with our assumptions, there are investors who hold no shares of a particular type because their deadweight costs for that type of share are too high. The appendix provides a derivation of the demand functions for the most general case considered in this paper. For the special case analyzed in this section, the demand for domestic shares from investor k, assuming that she holds positive amounts of domestic and foreign shares, is

$$D_{ka} = \frac{1}{(1-\rho^2)A\sigma^2}[E(p) - P_a(1+r+c_k) - \beta[E(p_F) - P_F(1+r+h_k)]],\tag{6}$$

---

[12] This assumption is made to reduce the investment in notation. As shown in Stulz (1981), without this assumption we would need to model separately long and short positions to take into account the fact that deadweight costs are positive both on long and on short positions. The assumption is not restrictive in the context of our model, since in equilibrium the foreign investors must hold the U shares long and the domestic investors must hold the R shares long if both types of shares are in positive net supply.

[13] The assumption that deadweight costs do not apply to risk-free lending and borrowing is generally made in the literature on international portfolio choice with investment barriers. A justification for this assumption might be the existence of a large offshore market for risk-free lending and borrowing, whereas there is no offshore market for equities.

where $a = U$ for a foreign investor and $a = R$ for a domestic investor, ρ is the coefficient of correlation between the payoffs of foreign shares and of domestic shares, $E(p)$ denotes the expected payoff of domestic shares, σ is the standard deviation of the payoff of domestic shares, and β is the beta coefficient of the payoff of domestic shares with respect to the payoff of F shares, $\text{cov}(p, p_F)/\text{var}(p_F)$. In this case, the demand for domestic shares of type a by investor k increases with her deadweight costs for F shares and falls with her deadweight costs for a shares. Equation (6) holds for a subset of foreign investors and a subset of domestic investors. Foreign investors with high deadweight costs for investing in the domestic country are assumed to never invest in the domestic country and consequently have no demand for domestic shares. Domestic investor j who invests only at home has the following demand for restricted shares:

$$D_{jR} = \frac{1}{A\sigma^2}\left[E(p) - P_R(1 + r + c_j)\right] \tag{7}$$

We can rewrite Equation (6) to emphasize its linearity in the domestic asset price:

$$D_{ka} = \alpha_k - \gamma_k P_a, \tag{8}$$

where

$$\alpha_k = \frac{1}{(1 - \rho^2)A\sigma^2}\left[E(p) - \beta[E(p_F) - P_F(1 + r + h_k)]\right]$$

$$\gamma_k = \frac{(1 + r + c_k)}{(1 - \rho^2)A\sigma^2}.$$

Equation (7) can be rewritten in the same way. Since all demand functions are linear, we can construct a domestic representative investor d whose demand function is a weighted average of Equations (6) and (7). Let f denote a foreign investor who invests in the domestic market. We assume that there are N_d investors of type d and N_f investors of type f.

With these assumptions, the entrepreneur chooses S_U and S_R to maximize from value V as in Section 1.1. From Equation (1), we have

$$V = D_U P_U + D_R P_R$$

$$= N_f D_{fU} P_U + N_d D_{dR} P_R$$

$$= \left(\frac{N_f \alpha_f - S_U}{N_f \gamma_f}\right) S_U + \left(\frac{N_d \alpha_d - S_R}{N_f \gamma_d}\right) S_R$$

$$= \left(\frac{N_f \alpha_f - S_U}{N_f \gamma_f}\right) S_U + \left(\frac{N_d - (S - S_U)}{N_d \gamma_d}\right)(S - S_U). \tag{9}$$

To get the second line, we replace the aggregate demands with the demands of the representative investors multiplied by the corresponding number of representative investors. We then use Equation (8) to substitute out the prices from the second line and the constraint that $S_R = S - S_U$ to obtain the last line. Note that with the definition of firm value in the last line, the only constraint on the entrepreneur's maximization problem is that $S \geq S_U \geq 0$. Solving for the optimal S_U, we get

$$S_U^* = \text{Min}\left[\frac{1}{2}\left[\frac{N_d\gamma_d N_f \alpha_f - N_d \alpha_d N_f \gamma_f + 2N_f \gamma_f S}{N_d \gamma_d + N_f \gamma_f}\right], S\right]. \tag{10}$$

If deadweight costs are the same for all investors who participate in the domestic market, the intercept and slope of the per capita asset demand functions are the same for all investors, so that there is no reason to price discriminate. In this case, $S_U^* = SN_f/(N_d + N_f) < S$, which is the first-best risk-sharing rule for the investors who participate in the domestic market. Hence, deadweight costs that depend on the country of residence of investors are a necessary condition for the optimal supply of U shares to differ from the first-best risk-sharing rule. In Equation (10), S_U^* increases with N_f and with h_f. When N_f and h_f are not too large, foreign investors as a group hold fewer domestic shares than they would in the absence of deadweight costs and the data on shareholdings exhibit a home bias. If the foreign investors who invest in the domestic country face sufficiently high deadweight costs on their home market, the degenerate case where foreign investors hold all of the firm's shares can be obtained. Henceforth, we do not consider this degenerate case.

To obtain a necessary and sufficient condition for price discrimination to maximize firm value, we now derive the difference between the price of unrestricted shares and the price of restricted shares. By substituting the optimal number of shares allocated to foreign investors from Equation (10) into Equation (8), we can solve for share prices assuming that the firm supplies positive quantities of each type of share. We obtain

$$P_U - P_R = \frac{1}{2}\left[\frac{\alpha_f}{\gamma_f} - \frac{\alpha_d}{\gamma_d}\right]. \tag{11}$$

To understand the implications of Equation (11), we define $P_a(D_a)$ as the inverse demand function for shares of type a. With this notation, $P_a(0)$ is the price corresponding to $D_a = 0$ in Equation (8), which is the price at which the linear demand function intersects the price axis in a graph of the demand function. Equation (11) implies that:

Result 2. *A necessary and sufficient condition for price discrimination to maximize firm value is that $P_R(0) \neq P_U(0)$.*

Proof. From Equation (8), $(\alpha_f/\gamma_f) = P_U(0)$ and $(\alpha_d/\gamma_d) = P_R(0)$. □

Result 2 follows in a straightforward way from Result 1 and from the linear demand functions obtained in Equation (8). Linear demand functions for which $P_R(0) = P_U(0)$ have the same elasticities because $\varepsilon_{fU} = P/[(\alpha_f/\gamma_f) - P]$ and $\varepsilon_{dR} = P/[(\alpha_d/\gamma_d) - P]$, so that $\varepsilon_{fU} = \varepsilon_{dR}$ when $(\alpha_f/\gamma_f) = (\alpha_d/\gamma_d)$ and $P_U = P_R = P$. It follows from Result 1 that if the demand functions have the same elasticities, there is no gain from price discrimination.

The empirical evidence shows that typically unrestricted shares sell at a premium. The next result provides a necessary and sufficient condition for this to be the case:

Result 3. *Firm value is maximized with $P_U > P_R$ if and only if*

$$
P_U - P_R = \frac{1}{2}[P_U(0) - P_R(0)]
$$

$$
= \frac{1}{2}\left[\frac{E(p) - \beta[E(p_F) - (1 + r + h_f)P_F]}{1 + r + c_f}\right.
$$

$$
\left. - \frac{E(p) - \beta[E(p_F) - (1 + r + h_d)P_F]}{1 + r + c_d}\right] > 0. \tag{12}
$$

Proof. Use Equation (8) to obtain the inverse demand functions and then substitute these functions in Equation (11). □

To understand better the implications of Result 3, it is useful to note first that taking the derivatives of $P_U - P_R$ with respect to the various deadweight costs shows that $P_U - P_R$ is an increasing function of c_d and h_f, and a decreasing function of c_f and h_d. Changes in deadweight costs which increase the demand of the domestic asset for one class of investors are equivalent to a decrease in the price elasticity of the demand for the domestic asset for that class of investors in the model we consider. Hence, any change in deadweight costs which increases the demand for the domestic asset from foreign investors increases $P_U - P_R$, and any change in deadweight costs which increases the demand for the domestic asset from domestic investors decreases $P_U - P_R$. With these comparative statics, one expects $P_U - P_R > 0$ when c_d and h_f are large relative to c_f and h_d. This will be the case if domestic investors face higher deadweight costs in the domestic country than abroad and/or the foreign investors who participate in the domestic market face higher deadweight costs in their home country than in the domestic country. Hence, $P_U - P_R > 0$ requires capital flight from domestic investors toward foreign securities or capital flight from foreign investors toward domestic securities. With either type of capital flight, foreign investors have a less price-elastic demand for domestic shares than domestic investors, and Result 3 implies that it is optimal for domestic firms to discriminate between domestic and foreign investors by restricting the supply of shares available to foreign investors.

Because of the well-known existence of a home bias in portfolio holdings, it cannot be the case that all foreign investors face greater deadweight costs at home than in the domestic country. If they did, one would have a situation where foreign investors hold mostly domestic shares if the foreign country is large, which would be inconsistent with the empirical evidence. If the foreign country of our model is the rest of the world, one would expect capital flight to affect only a small subset of foreign investors (those from Sweden or Colombia, but not those from Germany or the United States). For most other investors, price discrimination and deadweight costs in the domestic country make investments in unrestricted shares unadvantageous. This creates a situation which is quite different from the one typically assumed in models of international asset pricing.[14] Models without barriers to international investment predict that the demand for domestic shares from foreign investors is highly price-elastic relative to the demand for domestic shares from domestic investors because all foreign investors invest in the domestic country. Using Equation (8), we have

$$\varepsilon_U = \frac{N_f \alpha_f - S_U}{S_U}. \tag{13}$$

Hence, for a given supply of shares available to foreign investors, the price-elasticity of demand increases with the number of foreign investors participating in the domestic country, assuming that α_f is constant. In existing models, a large foreign country implies that N_f is large since all foreign investors participate in the domestic country. In this case, ε_U is large compared to ε_R and price discrimination such that $P_U/P_R > 1$ is not optimal given Result 1. In contrast, in our model, only a subset of foreign investors invests in the domestic country, so that N_f can be small even relative to N_d, and hence, price discrimination such that $P_U/P_F > 1$ can be optimal.

In our model, price discrimination with a higher price for unrestricted shares takes place only if the demand from foreign investors is less price-elastic than the demand from domestic investors. This means that for price discrimination to become unprofitable, the price elasticity of the demand for domestic shares from foreign investors has to increase so that it equals the price elasticity of the demand from domestic investors. In our model, price discrimination becomes unprofitable if the deadweight costs of foreign investors who participate in the domestic market become the same as the deadweight costs of domestic investors. As long as only a subset of foreign investors participates in the domestic market, though, removal of ownership restrictions has an adverse effect on the price of unrestricted shares because the price elasticity of the demand for these shares is limited.

As an example of a situation which would lead to the elimination of ownership restrictions, consider the following scenario. Suppose that initially

---

[14] For a review of models of international asset pricing, see Stulz (1994).

$h_d = c_d = c_f = 0, h_f > 0$. In this case, price discrimination so that $P_U > P_R$ is optimal. Consider now the effect of a decrease in deadweight costs so that the deadweight costs of foreign investors participating in the domestic country fall to zero and the deadweight costs of some foreign investors who do not participate in the domestic country fall to zero also. The effect of this fall in deadweight costs on $P_U - P_R$ is ambiguous because it decreases the demand for domestic shares from foreign investors who participate already in the domestic country but increases the demand for domestic shares from some foreign investors who currently do not hold domestic shares. Since the deadweight costs of the foreign investors who participate in the domestic country have fallen to zero, price discrimination is no longer optimal. Nevertheless, the fall in deadweight costs may have been accompanied by an increase in $P_U - P_R$. Finally, since, by construction, not all foreign investors invest in the domestic country, the demand for U shares is not perfectly price elastic and the price of these shares falls when ownership restrictions are removed.

The model developed in this section suggests that if there is a nontrivial fixed cost from imposing ownership restrictions, firms in sufficiently large countries do not impose such restrictions. To see this, note that the limit of S_U as N_d/N_f increases is zero. Hence, for sufficiently large countries, there is no benefit from charging a different price to foreign investors because foreign ownership is trivial. Similarly, if a country becomes sufficiently small, it becomes optimal for foreign investors to hold most shares. However, the country size which matters is not the total number of investors weighted by their wealth, but rather the number of investors weighted by their wealth willing to invest in the domestic country. Hence, N_d/N_f may be greater than one even though the foreign country is the rest of the world because only a few foreign investors invest in the domestic country.

Throughout our analysis, we have assumed that the foreign country does not discriminate against the investors from the domestic country. In some ways, our argument in this paper is similar to the optimal tariff argument of international trade.[15] Hence, one might expect the foreign country to discriminate against domestic investors if the domestic country discriminates against foreign investors. However, we have seen that price discrimination of the type discussed here requires that nonresident investors face unattractive deadweight costs in their country of residence. Typically, countries that benefit from capital flight are not countries that generate capital flight. Hence, if the conditions are met for the domestic country to discriminate against foreign investors by charging them a higher price, it is unlikely that at the same time the foreign country will find it worthwhile to discriminate against domestic investors by charging them a higher price.[16]

---

[15] See, for instance, Dixit and Norman (1980). Gordon and Varian (1988) extend optimal tariff considerations to asset markets by showing that if governments are not price-takers, they may affect terms of trade in asset markets through taxation to improve their country's welfare. Optimal tariff or tax arguments require the domestic country to be, in some sense made precise in the context of the model, large. Hence, they offer no basis for the existence of ownership restrictions in small countries.

[16] Note that both foreign country firms and foreign country investors are worse off if the foreign country discriminates against domestic investors in the absence of capital flight from the domestic

Our analysis so far has focused on a static model. Developing a dynamic model is beyond the scope of this article. Nevertheless, it is possible to reinterpret our model in a dynamic setting by assuming that the share supplies are fixed, that deadweight costs are paid period by period, and that the demand functions derived here hold period by period. In this case, nothing changes if deadweight costs are constant through time except that the end-of-period payoffs become next period's share prices, since markets are open and shares trade at the beginning of each period. If deadweight costs change randomly through time, next period's share prices depend on next period's deadweight costs and on the joint distribution of the share prices one period hence, which will depend on new information about the deadweight costs. In this multiperiod setting, next period's share prices will differ between U and R shares because these share prices are affected differently by changes in deadweight costs.

When the model is viewed from such a perspective, deadweight costs of a size consistent with tax rates can generate large differences between U and R shares. Consider the extreme case where F, U, and R shares all pay the same dividend each period and deadweight costs are constant over time. Suppose then that investors holding U shares are foreign investors who face deadweight costs at home and no deadweight costs in the domestic country. If deadweight costs are equal to $1/2$ the dividends at home for the foreign investors who invest in the domestic country, these investors are willing to hold U shares at a price equal to twice the price of F shares. Since domestic investors can hold F shares, R shares cannot sell for more than the price of F shares in equilibrium since otherwise they would not be held. With no short-sales, however, R shares can sell for less than the price of F shares.

Time-consistency problems might lead the static equilibrium derived here to unravel because foreign investors expect the firm to increase the supply of unrestricted shares immediately after they have bought some U shares. As in the durable monopolist problem, firms may be unable to commit not to act opportunistically. Since price discrimination is profitable, firms have incentives to make the elimination of price discrimination difficult. For instance, their charter can require the consent of holders of U shares for new issues of U shares. In addition, managerial incentives may be such that management maximizes total firm value rather than only the value of R shares, in which case management would change the relative supplies of shares if doing so increases firm value, but not if it only redistributes wealth across shareholders. If firms create obstacles to the elimination of price discrimination, price discrimination can persist even when it no longer maximizes firm value in the absence of obstacles to eliminate it.

country. This is because, in the absence of capital flight from the domestic country, the foreign country firms cannot benefit from price discrimination against domestic investors. Further, the imposition of ownership restrictions by the foreign country in this case makes it optimal for the domestic country to tighten its restrictions. This is because an increase in P_F for domestic investors increases α_d in Equation (8), and hence decreases S_U^* in Equation (10). This means that the foreign country investors are hurt by the imposition of ownership restrictions on domestic investors by foreign firms.

1.3. An Extension to Multiple Domestic Firms

In general, ownership restrictions affect the shares of many different firms in a country. Consequently, to investigate empirically the pricing implications of our model, an extension of the analysis to the case where there is a single foreign risky asset, but many domestic firms that issue U and R shares, is required. For this extension, we assume that the model of Section 1.2 holds period per period. In this case, the end-of-period payoffs of shares are their end-of-period prices. In a multiperiod model, the end-of-period prices of U and R shares may differ even though they always pay the same dividends, since deadweight costs could change. We provide in the appendix an extension of the analysis that leads to the following equations for the prices of U and R shares:

$$\underline{P}_U = \left(\frac{1}{1+r+c_f}\right)\left[E(\underline{p}_U) - \left(\frac{A}{N_f}\right)\left[V_{UU} - V_{UF}\frac{1}{\sigma_F^2}V_{FU}\right]\underline{S}_U\right.$$

$$\left. - \underline{\beta}_{U,F}[E(p_F) - (1+r+h_f)P_F]\right], \tag{14}$$

$$\underline{P}_R = \left(\frac{1}{1+r+c_d}\right)\left[E(\underline{p}_R) - \left(\frac{A}{N_d}\right)\left[V_{RR} - V_{RF}\frac{1}{\sigma_F^2}V_{FR}\right]\underline{S}_R\right.$$

$$\left. - \underline{\beta}_{R,F}[E(p_F) - (1+r+h_d)P_F]\right], \tag{15}$$

where $\underline{P}_a$ is the $n \times 1$ vector of share prices of type a when there are n domestic firms, $E(\underline{p}_a)$ is the $n \times 1$ vector of next period's prices of shares of type a, V_{aa} is the $n \times n$ variance–covariance matrix of next period's share prices of type a, V_{aF} is the $n \times 1$ vector of covariances between next period's share prices of type a and the price of F shares, V_{Fa} is the transpose of V_{aF}, $\underline{\beta}_{a,F}$ is the vector of beta coefficients of share prices of type a with respect to foreign shares, and $\underline{S}_a$ is the $n \times 1$ vector of supplies of a shares, where $a = R, U, F$. In each equation, the asset supplies are multiplied by a term in square brackets that corresponds to the variance–covariance matrix of next period's share prices hedged with positions in F shares. Since hedging cannot eliminate all the risk of domestic shares, it follows that the price of domestic shares falls as the supply of these shares increases. In addition, the price of domestic shares increases with deadweight costs on foreign shares and falls with deadweight costs on domestic shares.

With n domestic firms, it is still the case that price discrimination is optimal if demand elasticities differ due to heterogeneity in deadweight costs. Although we do not do this here, it would be possible, using Equations (14) and (15), to derive optimal supplies of R and U shares for each firm in one of two ways. One approach would be to assume that all firms in a country collude in choosing the supplies of R and U shares to maximize country wealth; to save on coordination costs, firms might prefer to have legislated restrictions on foreign ownership, though. The other approach would be to let each firm choose its supplies of R and U shares to maximize its value given that all firms choose their supplies to maximize their value.[17] Such an extension is beyond the scope of this article.

1.4. Alternative Explanations for the Existence of Ownership Restrictions

Our approach shows that ownership restrictions can be value-maximizing. In addition, since the ownership restrictions of individual domestic firms affect the cost of capital of other domestic firms, a case can be made that government-imposed ownership restrictions minimize the country's overall cost of capital because individual firms do not take into account the effects of their decisions on other firms' cost of capital.

Alternative explanations for ownership restrictions advanced in the literature mostly focus on control issues.[18] Governmental ownership restrictions could be motivated by a desire to keep control of home-country firms with home-country investors. This motivation, however, cannot explain why individual firms would choose to have ownership restrictions, and why restrictions do not simply preclude transfer of control to foreign investors rather than ownership of shares by foreign investors. To the extent that R shares as a control block have a majority of a corporation's voting rights, the fact that transfers of R shares have to be approved by the corporation essentially precludes a takeover of the corporation. Nevertheless, takeover deterrence does not explain restrictions on foreign ownership. Since the corporation can always control ownership of R shares, it is better off prohibiting ownership by potential raiders only, rather than investors at large, since doing so will result in higher share prices.

Suppose, however, that it is indeed true that ownership restrictions exist to enable management to keep control of the firm and that this is the only reason for these restrictions. In this case, one would still expect the demand for U shares to be almost perfectly price-elastic if the domestic country is small. Hence, removal of ownership restrictions would have almost no effect on U shares, except through the positive effect on cash flows resulting from the decrease in managerial entrenchment. One would expect ownership of R shares to be valuable if it enables investors to receive rents from control. In particular, if a control contest is ever going to take place, R shares would presumably receive greater compensation than U shares.[19] Further, restricted share owners can form a coalition to share with management the rents from control, which also would make R shares valuable. Yet, empirically, R shares generally trade at a discount relative to U shares so that the market price of R shares does not reflect the control advantages of these shares in a way that would justify their existence. It might be, however,

---

[17] For individual firms, strategic considerations become important in a context with multiple firms. This is because a firm's optimal supply of shares depends on the supplies of the other firms.

[18] For the case of Switzerland, this argument is advanced by Horner (1988) and Vock (1987).

[19] See DeAngelo and DeAngelo (1985).

that blocks of *R* shares transferred with the approval of the corporation trade at a price that is greater than the price of *U* shares. We do not have any data on transfers of blocks, but such data could provide evidence supporting the control hypothesis, given that this hypothesis fails to explain the pricing of *U* shares in general. In any case, with this control hypothesis, we would expect both the price of *R* and *U* shares to increase if ownership restrictions are removed because of the associated efficiency gain from less managerial entrenchment.

An alternative control hypothesis is that *R* shares provide the firm with a stable clientele of shareholders that are better monitors because they are closer to the firm. In that case, removing the ownership restrictions would decrease firm value unless, somehow, the value of monitoring has become less important. This argument also implies, however, that the removal of restrictions should have a trivial effect on *U* shares unless it reduces total firm value, since again one would expect the demand for *U* shares to be highly price-elastic.

Alternative explanations for the discount of *R* shares could be based on the argument that these shares are less liquid and/or that these shares have tax disadvantages. Since transfers of ownership of these shares are limited, it makes sense that a seller of *R* shares might find it more difficult to find a qualified buyer. Allowing foreign investors to hold *R* shares increases the liquidity of these shares, but it does not affect their possible tax disadvantages. In a standard asset pricing model, though, one would not expect that allowing foreign investors to hold *R* shares would have a significant impact on the price of *U* shares.

2. THE SWISS DATA

The Swiss evidence provides a sample for which it is possible to assess directly the valuation implications of ownership restrictions by constructing *R* and *U* securities that differ only in their ownership restrictions.[20] The sample includes 19 firms that have both *R* and *U* shares outstanding. All these firms had two types of *U* shares outstanding at the beginning of 1985: *U* shares with voting rights (bearer shares) and *U* shares with no voting rights (participation certificates). The *R* shares (registered shares) are available to Swiss citizens or to Swiss residents only depending on the firm. The ownership restrictions for these shares are enforced by the company through refusal to register owners of shares who do not meet its registration requirements. Owners of registered shares who are not registered do not exist as far as the company is concerned.[21] Our sample includes

[20] *R* and *U* shares in our sample differ also because *U* shares are bearer shares, whereas *R* shares are registered shares. Hence, shareholders who value anonymity will find *U* shares more valuable. However, in Switzerland, the tax advantage of anonymity is limited because dividends are subject to withholding taxes on all types of shares. Consequently, whereas this difference between share types implies a higher valuation of unrestricted shares, its value appears limited. An indication of this is that when the residency requirement for *R* shares is removed the ratio of the prices of *R* and *U* shares is very close to one as shown in Figures 1 and 2.

[21] Kaufmann and Kunz (1991) review the history of the legal status of registered and bearer shares.

8 of the 10 Swiss firms with the largest stock market capitalization in 1985 and all firms listed in the *Swiss Stock Guide* edited by Union Bank of Switzerland that had all three types of shares outstanding at the beginning of 1985, except for one, Bank Leu, for which stock data was lacking. The *Stock Guide* lists 98 firms which, on September 15, 1985, had a total capitalization of 126 billion SFr. The firms in our sample had a capitalization of 78 billion SFr on the same day, which amounts to about 62% of the total capitalization. Of the firms not in our sample, 17 seem to have only U shares; most of these companies are fairly small and are controlled by one shareholder.[22]

In Switzerland, dividends are the same fraction of face value for all share types and each voting share has one vote. Hence, a share type can gain a voting right advantage by having a lower face value. If registered and bearer shares have different face values, it is always the case that registered shares have a lower face value so that investors who hold registered shares have more voting rights for a given stake in the firm's cash flows than investors who hold bearer shares. To isolate the effects of ownership restrictions, we construct for each firm a portfolio of bearer shares and participation certificates which pays the same dividend and has the same voting rights as registered or restricted shares. We call these portfolios U shares in the following analysis. More formally, these U shares consist of one bearer share and $[F_R - F_B]/F_P$ participation certificates, where F_R, F_B, and F_P are, respectively, the face values of the registered shares, bearer shares, and participation certificates. Consequently, the face value of a U share is F_R so that it has the same face value as a registered share and therefore pays the same dividend. If a firm's bearer and registered shares have identical face values, its U shares have no short position in participation certificates.

Our empirical tests use portfolios which have short positions in participation certificates for some of the U shares. With this approach, we can match registered shares with portfolios which have identical dividends and voting rights. Since it may not be possible to implement the portfolio strategy that we assume, we distinguish in our empirical work between U shares that require short-sales of participation certificates and those that do not. This assures that we understand the sensitivity of our results to the use of short-selling in the construction of the U shares. In addition, we also show results which directly compare bearer shares versus registered shares; however, in this case we would be comparing shares that have different voting rights, except for nine firms for which there is no difference in face values between the bearer and registered shares. It is interesting to note, however, that the comparison of the price of bearer shares per Swiss franc of face value and the price of registered shares per Swiss franc of face value shows that the bearer shares are always more expensive. In cases where registered shares have a lower face value than bearer shares, an investment in restricted shares that

---

[22] An exception is F. Hoffmann-La Roche & Co. which, as of September 15, 1985, is the sixth largest firm in terms of capitalization. As of that date, Roche has shares with and without voting rights, but all shares are unrestricted.

pays the same dividends as an investment in bearer shares but has more voting rights always sells for less than the investment in bearer shares. Thus, voting rights considerations are always a second-order phenomenon.

Table 1 lists the firms in our sample and provides relevant information. The criteria used to register shareholders are those in effect at the end of the sample period as reported by the stock guide prepared by *Finanz und Wirtschaft* for 1989 and by Kaufmann and Kunz (1991). Hence, the requirements reported in the table are those in force after Nestlé decided to allow foreign investors to acquire *R* shares. In general, the cases where registration is at the discretion of the board should be interpreted as cases where foreign shareholders will not be registered. As far as we can ascertain, at the beginning of the sample period, Swiss residency was a requirement for registration for all firms, and for a number of firms the stronger requirement of citizenship was in place.[23] Note further that satisfying the residency or citizenship requirement might not be sufficient to ensure registration of registered shares, since a firm's board of directors generally has the right to reject registration for Swiss citizens. Finally, the information in Table 1 shows that holders of registered shares typically control the firm as a group.

In the empirical work, we use weekly share prices, more precisely Wednesday closing prices, over the period from January 2, 1985, to December 27, 1989. Besides the whole period, we distinguish three subperiods. The first one is from the start of our sample to the end of September 1987, that is, just before the stock market crash on October 16, 1987. The second subperiod extends from the beginning of November 1987 to the second week of November 1988, which is just before Nestlé announced on November 17, 1988, that it would no longer exclude foreign investors from ownership of *R* shares. The third subperiod starts in the third week of November 1988 and goes to the end of our sample. We consider the postcrash period separately to allow us to discern changes in the behavior of share prices following the crash.

Table 2 shows the values of the average ratio of the price of *U* and *R* shares. For many firms, the average price ratio before the removal of the registration restrictions by Nestlé exceeds two. In addition, for all firms but five, the minimum price ratio exceeds one, so that statistical tests for the existence of a price differential are superfluous. The price ratio exhibits substantial variation over time. Not surprisingly, the average values of the ratio fall for a number of firms in the last subperiod following the removal of the registration restrictions by Nestlé. In the absence of deadweight costs for foreign investors, ownership restrictions would appear to impose an extremely large cost on the corporations that have them. For instance, if the ratio is two and if the market for *U* shares has perfectly elastic demand curves, a firm whose value is divided equally between *R* and *U* shares could increase its value by one-quarter by removing the restrictions, assuming that the firm's cash flows are unchanged. Figure 2 plots the average price

---

[23] No stock guide with information on the ownership restrictions is available for the beginning of our sample period.

Table 1. *Characteristics of firms*

Firm	Symbol	Market value, Mio. SFr	Large shareholder	Registered share Ownership restrictions (1989)	Bearer share, face value (number)	Face value (number)	Participation certificate, face value (number)
Alusuisse	ALU	2421	No	Up to 3% per holder	250 (1351)	125 (1492)	25 (1624)
Brown-Boveri	BBC	5956	No	Up to 7% per holder	500 (1007)	100 (1007)	100 (1875)
Banca della Svizzera Italiana	BSI	987	2 holders jointly control	Residents only	500 (267)	100 (320)	100 (663)
Ciba-Geigy	CIG	15,790	No	Swiss only, up to 2% per holder	100 (749)	100 (3512)	100 (1138)
Feld-schlösschen	FEL	556	Several large holders	Swiss only	250 (38)	100 (192)	100 (100)
Georg Fischer	FIS	714	Employee fund holds 10%	Swiss up to 4000 shares, foreigners up to 400 shares per holder	500 (280)	100 (420)	100 (526)
Globus	GLO	699	Trust controls	Residents only	500 (44)	500 (22)	100 (267)
Haldengut	HAG	195	Large minority holder	Discretion	100 (20)	100 (40)	100 (20)
Jacobs	JAC	4887	Trust controls	Swiss only	500 (435)	100 (1066)	50 (632)
Konsumverein Zürich	KVZ	383	No	Residents only, up to 2% per holder	250 (41)	100 (160)	50 (65)
Nestlé	NES	26,218	No	Up to 3% per holder	100 (1073)	100 (2227)	20 (1150)
Oerlikon-Bührle	OEB	1716	Trust holds 45% of votes	Up to 50,000 shares per holder	250 (1000)	100 (1299)	100 (240)
Rückver-sicherung	RUK	1611	No	Swiss only, up to 3% per holder	100 (44)	100 (400)	20 (860)
Sandoz	SAN	14,407	No	Up to 2% per holder	250 (155)	250 (1043)	50 (1305)
Schweiz. Bank-gesellschaft	SBG	16,370	No	Residents only, up to 5% per holder	500 (3590)	100 (3800)	20 (9026)
Schweiz. Bank-verein	SBV	11,233	No	Swiss only, up to 2% per holder	100 (13,838)	100 (14,204)	100 (8936)
Schindler	SCH	1162	Trust controls	Residents only	500 (31)	100 (751)	100 (282)
Winterthur-Versicherung	WIN	4854	No	Swiss only, up to 10,000 shares per holder	100 (270)	100 (730)	20 (1760)
Zürich-Versicherung	ZUR	8462	No	Swiss only, up to 15,000 shares per holder	100 (400)	100 (1100)	50 (1100)

Note: Market value is the sum of the market values of bearer shares, registered shares, and participation certificates at average prices over 1989. Face values are in SFr at the end of 1989. Number of shares are in thousands.

Sources: Swiss Stock Guide (various issues) and Kaufmann and Kunz (1991).

Table 2. *Price ratios of unrestricted/restricted shares*

	Average price ratio				Maximum	Minimum
	Total period	Before crash	Crash–Nestlé	After Nestlé		
Firm						
ALU	1.62	1.66	1.72	1.43	2.01	1.23
BBC	1.83	1.77	2.27	1.56	2.65	1.07
BSI	1.66	1.59	1.63	1.84	2.55	1.06
CIG	1.91	2.12	2.02	1.27	2.42	1.17
FEL	1.24	1.21	1.25	1.31	1.50	0.93
FIS	2.08	2.12	1.78	2.26	2.86	1.00
GLO	1.17	1.26	1.14	1.00	1.70	0.90
HAG	1.05	1.06	1.05	0.99	1.36	0.87
JAC	1.34	1.02	1.86	1.57	2.46	0.24
KVZ	1.50	1.50	1.39	1.48	1.95	0.60
NES	1.76	1.94	2.00	1.07	2.17	1.00
OEB	2.40	2.57	2.69	1.67	3.21	1.37
RUK	2.20	2.61	2.03	1.37	3.21	1.20
SAN	2.23	2.60	2.38	1.17	2.89	1.03
SBG	1.34	1.29	1.44	1.35	1.66	1.02
SBV	1.24	1.29	1.25	1.12	1.50	1.06
SCH	2.12	1.70	3.29	1.97	3.87	0.94
WIN	1.87	2.05	1.98	1.30	2.37	1.16
ZUR	1.88	2.04	2.10	1.28	2.37	1.16
Portfolios						
All shares	1.71	1.76	1.86	1.42	1.99	1.35
Short sales	1.71	1.65	1.93	1.64	2.16	1.48
No short sales	1.70	1.88	1.77	1.18	2.10	1.12

Note: Price of unrestricted share/price of restricted share. Observations are weekly. Total period extends from January 2, 1985, to December 27, 1989. Subperiods: Before crash (January 2, 1985, through September 30, 1987), Crash–Nestlé (November 4, 1987, through November 16, 1988), after Nestlé (November 23, 1988, through December 27, 1989). Price ratios for portfolios are averages for individual shares. Short-sales (no short-sales) portfolios include all shares involving short-sales (no short-sales) of participation certificates to construct unrestricted share.

ratio for all firms, for firms where U shares require no short-sales of participation certificates, and for firms where U shares require such short-sales. In Figure 2, the fall in the price ratios following the announcement by Nestlé is quite dramatic.

Table 2 and Figure 2 show clearly the magnitude of the puzzle that has to be explained by any theory on the existence and pricing of ownership restrictions. In traditional asset pricing models, these restrictions imply a considerable cost without having an offsetting gain. Further, the advocates of the control hypothesis for the existence of R shares cannot point to control benefits impounded in the price of R shares that offset the loss in firm value resulting from ownership restrictions if the demand for U shares is highly price-elastic.

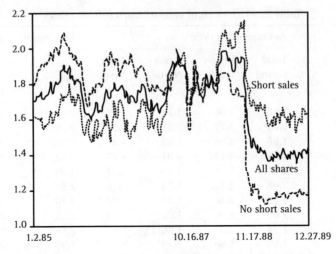

Figure 2. *Price ratio of unrestricted/restricted share prices*

Note: Wednesday closing Swiss francs prices from 1/2/85 to 12/27/89 are used to construct price ratios of unrestricted/restricted shares for each firm in the sample. Until 11/17/88, restricted shares are registered shares that cannot be held by foreign investors. After 11/17/88, restricted shares of Nestlé can be held by all foreign investors. The firms in the sample have two kinds of shares that can be held by all investors: bearer shares, which are shares with voting rights, and participation certificates, which are shares without voting rights. A firm's unrestricted share is a portfolio of bearer shares and participation certificates that pays the same dividend as that firm's registered shares and has the same voting rights. This portfolio has a short position in participation certificates when registered shares have a voting rights advantage relative to bearer shares or has no position in participation certificates if registered shares have no voting rights advantage relative to bearer shares. 'All shares' denotes an arithmetic average of all price ratios whether short positions are taken or not. 'Short sales' denotes the arithmetic average of the price ratios where unrestricted shares include short positions. The stock market crashed on 10/16/87.

Nor can they explain why the price of U shares fell following the Nestlé event shown in Figure 2. If removal of ownership restrictions decreases the private benefits of control, one would expect U shares to benefit since their holders get none of the private benefits from control. In addition, in the context of Gordon's growth model, a ratio of two essentially implies that the discount rate for R shares has to be twice what it is for U shares.

3. CROSS-SECTIONAL PROPERTIES OF THE RELATION BETWEEN THE PRICES OF UNRESTRICTED AND RESTRICTED SHARES

To investigate the usefulness of our model, we would like to know whether it helps to understand the cross-sectional variation in the relation between U and R

share prices compared to a model without deadweight costs. Without deadweight costs, the price of Nestlé U shares is determined in the same way as the price of IBM shares. Hence, in our mean–variance model, assuming that R and U shares are a trivial fraction of the world market portfolio, the price of U shares is determined by their beta with the world market portfolio. Thus the supply of U shares relative to the supply of R shares should not matter in the relative price of U shares relative to R shares.

Equations (14) and (15) of Section 1 provide formulas for the price level of U shares and R shares for the case where there are n domestic firms. When investigating the cross-sectional variation in the relation between U and R shares, however, we want to focus on the logarithm of the ratio of the price of U and R shares because the wide variation in the price of these shares makes comparison of the difference between the price of U and R shares meaningless across firms. To obtain a cross-sectional regression model, we derive an explicit formula for the log of the price ratio of U and R shares which is consistent with the model of Section 1. With this formula, the absolute level of share prices is irrelevant and cross-sectional regressions are meaningful. To derive that model, we assume that the model derived in Section 1 holds period by period and then use the log-linear approximation for the log of share prices derived in Campbell and Shiller (1987) and Campbell and Ammer (1993). With this approximation, the price of a share can be written as

$$\ln P_{ia}^t = E \sum_{j=0}^{\infty} \eta^j [(1 - \eta) d_{ia}^{t+j+1} - r_{ia}^{t+j+1}] + \theta, \tag{16}$$

where $\ln P_{ia}^t$ is the log of the price of the stock of type a of the ith firm at date t, d_{ia}^{t+j+1} is the log of the dividend at date $t+j+1$, and r_{ia}^{t+j+1} is the rate of return of the share from date $t+j$ to $t+j+1$. η is a parameter that comes from the approximation procedure and is slightly smaller than one, and θ denotes a constant that depends on η. Small changes in η have a trivial effect on the log of the price; hence, in the following, we assume that η is the same for R and U shares. With this notation and this additional approximation, the log price ratio is the discounted sum of the difference between the expected rates of return of the two types of shares:

$$\ln P_{iU}^t - \ln P_{iR}^t = E \sum_{j=0}^{\infty} \eta^j [r_{iR}^{t+j+1} - r_{iU}^{t+j+1}] \tag{17}$$

The log price ratio is positive, so U shares sell at a premium if the expected value of the sum of the discounted rates of return of R shares exceeds the expected value of the sum of the discounted rates of return of the U shares.

Table 3 presents evidence on the cross-sectional variation of log price ratios using the model of Section 1 extended to many firms to predict expected rates of return. The data available include the returns on the Swiss shares used so far, the returns on a broad Swiss index—the SBC index—and the returns in Swiss francs on the Morgan Stanley world index. We take the Morgan Stanley world index as the foreign asset in Section 1. In our empirical work, we estimate the relevant parameters using the precrash period and test the model using the period between the crash and the Nestlé event.

Equations (14) and (15) can be restated in return form for individual securities as follows:

$$
\begin{aligned}
E(r_{iR}) - r = c_d &+ \beta_{iR,RM}(AM_{RM}/N_d)\sigma_{RM}^2 - \beta_{iR,F}\beta_{RM,F}(AM_{RM}/N_d)\sigma_F^2 \\
&+ \beta_{iR,F}[E(r_F) - r - h_d],
\end{aligned} \tag{18}
$$

$$
\begin{aligned}
E(r_{iU}) - r = c_f &+ \beta_{iU,UM}(AM_{UM}/N_f)\sigma_{UM}^2 - \beta_{iU,F}\beta_{UM,F}(AM_{UM}/N_f)\sigma_F^2 \\
&+ \beta_{iU,F}[E(r_F) - r - h_f],
\end{aligned} \tag{19}
$$

where r_{ia} is the return of the ith share of type a, aM denotes the market portfolio of shares of type a, M_{aM} denotes the market value of portfolio aM, and σ_{aM} is the standard deviation of the return of the market portfolio of shares of type a. The beta coefficient of the ith share of type a with respect to Z is $\beta_{ia,Z}$. For instance, $\beta_{iU,F}$ is the beta coefficient from a regression of the return of the ith unrestricted share on the return on the foreign shares. Using the log approximation and Equations (14) and (15), we get the following testable equation:

$$
\ln P_{iU}^t - \ln P_{iR}^t \propto a_1 + a_2\beta_{iU,F} + a_3\beta_{iR,F} + a_4\beta_{iU,UM} + a_5\beta_{iR,RM} + \varepsilon_i \tag{20}
$$

Assuming that the model of Section 1 holds period by period, the regression coefficients correspond to

$$
\begin{aligned}
a_1 &= c_d - c_f, \\
a_2 &= -[E(r_F) - r - h_f - \beta_{UM,F}(AM_{UM}/N_f)\sigma_F^2], \\
a_3 &= E(r_F) - r - h_d - \beta_{RM,F}(AM_{RM}/N_d)\sigma_F^2, \\
a_4 &= -(AM_{UM}/N_f)\sigma_{UM}^2, \\
a_5 &= (AM_{RM}/N_d)\sigma_{RM}^2.
\end{aligned} \tag{21}
$$

We first consider the implications of a model without deadweight costs for the regression coefficients of estimates of Equation (21), assuming that the foreign country is large relative to the domestic country. First, we expect $a_1 = 0$. Second, since N_f is extremely large, a_2 becomes equal to minus the risk premium of foreign shares and hence should be negative. In addition, $a_2 + a_3 < 0$, $a_4 = 0$ as N_f becomes large enough, and $a_5 > 0$. The case which leads to price discrimination with a higher price charged to foreign investors requires $h_f > h_d \geq 0$ and c_f cannot be too large. In this case, one expects N_f to be much smaller than in the model without deadweight costs. Consequently, estimates consistent with that case are $a_1 \leq 0$, $a_2 + a_3 > 0$, $a_3 > 0$, $a_4 < 0$ and $a_5 > 0$.

Regression A of Panel A in Table 3 provides estimates of Equation (20) using as market portfolios of R and U shares the value-weighted portfolios of these shares in our sample. Because of our construction of U shares, we add a dummy variable to our regressions that takes a value of one if a share involves short-sales of participation certificates. We find that $a_5 > 0$ as predicted and that it is the only coefficient significant at the 0.05 level or better. The dummy variable is significant at the 0.10 level. Coefficients a_1 and a_4 have negative coefficients as expected, but they are not significant. The coefficient a_2 is not significantly different from zero, which is inconsistent with a model without deadweight costs. Coefficient $a_2 + a_3$ is nonnegative as expected in the model with deadweight costs. Note that over the estimation period for betas, $\beta_{UM,F} = 0.36$ with a t-statistic of 4.45 when we use the value-weighted portfolio of bearer shares as the market portfolio of U shares and $\beta_{RM,F} = 0.34$ with a t-statistic of 5.77. Hence, it is not the case that our failure to find $a_2 + a_3$ to be negative is due to betas equal to zero. It follows from this that Regression A is consistent with our model and does not provide support for a model without deadweight costs.

One reason for the lack of strength in our results might be that betas changed. The world beta coefficients seem substantially greater after the crash than before. After the crash, we have $\beta_{UM,F} = 0.95$ with a t-statistic of 10.48 and we have $\beta_{RM,F} = 0.72$ with a t-statistic of 9.67. Another reason why we estimate coefficients imprecisely is that we estimate six coefficients with 19 observations when, in addition, four of our explanatory variables are highly correlated. On average, the correlation coefficients between the various betas we estimate are greater than 0.50.

In Regression B, we include as additional explanatory variables the log of the market value of U shares, the log of the market value of R shares, and the total face value of U shares divided by the total face value of R shares. We find that none of these supply variables is significant, indicating that the size or relative size of a firm's outstanding supply of shares has little incremental explanatory power once betas are accounted for, and that adding these variables leads to a substantial fall in adjusted R^2.

In Regression C, we include only the log market value variables and find that these variables do not have significant coefficients. Interestingly, however, the signs of these coefficients are not supportive of liquidity arguments. One would expect shares to become more liquid, ceteris paribus, when their supply increases, so that an increase in the supply of U shares would increase the price ratio and an increase in the supply of R shares would decrease the price ratio if liquidity is an important determinant of the price ratio. Yet, in Regression C the coefficients have signs which are opposite to those predicted by the liquidity argument. The signs of the coefficients are consistent with the supply effects discussed in Section 2 and so is the relative magnitude of the absolute value of the coefficients.

The market values used in Regression C depend on the price ratio. An alternative relative supply measure that does not depend on the price ratio is the ratio of the aggregate face values of U to R shares. This relative supply measure is attractive because it tells us the relative supply of dividends offered in the form of U and R securities. In Regression D, we regress the log price ratio on this variable and find that it has the expected negative sign and is highly significant. Hence, using this variable, it is clear that relative supplies matter as implied by the model

Table 3. Cross-sectional regressions of the natural logarithm of the average estimation period price ratio between unrestricted and restricted shares

Panel A: The market portfolios of restricted and unrestricted shares are value-weighted portfolios from the shares in the sample

Regression	Constant a_1	Beta (U, F) a_2	Beta (R, F) a_3	Beta (U, UM) a_4	Beta (R, RM) a_5	Market value of R shares	Market value of U shares	Dummy for short-sales	Relative total face value	R^2 adjusted / F value
A	-0.09	0.40	0.20	-0.11	0.58*			0.30		0.25
	(-0.56)	(1.06)	(0.52)	(-0.33)	(2.24)			(1.92)		2.22
B	0.18	0.43	0.10	0.02	0.55	0.06	-0.08	0.36	0.00	0.10
	(0.15)	(0.93)	(0.15)	(0.03)	(1.05)	(0.27)	(-0.44)	(1.38)	(-0.14)	1.25
C	-0.93					0.17	-0.06	0.27		0.10
	(-1.43)					(1.60)	(-0.55)	(1.59)		1.64
D	0.60*							0.09	-0.02*	0.05
	(5.83)							(0.63)	(-3.39)	1.43
E	0.02				0.60*			0.28*	-0.01	0.29
	(0.11)				(3.70)			(2.24)	(-1.66)	3.50*

Panel B: The market portfolios of restricted and unrestricted shares are the SBC index, which is a broad-based index of Swiss shares

Regression	Constant a_1	Beta (U, F) a_2	Beta (R, F) a_3	Beta (U, D) a_4	Beta (R, D) a_5	Market value of R shares	Market value of U shares	Dummy for short-sales	Relative total face value	R^2 adjusted / F value
F	-0.05	0.33	-0.05	-0.28	0.90*			0.15		0.34
	(-0.29)	(1.08)	(-0.14)	(-1.13)	(2.75)			(0.96)		2.84
G	0.08	0.35	-0.19	-0.43*	1.02*					3.34
	(0.59)	(1.02)	(-0.43)	(-2.28)	(2.91)					3.31*
H	0.19	0.39	-0.32	-0.44*	0.99*				-0.01	0.35
	(1.08)	(1.05)	(-0.63)	(-2.39)	(2.59)				(-1.88)	2.98

Regression	Constant a_1	Beta (B, F) a_2	Beta (R, F) a_3	Beta (B, D) a_4	Beta (R, D) a_5	Market value of R shares	Market value of B shares	Dummy for short-sales	Relative total face value	R^2 adjusted F value
Panel C: The price ratios are calculated using bearer shares instead of unrestricted shares. The indices are the same as in panel B										
I	0.07 (0.42)	0.03 (0.18)	0.08 (0.23)	0.04 (0.09)	0.51 (0.94)			−0.26* (−2.23)		0.44 3.86*
J	0.21 (0.25)	0.05 (0.31)	−0.13 (−0.33)	0.04 (0.07)	0.64 (1.07)	0.09 (1.12)	−0.11* (−2.04)	−0.16 (−1.47)		0.47 3.31*
K	0.19 (0.95)	0.03 (0.19)			0.50* (2.24)			−0.25* (−2.16)	−0.03* (−2.41)	0.57 6.86*
L	0.08 (0.50)	0.04 (0.29)			0.57* (3.17)			−0.27* (−2.29)		0.52 7.39*

Note: The sample consists of weekly data for 19 Swiss firms. Regressions are estimated by ordinary least squares using the correction for heteroskedasticity developed by White (1980). The estimation period extends from 11/4/87 to 11/16/88. Beta (U, W) denotes the beta of U shares relative to the W portfolio. The other betas are defined analogously. The betas are estimated over the period from 1/2/85 to 9/30/87. The market portfolio of restricted (R) shares, RM, is the value-weighted portfolio of the registered shares in the sample. The market portfolio of unrestricted (U) shares, UM, is the value-weighted portfolio of the bearer shares in the sample. The world portfolio, F, is approximated by the Morgan Stanley Capital International World Stock Market Index, expressed in Swiss Francs. The domestic portfolio (D) is the SBC index. The parameters a_1 to a_5 correspond to Equations (20) and (21) in the text. Total market values of restricted (R) shares, unrestricted (U) shares, and bearer (B) shares are averages over the estimation period and expressed in natural logarithms. The dummy variable takes a value of one if there is a voting rights difference between restricted and bearer shares (i.e., if unrestricted shares can only be constructed by shorting participation certificates). A firm's relative total face value is the total face value of bearer shares plus participation certificates divided by the total face value of registered shares (participation certificates are not included in panel C). t-values are in parentheses below the estimated parameters. The F value tests for the joint significance of the estimated parameters. An * indicates significance at the 5 percent level (two-sided test).

of Section 1. In the model, however, relative supplies do not matter when Regression B is estimated, so that the insignificance of the supply measures in Regression B and the significance of the relative face values in Regression D are fully consistent with the model. It could be, though, the multicollinearity makes it difficult to estimate any of the coefficients precisely in Regression B.

In models without deadweight costs, relative supplies should not matter at all. The only supply variable one would expect to matter in that case is the supply of R shares. Another way to look at this is that in the model developed by Hietala (1989), the relative supply should be insignificant if one regresses the price ratio on the beta of R shares relative to the market portfolio of R shares and the relative supply variable. This is Regression E in Table 3, and we find that the relative supply variable has a negative coefficient with a t-statistic of -1.66, which is marginally significant. There, the coefficient on the beta coefficient of R shares is significant and positive as expected.

In Panel B of Table 3, we replace the market portfolios of R and U shares with a single proxy for the Swiss market portfolio—the SBC index. We find that doing so leads to stronger results. The dummy variable for short-sales is no longer significant. When we reestimate the equation without that dummy variable, we find that the beta of U shares with respect to the domestic portfolio has a significant negative coefficient, whereas the beta of R shares has a significant positive coefficient. In contrast, the world betas of R and U shares are insignificant. The adjusted R^2 of that regression is 0.34. The regression is inconsistent with a model of asset pricing in which Swiss shares are priced in an integrated world market except for the ownership restrictions. In the absence of deadweight costs, one would not expect the risk of U shares relative to the Swiss market portfolio to be important in the determination of the price ratio. In addition, the relative supplies have a significant negative effect on the price ratio. We estimated regressions with the logic of the levels of the supplies (i.e., similar to Regression A) and found the coefficients insignificant.

In Panel C, we use the ratio of the price of bearer shares to registered shares so that no short-sales are needed. In this case, there are voting rights differences for 10 firms as explained earlier. It is clearly the case that these voting rights matter when we estimate Equation (20) with a dummy variable that takes a value of one when the R shares have a voting rights advantage. In Regression I, the dummy variable takes a significant negative value, indicating that the voting rights advantage of R shares makes these shares trade at a smaller discount relative to the U shares. After including the log of the supplies in regression J, the dummy variable is no longer significant, but the log of the supply of bearer shares is. In Regression K, both the relative supply variable and the dummy variable are significant. Further, the beta of R shares is highly significant. All in all, this is the most significant regression we report, with an adjusted R^2 of 0.57. The last regression is Regression L, without the relative supply variable for comparison.

In summary, there is evidence from our regressions that world betas do not matter for the pricing of unrestricted shares, which we take as evidence of market segmentation induced by the existence of deadweight costs. Further, even controlling for betas, there is some evidence that asset supplies matter and that the price ratio is related to asset supplies as predicted by our model. The voting rights disadvantage of *U* shares reduces the price ratio as one would expect, but voting rights considerations do not help understand why *U* shares are priced at a premium and do not affect any of our conclusions.

4. THE NESTLÉ ANNOUNCEMENT OF THE RELAXATION OF OWNERSHIP RESTRICTIONS

On November 17, 1988, Nestlé announced that it would allow foreign investors to buy registered shares with a limit of 3 percent for any investor. This announcement more than doubled the number of shares of Nestlé with voting rights available to foreign investors. Viewed in another way, before the announcement, foreign investors could hold claims to, at most, slightly more than one-third of the total dividend payout of Nestlé. After the announcement they had the right to hold all of it.

Suppose that the announcement conveyed no other information than the information about share ownership. The model of Section 1.2 with deadweight costs set equal to zero implies that the change in the price of *U* shares following the announcement should be trivial since the distribution of future dividends is unchanged and since the demand for *U* shares in that case is highly price-elastic. In contrast, the value of *R* shares should increase because these shares are now priced on world markets, rather than on the market formed by Swiss investors. Figure 1 shows that the price of the *R* shares increased dramatically during the week of the announcement from 4245 SFr to 5782 SFr. It also shows, however, that the *U* shares fell by 2079 SFr from 8688 SFr to 6609 SFr. This fall of about 25 percent in the value of *U* shares cannot be understood in the context of a model without deadweight costs that limit access to the domestic market, but it makes sense viewed from the perspective of our theory. In Section 1.2, we argued that an increase in the supply of *U* shares leads to a fall in their price because foreign investors have a downward-sloping demand curve for *U* shares.

The drop in the price ratio of *U* to *R* shares associated with the announcement is dramatic also. Table 2 shows that the price ratio for Nestlé is about two before the announcement. After the announcement, it drops to an average of 1.07. To explain a decrease in the price ratio of this magnitude through changes in the risk premium of *U* shares would require, in the simplest dividend discount model, almost a doubling of the risk premium. Since there is no dramatic decrease in stock prices throughout the world at that time, one would have to explain the fall by a change in beta. There is no evidence of a dramatic fall in beta either.

The price ratio falls for other firms at the time of the Nestlé announcement, but not for all firms. The typical firm for which the average price ratio for the subperiod after the announcement is more than two standard deviations lower than the average price ratio for the subperiod before the announcement is a firm with an average price ratio for the subperiod before the announcement in excess of two. Hence, firms whose *U* shares were highly valued by foreign investors experienced a fall. This fall can be attributed to the increase in the supply of *U* shares and to the belief that other firms would follow Nestlé in relaxing the ownership restrictions.

We have not been able to locate other news that could explain such a drop in the price ratio for so many firms during the week of the Nestlé announcement.[24] For most of these firms, the price ratio had little volatility before the announcement. The average price ratio for Nestlé for the subperiod before the announcement was 2.0 with a volatility of 0.04. Hence, the drop in the price ratio is equivalent to a drop of more than 20 standard deviations!

The dramatic loss in value of the *U* shares takes place against an increase in the market value of Nestlé of 10 percent as measured by the total value of all three categories of shares. This increase is even more dramatic because during that week only two other firms experienced an increase in market value in our sample. Hence, the Nestlé announcement increases firm value as we would expect. The obvious question for which we have no answer is why Nestlé waited to make its announcement until it had such an impact on firm value and why other firms did not follow.

At least three explanations can be given for the increase in the market value of Nestlé that are not related to our theory. One view is that the ownership restrictions enable management to entrench itself. With this view, one could argue that the market reacted favorably because the announcement reflected confidence by management in how it would be evaluated by shareholders, and hence confidence in the future of the company.[25] The second explanation is that Nestlé made the move so it could be a more active player in the European Economic Community. The third possible explanation is that the Nestlé shares became more liquid. None of these arguments, however, can explain why the unrestricted shares fell so dramatically. The first two arguments suggest that the *U* shares should have increased in value because the information represents good news for the company; the third argument predicts little or no effect on the *U* shares because their liquidity would change little.

5. CONCLUDING REMARKS

In this article, we argue that in the presence of differential demands for domestic shares by domestic and foreign investors, firms will want to discriminate between these investors, and that this discrimination provides an explanation for why firms sometimes restrict foreign ownership of their shares. Price discrimination explains why shares available to foreign investors sell at a premium when (1) there is a home bias in asset holdings and (2) there is some capital flight from the foreign country. In the absence of a home bias, the price-elasticity of the

[24] Neither can Loderer and Jacobs (1994).
[25] This view has been put forward by Hermann and Santoni (1989).

aggregate demand from foreign investors exceeds the price-elasticity of the aggregate demand from domestic investors when the foreign country is large compared to the domestic country. Without capital flight, foreign investors do not have a sufficient preference for domestic shares to make it worthwhile to discriminate against them.

We explore a two-period model. Further work should study a multiperiod model to see under which conditions price discrimination holds when firms can change the supply of unrestricted shares over time. Most of the analysis in this article focuses on three assets. Hence, we ignore the strategic considerations that apply in a context where several firms have to decide on their supplies of unrestricted shares. These considerations could be usefully explored. Finally, our analysis does not derive explicitly why asset demands differ between investors from different countries. Modeling taxes and political risk explicitly could lead to a richer analysis.

Our cross-sectional evidence obtained using Swiss data is supportive of our model. The empirical analysis is limited by the nature of the database available and the small number of firms for which our experiment could be conducted. With more data, a time-series cross-sectional analysis that looks more directly at the optimal supplies of restricted and unrestricted shares for individual firms could provide useful evidence on our model. Although our model appears to be useful for the case of Switzerland, further work should explore whether it can explain the existence of ownership restrictions for other countries. Whereas historically, it seems clear that there has been a demand for Swiss assets motivated by political risk considerations which gave Swiss firms some monopoly power in supplying shares to foreign investors, it remains an empirical question as to whether political risk or tax effects on asset demands from foreign investors are important enough in other countries with ownership restrictions to make our theory appropriate for these countries.

Appendix

In this appendix, we derive Equation (14), which determines the prices of U shares. The derivation of Equation (15), which determines the prices of R shares, is similar. As in the text, we consider only the case where all shareholdings are strictly positive for simplicity. Since we only present results for the typical foreign investor who invests in the domestic country, we omit the subscript f. Using the notation in the text, Equation (5) can be written as an unconstrained equation through elimination of the holdings of the risk-free asset by substitution of Equation (4). For the case with many different unrestricted shares, the resulting unconstrained equation is

$$w = D_F[p_F - (1 + r + h_f)P_F] + \underline{D}'_U[\underline{p}_U - (1 + r + c_f)\underline{P}_U] + (1 + r)W.$$

$$(A.1)$$

We maximize the expected utility of terminal wealth using the definition of terminal wealth given in Equation (A.1):

$$E(w) - \frac{1}{2}AVar(w) = \underline{D}'_U[E(\underline{p}_U) - (1 + r + c_f)\underline{P}_U]$$
$$+ D_F[E(\underline{p}_F) - (1 + r + h_f)P_F]$$
$$+ (1 + r)W - \frac{1}{2}A[\underline{D}'_U V_{UU}\underline{D}_U$$
$$+ 2\underline{D}'_U V_{UF}D_F + D_F^2\sigma_F^2] \tag{A.2}$$

The first-order conditions are

$$\partial L/\partial \underline{D}_U = E(\underline{p}_U) - (1 + r + c_f)\underline{P}_U - A[V_{UU}\underline{D}_U + V_{UF}D_F] = 0,$$
$$\partial L/\partial D_F = E(\underline{p}_F) - (1 + r + h_f)P_F - A[D_F\sigma_F^2 + V_{FU}\underline{D}_U] = 0. \tag{A.3}$$

Solving for the demand functions yields

$$\frac{1}{A}V_{UU}^{-1}[E(\underline{p}_U) - (1 + r + c_f)\underline{P}_U] - V_{UU}^{-1}V_{UF}D_F = \underline{D}_U,$$
$$\frac{1}{A}\sigma_F^{-2}[E(p_F) - (1 + r + h_f)P_F] - \sigma_F^{-2}V_{FU}\underline{D}_U = D_F. \tag{A.4}$$

Substituting D_F in the equation for $\underline{D}_U$, we get

$$\frac{1}{A}V_{UU}^{-1}[E(\underline{p}_U) - (1 + r + c_f)\underline{P}_U]$$
$$- V_{UU}^{-1}V_{UF}\left[\frac{1}{A}\sigma_F^{-2}[E(p_F) - (1 + r + h_f)P_F] - \sigma_F^{-2}V_{FU}\underline{D}_u\right] = \underline{D}_U. \tag{A.5}$$

In equilibrium, the aggregate demand for unrestricted shares, N_f, times Equation (A.5), must equal their supply. After imposing this condition, we solve for $\underline{P}_U$ to obtain Equation (14).

REFERENCES

Bailey, W., 1994, 'Risk and Return on China's New Stock Markets: Some Preliminary Evidence,' *Pacific-Basin Finance Journal*, 2, 243–260.

Bagwell, L. S., 1991, 'Shareholder Heterogeneity: Evidence and Implications,' *American Economic Review, Papers and Proceedings*, 218–221.

Campbell, J. Y., and J. Ammer, 1991, 'What Moves the Stock and Bond Markets? A Variance Decomposition for Long-Term Asset Returns,' *Journal of Finance*, 48, 3–37.

—— and R. J. Shiller, 1987, 'The Dividend–Price Ratio and Expectations of Future Dividends and Discount Factors,' *Review of Financial Studies*, 1, 195–228.

Cooper, I. A., and E. Kaplanis, 1994, 'What Explains the Home Bias in Portfolio Investment?,' *The Review of Financial Studies*, 7, 45–60.

DeAngelo, H., and L. DeAngelo, 1985, 'Managerial Ownership of Voting Rights: A Study of Public Corporations with Dual Classes of Common Stock,' *Journal of Financial Economics*, 14, 33–69.

Deppler, M., and M. Williamson, 1987, 'Capital Flight: Concepts, Measurement, and Issues,' *Staff Studies for the World Economic Outlook*, International Monetary Fund, Washington D.C.

Dixit, A. K., and V. Norman, 1980, *Theory of International Trade*, Cambridge University Press, Cambridge, U.K.

Errunza, V., and E. Losq, 1985, 'International Asset Pricing under Mild Segmentation: Theory and Test,' *Journal of Finance*, 40, 105–124.

——, and E. Losq, 1989, 'Capital Flow Controls, International Asset Pricing, and Investors' Welfare: A Multi-Country Framework,' *Journal of Finance*, 44, 1025–1038.

Eun, C., and S. Janakiramanan, 1986, 'A Model of International Asset Pricing with a Constraint on the Foreign Equity Ownership,' *Journal of Finance*, 41, 897–914.

French, K. R., and J. M. Poterba, 1991, 'Investor Diversification and International Equity Markets,' *American Economic Review, Papers and Proceedings*, 222–226.

Gordon, R. H., and H. R. Varian, 1989, 'Taxation of Asset Income in the Presence of a World Securities Market,' *Journal of International Economics*, 34, 2107–2138.

Hermann, W., and G. J. Santoni, 1989, 'The Cost of Restricting Corporate Takeovers: A Lesson from Switzerland,' *Federal Reserve Bank of St. Louis Review*, November/December, 3–11.

Hietala, P. K., 1989, 'Asset Pricing in Partially Segmented Markets: Evidence from the Finnish Market,' *Journal of Finance*, 44, 697–715.

Horner, M., 1986, 'Ein Portfolio-Modell zur Erklärung des Preisabschlages der Namenaktien gegenüber den Inhaberaktien und Partizipationsscheinen,' *Schweizerische Zeitschrift für Volkswirtschaft und Statistik*, 61–79.

——, 1988, 'The Value of the Corporate Voting Right: Evidence from Switzerland,' *Journal of Banking and Finance*, 12, 69–83.

Kaufmann, H., and B. Kunz, 1991, *Vinkulterung von Schweizer Namenaktien*, Bank Julius Bär, Zürich, Switzerland.

Loderer, C., and A. Jacobs, 1995, 'The Nestlé Crash,' *Journal of Financial Economics*, 37 315–339.

——, and H. Zimmerman, 1988, 'Stock Offerings in a Different Institutional Setting: The Swiss Case, 1973–1983,' *Journal of Banking and Finance*, 12, 353–378.

Pigou, A. C., 1920, *The Economics of Welfare*, Cambridge University Press, Cambridge, U.K.

Stulz, R. M., 1981, 'On the Effects of Barriers to International Investment,' *Journal of Finance*, 36, 383–403.

——, 1994, 'International Portfolio Choice and Asset Pricing: An Integrative Survey,' working paper, National Bureau of Economic Research.

Tirole, J., 1988, *The Theory of Industrial Organization*, MIT Press, Cambridge, MA.

Vock, T., 1987, *Aspekte der Unternehmenskontrolle: Ein Analyse für die Schweiz*, ADAG Administration & Druck, Zürich, Switzerland.

Walter, I., 1990, *The Secret Money Market*, Harper & Row, New York.

Williamson, J., and D. Lessard, 1987, *Capital Flight: The Problem and Policy Responses*, Institute for International Economics, Washington, D.C.

White, H., 1980, 'A Heteroskedasticity-Consistent Covariance Matrix and a Direct Test for Heteroskedasticity,' *Econometrica*, 48, 721–746.

Index

Index